Teaching, Learning, and Schooling

A 21st Century Perspective

EUGENE F. PROVENZO, JR.
University of Miami

ALLYN AND BACON
Boston ■ London ■ Toronto ■ Sydney ■ Tokyo ■ Singapore

Executive Editor and Publisher: Stephen D. Dragin
Editorial Assistant: Barbara Strickland
Marketing Manager: Amy Cronin
Editorial-Production Service: Omegatype Typography, Inc.
Composition and Prepress Buyer: Linda Cox
Manufacturing Manager: Chris Marson
Photo Research: Elizabeth Wood and Katharine Cook
Cover Administrator: Linda Knowles
Electronic Composition: Omegatype Typography, Inc.

Copyright © 2002 by Allyn & Bacon
A Pearson Education Company
75 Arlington Street
Boston, MA 02116

Internet: www.ablongman.com

Between the time Website information is gathered and then published, it is not unusual for some sites to have closed. Also, the transcription of URLs can result in unintended typographical errors. The publisher would appreciate notification where these occur so that they may be corrected in subsequent editions. Thank you.

Many of the designations used by manufacturers and sellers to distinguish their products are claimed as trademarks. Where those designations appear in this book, and Allyn and Bacon was aware of a trademark claim, the designations have been printed with an initial capital. Designations within quotation marks represent hypothetical products.

Library of Congress Cataloging-in-Publication Data

Provenzo, Eugene F.
    Teaching, learning, and schooling : a 21st century perspective / Eugene F. Provenzo, Jr.
        p.   cm.
    Includes bibliographical references ( ) and index.
    ISBN 0-205-28970-3
    1. Educational anthropology—United States.   2. Postmodernism and education—United States.   3. Education—Social aspects—United States.   I. Title.

LC191.4 .P76   2002
306.43—dc21
                                                    2001034092

Printed in the United States of America

10 9 8 7 6 5 4 3 2 1   06 05 04 03 02 01

Credits: p. 3, National Archives; p. 5: National Archives; p. 73: Will Hart; p. 74: Will Hart; p. 118: Bob Daemmrich/Stock, Boston; p. 122: Brian Smith; p. 125: Rich Frishman/frishphoto.com; p. 149: Pearson Education; p. 200, bottom: Will Hart; p. 230: Library of Congress; p. 263: Corbis; p. 272: PhotoDisc, Inc.; p. 288: Will Faller; p. 291: David Young-Wolff/PhotoEdit; p. 323: Will Hart; p. 335: Tony Freeman/PhotoEdit; p. 344: Will Hart.

For my undergraduate students
at the University of Miami

CONTENTS

PART II
The Organization and Control of U.S. Schools

CHAPTER 6 Local and State Involvement in U.S. Education 113

CHAPTER 7 **Private Education and Religion in the United States   145**

PART III
Multiculturalism and the Family in U.S. Society

Conclusion   359

Appendix

Glossary   379

Index   387

Teaching, Learning, and Schooling: A 21st Century Perspective is written as a conscious challenge to many of the standard textbooks used in introduction to education and foundations of education courses. These books are vast encyclopedias of information that is often unconnected to contemporary schooling, culture, and society. One such book includes a chapter titled "World Roots of American Education" and topics ranging from education in ancient Indian civilization to the Enlightenment's influence on education (Ornstein and Levine, 2000).

These topics are important and worthy of careful study and reflection. But are they appropriate topics for beginning teachers? Do they have much immediate meaning for future professionals who will have to cope with students whose vision of the world is saturated by **media** such as television, video games, and the Internet and **World Wide Web**? Do they have much significance for beginning teachers faced with increasing pressures resulting from **cultural diversity** and from our country's avowed, but sometimes reluctantly pursued, desire to achieve greater

INTASC Standards
Principle #3

media
Sources of information such as television, movies, books, and newspapers. Media can be print or electronically based.

World Wide Web
A graphical user interface for the Internet, often confused with being the Internet.

cultural diversity
The idea of a culture or society being represented by many different cultural groups and their experiences.

INTASC Standards

The Appendix of this book includes the Model Standards for Beginning Teaching Licensing and Development that were developed by the Interstate New Teacher Assessment and Support Consortium (INTASC), Council of Chief State School Officers. The standards include ten basic principles each of which is divided into three subcategories (Knowledge, Performances, and Dispositions). The principles that are relevant to this book are listed as a marginal icon like the one you see above. You can identify each of the principles and then look at their detailed descriptions in the Appendix. As you read through this book, reflect on the basic knowledge, performances (skills), and dispositions (concepts) that these principles address.

equity and justice? Do these topics hold much meaning for administrators who are facing parents who are demanding increased involvement in their children's schools and who are challenging the traditional curriculum? Do they help administrators cope with the epidemics of drug abuse and teen pregnancy?

This book is written as an alternative to the traditional textbooks available for introduction to education and social foundation courses. It is intended to direct students toward many of the most interesting and vital issues in the field. It covers nearly all of the traditional content of introductory textbooks and is concerned with engaging and **empowering** the students who read it. Students do indeed need to know about the organization of schools, **stereotypes** about teaching, the separation of church and state, the impact of the **civil rights movement** on U.S. education, among other concerns. But they also need to understand these issues within the context of a changing and extremely complex culture.

This book presents and portrays a consciously postmodern perspective. (Postmodernism and its meaning for education is discussed in detail throughout this book.) I argue that no absolute answers exist, and that many traditions and **canons** need to be accepted and understood in a **pluralistic** society such as the United States. The psychiatrist and historian Robert Jay Lifton has described our condition as one of "fragmentation." According to him, as a culture,

> We are becoming fluid and many-sided. . . . We feel ourselves buffeted about by unmanageable historical forces and social uncertainties. Leaders appear suddenly, recede equally rapidly, and are difficult for us to believe in when they are around. We change ideas and partners frequently, and do the same with jobs and places of residence. Enduring moral convictions, clear principles of action and behavior: we believe that these must exist, but where? (Lifton 1993, 1)

For Lifton, human history has become "increasingly open, dangerous, and unpredictable" (Lifton 1993, 4). This is especially evident as people everywhere are bombarded by the "tragedies" and "achievements" of our culture as presented in the mass media (Lifton 1993, 1).

Lifton suggests that to cope with the challenges posed by our culture—and by inference in our schools—we must become **protean** in nature. The term *protean* comes from the ancient Greek god Proteus, who could change shape at will. In Homer's *Odyssey,* for example, Proteus takes on the forms of a lion, a serpent, a leopard, a boar, flowing water, and a tree. His changing shape allows him to cope with difficult and challenging sit-

---

INTASC Standards
Principle #1

INTASC Standards
Principle #9

empower
To give power to someone.

stereotype
A discriminatory judgment typically involving race, gender, or ethnicity.

civil rights movement
The movement of African Americans for political and social equality, particularly during the 1950s and 1960s.

canon
Traditional texts and respected sources.

pluralistic
Referring to the idea of coming from many sources.

protean
Changing and variable.

uations. The protean self is a shape-shifting self. It is a self that has relatively consistent features but can adapt to new conditions when needed. These new conditions, as this book demonstrates, are a constant in postmodern society and its schools.

For theorists such as Henry Giroux, working in such a society and its schools requires students who are training to be teachers, and teachers themselves, to become **"border crossers"** (Giroux 1992, 28). Crossing cultural borders requires thinking more like anthropologists than scientists, more like explorers than technicians. According to Giroux:

> . . . border pedagogy offers the opportunity for students to engage the multiple references that constitute different cultural codes, experiences and languages. This means educating students to both read these codes historically and critically while simultaneously learning the limits of such codes, including the ones they use to construct their own narratives and histories. (Giroux 1994, 29)

Crossing cultural borders, as must an African American from an urban background teaching in a rural white school, or a male high school English teacher reading a **feminist** text with male and female students in an honors course, requires that you be willing to reshape yourself. You must adapt to different conditions, understand in new ways, teach according to the conditions and circumstances required. Giroux argues that this requires understanding how fragile identity is as you enter "into borderlands crisscrossed within a variety of languages, experiences, and voices" (Giroux 1992, 34).

Such an approach is deeply **ecological,** not so much in the biological sense, but in the context of a social ecology. I argue in detail that we need to become social ecologists. We need to take a deeply ecological approach to schooling. Simply put, schools are connected to the larger culture and society of which they are a part. Education is a reflection of—and responds to—the larger culture. Thus, to understand schools we must understand their connection to the larger society. You must try to understand what the anthropologist Gregory Batson refers to as "the pattern, which connects" (Batson 1979, 8).

What are the patterns that connect schools to the larger society in the United States? What is the relationship between elementary schoolchildren watching approximately thirty to forty hours of television and movies a week and the knowledge they bring to school? How do changes in the structure of the family (divorce, women increasingly working outside the home) affect children in school? How are new technologies such as computers changing the traditional organization and meaning of

INTASC Standards
Principle #9

INTASC Standards
Principle #1

INTASC Standards
Principle #5
Principle #7
Principle #10

border crossers
Individuals who work across different cultural groups and settings.

feminist
A person who supports and promotes the idea of gender (usually female) equality.

ecological
Involving the interaction or the interrelationship of organisms and their environments.

knowledge? Our access to information? The meaning of work? The meaning of schooling? What it means to be a teacher?

These are just a few examples of the issues addressed in this book. It is intended as a starting point for discovery, reflection, and discussion. It can be used on a number of different levels. I hope that it is used mainly with other books and articles, as well as with films and computer programs, to establish a framework for thinking about schooling, teaching, culture, and society. Frankly, I also hope that this is a book students keep on their professional bookshelves long after they have completed their studies. I hope it is a book from which they obtain much useful information but, more importantly, from which they draw key concepts and ideas that stay with them and evolve as they develop as professionals.

One final note: a unique feature of this book is the attempt not only to analyze emerging technologies and their impact on education, but also to maximize their use as instructional resources. Addresses for websites that contain information on many of the issues discussed can be found throughout this book. A website for this book has also been created. The website Teaching, Learning, and Schooling: A 21st Century Perspective can be reached at http://www.ablongman.com/provenzo21st. Hopefully this site will be a valuable resource for students and teachers.

■ ACKNOWLEDGMENTS

This book reflects nearly three decades of researching and teaching in social and cultural foundations of education. My work has been influenced by many individuals—particularly my undergraduate students at the University of Miami. My colleagues in the Department of Teaching and Learning at the University of Miami have helped keep me grounded in classroom practice. Special thanks go to Beth Harry, Janette Klinger, Shawn Post, and Jeanne Schumm. Alan Whitney, as always, kept me on the straight and true with my discussion of computers.

Gary McCloskey, O.S.A. at Merrimack College, has been a constant friend and sounding board for new ideas. Cheryl Desmond, at Millersville University, took special time and effort to help improve this book. Asterie Baker Provenzo read and edited all the chapters of this book, providing insight at all stages of development. Her constant questioning and probing of its content has made it a better book. Virginia Lanigan began this project with me at Allyn and Bacon. Stephen Dragin took it under his wing as Virginia moved on to other responsibilities. I truly appreciate the professionalism that both have shown in their work on this book.

Finally, I thank the reviewers who provided comments on the manuscript as it went through its various iterations: Cheryl T. Desmond, Millersville State; Frank Guldbrandsen, University of Minnesota, Duluth; and Brent Wendling, University of Central Oklahoma. Their suggestions were almost always followed and have certainly enhanced this book.

■ SOURCES CITED ■

Batson, Gregory. 1979. *Mind and nature: A necessary unity.* New York: Bantam Books.

Giroux, Henry. 1992. *Border crossings: Cultural workers and the politics of education.* New York: Routledge.

———. 1997. *Pedagogy and the politics of hope: Theory, culture and schooling.* Boulder, Col: Westview Press.

Lifton, Robert Jay. 1993. *Human resistance in an age of fragmentation.* New York: Basic Books.

Ornstein, Allan C., and Daniel U. Levine. 2000. *Foundations of education.* 7th ed. Boston: Houghton Mifflin.

CHAPTER 1

Introduction

"We are come not only past the century's closing, he thought, *the millennium's turning, but to the end of something else. Era? Paradigm? Everywhere, the signs of closure.* Modernity was ending."

—William Gibson, *Virtual Light*

This book is entitled *Teaching, Learning, and Schooling: A 21st Century Perspective.* It is like the bearded and two-faced ancient Greek god Janus—the god of doorways and of beginnings—who looks both forward and backward at once. It assumes that although schools are still important institutions for learning, they are not the only means by which we educate people in U.S. culture. In fact, media such as television, video games, the Internet and World Wide Web, and rock music are as important as, and certainly more pervasive than, schools in teaching our youth.

INTASC Standards
Principle #1

The idea that learning goes on outside of traditional schooling is not new. The U.S. educational historian Lawrence Cremin, for example, argued throughout much of his work that schools are simply one of many institutions, including family, churches, museums, and newspapers, that shape the consciousness of our children. As he explained:

INTASC Standards
Principle #2

> Every family has a curriculum, which it teaches quite deliberately and systematically over time. Every church and synagogue has a curriculum, which it teaches deliberately and systematically over time . . . libraries have curricula, museums have curricula, Boy Scout troops have curricula, and most important, perhaps, radio and television have curricula. (Cremin 1976, 22)

multiculturalism
The idea of a state or society, such as the United States, being represented by diverse cultural groups and belief systems.

equity
Freedom from bias or favoritism and correspondingly equal treatment.

gay
Of, or relating to, homosexuals.

postmodern perspective
A point of view reflective of the postmodern experience.

Renaissance
The historical period in Europe between medieval and modern times, beginning in the fourteenth century and continuing into the seventeenth century.

The fact that schools are not the only institution that shapes the consciousness of our children was also recognized by the radical educator Ivan Illich. According to Illich:

School is not, by any means, the only modern institution that has as its primary purpose the shaping of man's vision of reality. The hidden curriculum of family life, draft, health care, so-called professionalism, or of the manipulation of the media play an important part in the institutional manipulation of man's world-vision, language and demands. (Illich 1971, 47)

Yet Illich argues that whereas family and media are important, schools are even more important in shaping the consciousness of children because they are solely devoted to that task. According to Illich, "school touches us so intimately that none of us can expect to be liberated from it by something else" (Illich 1971, 47).

Perhaps we should not be arguing about whether media are more important than schools, or schools are more important than media, but instead should try to understand how they combine to shape and educate our children. In this sense, our inquiry is based on a social/ecological approach—an approach that is outlined in more detail in Chapter 3. As a result, this book concerns itself with both traditional and nontraditional modes of education and schooling. In a traditional context, this book deals with questions such as the organization and control of U.S. schools, **multiculturalism,** inclusion, **equity** and schooling, feminist issues, the changing meaning of family and work, and the content of textbooks. In a nontraditional context, it deals with questions ranging from the impact of media on children and youth, to such contemporary issues as AIDS and the rights of **gay** students and teachers.

What ties the discussion together is a **postmodern perspective.** It is my belief that U.S. and world culture have recently crossed a profound cultural divide—the type of change that occurs rarely in our history. A similar divide of this type took place five hundred years ago during the **Renaissance** when we moved from an **oral culture,** based on the spoken word, to a **typographic culture,** based on the printed word. More recently, the explosion of the first **atomic bomb** in 1945, the invention of the **electronic computer,** or more recently **cloning** and **nanotechnology,** would represent similar types of events—what the science fiction author Vernor Vinge refers to as a **"singularity"**—an event so profound that everything that follows it is changed (Vinge 1989, 116).

We have now moved beyond a traditional typographic culture into what I described in *Beyond the Gutenberg Galaxy: Microcomputers and*

FIGURE 1.1 ■ The walls of a two-story brick building in Hiroshima, Japan, 0.8 mile from ground zero. The dropping of the first atomic bomb in August 1945 represents a "singularity" of the type described by Vernor Vinge.

Source: Courtesy National Archives.

the Emergence of Post-Typographic Culture as a **post-typographic culture** (Provenzo 1986). In describing the transition from a typographic to a posttypographic culture, I was primarily concerned with the microcomputer and its role in transforming contemporary education and culture. I have subsequently come to the conclusion that the revolution in information and learning, brought about as a result of the introduction of new models of computing, is in fact part of a much larger **postmodern** phenomenon.

What do we mean when we use the term *postmodern*? In *Postmodernism, Feminism and Cultural Politics: Redrawing Educational Boundaries,* the educational theorist Henry A. Giroux argues that we have entered a new period of historical time, one that is characterized by a

oral culture
A culture or society based primarily on the oral rather than the written word.

typographic culture
A culture based on the printed word or on books.

atomic bomb
A bomb whose force is a result of the sudden release of energy resulting from the splitting of nuclei of a heavy chemical element such as plutonium or uranium by neutrons in a very rapid chain reaction.

electronic computer
A computer or calculating device whose mechanics are electronic.

cloning
The replication of genetic material.

nanotechnology
The creation of materials on an atomic or molecular scale in order to build microscopic machines.

singularity
An event of such importance that everything that follows it is changed or altered.

post-typographic culture
The contemporary information age in which the printed word has been superseded by electronic media.

postmodern
A model describing the current historical period as being distinct from the modern era. A postmodern society is fragmented, complex, and diverse.

FIGURE 1.2 ■ The introduction of the printing press and moveable type technology into Western Europe five hundred years ago represents a singularity of comparable importance to the dropping of the atomic bomb in 1945.

Source: Courtesy Dover Pictorial Archives.

crisis of power, patriarchy, authority, identity, and ethics (Giroux 1991, 1–2). This new historical era, loosely referred to as postmodernism, is a period in which "science, technology, and reason are associated not only with social progress but also with the organization of **Auschwitz** and the scientific creativity that makes Hiroshima possible" (Giroux 1991, 2). According to Giroux:

> . . . postmodernism in the broadest sense refers to an intellectual position, a form of cultural criticism, as well as to an emerging set of social, cultural, and economic conditions that have come to characterize the age of global capitalism and industrialism. In the first instance, postmodernism represents a form of cultural criticism that radically questions the logic of foundations that has become the epistemological cornerstone of modernism. . . . postmodernism refers to an increas-

Auschwitz

A concentration camp near Munich, Germany, during World War II (1939–1945).

ingly radical change in the relations of production, the nature of the nation-state, the development of new technologies that have redefined the fields of telecommunications and information processing, and the forces at work in the growing globalization and interdependence of the economic, political and cultural spheres. (Aronowitz and Giroux 1991, 62)

Giroux's definition is fairly intimidating. In many respects the idea of postmodernism is fairly straightforward. In the context of this textbook, it refers to the profound social, political, technological, and cultural changes that have taken place in the United States and in the world since the 1960s—changes that almost certainly affect your work as teachers.

FIGURE 1.3 ■ Jewish civilians being rounded up for deportation to concentration camps during the destruction of the Warsaw Ghetto, Poland, 1943.

Source: Courtesy of the National Archives

INTASC Standards

Principle #9

Look at the following list of modern versus postmodern comparisons to get a better idea of the shifts that are taking place. Then consider how they might affect your work as a teacher, or simply your life in general. What could you add to the list?

Modern	Postmodern
Mothers working in the home	Mothers in the work force
Staying married for the children	Divorcing to find one's self
Traditional nuclear families	Complex or blended families
Radio and television	Internet and World Wide Web
Broadcast	Cable and satellite
Passive entertainment	Interactive entertainment
East versus west politically	Global economy and politics
Telephones	Cell phones
Personal calendars	Personal digital assistants
Board games	Video games
Venereal diseases	AIDS
Roller skates	roller blades
X-ray	CAT scan
Segregation	Integration
Heterosexuality	Bisexuality
Smoke-stack industries	Service economy
Commuting	Telecommuting

Some theorists use terms other than *postmodernism* to describe the complex culture and economic system that is coming into existence at the beginning of the new millennium. **Post-Fordism,** an awkward and somewhat problematic phrase, describes many of the elements of the new culture. According to Stuart Hall:

"Post-Fordism" is a [broad] term suggesting a whole new epoch distinct from the era of mass production. . . . it covers at least some of the following characteristics: a shift to the new information "technologies"; more flexible, decentralized forms of labor process and work organization; decline of the old manufacturing base and the growth of the "sunrise," computer-based industries; the hiring off or contracting out of functions and services; a greater emphasis on choice and product differentiation, on marketing, packaging, and design, on the "targeting" of consumers by lifestyle, taste, and culture rather than by the categories of social class; a decline in the proportion of the skilled, male, manual working class, the rise of the service industry and "white-collar classes and the "feminization" of the work force; an economy dominated by

post-Fordism
The present era following the period of modern industrial production.

the multinationals, with their new international division of labor and their greater autonomy from nation-state control; and the "globalization" of the new financial markets, limited by the communications revolution. (Quoted by Giroux 1994, 12)

Whether we use the term *postmodernism* or *post-Fordism* to describe the changes that are taking place in the culture, and in turn our schools, is not that important. Recognizing the changes that we are living through is what is critical. It is sufficient to argue that our culture, and more specifically the schools and educational system that are part of it, has been profoundly redefined in recent years. This process, which is ongoing, is reflected in a wide range of phenomena—phenomena that comprise much of the description and discussion in this book.

When the author of this book began teaching social foundations courses at the University of Miami in 1976, many of the issues currently confronting schools and the educational system did not then exist. **Microcomputers/Personal computers**—with all their potential and problems for the educational system—were not invented until 1978. By the mid-1990s, the Office of Technological Assessment reported that approximately 5.8 million computers were in use in schools in the United States, or approximately one machine for every 9 students (Office of Technological Assessment 1995, 89). By 1998, these numbers had reached 6.4 students per computer (Market Data Retrieval 2001). Think about how the World Wide Web has changed both education and the culture in general since its introduction in 1992. AIDS wasn't identified as a disease until 1981. Today AIDS prevention is a major component in school curricula across the country. **Crack cocaine** was not introduced to the streets until the mid-1980s. Now we have special education programs that focus on the medical and educational needs of children who have been exposed to crack cocaine in utero.

Think for a moment about the rights of ethnic minorities, women and the physically challenged. What were the rights of these groups in the 1950s and 1960s as compared to today? Think about **perestroika** and the end of the Soviet Empire and the fall of the **Berlin Wall,** or the rise of Japan as a cultural and economic force. Think about the changes that have taken place in China since the 1960s. What role have all these events had in the creation of a new world order?

What does it mean for the United States to be the only military superpower in the world? What does it mean when U.S. children spend more time watching television than going to school? What does it mean when sushi (not just hot dogs, peanuts, and popcorn) is sold as a snack at the San Diego Padres baseball games? These phenomena are

---

microcomputers/ personal computers
Small computers introduced in the 1970s for personal and small business use.

crack cocaine
A crystallized form of the drug cocaine.

Perestroika
The policy of economic and governmental reform that contributed to the dissolution and end of the Union of Soviet Socialist Republics (USSR).

Berlin Wall
The guarded wall built by East Germany in 1961 in Berlin to prevent people from passing between East and West Germany during the Cold War.

INTASC Standards
Principle #9

INTASC Standards
Principle #9

FIGURE 1.4 ■ Photograph of the Berlin Wall before its fall in 1989 with the Brandenberg Gate in the background.

Source: Courtesy of Frederik Ramm. (Available online at http://www.remote.org/frederik/culture/berlin/)

INTASC Standards

Principle #3

modernism
The historical period having its origins in the French Enlightenment.

indications of the emergence of a new culture and society in the United States.

Perhaps you find all this unsettling, maybe even profoundly disturbing. This book is not a celebration of the changes taking place in our culture and our schools. It simply maintains that we have entered a new phase of our culture, and in doing so the meaning and nature of schooling has changed as well. Holding on to the old model of **modernism** does not ensure that the changes taking place in our culture and their influence on the schools will go away or diminish. The number of women of childbearing age in the work force has increased by approximately 25 percent since the early 1960s. By definition, this changes the experience of children and how they are raised. This is not a value judgment; it is simply a reality we can observe as sociologists, social historians, and critically thinking and reflective educators.

Likewise, more than three times the number of single parents exists today than did in the early 1960s. The reality is that the conditions of schooling reflect profound changes in the society. In turn, the possibilities of schooling, the role of the teacher, and the needs of the curricula are all affected by the emergence of postmodern phenomena. What is being experienced in contemporary and postmodern culture is not necessarily negative. It is simply different. Much of it is also positive. Ask any African American whether he or she would rather be living in the United States in the 1990s or in the 1950s. Ask a woman in a profession such as law whether she would prefer the possibilities open to her today or the ones that were available in the 1940s, 1950s, or even 1960s. Ask an older person who has been wheelchair bound most of his or her life whether it is easier to get around now than thirty or forty years ago.

INTASC Standards
Principle #9

In addition, a great deal of the technology that has emerged as part of postmodern and contemporary culture serves us well. Few professional writers would trade in their computers and word-processing programs for a typewriter or a pen. Think about accountants using spreadsheets to do their work or architects doing their designs and drawings on computers. Think about our worldwide telephone and computer network systems. Think about a blind child who can use a computer to scan printed text from a book, which is then read aloud to the child. Few people would argue that, overall, these postmodern technological applications have not served us well. Yet they have also changed our world and not always in ways that are clear or necessarily positive. What do we gain by having access to technologies such as television or the Internet and World Wide Web? What do we lose? Cars are a useful means of transportation, but they also pollute, isolate us from our neighbors, and cost large amounts of money to maintain.

This book challenges the reader to seek new perspectives as our culture and society are redefined. The signs of postmodernism are everywhere but often difficult for many of us to recognize or accept. We are surrounded by our culture. It is hard to imagine anything other than what we are used to, even when something is in the process of changing profoundly. As the physicist Albert Einstein suggested, the fish are the last creatures to consider the water that surrounds them.

Postmodernism brings with it the question of whether schools, as we traditionally know them, need to exist. In fact, the question of whether we need to "deschool" society (literally, eliminate formal schooling as we know it) has already been addressed by many radical educators, such as Paul Goodman and Ivan Illich (Goodman 1964; Illich 1970). Although their work is dated in some respects, many of their ideas are even more relevant in a contemporary and postmodern context. Should schooling be compulsory? Do we need a graded system of schooling? What is the relevance and meaning of standardized testing?

This book assumes not only a postmodernist perspective about schools, but also that what goes on in schools—the values and knowledge children bring to the classroom and the content included in textbooks and the curriculum—ultimately reflects the values and beliefs of the society of which they are a part. This idea is not new. The ancient Greeks had a special word to describe it—*paideia*. Significantly, the meaning of *paideia* has changed over the course of time. In the fifth century BC it suggested the idea of raising a child or childrearing. A century later, in the fourth century BC, it came to mean education as reflecting the ways of a culture (Jaeger 1943; Curren 1996).

The idea of education reflecting culture—reflecting U.S. society—is the second theme that ties together the discussions and issues raised in this book. Schools are sensitive measures of the forces and conflicts and the issues and concerns at work in society. If television and video games influence children, they bring these experiences and perceptions with them into the classroom. If drug abuse or violence is a problem in a local community, children bring these problems with them into the schools. Likewise, if children feel secure in their families, their culture, and their traditions, they carry these feelings into their classroom experience.

Simply stated, problems, conditions, and issues in the larger society tend to be reproduced in the schools. Thus, prejudice against African Americans, women, or people with disabilities is reflected in the day-to-day reality of the school. If **homophobia** is allowed in the community, it is perpetuated in the classroom, the gymnasium and the cafeteria.

In the end, the purpose of *Teaching, Learning, and Schooling: A 21st Century Perspective* is to introduce students interested in U.S. schools to the forces at work within the educational system. The approach is interdisciplinary, drawing on historical, philosophical, anthropological, and sociological approaches, as well as on sources from popular culture. Because of the importance of technology in defining the postmodern condition, we are also concerned with models of analysis normally associated with media studies and computer studies. The approach taken in this book is topical in nature. It reflects the concerns of a single author, scholar, or teacher at a particular moment in time. As such, its interpretations are ultimately subjective and, perhaps, inevitably limited.

The intent of this book is to engage the reader in the process of questioning: the role of teaching, learning, and schooling in U.S. culture; the

INTASC Standards

Principle #2

paideia
The ancient Greek word for education—literally meaning education is a reflection of the culture of which it is a part.

significance of postmodernism in shaping what it means to teach and be taught in our schools; and the relationship between our schools and the larger social, cultural, and economic forces at work in our society.

■ DISCUSSION QUESTIONS ■

1. Given that schools are not as important in the education of children today as they were in the past, why are they still important?
2. What have been the issues and forces in your own experience that have been most influential in determining what you know and how you view the world (family, school, religion, peer group, television, etc.)?
3. What are some of the issues facing schools and contemporary children that did not exist a generation ago?
4. Singularities have appeared rarely throughout our history. The increasing appearances of singularities, such as dropping the first atomic bomb, electronic computing, cloning and nanotechnology, suggest that profound change is occurring at an unprecedented speed in our culture. What implications do you think these emerging technologies have for the culture and for education in general?
5. What are the essential differences between a typographic and post-typographic culture?
6. Can you describe some phenomena that are distinctly modern? Can you describe some that are postmodern? How are they different?
7. How do you think technologies like microcomputers and personal computers have changed U.S. culture, and more specifically, public schools?
8. How would your life and experience have been different if you lived fifty years ago?
9. Can you provide some examples from your own experience that illustrate how schools reflect the culture or society of which they are a part?

■ SOURCES CITED ■

Aronowitz, Stanley, and Henry A. Giroux. 1991. *Postmodern education: Politics, culture, and social criticism.* Minneapolis: University of Minnesota Press.

Best, Steven, and Douglas Kellner. 1991. *Postmodern theory: Critical interrogations.* New York: Guilford Press.

———. 1997. *Postmodern turn.* New York: Guilford Press.

Cremin, Lawrence. 1976. *Public education.* Foreword by Maxine Green. New York: Basic Books.

Curren, Randall R. 1996. *Paideia. Philosophy of education: An encyclopedia.* New York and London: Garland Publishing.

Gibson, William. 1995. *Virtual light.* New York: Bantam Books.

Giroux, Henry A. 1992. *Border crossings: Cultural workers and the politics of education.* New York, London: Routledge.

———. 1994. *Disturbing pleasures: Learning popular culture.* New York: Routledge.

———. 1991. *Postmodernism, feminism, and cultural politics: Redrawing educational boundaries.* Albany: State University of New York Press.

Giroux, Henry A., and Peter McLaren. 1994. *Between borders: Pedagogy and the politics of cultural studies.* New York, London: Routledge.

Illich, Ivan. 1971. *Deschooling society.* New York: Harper & Row.

Jaeger, Werner W. 1943. *Paideia: The ideals of Greek culture.* Translated from the German by Gilbert Highet. New York: Oxford University Press.

Kincheloe, Joe. 1993. *Towards a critical politics of teacher thinking: Mapping the postmodern.* Westport, CT: Begin & Garvey.

Market Research Data. *Computer use in schools, 1984–1985 and 1997–1998.* Available online at http://www.infoplease.com/ipa/A0193911.html. Accessed May 21, 2001.

Marrou, H. I. 1956. *A history of education in antiquity.* Translated by George Lamb. London: Sheed and Ward.

Murray, Robin. 1992. Fordism and post-Fordism. In *The postmodern reader,* edited by Christopher Jencks, 267–276. New York: St. Martin's Press.

Office of Technology Assessment, Congress of the United States. 1995. *Teachers & technology: Making the connection.* OTA-EHR-616. Washington, D.C.: U.S. Government Printing Office.

Provenzo, Eugene F., Jr. 1986. *Beyond the Gutenberg galaxy: Microcomputers and the emergence of post-typographic culture.* New York: Teachers College Press.

Vinge, Vernor. 1987. *True names . . . and other dangers.* New York: Baen Books.

CHAPTER 2

Schools as Cultural Institutions

In this chapter, we begin to look at schools as cultural institutions. **Culture** is part of the postmodern condition that is undergoing a major process of redefinition. **Postmodern culture** represents a direct challenge to the **modernist tradition** in which legitimate knowledge is seen as being drawn almost exclusively from a European, and largely male, social, and cultural, tradition. Before we can proceed with our discussion, it is essential that we define what is meant by culture.

■ WHAT IS CULTURE?

The English poet T. S. Eliot defined culture as "all the characteristic activities and interests of a people." In the United States this definition could include the murder trials of O. J. Simpson or Timothy McVeigh (the "Oklahoma Bomber"), the novels of William Faulkner, the television program *Baywatch,* the rock group Aerosmith, and the New York Philharmonic.

    This definition includes what is sometimes called **high culture**—works of great art (Da Vinci, Michelangelo, Durer, Degas, Picasso), poetry (Shakespeare, Tennyson, Frost), and music (Bach, Beethoven, Hindemith). It also includes popular culture—rock music, hamburgers, television, and the World Wide Web. Schools deal with culture at many levels, both high and popular culture. In terms of high culture, we try to introduce students to the most noble and meaningful of humankind's creations. These could include a symphony by Brahms or an anonymous African American spiritual. At a more basic level, schools introduce

INTASC Standards
Principle #1

culture
The social values and beliefs that define being human and create a society.

postmodern culture
Culture or society created in the postmodern era.

modernist tradition
Traditions based on values and traditions from the modern period.

high culture
Those artifacts of music, art, and literature traditionally associated with the most highly regarded traditions of a culture.

students to culture in terms of the fundamental values and beliefs that are assumed to be the norms of the society.

The anthropologist Edward T. Hall describes the importance of culture in the following way:

> Culture is man's medium; there is not one aspect of human life that is not touched and altered by culture. This means personality, how people express themselves (including shows of emotion), the way they think, how they move, how problems are served, how their cities are planned and laid out, how transportation systems function and are organized, as well as how economic and government systems are put together and function. However, it is frequently the most obvious and taken-for-granted and therefore the least studied aspects of culture and influence behavior in the deepest and most subtle ways. (1981, 16–17)

Schools are some of our most important and complex cultural systems. As mentioned in Chapter 1, schools reflect the culture of which they are a part. They in turn socialize students to accept that culture and to become functioning members of the social system. In the United States this includes making a living, raising the next generation, paying taxes, voting in elections, and so on.

The fact that schools socialize students is not necessarily a bad thing, but it is something that must be understood. It is naïve to assume that the schools have as their primary purpose the interests of the student above all else. As the French educational theorist and sociologist Emile Durkheim noted nearly a century ago:

> . . . education, far from having as its unique or principal object the individual and his interests, is above all the means by which society perpetually recreates the conditions of its very existence. . . . It consists, then, in one or another of its aspects of a systematic socialization of the young generation. (Durkheim 1956, 123–124)

INTASC Standards

Principle #9

One of the critical issues that arises concerning the role of schools in transmitting culture from one generation to the next is the question of whose culture is going to be passed on. Historically, the United States has been a racist and sexist culture. African Americans were enslaved until the middle of the 1860s; women were denied the vote until 1918. We have never had a woman president or even vice president, yet women represent more than 50 percent of the population. Likewise, we have never had an African American or Hispanic president or vice president. Much of our history has been focused on European traditions, yet we are a pluralistic culture representing a veritable rainbow of people and cultures.

Whose history should be taught? Are the fables of **Aesop** (an ancient Greek slave) more important than the African **Anansi** or **Spiderman** stories? Should European traditions be emphasized because they are the traditions out of which most of our laws and religious beliefs evolved? These are difficult questions and relate to what is commonly known as **cultural capital.**

INTASC Standards
Principle #1
Principle #9

Aesop
Ancient storyteller(s) associated with the telling of animal fables.

Anansi or **Spiderman**
Trickster figure in central African folktales.

cultural capital
The knowledge and ideas in which a culture or society invests.

curriculum
The content of what is taught. It can be both formal and informal.

INTASC Standards
Principle #5

■ EDUCATION AS CULTURAL CAPITAL

What we teach reflects the realities of power and influence within our culture. The selection of **curriculum** is in fact a cultural and, ultimately, a political act, whether we are conscious of it or not. According to Henry Giroux, most discussions of culture, and in turn education, have been stripped of their political dimension. More often than not the discussion of culture and education has little or no political or social meaning and simply becomes an apology for the existing system or status quo (Giroux 1981, 26).

The reality is that the United States is not a single culture, but instead a group of competing cultures. Nearly all the conflicts within the contemporary educational system reflect these competing cultures. In this context, according to Giroux, culture

> . . . would be defined not simply as lived experiences functioning within the context of historically located structures and social formations, but as "antagonistic relations" situated within a complex of socio-political institutions and social forms that limit as well as enable human action. . . . Culture is more than an expression of experiences forged within the social and economic spheres of a given society, . . . [it is also] a complex realm of antagonistic experiences mediated by power and struggle. . . ." (Giroux 1981, 26)

INTASC Standards
Principle #5

Schools reflect the social, political, and economic configurations of a culture. To see how true this is, observe a class in a poor inner-city school and compare what goes on in that class to what goes on in its affluent suburban counterpart. Schools, according to Giroux, are in fact battlegrounds upon which various groups fight over different cultural points of view. The language teachers use, the curricula they employ, and the values they hold represent what Giroux and other theorists, such as Pierre Bourdieu, have described as "cultural capital" (Bourdieu 1977). According to Giroux:

> Just as a country distributes goods and services, what can be labeled as material capital, it also distributes and legitimates certain forms of knowledge, language practices, values, modes of style and so forth, or what can be labeled as cultural capital. . . . the concept of cultural capital also represents certain ways of talking, acting, moving, dressing, and socializing that are institutionalized by schools. Schools are not merely instructional sites but also sites where the culture of the dominant society is learned. . . . (Giroux 1988, 5–6)

In a relatively homogeneous culture such as France or Norway, this does not necessarily present a serious problem; but in a diverse culture such as the United States, where different values, traditions, and worldviews separate the students from the teachers, conflict is inevitable.

The value of the work of Giroux and other educational theorists like Bordieu is that they recognize that any education embodies specific values and purposes. Instead of seeing the educational process as being neutral and apolitical, they perceive education as existing within a larger social, economic, and political context subject to the personal needs and interests of those in power.

What does this mean on a practical level for teachers and students? In a society dominated by men, it might mean that women receive specific messages as part of their education that discourage them from seeking positions of leadership or high status. Language minorities (Native Americans, Chinese Americans, Hispanic Americans, and so on) may have the message communicated to them, subtly or not so subtly, that their native languages and cultural traditions are inferior to the mainstream language and culture.

In a postmodern culture, schools become arenas in which different values are debated and negotiated. The increased empowerment of minority groups that has characterized the history of U.S. society over the last thirty or forty years has resulted in increasing demands that new models of culture be represented in the curriculum and activities of schools. Whether we take time to celebrate Martin Luther King's or Lincoln's birthday, **Hanukkah, Kwanza,** or Christmas, and so on, represents a series of cultural choices that ultimately reflect different investments in cultural capital.

INTASC Standards

Principle #6

Principle #9

Hanukkah
A Jewish holiday commemorating the rededication of the Temple of Jerusalem after its defilement by Antiochus of Syria.

Kwanza
A recently developed holiday introduced by African Americans celebrating African traditions and the family.

■ CULTURAL LITERACY

In 1987, the literary scholar E. D. Hirsch, Jr. published *Cultural Literacy*. In it, and in his 1996 book *The Schools We Need and Why We Don't Have Them,* Hirsch argues that U.S. schools need to develop a model of literacy that focuses the attention of children on a common western cultural heritage. According to Hirsch, "to be culturally literate is to possess the basic information needed to thrive in the modern world" (Hirsch 1987, xiii).

Hirsch has promoted his ideas not only through works such as *Cultural Literacy* and *The Schools We Need and Why We Don't Have Them,* but also through the establishment of the Core Knowledge Foundation (http://www.coreknowledge.org/) and a series of curriculum guides and reference books, including *What Your First Grader Needs to Know* (1991), *What Your Second Grader Needs to Know* (1991), *What Your Third Grader Needs to Know* (1992), *What Your Fourth Grader Needs to Know* (1992), *What Your Fifth Grader Needs to Know* (1993), *What Your Sixth Grader Needs to Know* (1993), and *A First Dictionary of Cultural Literacy: What Our Children Need to Know* (1989).

INTASC Standards
Principle #7
Principle #9

Core Knowledge Foundation

Hirsch correctly recognizes that literacy involves more than just obtaining reading and writing skills. Reading a newspaper article, for example, requires the reader to identify and decode not only specific words and phrases, but also their context and meaning. Look, for example, at the following two sentences:

> With Fidel Castro's assumption of power in Cuba in 1959, the era of U.S. domination of Cuban culture came to an end, and a new government based on the needs of the people was set in motion.

> With Fidel Castro's assumption of power in Cuba in 1959, the era of U.S. involvement in Cuban culture came to an end, and a new government based on communist principles was set in motion.

Each sentence represents a very different political point of view. In addition, the reader has to decode the meaning of each sentence. This requires knowledge on the part of the reader of who Fidel Castro is, where and what Cuba is, and so on. These things are not explained in the sentences; instead they are assumed by the writer to be understood by the reader.

cultural literacy
Knowledge of cultural events and facts. In recent years this term has taken on significant political overtones.

INTASC Standards

Principle #9

For Hirsch, a common core of knowledge is essential for any culture. In this context, literacy is larger than just the ability to read and write—in other words it includes **cultural literacy.** Facts, and other types of information that constitute cultural literacy, are not neutral, however, but represent an investment in specific ways of understanding and interpreting the world. According to Hirsch, "cultural literacy constitutes the only sure avenue of opportunity for disadvantaged children, the only reliable way of combating the social determinism that now condemns them to remain in the same social and educational condition as their parents" (Hirsch 1987, xiii).

In reading Hirsch, and many other cultural conservatives like him (William Bennett, Chester Finn, Diane Ravitch), we get the idea that the knowledge they promote is noble, altruistic, and neutral. As Joe Kincheloe and Shirley Steinberg argue, however, this type of "view dismisses the cultural and power-related dimensions of knowledge" (Kincheloe and Steinberg 1997, 51).

No curriculum is neutral. Instead, every curriculum represents a set of specific values and a conscious investment in specific models or types of cultural capital. Although the Western canon may be an important and valuable body of knowledge—one that is essential to understanding who we are as Americans—it is not the only body of cultural knowledge our children need to know. In addition, as a body of knowledge, many of its assumptions need to be challenged if we are to achieve a more just and equitable society. Although much of what Hirsch and other conservatives argue for is important, it is not sufficiently inclusive. The position that needs to be taken is more like the one taken by the critical multicultural teachers described by Kincheloe and Steinberg, who refuse to accept automatically the status of Western knowledge, and who,

> . . . as scholars of Western knowledge, non-Western knowledge and subjugated and indigenous knowledge, . . . are not content to operate in socio-educational frameworks often taken for granted. As critical multiculturalists, they seek to rethink and recontextualize questions that have been traditionally asked about schooling and knowledge production in general. While they respect earlier insight and are reverential in respect to the genius of past eras, such educators display their veneration by continuing to question the work of their intellectual ancestors. (Kincheloe and Steinberg 1997, 57)

Hirsch's failure is that he does not adequately recognize the extent to which his construction of the Western cultural tradition is driven by a set of specific **ideological,** political, and social values.

WHAT DO YOU THINK?

What Does It Mean to be Culturally Literate?

E. D. Hirsch Jr. believes that the chief beneficiaries of the educational reforms that he advocates are disadvantaged children (Hirsch 1987, xiv). He also believes that his proposed reforms will be helpful to children from middle-class homes. According to him, "the educational goal advocated is that of mature literacy for *all* our citizens" (Hirsch 1987, xiv).

Hirsch's use of the idea of a "mature literacy" for all our citizens is an interesting one. It seems to assume that an "immature literacy" is at work in our culture as well. In an electronic information and market-oriented culture, is media literacy an "immature" literacy? In an increasingly multicultural and diverse society, is knowledge of some concepts more or less important than others? Consider the following list of items: acupuncture, Douglas Addams, Theodor Adorno, Affirmative Action, Afrocentrism, Aid for Dependent Children, AIDS, *Alice's Adventures in Wonderland,* the Altair computer, Louis Althusser, the American Association of University Women, anarchy, Maya Angelou, Susan B. Anthony, anti-intellectualism, Apple (the corporation), Hannah Arendt, Louis Armstrong, Stanley Aronowitz, the ARPAnet, *Art in the Age of Mechanical Reproduction,* artificial reality, the Aspen Movie Map, Atari, Atavars, authority and autonomy—just to name a few things that begin with the letter *A*. Are these concepts less important than those found at the beginning of Hirsch's list: Hank Aaron, abbreviation, Aberdeen, abolitionism, abominable snowman, abortion, absenteeism, absolute monarchy, absolute zero, abstract art, abstract expressionism, academic freedom, a capella, particle accelerator, accounting, acculturation, AC/DC, Achilles, Achille's heel, acid, acquittal, acronym, acrophobia, Acropolis, act of God, or actuary (Hirsch 1987, 152)?

Is the quote "Abandon hope, all ye who enter here" from the beginning of Dante's *Inferno* more meaningful from the viewpoint of being culturally literate than the quote "Math class is tough" (Barbie), or "The street finds its own uses for things" (William Gibson in *Neuromancer*), or "The problem of the Twentieth century is the problem of the Color Line" (W. E. B. DuBois in *The Souls of Black Folks*)? What constitutes a valid curriculum from a cultural point of view? What do people need to know to be truly "culturally literate"? What do you think?

■ CAN SCHOOLING BE NEUTRAL?

Up until the 1970s, most educators assumed that education and schooling could be neutral. All that was needed was to present the facts. People

INTASC Standards

Principle #7

hidden curriculum
Curriculum that is
not taught directly or
consciously.

could judge for themselves what was good or bad. Yet curriculum (i.e., the content of schooling) cannot be separated from the culture in which it occurs. The very selection of one subject—African American folktales versus European fairy tales—represents a cultural and, ultimately, political decision. Curriculum must be viewed in context. Isolating "curriculum from its multiple, interacting contexts is an absurdity" (Cornbleth 1991, 85).

No type of schooling or education is neutral. Underlying every educational curriculum is a structure of values and beliefs. Think for a moment about why many people send their children to a private Catholic school. It is to receive an education in specific values involving religion, community, and politics. Why do people attend certain public rather than private universities? The reason often lies in the value structures of the different institutions. Some African American students, at least in part, attend historically Black colleges and universities like Tuskegee or Howard to be involved in curricula that are more oriented toward African American traditions, history, and culture. An undergraduate at Vassar, Harvard, or Yale, whose father or mother also attended the school, may be connecting to traditions of power and prestige that have been part of the university's history. This raises the interesting question of how schools at all levels are involved in what theorists have come to describe as the **hidden curriculum.**

■ THE HIDDEN CURRICULUM

The concept of the hidden curriculum is drawn largely from the work of Philip Jackson. In his 1968 book *Life in Classrooms,* Jackson argued that what actually went on in classrooms was insufficiently understood. In fact, many things were being taught besides the formal subject matter. As part of the hidden curriculum students learn how to behave in class and who warrants special attention (boys or girls, brown-skinned children or white-skinned children, and so on).

INTASC Standards

Principle #7

Principle #9

According to Peter McLaren: "The *hidden curriculum* refers to *the unintended outcomes of the schooling process*"(McLaren 1998, 186). For McLaren, critical educators must be aware of the fact that schools shape students in many different ways including standard learning situations, rules of conduct, classroom organization, informal activities, and so on (McLaren 1998, 183–184).

Think for a moment about your own experience in school. In your senior year of high school, what did you learn as part of the **formal cur-**

riculum? What did you learn informally from teachers (e.g., how to be polite, how not to "give lip," how to "brown-nose" for a grade)? What did you learn from peers (e.g., how to perceive the opposite sex; how to decide who was cool or who wasn't; how to "cram" for a final)? What did you learn about **bureaucracies** and power from the administrators in your school?

The hidden curriculum is something that is rarely discussed in most schools or courses in education. It is too ephemeral, too hard to identify, but it nonetheless exists. Anyone planning to become a teacher needs to be aware that hidden curricula are an inevitable part of almost every educational situation—that they are part of the reality that schooling is not neutral.

■ THE NULL CURRICULUM

Even less discussed than the concept of the hidden curriculum is the **null curriculum**. The null curriculum is the curriculum that does not exist. Think of the hole in a doughnut. It is something that is there but does not exist. The idea of the null curriculum is that we teach things by excluding them from the curriculum—by not teaching them. The curriculum theorist Elliot Eisner explains this phenomenon the following way:

> . . . what schools do not teach may be as important as what they do teach. . . . ignorance is not simply a neutral void; it has important effects on the kinds of options one is able to consider, the alternatives one can examine, and the perspectives from which one can view a situation or problems. (Eisner 1985, 97)

If, according to Eisner (1985, 96), one of the purposes of schooling "is to foster wisdom, weaken prejudice, and develop the ability to use a wide range of modes of thought," then we ought to look carefully at what the schools do not include in the curriculum.

Historical models are useful. Before the 1970s, very little discussion of African Americans or women was included in high school U.S. history courses and textbooks. As I think back to my own privileged education in the mid-1960s, for example, I realize how little I was taught about either of these subjects. I used a textbook that included no references to African American history, except in the context of slavery or Booker T. Washington and George Washington Carver. I learned about W. E. B. DuBois by reading about him outside of class. Topics such as Eldridge

formal curriculum
The curriculum that is consciously taught.

bureaucracy
A highly structured social organization such as a school, the government, or a large business, which includes a hierarchical system of administration and strict rules for its governance.

null curriculum
The idea that something is taught by not being taught and is excluded from the curriculum.

INTASC Standards

Principle #7
Principle #9

INTASC Standards

Principle #9

Cleaver or the Black Panther Movement were introduced outside of the traditional curriculum.

I remember when a visiting African American scholar from the University of Buffalo came to my school to talk with us. I asked him how it was possible for there to be African American history when no written records were left by African Amercian people. It is hard to believe that I could have asked a question so naïve, except for the fact that it reflected the Eurocentric tradition of my education.

Likewise, women were excluded from my early historical training. Other than the brief mention of the suffrage movement, I have no memory from my courses in high school of reading or learning anything about the role of women in U.S. history or culture. Yet the education I received was considered among the best in the region. Being educated in a closed system, I did not know about other traditions. On the rare occasions I was introduced to these traditions, I dismissed them as secondary, as not holding up to the substance of the works from the Western canon.

I refer to my personal experience because I think it is a clear demonstration of the null curriculum at work. Who knows what its effects were? I am sure, however, that much of what I understood about the world was a result of what I had not been taught.

KEY SUPREME COURT CASES

Religion and the Null Curriculum

In 1962, the Supreme Court banned mandatory prayer in the public schools. The decision to do so was based on the principle of the separation of church and state, which precludes specific religious activities in the public sphere to ensure individual citizens the right to practice the religion of his or her choice. Since the early 1960s, many people have felt that, as a result of banning prayer and Bible reading in schools, U.S. education has lacked a necessary moral focus.

Various unsuccessful attempts have been made to reintroduce religion in the schools. Most school districts avoid the discussion of religion because of its potentially controversial nature. Significantly, the Supreme Court did not prohibit religion from being taught in the schools if it was taught from a historical, rather than a religious or doctrinal, point of view. Many religious leaders believe that to avoid controversy, public schools ignore or trivialize the religious elements of U.S. culture. This represents a type of null curriculum because to teach nothing about religion is, in effect, to teach something about it (that it is trivial, not worth serious study and so on). In doing so, it can be argued, an integral and important part of our cultural tradition is being ignored.

Is the exclusion of religion as a topic a mistake? Can it be discussed without violating issues of the separation of church and state? Does not including it, in fact, represent a type of null curriculum at work? What do you think?

Concepts such as the hidden curriculum and the null curriculum suggest that what is learned in school settings is complex. Students play a critical role in what is learned as well. This is particularly true in the case of **resistance theory** and learning.

resistance theory
The idea that oppressed or dominated groups often develop strategies and effective means to oppose or counter their domination.

■ RESISTANCE THEORY AND LEARNING

Much of the contemporary thinking about schools includes a tendency to believe that schools simply reproduce the existing class and social formations of the culture of which they are a part. The 1981 publication of Paul Willis's book *Learning to Labor* suggests that such attempts by the schools to impose specific cultural and class-oriented values on students often result in a great deal of resistance.

INTASC Standards
Principle #7

Willis studied a group of twelve nonacademically oriented, working-class English adolescents during their final two years of school and the first six months of their work careers. In his research Willis discovered that his subjects consciously rejected the values emphasized as part of the traditional schooling process. In doing so, they asserted their own identities and the traditions of their social group.

This type of resistance is extremely important to understand. An inner-city student of African American origin may reject the traditional curriculum, not because he or she is not smart enough to succeed in his or her work, but because it does not represent their family and culture. Speaking "correct English" may be seen as acting too much like "the white man." Considering their opportunities in life to be extremely limited, many inner-city youths see no point in embracing a curriculum that promises rewards later in life (after completing a college education).

According to Peter McLaren, "for many economically disadvantaged students, success in school means a type of forced cultural suicide, and in the case of minority youth racial suicide" (McLaren 1994, 215). In a study of students in the South Bronx, Michelle Fine found that those minority students who stayed in school were significantly more depressed, less politically aware, less likely to be assertive, and more conformist than their counterparts who had dropped out (cited by McLaren 1994, 215).

critical pedagogy
Teaching that involves a critical social and political awareness of issues.

Think, for a moment, how the arguments of Willis, McLaren, and Fine might affect your work as an inner-city teacher. To what extent will your own class and social background affect how students respond to you? Will curriculum that you think is important necessarily be important to your students? If students drop out or resist learning, does it necessarily mean that they are stupid or incapable of learning? What are the strategies you will have to employ to be an effective teacher?

■ DEVELOPING A CRITICAL PEDAGOGY

Nearly all the issues that have been raised thus far in this book in fact relate to the problem of developing a **critical pedagogy.** Pedagogy is an old-fashioned word. It comes from the Greek word *paidagōgia,* and refers to the "function or work of a teacher"—that is, teaching. *Paidagōgia* is obviously etymologically related to the word *paideia.* Think back about the discussion in the previous chapter concerning *paideia. Paideia* refers to the idea of education being a reflection of the culture or society of which it is a part. A critical pedagogy understands the role and function of education in the society or culture in which it functions.

As you will discover later in this book, the question of what should be taught in K–12 schools, colleges, and universities—including, of course, departments, schools, and colleges of education—is actively being debated in the educational field and the larger culture. Pedagogy, in its most narrow context, reduces teaching to instrumental skills, techniques, and objectives. In doing so, the "instrumentalization of teaching erases questions of power, history, ethics, and self-identity" (Giroux 1992, 98).

In contrast, critical pedagogy is concerned with the realities of what goes on in the classroom: the connections between the school and society, the child and the media, and the teacher and the students and parents they serve. Critical pedagogy, according to Giroux is

INTASC Standards

Principle #7

Principle #9

> . . . a pedagogy that rejects the notion of culture as an artifact immobilized in the image of a storehouse. Instead, the pedagogical principals at work here analyze culture as a set of lived experiences and social practices developed within asymmetrical relations of power. (Giroux 1992, 99)

To be meaningful, teaching must realize that what is taught more often than not reflects traditions of power, authority, and domination in the culture. Effective teaching must take into account the fact that education, pedagogy, teaching, and instruction are cultural and political acts. As discussed previously in this chapter, no such thing as neutral education exists. Critical pedagogy has as its purpose "developing pedagogical practices informed by an ethical stance that contests racism, sexism, class exploitation, and other dehumanizing and exploitative social relations as ideologies and social practices that disrupt and devalue public life" (Giroux 1992, 101).

Critical pedagogy is related to what Giroux refers to as "border pedagogy" and in turn "border crossing"—a concept introduced in the Preface to this book. Border pedagogy, implies a critically based multiculturalism, or what Giroux refers to as an "insurgent multiculturalism" (Giroux in Duarte 2000, 206). Both border pedagogy and insurgent multiculturalism, should, according to Giroux,

> ... promote pedagogical practices that offer the possibilities for schools to become places students and teachers can become border crossers engaged in critical and ethical reflection about what it means to bring a wider variety of cultures into dialogue with each other, to theorize about cultures in the plural, within rather than outside "antagonistic relations of domination and subordination." (Giroux in Duarte 2000, 206)

Practicing border pedagogy and, as a result, being a critical educator implies asking a number of questions: Who creates knowledge? Who is empowered by it? How are different groups subordinated, marginalized, and excluded in U.S. education and culture? What are the possibilities for resistance? What are the possibilities for achieving a more just and equitable society through the act of teaching? These are highly complex and difficult questions. They are questions that must be asked by those working in postmodern schools and classrooms. To ignore such questions is to ignore one's students, the changing nature of contemporary culture and society, and to fail in one's moral, ethical, and, ultimately, curricular mission as a teacher.

INTASC Standards

Principle #2

Principle #7

■ SUMMARY

This chapter has examined the meaning of culture and the role that schools play in reproducing the values and beliefs of a culture or society. We have addressed the issue of whether schools are neutral, and whether it is possible to have such a thing as a curriculum that is value free. Finally, we have considered questions of cultural capital, the hidden curriculum, the null curriculum, and the extent to which cultural resistance plays an important part in contemporary schooling. We have also looked at the meaning of critical pedagogy.

All this discussion suggests that schools are complex social settings—inherently fascinating, messy, and full of surprises. As a teacher you will, by definition, have to negotiate your way through a wide range of cultures. Even in the most rural and isolated classrooms in the United States, you will find diversity and will need to know the extent to which you as a teacher are promoting certain values and ways of looking at the world.

You will also need to understand how your students, classroom, and school are connected to larger social, economic, and cultural structures within the community. In the next chapter (Chapter 3), we look at the connection between education and the creation of a sustainable culture and society.

■ DISCUSSION QUESTIONS ■

1. Define what is meant by the term *culture*. What is the difference in your mind between high and low culture in U.S. society? Is one better than the other? If so, why?
2. Can you think of examples of how you were socialized in your experience as a student? What were the sources of that socialization?
3. Do you think that it is bad that schools socialize people? If yes, why? If no, why?
4. In a democratic culture like the United States, how do we determine what should be taught in the schools?
5. Can you describe examples of cultures competing with one another in your own community?
6. What is distinctly American about American culture? Can you provide examples?
7. What do you think is meant by the idea of cultural capital?
8. Do you think that education can be a neutral process? If yes, why? If not, why?
9. What does it mean to be literate? Is literacy limited just to reading books?
10. Give examples of the hidden curriculum from your own experience as a student in the schools.
11. Can you remember examples of the null curriculum from your own experience?
12. Why might students from minority groups be justified in resisting traditional schooling?

13. What are the good things about contemporary or postmodern culture? What things are problematic?
14. What would U.S. culture be like if we did not have schools—if society were deschooled, as suggested by Ivan Illich?
15. Why is the concept of *paideia* a useful one in understanding education and its role in our culture?
16. Why are critical and border pedagogy important concepts for educators?

■ SOURCES CITED ■

Bourdieu, Pierre. 1974. *Outline of theory and practice.* Cambridge: Cambridge University Press.

Cornbleth, Catherine. 1991. *Curriculum in context.* London: Falmer Press.

Duarte, Manuel, and Stacy Smith, editors. 2000. *Foundational perspectives in multicultural education.* New York: Longman.

Durkheim, Emile. 1956. *Education and sociology.* Glencoe, Ill.: The Free Press.

Eisner, Eliot W. 1985. *The educational imagination: On the design and evaluation of school programs.* New York: Macmillan.

———. Insurgent multiculturalism and the promise of pedagogy. In *Foundational perspectives in multicultural education,* edited by M. Duarte and S. Smith, 195–212. New York: Longman.

Giroux, Henry. 1992. *Border crossings: Cultural workers and the politics of education.* New York: Routledge.

———. 1981. *Ideology, culture and the process of schooling.* Philadelphia: Temple University Press.

Hall, Edward T. 1981. *Beyond culture.* Garden City, New York: Anchor/Doubleday.

Hirsch, Edward Donald, Jr. 1987. *Cultural literacy.* Boston: Houghton Mifflin.

———. 1989. *A first dictionary of cultural literacy.* Boston: Houghton Mifflin.

———. 1989. *The dictionary of cultural literacy.* Boston: Houghton Mifflin.

———. 1991. *What your first grader needs to know.* New York: Doubleday.

———. 1991. *What your second grader needs to know.* New York: Doubleday.

———. 1992. *What your third grader needs to know.* New York: Doubleday.

———. 1992. *What your fourth grader needs to know.* New York: Doubleday.

———. 1993. *What your fifth grader needs to know.* New York: Doubleday.

———. 1993. *What your sixth grader needs to know.* New York: Doubleday.

———. 1996. *The schools we need and why we don't have them.* New York: Doubleday.

Jackson, Philip. 1968. *Life in classrooms.* New York: Holt, Rinehart and Winston.

Kincheloe, Joe, and Shirley Steinberg. 1997. *Changing Multiculturalism.* Buckingham, Great Britain: Open University Press.

McLaren, Peter, ed. 1994. *Schooling, politics and cultural struggle.* New York: State University of New York Press.

———. 1998. *Life in schools: An introduction to critical pedagogy in the foundations of education.* New York: Longman.

Willis, Paul. 1977. *Learning to labor: How working class kids get working class jobs.* Westmead, England: Gower.

CHAPTER 3

Sustaining Our Culture and the Goals of Education

Sustainability is a fundamental concept in the field of ecology. It is based on a relatively simple idea: a viable system, whether biological or social, should be able to sustain itself over the course of time. What does this mean? In the case of fishing in a lake, it would mean only taking the fish we actually need and not taking so many that the ability of the fish population to maintain itself is threatened. In the case of a forest, we would look at the number of trees that could be harvested without threatening the existence of the forest as a viable ecological system.

Sustainability is a concept that can be applied to a culture, and more specifically, to an educational system and the students who attend its schools. This approach represents what some theorists describe as **social ecology.**

This chapter examines how the ecology of schools has changed as a result of postmodern trends. It also discusses the idea that among the major obligations of schools and the teachers who work in them is the need to help in the creation of a just and sustainable culture and educational system. In doing so, we reflect on the goals and purposes of education, and examine how schools fit into a larger social and cultural system.

The idea of creating a just and sustainable culture and educational system simply means living in a balanced and sensible way. It means that we take full advantage of the human resources we have available in our society. In other words, we do not waste **human capital,** but instead maximize the potential of individuals to become all that they are capable of becoming.

social ecology
The interrelationship of individuals and their cultures with their cultural, social, and political environments.

human capital
The idea that we invest in humans as resources much as business people invest in money and goods.

We are faced then, as **critical pedagogists** and educators—individuals concerned with understanding and critically addressing issues and problems in our schools and culture—with the problem of defining what we believe should be the goals of U.S. education.

■ GOALS OF U.S. EDUCATION

The educational historian Lawrence Cremin has defined education "as the deliberate, systematic, and sustained effort to transmit, evoke, or acquire knowledge, attitudes, values, skills, or sensibilities, as well as any outcomes of that effort" (Cremin 1976, 158). Cremin's definition stresses intentionality, and it is in this context that we examine the traditional goals of U.S. education.

In his famous *Rockfish Gap Report* (1818) on the program of the University of Virginia, Thomas Jefferson outlined the aims of an elementary educational system within a democracy. According to Jefferson the schools should

- Provide each citizen with the means by which he can transact his own business
- Provide each citizen with the means by which he can calculate for himself and preserve his ideas, contracts, and accounts in writing
- Improve by reading the citizen's morals and faculties
- Help the citizen understand his duties to his neighbors and country—and how to fulfill his obligations and duties as a neighbor and a member of the culture
- Provide the citizen an understanding of his rights and the ability to choose wisely those who represent his interests
- Provide the citizen with an understanding of various social relationships (adapted from Cremin 1965, 37–38)

critical pedagogists
Teachers and educators who support a philosophy of critical pedagogy.

common school
A movement in the 1830s and 1840s calling for common public education for all people.

Looking at U.S. education from the **common school** movement of the 1830s and 1840s to the present, we can argue that the schools have achieved these ends for many people, but more often for men than for women, and more often for whites than for blacks or other minority groups.

Historically, Americans have had an almost boundless faith in popular education as a vehicle of social reform and progress. For many people this faith has been justified. But at the same time, it has often oversimplified the complexities of education as a social and cultural phe-nomenon. Now, as in the past, the public school system and an "educa-tion" mean different things to different people. Although the United States has had a system of free universal public education for nearly 150 years, the educational experiences of individuals within that system have not necessarily been uniform. Instead, those experiences have been shaped by forces outside the educational system, forces at work within the larger society.

As a culture, we have assumed that schooling is a universally posi-tive experience—that it serves all our citizens equally well. This faith in schooling is part of the idea that the United States is a **meritocracy**. Un-der a meritocracy all individuals are given the opportunity to compete fairly and equally. In a meritocracy, those who are at the lower end of the social and economic scale are assumed to be there because they lack the intelligence, drive, and ability to succeed in the more general culture. Authors such as Richard J. Herrnstein and Charles Murray have argued in *The Bell Curve* (1994)that biological factors, rather than factors of race, gender, or geography, are responsible for why people do or do not succeed in U.S. society.

In a meritocracy, it is assumed that the best people rise to the sur-face, just as cream does in milk. It is also assumed that the most meri-torious citizens work for the betterment of the society. They are perceived as being neutral. Underlying the mythology is the belief that the leadership of the culture is disinterested in power—that they are be-nign "and because of the merit and wisdom of their members, such groups provide the best leadership, the most disinterested (objective) social management available" (Kincheloe and Steinberg 1997, 118). This leadership—as reflected in a largely white, male House of Repre-sentatives and Senate, as well as in corporate leadership drawn mainly from the same group—is what the cultural theorist John Fiske refers to as the **power bloc**.

According to Fiske, the power bloc is not made up of a specific class or well-defined social group. Power blocs constantly shift their strategic and social alliances. They involve the pursuit of privilege and power, and are often created around formations of race, class, gender, and ethnicity (Kincheloe and Steinberg 1997). Power is the key to understanding the idea of a power bloc. According to Fiske, power represents "a system-atic set of operations upon people that works to ensure the maintenance of the social order . . . and ensure its smooth running" (Fiske 1993, 11). Therefore, the power bloc can be better described by "what it *does* than what it *is*" (Kincheloe and Steinberg 1997, 77).

meritocracy
A political system based on merit.

power bloc
Political and social groups who subtly hold and maintain power in a cul-ture such as the United States.

INTASC Standards
Principle #9

INTERNET @ CONNECTIONS

Educational Lobbying Groups

Education is a hotly contested subject in U.S. society. There are many different views about how children should be taught. Should we have school vouchers? Does a local community have the right to limit the selection of books used by teachers in their classrooms? Does a teacher have the right to have an alternative sexual orientation? Political lobbying groups represent different perspectives on these issues. Among the most important lobbying groups in Washington, D.C. are People for the American Way and The Heritage Foundation.

The Heritage Foundation is a conservative religious group based in Washington, D.C. It describes itself as being "committed to rolling back the liberal welfare state and building an America where freedom, opportunity, and civil society flourish" (Heritage Foundation website).

People for the American Way, in contrast, is a liberal policy group that describes itself as working "to protect the heart of democracy and the soul of the nation. In Congress and state capitals, in classrooms and in libraries, in courthouses and houses of worship, on the airwaves and on the printed page, on sidewalks and in cyberspace, we work to promote full citizen participation in our democracy and safeguard the principles of our Constitution from those who threaten the American dream" (People for the American Way website).

Visit each organization's website to look at the sections devoted to education. Compare and contrast their points of view. What type of useful information does each group provide? How is the information they provide slanted politically? Which perspective is closest to your own?

People for the American Way
http://www.pfaw.org/

The Heritage Foundation
http://www.heritage.org/

Significantly, the power bloc can include individuals who are from backgrounds that are not representative of the more general populations within the power bloc. Thus, former Secretary of State Madeline Albright can be of immigrant origin and a woman and still be part of the power bloc. Likewise, General Colin Powell can be an African American and yet function as an extremely privileged and powerful member of the power bloc.

The power bloc, as a concept, may be difficult to understand. It is a concept that many people are uncomfortable talking about. The existence of the power bloc, and the belief in the United States as an essentially fair and just culture, is reinforced by many cultural myths and assumptions. Among the most interesting and important to know about among educators is the **"Great School Legend."**

Great School Legend
The tradition or myth that the public schools have provided students an equal means by which to advance and improve themselves in the culture.

? **WHAT DO YOU THINK?**

Who Is in Leadership?

Many people would argue that leadership in a democracy does not reflect class, race, or gender. Is this actually true? Who has economic and social power in the United States? Who has privilege? Think for a moment about who most of your teachers were in school. What was their racial or social background? What was their gender? Who were most of your principals? What was their race, social background, and gender? In your university or college, what is the gender of your school's dean? Of its provost or main vice president? Of its president? Who serves on the board of your university or college? What about the local school board in your hometown? Is there a relationship between race, social background, and gender, and economic and social power in U.S. society? Is the situation the same in the United States as in other countries, or is it different? What is your experience? What do you think?

■ THE GREAT SCHOOL LEGEND

Simply stated, the Great School Legend argues that the public schools have functioned as the great equalizing force in U.S. culture. If you were poor, if your parents were not well educated, then the public schools would provide you the opportunity to prove your merit. According to Colin Greer, the Great School Legend is like a fairy tale in which

INTASC Standards
Principle #9

> once upon a time there was a great nation that became great because of its public schools. . . . The public school system, . . . built American democracy. It took the backward poor, the ragged, ill-prepared ethnic minorities who crowded into the cities, educated and Americanized them into the homogeneous productive middle class that is America's strength and pride. (Greer 1972, 3–4)

Greer argues that instead of helping the poor and minorities advance within society, schools have actually held people back. He asserts that the Great School Legend has hidden the fact that racial and ethnic minorities have failed to achieve social and economic advancement. The Great School Legend has been widely believed by many people in U.S. culture going back to the beginning of this century. As an idea, it was widely promoted in the work of the educational historian Ellwood P. Cubberley.

FIGURE 3.1 ■ Standards of America.
Lithograph by Henry F. Heidrich, 1897.

Source: Courtesy of the Library of Congress.

Cubberley was dean of education at Stanford University. In 1919 he published *Public Education in the United States,* which argued that the public schools in the United States were society's main tool for democracy and social improvement. Cubberley's interpretation dominated U.S. education until the early 1960s when historians such as Bernard Bailyn, Lawrence A. Cremin, and Raymond Callahan began to demonstrate in their writings that despite many accomplishments, the schools had not achieved all they had been given credit for.

Beginning in the late 1960s, a group of radical historians, philosophers, economists, and social theorists known as the "revisionists" explored this issue in even greater detail. Under the leadership of scholars such as Michael Katz, Clarence Karier, Paul Violas, Walter Feinberg, Samuel Bowles, Herbert Gintis, Joel Spring, and Colin Creer, the revisionists criticized the role of the schools in the development of U.S. culture. Michael Katz, for example, in referring to figures like Cubberley, has written that

revisionist
Refers to the group of historians who revised the traditional and highly positive interpretation of the role of education in U.S. culture.

radical revisionist
The most critical of the revisionist theorists.

Americans share a warm and comforting myth about the origins of public education. For the most part historians have helped to perpetuate this essentially noble story, which portrays a rational, enlightened working class, led by idealistic and humanitarian intellectuals, triumphantly wresting public education from a selfish wealthy elite and from the bigoted proponents of orthodox religion. (Katz 1968, 1)

The **revisionist** and **radical revisionist** interpretations of U.S. educational history assume that public schools have served different social, economic, racial, and gender groups differently. Their interpretation suggests that there have indeed been power blocs in U.S. culture, and that different groups have been given a different education for different purposes. I feel strongly that this interpretation is valid, and the historical and sociological record confirms it. Does this mean that the public schools simply replicate class, social, and gender structures—that they are simply tools of the power bloc?

The answer is yes, but only in part. Schools are also centers of resistance. Students do not simply accept everything that is taught them. Typically, they use the portion of what they are being taught that is applicable to their lives. Learning to read, for example, does not mean that students read just what is in their textbooks. Nor do they uncritically accept what they read in their books.

Bernardo Gallegos, a well-known educational theorist and "Mexican American," for example, talks about how as a teenager he tried "to wash the brown off my skin with Comet bleach powder" (Gallegos 2000, 359). At the same time, he began to construct a self that asked questions about whom he was and the culture he came from. In doing so, he began to become aware of the possibilities of **counternarratives** to the stories he learned from the mainstream culture.

Counternarratives, in this context, would involve **postcolonial themes.** These are themes that recast traditional narratives and ways of constructing the world. Gallegos, for example, points out how in the Mexican American community this takes the form of creating new folk heroes and folk saints, such as Malverde, the patron saint of people who function outside the law—among the most popular deities found in **botanicas** throughout the Southwest. Another example of a counternarrative provided by Gallegos is of thousands of furious Latino high school and junior high school students storming out of class after the passage of the anti-immigration–oriented **Proposition 187**, most of Mexican background declaring: "We didn't cross the border, the border crossed us" (Gallegos 2000, 355).

According to Gallegos, the preceding statement represents a **discursive** counternarrative, one that locates "both Mexico and the United States as agents of the Western imperialist project, ultimately resulting in European occupation of Native North American territory and the subjugation of its people" (Gallegos 2000, 357). Gallegos talks about his own personal experience as someone of Mexican origin living in the United

counternarratives
Stories or cultural patterns of belief out of the mainstream and opposing traditional values and interpretations.

INTASC Standards
Principle #9

INTASC Standards
Principle #3

postcolonial themes
Themes that have emerged as part of the postcolonial era, typically in opposition to models of colonial power and control.

botanicas
Shops that sell medicinal herbs and spiritual material for the practice of various folk religions such as Santeria.

Proposition 187
A 1994 legal effort in California to restrict the education of undocumented children in the public schools.

discursive
Involving discourse and interaction.

? WHAT DO YOU THINK?

Should People Be Compensated for Past Injustices?

Many peoples and cultures inhabited North America before the European settlement. Indigenous people had their lands taken away from them as part of a conquest of the continent. Africans were brought against their will as slaves to North America. Much of the southwestern portion of the United States was annexed from Mexico in the first half of the nineteenth century. During the Second World War Japanese Americans (Nisai) were imprisoned and cheated out of much of their land and property in places such as California, Oregon, and Washington. In the case of the Japanese, limited compensation for their losses has been made in recent years. Do other groups deserve compensation? What constitutes sufficient compensation? Is it even possible to redress past wrongs? What do you think?

States and experiencing the pain caused by the contradiction between the "myriad of events, memories, conditions, and stories, that he carries with him through his native culture, and the representations of the same events in the mainstream and academic culture (Gallegos 2000, 360). He quotes the cultural theorist Stuart Hall, who in a similar vein describes how

> When I look at the snapshots of myself in childhood and early adolescence, I see a picture of a depressed person. I don't want to be who they want me to be, but I don't know how to be somebody else . . . Gradually, I came to recognize, I was black West Indian, just like everybody else, I could relate to that, I could write from and out of that position. It has taken me a very long time to write in that way, personally. Previously, I was only able to write about it analytically. In that sense, it has taken me fifty years to come home. It wasn't so much that I had anything to conceal. It was the space I couldn't occupy, a space I had to learn to occupy. (Cited in Gallegos 2000, 359)

Assuming a "cultural location" outside of the mainstream by definition represents a form of resistance—and an attempt to construct the world in a broader and more inclusive way.

Such experiences are not limited just to students in the schools. Likewise, teachers can resist the oppressive aspects of the culture and schooling. They can do so in their relationships with their students and their students' parents. They can do so in their interactions with their colleagues and by assuming the role of critical educators and pedagogists.

INTASC Standards

Principle #9

To do so, however, they must critically confront difficult questions. How do schools help children grow and develop their full potential? How do schools perpetuate existing power structures and prejudice within the culture? How can they limit the potential of certain children while helping others? What are the genuine accomplishments of the educational system? What are its limitations?

To begin to address these questions, teachers need to understand the context in which the schools they teach function. They need to understand the cultural background of their students and the ways in which their families and communities understand and organize knowledge. In doing so, they have the foundation necessary to be "border crossers."

INTASC Standards

Principle #7

What every teacher needs to know to function effectively as an educator differs from setting to setting and community to community. To teach effectively in a country like the United States requires educators to understand the relationship between the students they teach and the communities in which they live. Working with a child from a conservative Protestant religious orientation requires that the teacher understand something of that child's family and its values. A teacher, working with newly arrived Nicaraguan or Chinese immigrants, needs to have an understanding of the economic needs and the social and cultural traditions of the students with whom he or she is working.

Teachers also need to understand the changing structures of families and the demands that are increasingly being placed on children and their parents as part of the emergence of a postmodern culture and society. Many teachers, for example, meet parents for conferences about their children before school rather than after school to accommodate work schedules of busy two-parent working families. Teachers must cope with changing social situations in which, instead of writing a Father's Day card to their biological father, many children may also need to create a card for a stepparent or a guardian.

Situations such as these suggest that teachers need to have a deep understanding of the relationships and forces at work in the communities in which they teach. Such an understanding goes beyond simply knowing teaching methods and techniques, but also understanding teaching in a cultural context.

■ ECOLOGICAL PRINCIPLES APPLIED TO SCHOOLS

Think for a moment about a biological system such as a pond. As a natural system almost everything in the pond is interconnected. Small

INTASC Standards

Principle #9

Native American
The populations often equated with the colonial term *Indian,* who occupied North and South America prior to the arrival of the Europeans.

insects feed on plants and waste from large fish. Large fish feed on small fish and so on. Things are connected and dependent on one another—interrelated and linked.

Human beings live in an ecological system, just as do fish in a pond. Human systems are even more complex because they include not only biological elements, but also social, political, and cultural elements as well. How a child behaves in school, and more specifically in an individual teacher's classroom, is critically influenced by his or her socioeconomic status, the work and marriage patterns of their parents, and their race and ethnicity. They also are influenced by the type of neighborhood they live in, the country they come from, or even the region of the country they come from, the opportunities they have for meaningful work in the culture, and so on.

A privileged child (no matter what his or her racial or ethnic background may be), living in the suburbs, whose parents are members of the power bloc, probably finds the content of traditional curriculums easier to understand than does a child from an inner-city neighborhood whose parents are recently arrived immigrants from El Salvador or Estonia. The same child may not need much convincing about the importance of studying and striving for good grades to his or her long-term economic and social well-being. Such children probably are confident that if they graduate with good grades, they can almost certainly find a meaningful and high-paying job.

The privileged child at the high school level may strive for acceptance into an elite college that takes them far away from their home and family. They may be confident that their family is able to provide the necessary funds to pay for expensive tuition and so on. Imagine a talented young woman from a traditional **Native American** culture—perhaps an Inuit from Alaska. Going off to college for her may mean leaving her family, her traditions, and her culture. Paying for college, even with scholarships and loans, may place an enormous financial and psychological burden on her. The payoff provided by a college education may not be that much—jobs for highly educated individuals in her hometown may be very limited.

Likewise, a bright high school student who has arrived alone in this country, with family back home in a country like Cuba, Haiti, or Nicaragua, may think that getting a job flipping hamburgers or working on a construction crew is more important than staying in high school. Physical survival in this country may depend on making a basic salary. The ability to send some money back to one's family in his or her home country may be critical to that family's survival.

Taking these factors into account, the teacher must understand where his or her students are from within the cultural system. They must un-

INTASC Standards
Principle #10

derstand what forces outside the schools are shaping their perception of learning. What then is a teacher to do? Can teachers make a difference in the lives of their students despite the tremendous forces that are at play in the culture and in the individual environment where the students live?

The answer is yes. But to do so requires a sophisticated understanding of the cultural context of learning. In this context, insights from the field of biological ecology are helpful. Among the most important works in this field is Aldo Leopold's *A Sand County Almanac*. Originally published in 1949, *A Sand County Almanac* contains reflections about experiences in rural Wisconsin by one of the great U.S. naturalists and pioneering ecologists. In this work, Leopold establishes a series of remarkably simple but profound arguments about how biological systems function, and, in turn, how we should behave. He argues, for example, that "a thing is right when it tends to preserve the integrity, stability and beauty of the biotic community. It is wrong when it tends otherwise" (Leopold 1970, 262).

Apply this same concept to education. Apply it to the children in our culture. We are the richest nation in the world. One percent of our families own 42 percent of our wealth. Twenty percent of our children live below the poverty line. This poverty rate, which is shared with South Africa, is the highest in the industrialized world. We are the only nation in the industrialized world that does not provide universal health care for pregnant women and children (Giroux 1992, 162). Look at the following figures from the child advocacy group the Children's Defense Fund. What do they tell you about U.S. culture and the experience children bring with them to the schools?

> **INTASC Standards**
> Principle #9

- One in 2 preschoolers has a mother in the labor force.
- One in 2 will live in a single parent family at some point in childhood.
- One in 2 never completes a single year of college.
- One in 3 is born to unmarried parents.
- One in 3 will be poor at some point in their childhood.
- One in 3 is behind a year or more in school.
- One in 4 lives with only one parent.
- One in 4 was born poor.
- One in 5 is poor now.
- One in 5 lives in a family receiving food stamps.
- One in 5 is born to a mother who did not graduate from high school.
- One in 5 has a foreign-born mother.
- One in 6 is born to a mother who did not receive prenatal care in the first three months of pregnancy.
- One in 6 has no health insurance.

- One in 7 has a worker in their family but still is poor.
- One in 8 never graduates from high school.
- One in 8 is born to a teenage mother.
- One in 12 lives at less than half the poverty level.
- One in 12 has a disability.
- One in 13 was born with low birthweight.
- One in 24 lives with neither parent.
- One in 26 is born to a mother who received late or no prenatal care.
- One in 60 sees their parents divorce in any year.
- One in 138 will die before their first birthday.
- One in 910 will be killed by guns before age twenty. (Children's Defense Fund, 2000)

INTERNET @ CONNECTIONS

The Children's Defense Fund

The Children's Defense Fund is the United States leading organization concerned with improving the lives of children. Its publicly stated mission is "to leave no child behind" and to ensure every child "a healthy start," "a head start," "a fair start," and "a safe start" in their passage to adulthood. The Children's Defense Fund website at http://www.childrensdefense.org/ provides a wealth of information on subjects such as children's health, children and domestic violence, and children and gun violence.

INTASC Standards

Principle #9

Leopold argued more than fifty years ago "that land is a community is the basic concept of ecology, but that land is to be loved and respected is an extension of ethics. That land yields a cultural harvest is a fact long known, but latterly often forgotten" (Leopold 1970, xix). Likewise, doesn't the same hold true for our children? Don't we as a society reap a cultural harvest by how we treat them? Are we too concerned in our society with the individual, rather than the community? Are we more interested in wealth and consumption than human relationships and the family? Leopold warned us years ago that

> . . . our bigger-and-better society is now like a hypochondriac, so obsessed with its own economic health as to have lost the capacity to remain healthy. The whole world is so greedy for more bathtubs that it has lost the stability necessary to build them, or to even turn off the tap. Nothing could be more salutary at this stage than a little healthy contempt for a plethora of material blessings. (Leopold 1970, xix)

I agree with Leopold that we must reverse our tendency toward specialization: "instead of learning more and more about less and less we must learn more and more about the whole biotic landscape" (Leopold 1970, 189). Likewise, to be effective as teachers, we must understand where the students we teach are located in the broader social and cultural system (i.e., the ecological system). We must know this to be able to help them acquire the economic, social, and political skills that allow them to protect themselves and to develop to their full potential.

We need to be shocked by and morally responsible for what is happening to the children we teach. When we talk about young African American students, for example, what is the meaning for our society of the following facts?

■ African American children ages twelve to fourteen are 4.5 times more likely to be murdered than their white counterparts. African American children ages fifteen to seventeen are murdered at a rate almost seven times higher than white juveniles the same age.
■ In 1995, the largest group of murdered children ages twelve to seventeen was composed of African American males.
■ Firearms took the lives of 2,167 African American children in 1995.
■ Suicide rates involving a firearm almost tripled among young African American males between 1979 and 1994. This increase made 1994 the first year that youth suicides involving firearms were greater for African American males than for white males. (Children's Defense Fund, 1998)

Throughout this book, we look at sociological and historical data with the intention of better understanding the forces at work that shape the experience of the students in our schools. In doing so, we assume that knowledge provides a critical foundation for our work as teachers.

Although many aspects of this book seem to be negative and highly critical of U.S. culture and society, its basic assumption is that teachers and the work they do can make a difference in the lives of the children they teach. But this is only possible if they truly understand the populations they are working with and the social/historical forces that define who we are as a people.

As teachers, we must teach students to identify the forces that shape and mold their lives. The privileged child from the wealthy suburb whose parents and family are part of the power bloc must understand the privilege and opportunities he or she has been given. These children need to understand how others are situated compared to themselves. They need to be compelled to ask what is the basis and justification for their privileged position in society.

INTASC Standards
Principle #9

Likewise, the female student from rural Appalachia needs to understand where she is situated in the economic system, how traditions involving gender and patriarchy affect her life and the possibilities she has for the future. We must work with students to obtain a clear idea of their culture and traditions. If we do so effectively, we have the potential to help create, through the schools, a new and more just social order.

■ DARE THE SCHOOL BUILD A NEW SOCIAL ORDER?

INTASC Standards

Principle #9

In 1932 George S. Counts, a professor at Teachers College, Columbia University, published a short pamphlet, *Dare the School Build a New Social Order*, in which he explained that he was

> . . . prepared to defend the thesis that all education contains a large element of imposition, that in the nature of the case this is inevitable, that the existence and evolution of society depend upon it, that it is consequently eminently desirable, and that the frank acceptance of this fact by the educator is a major professional obligation . . . (Counts 1932, 12)

Counts further argued that teachers had a special role in defining the direction and purpose of U.S. society. He believed teachers should deliberately assume power—power they would use "fully and wisely and in the interests of the great masses of the people . . . " (Counts 1932, 12). Counts felt that the schools could be truly effective only if they became the centers for reconstructing or building—not merely contemplating—our culture. But he did not believe that teachers should impose their dogmatic views on students:

> This does not mean that we should endeavor to promote particular reforms through the educational system. We should, however, give to our children a vision of the possibilities which lie ahead and endeavor to enlist their loyalties and enthusiasms in the realization of the vision. Also, our social institutions and practices, all of them, should be critically examined in the light of such a vision. (Counts 1932, 37)

Counts clearly saw the limited possibilities of educational reform. He did not believe the schools could single-handedly redirect or reconstruct the culture. He did believe, however, that teachers could focus on issues in their classrooms that related to larger problems in the society.

Counts's ideas still ring true today. It is clear that U.S. society—in its various postmodern manifestations—is going through a period of remarkable and difficult change. It is also clear that we must reexamine the foundations of our educational system, and to do so we must understand something of the social and cultural forces that focus and direct it. As the educational historian David Tyack writes: ". . . what we need among other things, in American education is a tough-minded attempt to reformulate the purposes of public education in order to enlist the support this basic institution will need in the next generation" (Tyack 1980, 50). Such a reformulation requires us to ask critical questions about the nature and purpose of schooling in a postmodern culture.

■ CRITICAL QUESTIONS ABOUT THE NATURE AND PURPOSE OF SCHOOLING

If we are going to be critically engaged as educators; if we are to practice border pedagogy; if we are going to help our students achieve their full potential; and if we are going to work for the creation of a just and sustainable culture and educational system, we must face certain critical questions about the nature and purpose of schooling. In attempting to answer them we are in fact addressing a series of much larger questions that have profound importance not only for those entering the teaching profession, but also for our society as a whole. Consider the following:

INTASC Standards
Principle #9

1. **What is taught in the schools?** Who determines the curriculum? Does the content reflect a specific social or political set of values? Is the censorship of certain ideas necessary to protect students from "dangerous" or inappropriate ideas? What should be included in textbooks?
2. **Should the schools act as agents for social change or as a means of maintaining the status quo?** To what extent should teachers act as agents for promoting change or for maintaining the dominant values and beliefs of the culture? Should teachers be restricted in what they are allowed to teach their students?
3. **Who is to be educated?** In a democratic society such as the United States, is equal education for all possible or even desirable? Does the gifted child need the same support and resources as the average child or the handicapped child? What is equitable? Should ethnic groups and language minorities receive different training than other groups?
4. **What makes a good school?** Does the definition of a good school differ depending on the social and economic background of its students?

Can we compare schools with different types of clients who have different types of needs?

5. **What narratives should be emphasized in the curriculum of the schools?** Whose stories are to be told? What cultures are to be represented? What should be the end and purpose of instruction?

6. **What types of obligations do the schools have beyond simply educating students?** Should schools address the moral development of students, for example, or provide health services? What should be the focus of the school?

7. **Should schooling be compulsory?** If so, for how long? What is considered a sufficient education? Should students be compelled to learn things they or their parents oppose on moral and personal grounds?

8. **Should private schools be encouraged or discouraged?** Should they receive direct or indirect support from the government?

9. **What role should religion play in schooling?** Should selected religious practices or sects be allowed in the schools? Should certain religious groups be excluded? What is equitable?

10. **Who should control the schools?** Should the schools be controlled by parents, administrators, or state and federal governments? Who is capable of making the most informed decisions concerning what is needed by the educational system?

11. **What constitutes the necessary and proper means of training teachers?** Who should be allowed to teach? To what extent should teachers have the right to act according to the dictates of their own values?

12. **To what extent should the schools be used as a means of correcting or compensating for past social injustices?** Should the schools be used to desegregate the society and bring about greater equality?

13. **To what extent should the schools provide instruction that has in the past been provided by the family and other social groups?** Should subjects such as sex education or personal ethics and values be taught in the schools?

14. **To what extent is the media, in the form of television, movies, popular music, video games, and computers, taking the place of more traditional family and school-based instruction?** Is most of the education children receive coming from media sources? How is this type of education different from other types of learning? How is it related to commercial interests in our society?

15. **Who benefits most from new educational technologies such as computers?** Do the privileged have the most to gain from new computer technologies such as the Internet? Are there differences in the services provided students based on their social or economic class? Is the use of technology encouraged more for boys than girls?

16. **What is considered useful knowledge?** Whose knowledge is taught in the classroom? Is a particular canon taught? Where does it come from?

17. **How does race affect what goes on in the schools?** Does the racial background of the student affect how and what they are taught?

18. **How does ethnicity affect what goes on in the schools?** Are certain ethnic groups treated differently based on their background and experience? Or are all ethnic groups treated the same?

19. **How does gender affect what goes on in the schools?** Are men educated differently than women? Are women subjected to different treatment and experiences than men?

20. **How does social class affect the experience of students in the schools?** Are students from lower socio-economic groups treated differently than children whose parents are part of the culture's power bloc?

21. **What types of citizens do our schools want to create?** What knowledge is necessary to make people active and productive citizens?

22. **What constitutes good teaching?** How are teachers trained? What is considered good teaching?

23. **Why are the majority of teachers women?** Why are there fewer men and minorities in the teaching profession than in the general population?

24. **Should religion play a role in the educational system?** Why has religion been excluded from the schools? Should this practice continue?

25. **Should schools provide social services?** Is it the obligation of schools to provide free lunch and health care programs for students in need?

26. **What are the rights of teachers?** What can teachers do or not do? How much control should the society have over teachers in the classroom? In their private lives?

27. **What is the role of business in shaping and influencing the content of education?** What type of influence should business have in shaping the curriculum of the schools? Should students be trained for specific jobs demanded by the business system?

28. **What is the significance of the fact that women have dominated the teaching profession since the middle of the nineteenth century?** Has the fact that teaching has been a feminized profession affected the status of teachers—both historically and in contemporary culture?

29. **Should there be national standards and guidelines for the curriculum of the schools?** Should the content of curriculum be controlled at the local and state level or by the Federal government? Who should determine what gets taught in the schools?

30. **Should teachers be nationally licensed and certified?** Should teachers be "board certified" the way a specialist is in the field of medicine? What should constitute certification?

There are no easy answers to these questions, but the following chapters offer some perspective on these and many related issues. Use these questions as a starting point to begin your exploration of teaching as a profession and to reflect on your goals as a teacher.

■ SUMMARY

This book assumes that schools are important institutions in U.S. culture. As reflections of the social and economic tensions and forces within society, schools can provide us with a laboratory for understanding the values and beliefs at work in our culture. Schools also work in ways that are highly positive or very negative for students who attend them. Schools represent complex social systems in which issues of economic privilege, race, and gender are negotiated.

In a positive light, as David Tyack has pointed out, schools have served the important function of providing not just education but also social services across the entire society. The universality of elementary and secondary schooling allows, however imperfectly, the chance to compensate children who have a less than equal start in life. When they work well, schools can make a difference for the child from the broken home, or the poorly fed child, or the child with mental or physical disabilities just as they do for the well cared for and "normal" child.

Race, class, sex, and ethnicity can also restrict the ways in which people participate in and benefit from public education. Schools can function as instruments to perpetuate a wide range of discriminatory and essentially undemocratic practices. Teachers working in the schools must realize that they are part of a much larger social system. It is a system rooted in a complex set of historical experiences and power relationships. It is also a system that is influenced by media, technology, and a myriad of forces at work in society.

This book assumes that teachers have an important role in shaping and defining who we are as a people, and what we might become. In this context, we need to return to the idea of creating a just and, ultimately, a sustainable culture in which each citizen is given the opportunity to achieve his or her full potential. To do so, we must understand the larger social system in which our schools are located as well as what social, economic, and cultural forces are at work in the lives of the students whom we teach.

To do so, teachers must understand that teaching and schooling is ultimately a political and a social act. It is not neutral. It is not dispassionate. Teaching requires the individual to think critically and act and be. Teaching is an active verb. It is my belief that the complexities of teaching in a postmodern culture require a sophistication and insight that go far beyond what was demanded of teachers in the past. Without a reasonable understanding of the social foundations of our educational system and its relationship to U.S. society, your potential as a teacher will be limited.

Thus, what is described in this book is as essential to your success as a teacher as is learning how to plan a lesson, file a grade report, discipline a student, or get along with your colleagues. Although what we deal with in subsequent pages may at times seem abstract and somewhat distant from helping or loving children, it is nonetheless essential.

■ DISCUSSION QUESTIONS ■

1. Do you believe that thinking of schools as an ecological system is a useful model? If yes, why? If not, why?

2. What should be the primary purpose of schools—to educate people for the world of work or for life? Should a distinction be made between the two?

3. How does power manifest itself in schools? Think about this question at a number of different levels.

4. Based on your own personal experience in the schools, what can you remember that would confirm or contradict the "Great School Legend"? Can a case be made both for and against the legend?

5. What do you think schools in U.S. culture have done that is good? What have they done that has not been so good?

6. Should schools provide social services to needy students? Should free breakfast and lunch programs or health care programs be provided to needy schoolchildren? How might providing such programs affect school operations?

7. Can we expect schools to address social issues that the culture itself has difficulty addressing (equality of opportunity and so on)?

8. What do you understand by the idea of postcolonial thought? Do you think groups that have been discriminated against historically need to be compensated by the mainstream culture for past injustices? If yes, what is appropriate compensation?

9. Should schools attempt to reformulate or reconstruct society?
10. Why is it important, or perhaps unimportant, that U.S. society support a system of public and private education?

■ SOURCES CITED ■

American Federation of Teachers. Teachers salaries fail to keep up with inflation. Press release, May 17, 2001.

Bestor, Arthur. 1953. *Educational wastelands: The retreat from learning in our public schools.* Urbana: University of Illinois Press.

Bowles, Samuel, and Herbert Gintis. 1976. *Schooling in capitalist America: Educational reform and the contradictions of economic life.* New York: Basic Books.

Button, H. Warren, and Eugene F. Provenzo, Jr. 1983. *History of education and culture in America.* Englewood Cliffs, N.J.: Prentice-Hall.

Children's Defense Fund. 1998. *The state of America's children yearbook 1998.* Washington, D.C.: Children's Defense Fund.

———. 2000. *The state of America's children yearbook 2000.*

Counts, George. 1932. *Dare the schools build a new social order?* New York: Day.

Cremin, Lawrence A., ed. 1951. *The republic and the school: Horace Mann and education of free men.* New York: Teachers College Press.

———. 1965. *The genius of American education.* New York: Vintage Books.

———. 1976. *Public education.* New York: Basic Books.

———. 1977. *Traditions of American education.* New York: Basic Books.

Cubberley, Ellwood P. 1919. *Public education in the United States.* Boston: Houghton Mifflin.

Feinberg, Walter. 1975. *Reason and rhetoric: The intellectual foundations of twentieth century liberal educational policy.* New York: Wiley.

Feinberg, Walter, and Henry Rosemont. 1975. *Work, technology and education: Dissenting essays in the intellectual foundations of American education.* Urbana: University of Illinois.

Fiske, John. 1993. *Power plays, power works.* New York: Verso.

Ford, Paul Leicester, ed. 1982–1999. *The writings of Thomas Jefferson.* 10 vols. New York: G. P. Putnam's Sons.

Gabbard, David, ed. 2000. *Knowledge and power in the global economy: Politics and the rhetoric of school reform.* Mahwah, N.J.: Lawrence Erlbaum.

Gallegos, Berbardo. 2000. Postcolonialism. In *Knowledge and power in the global economy: Politics and the rhetoric of school reform,* edited by David Gabbard, 353–362. Mahwah, N.J.: Lawrence Erlbaum.

Giroux, Henry. 1992. *Border crossings: Cultural workers and the politics of education.* New York: Routledge.

Greer, Colin. 1972. *The Great School Legend: A revisionist interpretation of American public education.* New York: Basic Books.

Herrnstein, Richard J., and Charles Murray. 1994. *The bell curve*. New York: The Free Press.

Karier, Clarence J., Paul Violas, and Joel Spring. 1973. *Roots of crisis: American education in the twentieth century*. Chicago: Rand McNally.

Katz, Michael B. 1968. *The irony of early school reform: Educational innovation in mid nineteenth century Massachusetts*. Boston: Beacon Press.

Kincheloe, Joe, and Shirley Steinberg, editors. 1995. *Thirteen questions*. New York: Peter Lang.

———. 1997. *Changing multiculturalism*. Buckingham, Great Britain: Open University Press.

Maeroff, Gene I. 1982. *Don't blame the kids: The trouble with America's public schools*. New York: McGraw-Hill.

National Center for Educational Statistics (NCES). 1994. *The condition of education 1994*. Washington, D.C.: U.S. Government Printing Office.

National Commission on Excellence in Education. 1983. *A nation at risk: The imperative for educational reform*. Washington, D.C.: U.S. Government Printing Office.

Provenzo, Eugene F., Jr. 1985. Education in a post-revisionist era: A note. *The educational forum* 49(2): 227–232.

Ravitch, Diane. 1974. The revisionists revised: Studies in the historiography of American education. *Proceedings of the National Academy of Education* 4: 1–84.

Spring, Joel. 1972. *Education and the rise of the corporate state*. Boston: Beacon Press.

Tyack, David. 1980. Reformulating the purposes of public education in an era of retrenchment. *Educational Studies* 11(1): 49–64.

Tyack, David, and Elizabeth Hansot. 1982. *Managers of virtue: Public school leadership in America, 1820–1980*. New York: Basic Books.

United States Department of Commerce. 1999. *Statistical Abstracts of the United States*. Washington, D.C: U.S. Government Printing Office.

Yaffe, Elaine. 1980. Public education: Society's band-aid. *Phi Delta Kappan* 61(7): 452–454.

CHAPTER 4

Education and U.S. Society

Since the colonial period Americans have placed great faith in formal education. The ideal of every citizen having an equal opportunity to attend a school and receive an education has been an important part of the U.S. democratic tradition and has led to the development of a massive public school system extending from the elementary grades through the college level. The number of people attending public schools throughout the country illustrates the magnitude of this educational effort.

INTASC Standards
Principle #9

Virtually all children between the ages of six and fifteen are enrolled in public or private schools. Public school enrollment in kindergarten through eighth grade increased from 29.2 million in fall 1989 to an estimated 33.7 million in fall 1999. Enrollment in the upper grades decreased from 11.4 million in 1989 to 11.3 million in 1990. By 1999, however, this figure had risen to 13.5 million (*Digest of Education Statistics, 1999*). By 2007, the total number of students in the public schools is projected to rise to 48.3 million. Total private school enrollment is expected to be 6.1 million—approximately a 3 percent increase from 5.9 million students in the mid-1990s (*Condition of Education 1997*).

Total costs for public and primary education, from preprimary through graduate school were $619 billion for the 1998–1999 school year. Elementary and secondary schools spent about 60 percent of this total, and colleges and universities accounted for the remaining 40 percent. Elementary and secondary schools and colleges and universities spent an estimated 7.3 percent of the gross domestic product in 1998–1999 (*Mini Digest of Education Statistics 1997; Statistical Abstract of the United States 1998, Digest of Educational Statistics 2000*).

Per pupil investment in education varies significantly from one state to another. In 1994–1995 New York invested a total of $8,311 in each

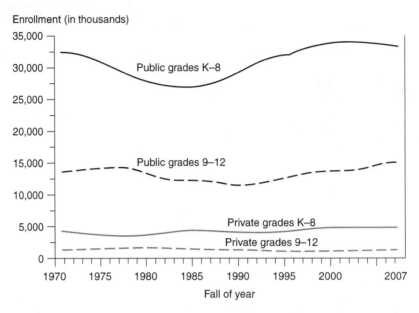

FIGURE 4.1 ■ **Elementary and secondary enrollment, by control and level of school: Fall 1970–2007.**

Source: U.S. Department of Education, National Center for Education Statistics, *Digest of Education Statistics, 1996* (based on Common Core of Data) and *Projections of Education Statistics to 2007,* 1997.

student and Connecticut invested $8,380. These amounts were more than twice as much as Utah ($3,109) and Mississippi ($3,798) invested per pupil (National Center for Education Statistics 1994–1995).

An estimated 3.3 million elementary and secondary school teachers worked in public and private schools in the fall of 2000. About 2.9 million men and women taught in public preprimary, elementary, and secondary schools across the country. In addition, 0.4 million worked in private schools. About 2.0 million teachers were teaching in elementary schools and 1.3 million at the secondary level (*Digest of Education Statistics 2000,* 6).

This extraordinary commitment of people and financial resources to the schools reflects the importance of formal education in U.S. society. Schools do much more than educate people to be citizens. In fact, as I have already suggested in this book, meeting the needs of the individual may be a secondary, rather than a primary, function of public schools. In the past, and perhaps even more so today, schools trained people for the world of work. They also communicated to people their status within society and what was expected of them. Almost always this was done as part of a hidden or null curriculum.

Enrollment, in millions

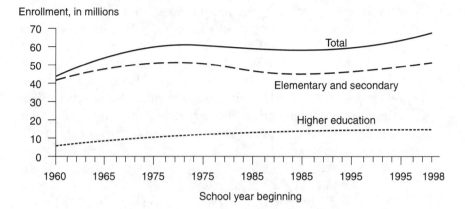

Enrollment, in billions of current dollars

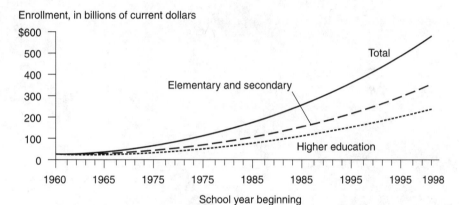

Enrollment, in billions of constant 1998–99 dollars

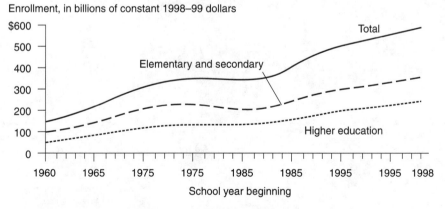

FIGURE 4.2 ■ Enrollment and total expenditures in current and constant dollars by level of education: 1960–1961 to 1998–1999.

Source: Digest of Education Statistics, 1999.

How do Americans actually feel about their schools? In the "31st Annual Phi Delta Kappan/Gallup Poll of the Public's Attitude toward the Public Schools" (1999), respondents indicated strong support for their local schools and more general dissatisfaction with the schools nationally. This is consistent with responses from earlier polls. Interestingly, considerably greater doubts are held about schools at the national level. When asked to grade the schools nationally, respondents to the 1999 Gallup Poll gave the nation's schools much lower grades than their local schools.

When respondents to the 1999 Gallup Poll were asked what they saw as being the "biggest problems" facing public schools in their community, they talked about the use of drugs (46%) and the lack of discipline (18%). This is compared to previous percentages in 1992 of 22 percent and 28 percent for the use of drugs, and 17 percent in 1992 and 24 percent in 1986 for lack of discipline.

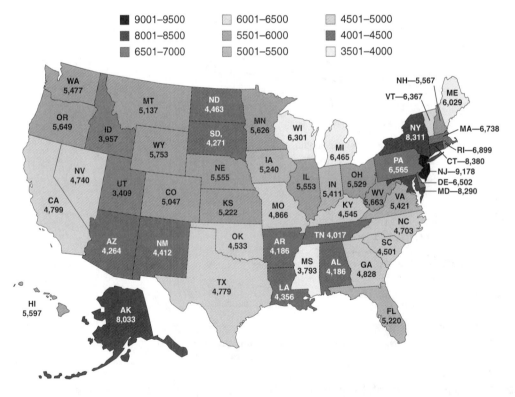

FIGURE 4.3 ■ Current per-pupil expenditures for elementary and secondary schools, school year 1994–1995.

Source: U.S. Department of Education, National Center for Education Statistics, Common Core Data, "National Public Education Financial Survey, School Year 1994–1995."

TABLE 4.1 ■ Grades Given Local Public Schools by the General Public

	1999	1992	1986
A & B	49%	40%	41%
A	11	9	11
B	38	31	30
C	31	33	28
D	9	12	11
Fail	5	5	5
Don't Know	6	10	15

Source: Adapted from *Phi Delta Kappan*'s 1999, 1992, and 1986 "Annual Gallup Polls of the Public's Attitude Toward the Public Schools." Used with permission.

INTERNET @ CONNECTIONS
Online Information about Education

There any many outstanding online resources currently available to educators to help them conduct research on schools and the teaching profession. The National Center for Educational Statistics, at http://nces.ed.gov/, is one of the best places to begin any general research. The purpose of the Center is to collect and report "...statistics and information showing the condition and progress of education in the United States and other nations in order to promote and accelerate the improvement of American education" (NCES Website).

Compendia put together by the Center include the *Digest of Education Statistics;* the *Condition of Education;* Youth Indicators; the *Mini Digest of Education Statistics and Projections of Education Statistics to 2007* (a collection of projections to the year 2007 related to education, including enrollment, graduates, classroom teachers, and expenditures). Most of these sources are updated on an annual basis. Also worth consulting for educational information is the *Statistical Abstract of the United States.* Published each year, the *Abstract* is the country's main national data book and contains statistics on the social and economic conditions in the United States, as well as related international data. It is also available online, http://www.census.gov/statab/www/, and is an invaluable resource for general information and data.

TABLE 4.2 ■ Grades Given National Public Schools by the General Public

	1999	1992	1986
A & B	24%	40%	41%
A	2	9	11
B	22	31	30
C	46	33	28
D	16	12	11
Fail	4	5	5
Don't know	10	10	15

Source: Adapted from *Phi Delta Kappan*'s 1999, 1992, and 1986 "Annual Gallup Polls of the Public's Attitude Toward the Public Schools." Used with permission.

TABLE 4.3 ■ Biggest Problems with Which the Public Schools of Your Community Must Deal (national totals)

	1999	1992	1986
Lack of discipline/more control	18%	17%	24%
Lack of financial support/funding/money	9	22	11
Use of drugs/dope	46	22	28
Overcrowded schools	16	9	5
Crime/vandalism	4	3	3
Difficulty getting good teachers	4	5	1
Parents' lack of support/interest	2	5	4
Low pay for teachers	2	3	3
Poor curriculum/low standards	2	9	8
Busing	2	4	3
Pupils' lack of interest/attitudes/truancy	2	3	3

Source: Adapted from *Phi Delta Kappan*'s 1999, 1992, and 1986 "Annual Gallup Polls of the Public's Attitude Toward the Public Schools." Used with permission.

Figures add to more than 100 percent in some cases because of multiple answers.

INTERNET @ CONNECTIONS

What Does the Public Think about Its Schools?

Every September since 1969, *Phi Delta Kappan* magazine, together with the Gallup Organization, has published a poll of U.S. public attitudes toward schools. Beginning in 1974 respondents to the education polls have been asked to grade the public schools in their communities on a scale of A to F. In 1981, people were first asked to rate the "nation's public schools" using the same scale.

You can look at the results of the most recent *Phi Delta Kappan*/Gallup Poll by visiting the magazine's website at http://www.pdkint.org/kappan/ktoclist.htm. Look at the most recent September issue of the magazine to find the results for the poll. By comparing results from earlier surveys, you will be able to see historical trends in the public attitude toward education.

Traditionally, we have assumed not only the importance, but also the necessity, of education in defining a society. Yet if education recreates the society of which it is a part, we face a number of dilemmas. What if the society is unjust? Inequitable? What if its ideas are sterile or corrupt? Would the educational system help to perpetuate a society that needs to be changed and redefined (Greene 1973b, 3–4)? These are crucial questions for those interested in teaching. The answers are not simple. Most teachers enter the profession as idealists. They want to find meaning in their own lives and help others find meaning as well. Often teachers perceive themselves as agents of change concerned with improving the quality of life in our society.

INTASC Standards
Principle #9

Romantic educational critics, such as Jonathan Kozol, have pointed out that teachers who have carefully examined the U.S. public school system face a number of difficult and painful realities. Much of what goes on in the schools on a day-to-day basis is archaic, and often education is dehumanizing. Many teachers continue to work as teachers despite obvious limitations and problems; often they feel they can overcome the limitations of the school system in which they work. As Kozol has explained, many teachers live and work

> . . . in somewhat the state of mind as intellectual guerrillas, determined somehow to awaken students, to spark their curiosity and to open their minds, yet no less determined to *remain* as teachers in the schools. We live and work with a strong resolve to raise some basic, and challenging and perhaps subversive questions in the consciousness of children. At the same time we have got to keep in mind the needs of our families, health care, food and mortgage and the rest. (Kozol 1981, 3)

Kozol's final point relates to a fundamental issue students and the public often forget—that teachers are people and have normal human problems. Along with his desire to do what is best for his students, the typical teacher has to worry about problems like paying the rent, keeping the automobile fixed, and worrying about why his son or daughter is coming home late from a Saturday night date.

The teacher, like any other individual, must come to grips with the contradictions and problems inherent in our society. On a day-to-day basis this means recognizing the realities of power and influence within the school system. Teachers must determine what they can and cannot accomplish; they must know their strengths and weaknesses. But while realizing their own limitations as well as the limitations of the school system, they must understand they are not powerless to bring about change. The anthropogist Jules Henry explains:

> . . . we must know our strength. Nobody is invulnerable, but nobody is as weak as he thinks he is either. Let everyone instead of saying to himself, "I am afraid," say instead, "I may be stronger than I think." (Henry 1972, 24)

■ EDUCATION AND POWER

Power is rarely discussed in an educational context. We are embarrassed to discuss the realities of power openly, but power in one form or another shapes what can or cannot be done in schools. Power is fundamental in all human experience, and education and schooling are no exception. David Nyberg has commented on this failure to address the question of power:

> The idea of power has lain more completely neglected in educational studies than in any other field of thought that is of fundamental social interest. Power talk is conspicuously absent from schools and from educational literature. There is no theory of power that contributes much at all to understanding education and its importance in American society. It would seem that the customs and cultures of educators prohibit the mere mention of power and censor the impulse to think seriously about it. One is more likely to hear singing in a bank than serious talk of power in relation to education. (Nyberg 1981a, 536)

Bertrand Russell has argued that "the fundamental concept in social science is Power, in the same sense in which energy is the fundamental concept in physics" (Russell 1938, 12). Why then does educational theory ignore the issue? Why is power not a concept discussed more often within the schools and departments of education (Nyberg 1981a, 536)?

Power is a reality in nearly all of our social relationships. It determines what we may or may not accomplish as educators. Teachers have power over students. Administrators have power over teachers. The community has power over them all. Yet the idea of one simply dominating the other does not conform to reality. Instead, there is a subtle interplay of force versus counterforce, of compromise and exchange. Teachers may demand certain standards of excellence from their students, who in turn may either accept or reject what is demanded of them.

With the exercise of power there is also an inevitable testing of power. A teachers' union may demand higher wages and threaten to strike if its requests are not met. If those requests are unreasonable, a community may counter this exercise of power by not acceding to the union demands and letting the strike take its course. The ultimate outcome of the strike—the surrender of the union, accession by the community to its demands, or a compromise between the striking teachers and the community—reflects the realities of power.

The **desegregation** of schools, the hiring and firing of teachers, the extent to which a community has control over the content of the curriculum in its schools, and whether a teacher permits students to leave their desks to go to the bathroom are all ultimately issues of power and authority. Who has power is critically important for education and schooling in general.

desegregation
The process of eliminating racially and ethnically segregated social institutions.

culture of silence
A concept developed by the Brazilian educator Paulo Freire in which the poor are silenced by not having a voice or a critical role in their own affairs.

■ PAULO FREIRE—EDUCATION AS CULTURAL ACTION FOR FREEDOM

In our discussion thus far, we have emphasized that educational practice implies a cultural and, in turn, a political and an ideological point of view. This argument has been basic to the work of a number of educational theorists, among whom the most interesting is the Brazilian educator Paulo Freire. Freire's experience as an educator came primarily from working with the poor in South America. According to him the poor live in a **"culture of silence"** dominated by the ideas and values of others. As a revolutionary educator Freire saw learning as a process of liberation; for him, education is "an act of cultural action for freedom—an act of knowing and not of memorization" (Freire 1970, 1).

What does Freire mean by education as cultural action for freedom? And why do his ideas have importance for U.S. education? Freire recognized that if learning is to have any meaning for the student, it must relate to his or her experience and life. This is not a new idea. John

INTASC Standards
Principle #9

Dewey discussed its importance nearly a hundred years ago. Learning, according to Freire, involves a **dialogue** between the teacher and the student. Learning also involves the development of a critical consciousness on the part of the student. Instead of being simply acted on and reacting to the world in which he or she lives, the student learns to reflect and act on the events of his life.

Freire put his ideas into action while working with illiterate peasants in Brazil. Instead of imposing information on them from outside their experience and culture, Freire drew on the experience and interests of those being taught to create the conditions for dialogue. Vocabulary words were of a **generative** nature, and came from the experience of and reflected the needs of those being taught to read. How and why questions took precedence over questions of who and what. Instead of domestication, education became an act of liberation, what Freire described as "conscientization," or education for critical consciousness.

Having learners become engaged in a process of critical consciousness is a radical shift from the more traditional **banking model** of education. Under a banking model of education, students are considered to be empty containers or vessels into which the teacher (and the society) "pour" knowledge and information. In an educational system that has a banking model at work, students do not function critically but, instead, have information imposed on them from the outside. As Freire explained in *Pedagogy of the Oppressed*:

> To achieve [domination] the oppressors use the banking concept of education in conjunction with a paternalistic social action apparatus within which the oppressed receive the euphemistic title of "welfare recipients." They are treated as individual cases, as marginal persons who deviate from the general configuration of a "good, organized, and just" society. The oppressed are regarded as the pathology of the healthy society, which must therefore adjust these "incompetent and lazy" to its own mentality by changing their mentality. . . . Translated into practice the concept of banking education is well-suited to the purposes of the oppressors, whose tranquility rests on how well humans fit the world the oppressors have created, and how little they question it. (Freire 1972, 47–48)

For Freire, formal schooling has too often involved the domination of the student instead of his or her liberation. Educational theorists such as Martin Carnoy, as well as Gail P. Kelly and Phillip Altbach, have described this situation as one of "cultural imperialism" or "educational colonialism."

INTASC Standards

Principle #4

INTASC Standards

Principle #4

---

dialogue
As defined by Paulo Freire, the genuine and meaningful exchange of information and ideas between people—one which leads to greater knowledge and insight for all of those involved.

generative
Referring to words or concepts that generate meaning and which ultimately empower their users.

banking model
An idea developed by Paulo Freire in which ideas and information are deposited in people, much like money is deposited in a bank.

■ EDUCATIONAL COLONIALISM

According to Kelly and Altbach, **educational colonialism** manifests itself in three different ways. In a traditional colonial setting schools emerge that in most instances "reflect the power and the needs of the colonizers" (Kelly and Altbach 1978, 2). Typically, the aspirations and needs of those being dominated are ignored: "The thread that ran through all colonial education was the fact that it was offered by the colonizer without the input or the consent of the colonized" (Kelly and Altbach 1978, 2). Citing examples in Africa, Asia, and Latin America prior to independence, Kelly and Altbach argue that traditional colonial schools neither provided the opportunity for integration into the dominant culture for those of the colonized population who attended them, nor prepared those who were colonized for positions of leadership within their indigenous cultures.

In a colonized educational system the individual becomes increasingly alienated from his or her native culture. Colonized people are directed; they do not direct themselves. Their creative power is impaired; they are objects, not subjects. A number of contemporary educational critics have argued that throughout their history U.S. schools have attempted to colonize many of the groups whom they teach. In particular, the experiences of women, African Americans, and Native Americans have often been cited as demonstrations of a colonial system of education at work in U.S. society.

We must ask ourselves whether the concept of colonialism can be fairly applied to U.S. education. From the evidence available, we must conclude that for many students schooling in the United States has often fit a colonial model. Consider for a moment the points made by Kelly and Altbach:

1. That those who are colonized are considered intellectually, physically, and morally inferior when compared with the colonizers
2. That colonial education is controlled by the colonizer and is detached from both the educational system of the colonizer and the colonized
3. That the history of the colonized group is denied or reinterpreted in such a way that the fundamental identity of the colonized group is significantly obscured or diminished
4. That the content of colonial education is different from that given the colonizer
5. That the colonized group eventually comes to identify with the values and beliefs of the colonizer and to assume their superiority (Kelly and Altbach 1978, 1–44)

INTASC Standards
Principle #2

educational colonialism
In colonized educational systems a dominant culture imposes its educational ideas and values on a subordinated culture.

INTASC Standards
Principle #9

INTASC Standards

Principle #3

Kelly and Altbach's arguments clearly conform to the educational experience of various minority groups in U.S. culture. Take, for example, the case of the African American population, which demonstrates each of Kelly and Altbach's points:

1. Until recently, and unfortunately still in many instances, the dominant white culture has considered itself superior in almost every way to African American culture.
2. African American students have only recently been integrated into the general educational system of the culture.
3. Until the 1960s the contributions made by African Americans to U.S. culture and society were rarely recognized or discussed.
4. The type of education provided to African Americans was frequently different from, and most often inferior to, that provided in the mainstream school system.
5. As a result of the tradition of domination and oppression, many African Americans have looked on the mainstream white culture as being superior to their own.

Certainly the inequities of the educational system are fewer than they were a generation ago. The desegregation of schools and the passage of the various civil rights acts of the 1960s have greatly expanded the possibilities for genuine equality in our society. Yet discrimination can also function at a very subtle, and sometimes almost undetectable, level. One can see this in the case of **hegemony.**

■ EDUCATION AND HEGEMONY

hegemony
A concept in which a dominant group maintains its control of a subordinate group or class of people through consensual practices, social forms, and structures. This control can be exercised through educational institutions such as schools, mass media, the political system, and the family.

Hegemony, as a cultural and educational concept, is difficult to explain. It involves a dominant culture dominating or subordinating a class or group of people. Peter McLaren defines the term:

Hegemony refers to the maintenance of domination not by the sheer exercise of force *but primarily through consensual social practices, social forms, and social structures produced in specific sites such as the church, the state, the school, the mass media, the political system and the family. . . .* Hegemony refers to the moral and intellectual leadership of a dominant class over a subordinate class achieved not through coercion (i.e., threat of imprisonment or torture) or the willful construction of rules and regulations (as in a dictatorship or facist regime), but rather through the general winning of consent of the subordinate class to the authority of the dominant class. (McLaren 1998, 177, 178)

Hegemony is particularly interesting because the very people whom it oppresses often embrace it. In high schools, for example, a hegemony is at work in the power and influence of sports and athletes. Many students are put down and mocked if they are different from the athletes and cheerleaders (not as pretty or handsome in a mainstream way, not as interested in team sports like football and basketball, and so on), who dominate the elite sports culture of many high schools. Yet the very individuals who are teased by the jocks, humiliated by the coaches, and ignored by the cheerleaders attend school sports matches and often live vicariously through the experiences of those who exclude them.

Think back to your own high school experience. Do you remember a water-boy for the football team or a record keeper or manager for the basketball team who was constantly being mocked and taken advantage of by members of the team? Do you remember the shy or awkward kid who was never accepted by the jocks and the cheerleaders but who always wanted to be accepted by them?

Hegemony can enter the curriculum in terms of what is taught. When the author of this book, for example, was attending elementary school in the mid- to late 1950s, none of the reading books he learned to read from included illustrations of African American or ethnic children or adults, nor individuals who were anything other than middle or upper class. When he went to high school during the mid- and late 1960s, none of his U.S. history textbooks had much to say about African American history, women's rights or the rights of gays. The historical culture that was presented to him was primarily white male and Western European. A null curriculum was in place that excluded people of color and ethnicity and lower socioeconomic class.

That was part of the hegemony of the dominant political and social groups in the culture. In the case of gay students, a hegemony of **heterosexuality** has historically dominated, and continues to dominate, most schools. Gay students and teachers may be invisible in the culture of schools—largely to protect themselves from the discrimination and oppression that often faces them.

Hegemonic systems, according to Douglas Kellner, try "to define the limits of discourse, by setting the political agenda, by defining the issues and terms of debate, and by excluding oppositional ideas" (quoted by Giroux 1981, 23). Such efforts often meet with resistance. Even though a hegemonic system is in place, it does not mean that it is necessarily

heterosexuality
Sexual relationships and activities between males and females.

gothic
A romantic popular culture grouping in which individuals dress in black and focus on themes involving death.

oppositional groups
Groups that consciously oppose or challenge traditional cultural models.

accepted. At the same time, organizing or sometimes even being aware of the need for resistance is difficult for oppressed groups to do.

One of the most common places for resistance is found in popular culture. Songs, movies, clothing, and other cultural representations act as a means by which to protest or promote an alternative model. Thus, high school students wearing black **"gothic"** dress, or piercing their ears, noses, tongues, and belly buttons, may actually be making a deliberate statement against dominant groups. Schools are active sites for contesting dominant cultures. As Peter McLaren argues: "People *do* resist. Alternative groups do manage to find different values and meanings to regulate their lives. **Oppositional groups** do attempt to challenge the prevailing culture's model of codifying representations and meanings" (McLaren 1998, 179).

KEY SUPREME COURT CASES

The Pledge of Allegiance

The First Pledge

> *I give my hand and heart to my country, one nation, one language, one flag.*
> —Traditional pledge used throughout the nineteenth century at public ceremonies (author unknown)

1892

> *I pledge allegiance to my Flag and to the Republic for which it stands—one Nation indivisible, with liberty and justice for all.*
> —Francis Bellamy

1923

> *I pledge allegiance to the Flag of the United States of America and to the Republic for which it stands, one Nation indivisible, with liberty and justice for all.*
> —National Flag Conferences of 1923–1924

1954

> *I pledge allegiance to the Flag of the United States of America and to the Republic for which it stands, one Nation under God indivisible, with liberty and justice for all.*
> —United States Congress

The history of the Pledge of Allegiance can be traced back to the early 1890s when James Upham, circulation head of the popular children's magazine *Youth's Companion,* developed a plan to encourage patriotism among U.S. schoolchildren. In a series of articles Upham encouraged thousands of children across the country to raise money to buy flags for their classrooms. More than 30,000 flags were eventually purchased for classrooms.

Spurred on by the success of the flag purchasing program, Upham decided to create a pledge of allegiance that students would recite each morning as the flags in their classrooms were raised. The Pledge itself was actually written by Francis J. Bellamy, one of the editors of the *Youth's Companion.*

Bellamy also devised a plan that would include schoolchildren across the nation in the Columbus Day celebrations. He urged that the dedication day of the World's Columbian Exposition, October 12, 1892, be set aside as a national holiday. To make the Columbus Day celebrations truly national in character, copies of the pledge were circulated to teachers throughout the country by the U.S. Department of Education.

The use of the Pledge as part of the daily routine of the public schools became widespread following its introduction in 1892. Alterations were made to Bellamy's original version of the pledge in 1923 and 1924 by the National Flag Conferences. In 1954 the words "under God" were added. A resolution approving this change was signed by President Dwight D. Eisenhower.

Considerable controversy has surrounded the Pledge. State laws mandate that the Pledge be recited daily in the schools. In 1940 the Supreme Court ruled in *Minersville School District v. Gobitis,* 310 U.S. 586, that two children who refused to salute the flag as part of a daily exercise could be required to do so. This decision was overturned in 1943 in the case of *West Virginia State Board of Education v. Barnette,* 319 U.S. 624. In *Barnette,* Justice Robert Jackson argued that " . . . no official, high or petty, can prescribe what shall be orthodox in politics, nationalism, religion, or other matters of opinion or force citizens to confess by word or act their faith therein."

The *Barnette* ruling was generally understood as maintaining the religious rights of individuals not to have to salute or pledge to the flag—in this case a principal rejected by Jehovah's Witnesses who were plaintiffs in the case. In the late 1960s an important test case came to light after two students in High School 217 in Briarwood, New York, refused to say the Pledge of Allegiance and stand for the salute to the flag. Under New York State Education Law, students were required to participate in the Pledge. In this case the students' actions were motivated by their political convictions and dissatisfaction with the government's pursuit of the war in Viet Nam. In May of 1970, Governor Mandel of Maryland signed a bill requiring teachers to lead their classes in the Pledge. Implementation of this law was delayed by the circuit court until pending legal cases were decided.

Eventually, clarification of the controversies surrounding the Pledge of Allegiance occurred in 1973 with the case of *Goetz v. Ansell,* 477 F. 2d. 636. Building on *Barnette,* this decision assured teachers that students had the right to remain silent and seated, without having to leave the room, while the Pledge was being recited by other students (Provenzo and Provenzo 1991).

▪ SCHOOLS AS SOCIAL SYSTEMS

INTASC Standards

Principle #1

Schools and the teachers and administrators who work in them tend to be optimistic by nature. Most people involved in the educational process buy readily into the idea that if we try hard enough, we can improve the education and lives of the children we teach. This idea, although noble, may not be entirely realistic. As critical educators, we need to understand the extent to which schools function as part of a larger social, cultural, and economic system.

The previous chapter introduced the concept of schools being ecological systems—systems clearly connected to the larger culture and society of which they are a part. As argued earlier, our social systems, including schools, can be looked at in much the same way that we look at natural and biological systems. Social theorists can provide us with the means to interpret the complexity of schools and their relationship to the larger culture. In this context, the work of the German social theorist Jürgen Habermas and his work *Legitimation Crisis* are particularly relevant.

Habermas's reputation is based on works such as *The Theory of Communicative Action, Toward a Rational Society, Knowledge and Human Interests, Theory and Practice,* and *Communication and the Evolution of Society.* In *Legitimation Crisis* Habermas draws on systems theory to develop his own theory of social crisis. According to a systems approach, "crises arise when the structure of a social system allows fewer possibilities for problem solving than are necessary to the continued existence of the system" (Habermas 1973, 2).

Crises in social systems do not occur by accident, but are a result of "system-imperatives" that cannot be integrated into the social system. Drawing on an analogy with biological systems, Habermas argues that a crisis occurs when an organic system reaches an impasse where the various systems that make up an organism no longer integrate with one another and a malfunction leads to the death of the organism or a reestablishment of a new equilibrium or balance in the system.

A social system such as the United States is "steered" by subsystems that include (1) a "political administrative system" (government), (2) an economic system, and (3) a sociocultural system (Habermas 1973, 5). The sociocultural system is of particular interest from an educational point of view in that it legitimizes the political and economic system through the education and socialization of our children. In this context, a capitalist culture such as the United States educates children to be consumers and producers in the economic system, to value democratic political values, and to assume that a free market economy is of greatest benefit to us as a culture and society.

NOTABLE QUOTES

What Are Education and Schooling Really About?

There are lots of famous quotes about what education and schooling are all about. Look at the examples provided below. Which, if any, is the most meaningful to you. Are these quotes really meaningful to people involved in the day-to-day work of schools? Are they more than just platitudes? What do you think?

> *At its best, schooling can be about how to make a life, which is quite different from how to make a living.*
>
> —Neil Postman

> *The classroom—not the trench—is the frontier of freedom now and forevermore.*
>
> —Lyndon B. Johnson

> *Education is not a preparation for life; education is life itself.*
> —John Dewey

> *The chief object of education is not to learn things but to unlearn things.*
> —G. K. Chesterton

> *I have never let schooling interfere with my education.*
> —Mark Twain

> *Schools are the workshops of humanity.*
> —Johann Amos Comenius

> *Only the educated are free.*
>
> —Epictetus

Using the biological model, these three subsystems: political administration, economic, and sociocultural—form an organic whole. In fact, more than these three systems may be at work, but these three are essential to any advanced capitalist system such as the United States. To understand ourselves as a culture and to understand our schools, we must be aware of how these three systems interact with one another to make us who we are.

No one would argue that these three systems are not necessary or desirable. How they should interact with one another, however, is open to considerable debate. What norms are to be established? How is the system to be brought into equilibrium and balance? In fact, these three subsystems, which make up the larger cultural system, are in constant tension with one another. Each affects and shapes or steers the other, often in ways that are not immediately evident or visible.

Within this context, return to the model of the social system as a body: if there is something wrong with the circulatory system, it may not necessarily manifest itself as a problem with the blood or the heart, but may appear as a pain in the leg, the gradual withering of a limb, or a lack of strength or endurance. Thus, Habermas associates "with crises the idea of an objective force that deprives a subject of some part of his normal sovereignty" (Habermas 1973, 1). The resolution of a physical, or in turn social, crisis "effects a liberation" of the individual who is caught up in it.

Thus, according to Habermas, the systems that make up the human body, and in turn the political, economic, and sociocultural body, are interdependent. As a result, an illness exists within a larger body or system. So too is this the case with the society at large. Thus, failures in the economic system may manifest themselves in the political and socioeconomic subsystems. Drug abuse may actually be a systemic response to despair over a lack of economic opportunity. Certain types of criminal behavior may in part be a result of the failure to empower politically certain ethnic and social groups.

■ SUMMARY

INTASC Standards
Principle #9

What is important in terms of Habermas's theory is to realize that society and culture, and in turn the public schools, operate as part of a larger social system. It is this idea that we continue to return to throughout the subsequent sections of this book. As critical educators we must develop the insights necessary to understand the context in which schools function—their role and relationship to the larger social systems. In doing so, we potentially become not only more sophisticated interpreters of the culture that surrounds us, but also more able to act as border crossers in our work as teachers.

■ DISCUSSION QUESTIONS ■

1. Why do you think power is a topic that is avoided in discussions about education?
2. Do you think that the idea of dialogue and critical consciousness are encouraged in U.S. schools?
3. What would be the arguments in favor of and against a banking model of education?

4. Do you think that the United States has elements of a colonized educational system?
5. Why do you think that sports are so heavily emphasized in U.S. public education? What is good and bad about this emphasis?
6. How does resistance manifest itself in the actions of students in schools?
7. How, in your opinion, do schools function as social systems?
8. Does Habermas provide a useful model for explaining how a system such as the public schools function?
9. Explain what Habermas means by the idea of a "legitimation crisis"?

▪ SOURCES CITED ▪

Freire, Paulo. 1970. *Cultural action for freedom.* Cambridge: Harvard Educational Review Monographs.
———. 1973. *Education for critical consciousness.* New York: Seabury Press.
———. 1970. *Pedagogy of the oppressed.* New York: Herder & Herder.
Gallup Organization. 1999. 31st Annual Phi Delta Kappa/Gallup Poll of the public's attitudes toward the public schools. *Phi Delta Kappan* 81: 41–56.
———. 1992. 24th Annual Phi Delta Kappa/Gallup Poll of the public's attitudes toward the public schools. *Phi Delta Kappan* 74: 41–53.
———. 1986. 18th Annual Phi Delta Kappa/Gallup Poll of the public's attitudes toward the public schools. *Phi Delta Kappan* 68: 43–59.
Giroux, Henry. 1981. *Ideology, culture and the politics of schooling.* Philadelphia: Temple University Press.
Greene, Maxine. 1973. *Teacher as stranger.* Belmont, Calif.: Wadsworth.
Habermas, Jürgen. 1973. *Legitimation crisis.* Boston: Beacon Press.
Henry, Jules. 1972. *On education.* New York: Vintage Books.
Kelly, Gail P., and Phillip Altbach. 1978. *Education and colonialism.* New York: Longman.
Kozol, Jonathan. 1981. *On being a teacher.* New York: Continuum.
McLaren, Peter. 1998. *Life in schools: An introduction to critical pedagogy in the foundations of education.* 3d ed. New York: Longman.
Mini Digest of Education Statistics. 1997. Washington, D.C.: U.S. Government Printing Office.
Nyberg, David. 1981a. A concept of power for education. *Teachers College Record* 82(4): 535–551.
———. 1981b. *Power over power.* Cornell, N.Y.: Cornell University Press.
Provenzo, Eugene F., Jr., and Asterie Baker Provenzo. 1991. Columbus and the Pledge. *The American School Board Journal* 178(10) 24–25.
Statistical Abstract of the United States. 1998. Washington, D.C.: U.S. Government Printing Office.

U.S. Department of Education, National Center for Education Statistics. 1996. *Digest of Education Statistics, 1996.* Washington, D.C.: U.S. Government Printing Office.

———. 2000. *Digest of Education Statistics, 2000.* Washington, D.C.: U.S. Government Printing Office.

———. 1997. *Projections of Education Statistics to 2007.* Washington, D.C.: U.S. Government Printing Office.

CHAPTER 5

Teachers in U.S. Society

Schools are complex **social institutions**. Besides the brick and mortar of their buildings, they are made up of students, teachers, and administrators. Teachers, in particular, determine what can or cannot be done in the educational system. Their training, experience, and ideals largely determine the possibilities and limitations of a school.

Teachers are subject to community pressure and influence, yet at the same time they exert their own influence on the students they teach and on the communities in which they live. Their day-to-day activities in the classroom represent one obvious influence. In recent years, teachers have also come to assert their influence through the organization of unions and other less formal power structures.

INTASC Standards
Principle #7

■ TEACHING IN THE UNITED STATES: AN OVERVIEW

As of the mid-1990s the United States had approximately 3.1 million public and private schoolteachers. Of the teachers in public elementary and secondary schools in 1993–1994, 73 percent were women and 27 percent men. Some 65 percent of these teachers had at least 10 years of full-time teaching experience and almost all teachers held at least a bachelor's degree (*Mini Digest of Education Statistics 1995,* "Numbers of Teachers").

The national average salary for public schoolteachers has grown rapidly in recent years, reaching $41,820 in 1999–2000. The highest average salaries in the country were in Connecticut ($52,410) and New York ($51,020) whereas the lowest were in South Dakota ($29,072) and

TABLE 5.1 ■ Characteristics of Teachers in Public Schools: 1993–1994

Selected Characteristics	Number (in thousands)	Percent
Total	2,561	100.0
Men	694	27.1
Women	1,867	72.9
Race/ethnicity		
White, non-Hispanic	2,217	86.5
Black, non-Hispanic	188	7.4
Hispanic	109	4.2
Other minorities	48	1.9
Experience		
Less than 3 years	249	9.7
3 to 9 years	653	25.5
10 to 20 years	897	35.0
More than 20 years	762	29.8
Highest degree		
Less than bachelor's	8	0.8
Bachelor's	1,331	52.0
Master's or above	1,212	47.3

Source: *Mini Digest of Education Statistics 1995,* "Numbers of Teachers." (Available online at http://nces.ed.gov/pubs/MiniDig95/teach.html#14)

Oklahoma ($29,525) (American Federation of Teachers, 2001). Over the past ten or fifteen years, teacher salaries have generally increased. After adjustments for inflation, for example, teachers' salaries rose 9 percent between 1984–1985 and 1994–1995 (*Mini Digest of Education Statistics 1995,* "Numbers of Teachers").

The number of elementary and secondary schoolteachers in the United States has risen in recent years, up about 16 percent since the mid-1980s. In the fall of 1994, the ratio of pupils per public school teacher was 17.3 compared with 18.1 pupils per teacher ten years earlier. During the same time period, the pupil–teacher ratio in private schools fell from 16.8 to 15.2 pupils per teacher (*Mini Digest of Education Statistics 1995,* "Numbers of Teachers").

Teachers are the single largest group of people working within the public sector. They reflect a wide range of backgrounds and interests and are as diverse as the schools and communities they serve. Two-thirds of all teachers are women. The median age for male teachers is thirty-eight and for female teachers, thirty-six. Approximately 73 percent are married and 8.5 percent are widowed, divorced, or separated (NEA 1981, 90, 95).

FIGURE 5.1 ■ Modern teacher.

Public schoolteachers are considered public servants. Unlike other professionals, such as doctors and lawyers, their licensing and certification is under the control of state legislatures. It is interesting to note that certification restrictions do not apply to other types of teaching. To teach in a public school in the United States, a person needs to present evidence that he or she has attended an accredited teacher-training program at a college in the United States and has met various requirements including student or associate teaching. In contrast, to teach at the university level, he or she needs only a doctorate (which in special circumstances can be waived). Colleagues' judgments, not some outside accrediting agency, determine acceptance and advancement.

■ TEACHERS AS PROFESSIONALS

One of the criteria cited by sociologists for deciding whether a job is a profession is whether it possesses a specialized body of knowledge. In this respect teaching does not strictly represent a profession. Teachers

FIGURE 5.2 ■ Modern teacher.

claim their professional status on the basis of their experience and technical skills. They do not possess a specialized body of knowledge as do doctors, nurses, or lawyers (Campbell et al. 1980, 278–279). A second criterion that is used to define professionalism is whether a group regulates itself through a peer review process. This is the case with both medical doctors and lawyers. In the case of teachers, regulation and control is maintained by local, state, and national accrediting agencies that are not controlled by teachers (peers) but instead by the public or their representatives.

INTERNET @ CONNECTIONS

National Board Certification for Teachers

Among the most interesting developments in teaching has been the establishment of the National Board for Professional Teaching Standards. The NBPTS (http://www. nbpts.org/nbpts/) is a private, nonprofit, nongovernmental organization founded in 1987. Its purpose is to improve U.S. education and the teaching profession through voluntary advanced certification of elementary and secondary schoolteachers. The mission of the NBPTS is to establish national standards and advanced licensing for U.S. teachers.

According to the NBPTS, there are five propositions of accomplished teaching: 1. Teachers are committed to students and their learning; 2. Teachers know the subjects they teach and how to teach those subjects to students; 3. Teachers are responsible for managing and monitoring student learning; 4. Teachers think systemically about their practice and learn from experience; and 5. Teachers are members of learning communities.

To review the National Board for Professional Teaching Standards in more details, visit their website at the address above.

In K–12 settings, teachers do not select the textbooks they use or the curriculum they teach. Instead, they are subject to specific guidelines and directions from local school boards and administrators. In reality, teachers do have significant input into what they teach, as well as the instructional materials they use. The act of teaching at any level is highly individualistic. Good teaching also involves the use of careful professional judgment and reflection.

So the questions remain, Is teaching a profession? Are teachers professionals? The educational sociologist Dan Lortie argues that teaching is a "semi-profession" (Lortie, 1975). Whereas it has many of the characteristics of what we commonly associate with a profession, it is also significantly different. Teachers constantly function in a professional context, have expert knowledge, and make professional decisions. Certainly in this context, teachers are professionals.

> **INTASC Standards**
> Principle #9

Teaching is a service profession. Whereas it involves expert knowledge in areas ranging from subject expertise to classroom management and instructional methods, it is also highly intuitive. In this context, teaching can be seen as a type of artistry in which rules are followed but not always consciously. The problem with describing teaching as simply artistry is that it does not adequately emphasize the extent to which different types of knowledge shape and define what a successful teacher does.

National Education Association Code of Ethics of the Education Profession

Preamble

The educator, believing in the worth and dignity of each human being, recognizes the supreme importance of the pursuit of truth, devotion to excellence, and the nurture of the democratic principles. Essential to these goals is the protection of freedom to learn and to teach and the guarantee of equal educational opportunity for all. The educator accepts the responsibility to adhere to the highest ethical standards.

The educator recognizes the magnitude of the responsibility inherent in the teaching process. The desire for the respect and confidence of one's colleagues, of students, of parents, and of the members of the community provides the incentive to attain and maintain the highest possible degree of ethical conduct. The Code of Ethics of the Education Profession indicates the aspiration of all educators and provides standards by which to judge conduct.

The remedies specified by the NEA and/or its affiliates for the violation of any provision of this Code shall be exclusive and no such provision shall be enforceable in any form other than the one specifically designated by the NEA or its affiliates.

PRINCIPLE I—Commitment to the Student

The educator strives to help each student realize his or her potential as a worthy and effective member of society. The educator therefore works to stimulate the spirit of inquiry, the acquisition of knowledge and understanding, and the thoughtful formulation of worthy goals.

In fulfillment of the obligation to the student, the educator—

1. Shall not unreasonably restrain the student from independent action in the pursuit of learning.
2. Shall not unreasonably deny the student's access to varying points of view.
3. Shall not deliberately suppress or distort subject matter relevant to the student's progress.
4. Shall make reasonable effort to protect the student from conditions harmful to learning or to health and safety.
5. Shall not intentionally expose the student to embarrassment or disparagement.
6. Shall not on the basis of race, color, creed, sex, national origin, marital status, political or religious beliefs, family, social or cultural background, or sexual orientation, unfairly—
   a. Exclude any student from participation in any program
   b. Deny benefits to any student
   c. Grant any advantage to any student.
7. Shall not use professional relationships with students for private advantage.
8. Shall not disclose information about students obtained in the course of professional service unless disclosure serves a compelling professional purpose or is required by law.

PRINCIPLE II—Commitment to the Profession

The education profession is vested by the public with a trust and responsibility requiring the highest ideals of professional service.

In the belief that the quality of the services of the education profession directly influences the nation and its citizens, the educator shall exert every effort to raise professional standards, to promote a climate that encourages the exercise of professional judgment, to achieve conditions that attract persons worthy of the trust to careers in education, and to assist in preventing the practice of the profession by unqualified persons.

In fulfillment of the obligation to the profession, the educator—

1. Shall not in an application for a professional position deliberately make a false statement or fail to disclose a material fact related to competency and qualifications.
2. Shall not misrepresent his/her professional qualifications.
3. Shall not assist any entry into the profession of a person known to be unqualified in respect to character, education, or other relevant attribute.
4. Shall not knowingly make a false statement concerning the qualifications of a candidate for a professional position.
5. Shall not assist a noneducator in the unauthorized practice of teaching.
6. Shall not disclose information about colleagues obtained in the course of professional service unless disclosure serves a compelling professional purpose or is required by law.
7. Shall not knowingly make false or malicious statements about a colleague.
8. Shall not accept any gratuity, gift, or favor that might impair or appear to influence professional decisions or action.

—Adopted by the NEA 1975 Representative Assembly

Source: Used with permission from the National Education Association. (Available online at http://www.nea.org/info/code.html)

■ TEACHING AS A "MORAL CRAFT"

Alan Tom in *Teaching as a Moral Craft* argues that teaching is a moral craft. Drawing on the work of Popkewitz and Wehlage, who believe that "teaching should be viewed as a craft that includes a reflective approach toward problem, a cultivation of imagination, and a playfulness toward words, relationships and experiences" (quoted by Tom 1984, 127), Tom adds to their definition "an explicit concern for desirable ends" (Tom 1984, 127).

Tom integrates the idea of moral craft into this argument by defining it as a "reflective, diligent, and skillful approach toward the pursuit of desirable ends" (Tom 1984, 127). Thus, he defines teaching as "a reflective, diligent, and skillful approach (conducted in a social setting) towards the pursuit of desirable ends" (Tom 1984, 129).

Tom contrasts his model with the idea of teaching-as-art, which he feels is inadequate because artists, such as actors and painters, are subject to different rules and conditions for their work than teachers are. An actor, for example, plays a role and does not necessarily have to become involved with his or her audience. This is not the case with a teacher. Artists, whether painters, sculptors, or actors, have considerably greater freedom than do teachers (Tom 1984, 131).

? WHAT DO YOU THINK?
The Teacher as a Moral Force

In Muriel Spark's 1962 novel, *The Prime of Miss Jean Brodie* (later made into a film starring Maggie Smith), a seemingly dedicated Scottish schoolteacher of the 1930s carefully inculcates her students at an exclusive girl's school with her own social and political values. These include a romantic idealization of the Italian fascist movement under the dictator Mussolini and a belief in free love. As a result of her teaching and private encouragement, one of her students goes off to fight in the Spanish Civil War and dies tragically and uselessly; another is propelled into a destructive love affair with a married man.

Although fiction, *The Prime of Miss Jean Brodie* raises an important distinction between teaching and indoctrination. Where does one end and the other begin? How much should teachers project their own social, political, and moral views onto their students? Is it inevitable that teachers communicate private and personal beliefs to their students, or can they remain neutral? Should teachers be able to talk about their political beliefs in class? Or talk about their religious or moral values? What do you think?

Tom also discusses the metaphor of teaching being an applied science. This is similar to a medical model in which the student is "treated" for his or her educational needs. Such a model is extremely limiting in that it fails to take into account the social dimensions of teaching and learning. Teaching as an applied science fits Paulo Freire's definition of a banking model, in which information is literally deposited (poured or dumped) into the mind of the learner.

Although the teaching as an applied science model is tempting because it can be systematized and carefully regulated, it is ultimately inadequate. Tom's model of teaching as a moral craft seems much more powerful. Other related models can also be employed. David Hansen, for example, talks about teaching as a vocation, as "a form of public service that yields enduring personal fulfillment to those who provide it" (Hansen 1995, xiii).

Such an approach can be integrated into Tom's model. For those who are entering the teaching profession, the challenge is to understand the extent to which being a teacher is subject to a wide range of social and cultural forces. The rest of this chapter attempts to provide a context for understanding the latitude and freedom teachers have in their work, and what it means to be a teacher in U.S. society. We begin by trying to set the profession of teaching in a historical context.

The American Federation of Teachers

A Bill of Rights and Responsibilities for Learning: Standards of Conduct, Standards for Achievement

The traditional mission of our public schools has been to prepare our nation's young people for equal and responsible citizenship and productive adulthood. Today, we reaffirm that mission by remembering that democratic citizenship and productive adulthood begin with standards of conduct and standards for achievement in our schools. Other education reforms may work; high standards of conduct and achievement do work—and nothing else can work without them.

Recognizing that rights carry responsibilities, we declare that

1. All students and school staff have a right to schools that are safe, orderly, and drug free.
2. All students and school staff have a right to learn and work in school districts and schools that have clear discipline codes with fair and consistently enforced consequences for misbehavior.
3. All students and school staff have a right to learn and work in school districts that have alternative educational placements for violent or chronically disruptive students.
4. All students and school staff have a right to be treated with courtesy and respect.
5. All students and school staff have a right to learn and work in school districts, schools, and classrooms that have clearly stated and rigorous academic standards.
6. All students and school staff have a right to learn and work in well-equipped schools that have the instructional materials needed to carry out a rigorous academic program.
7. All students and school staff have a right to learn and work in schools where teachers know their subject matter and how to teach it.
8. All students and school staff have a right to learn and work in school districts, schools, and classrooms where high grades stand for high achievement and promotion is earned.

9. All students and school staff have a right to learn and work in school districts and schools where getting a high school diploma means having the knowledge and skills essential for college or a good job.

10. All students and school staff have a right to be supported by parents, the community, public officials, and business in their efforts to uphold high standards of conduct and achievement.

Source: Used with permission from the American Federation of Teachers. (Available online at http://www.aft.org/lessons/rights.html)

■ TEACHING IN THE UNITED STATES: HISTORICAL DEVELOPMENT

Teachers have been part of U.S. life from the earliest colonial times. In Boston, private teachers were instructing children as early as 1630. The first publicly supported teacher in Boston was hired in 1636 (Seybolt 1935, 3). Newspaper advertisements (Seybolt 1935, 12, 14–15) dating from 1709 and 1718 describe typical duties for public or private schoolteachers during the colonial period:

master
Name used for a male teacher during the colonial period in America.

school dame
Female teacher during the colonial period in America.

governess
A female tutor assigned to the care and instruction of children—almost always within a single family.

tutor
A male instructor assigned to the instruction of children—mostly males and usually within a single family.

> **1709**
>
> Reading, Writing, Arithmetick, Merchants Accompts, Geometry, Trigonometry, Plain and Sphaerical, Dyalling, Gauging, Astronomy and Navigation are Taught: And Bonds, Bills Indentures, Charter-parties, &c. are Drawn; and Youth Boarded, in Cross-Street, Boston. By John Green.

> **1718**
>
> These are to give Notice, that there is just arrived here a Certain Person and his Wife fit for any Town, to teach School, both Latin, and to Read and Write English, and his Wife for teaching Needle Work, any person that wants may be informed at the Post-Office in Boston.

During the colonial period teachers were known by various names; the most common was **master,** although there were also **school dames, governesses, tutors.** Largely self-explanatory, the different terms denote the different types of activities involved. They also suggest the social status and authority afforded to teachers prior to the nineteenth century.

Differences in how teachers are perceived, based on what they are called, continue into our own era. Think for a minute about those who teach at the university and college level versus those who teach in elementary or secondary schools. A college or university instructor is a **professor;** an elementary or secondary instructor is a **teacher.** The difference may not seem important at first but in fact represents significantly different perceptions by society of the teachers' expected roles and functions.

In colonial times most teachers worked on a fee-for-instruction basis; a student would pay a teacher a specific fee for a lesson or set of lessons. In the nineteenth century, however, this situation changed as local governments became more involved in setting up public schools. Increasingly, local school boards became responsible for raising taxes, erecting school buildings, and hiring teachers. Teachers were paid salaries by the school boards, given a place to teach, and were supervised.

> **INTASC Standards**
> Principle #9

> **professor**
> A teacher at the university or college level.
>
> **teacher**
> Usually used to define an instructor at the elementary or secondary level.

FIGURE 5.3 ■ A young male teacher providing instruction in spelling.

Source: Frontispiece from J. Madison Watson's *The National Elementary Speller* (New York: A. S. Barnes & Burr, 1862).

As public schools grew more numerous during the first half of the nineteenth century, other important changes took place. Until that time, teaching had been a largely male profession. Increasingly, however, teaching became an occupation popular with women. In 1870, for example, 123,000 women and 78,000 men were teaching. By 1930 five times as many women as men were teaching. Most male teachers taught at the secondary level (Lortie 1975, 8).

Women were hired as teachers during the nineteenth century because they could be paid less than men and because teaching was seen as a nurturing task. Still, teaching was an attractive profession for women. It commanded great respect and was one of the few professions open to them. An elementary schoolteacher, for example, typically needed to complete a two-year training program at the high school level; in many parts of the country requirements were even less stringent. It was not until well into the twentieth century that schools required teachers to have a college degree.

The fact that most teachers have been women has had important implications for teaching in the United States. Traditionally women have re-

FIGURE 5.4 ■ The new school mistress.

Source: From *Harper's Weekly,* 17, 817.

FIGURE 5.5 ■ African American kindergarten teachers, St. Louis public schools, 1904.

ceived less pay and recognition than men for their contributions to society. The domination of the profession by women has undoubtedly affected the public's perception of teaching—making it less valued than professions dominated by men. With women achieving greater equality in the workplace in recent years, it is hoped that the job's status and salary improve.

EDUCATION AND LITERATURE

The New Teacher

The board walls were not battened. Streaks of sunshine streamed through the cracks upon a row of six homemade seats and desks that marched down the middle of the room. Beyond them on the studding of the opposite wall, a square of boards had been nailed and painted black, to make a blackboard.

In front of the seats stood a big heating stove. Its round sides and top were cherry-red from the heat of the fire, and standing around it were the scholars that Laura must teach. They all looked at Laura. There were five of them, and two boys and one girl were taller than she was.

"Good morning," she managed to say.

They all answered, still looking at her. A small window by the door let in a block of sunshine. Beyond it, in the corner by the stove, stood a small table and a chair. "That is the teacher's table," Laura thought, and then, "Oh my; I am the teacher."
—Laura Ingalls Wilder, *These Happy Golden Years* (1943)

Other situations have also influenced teaching and its development in the United States. In contrast to other professionals, teachers have a relatively limited path for career development. Unlike university instructors who can follow a number of different career options (teaching, research, administration, or some combination of those activities) and advance through various ranks (instructor, assistant, associate, and full professor), the elementary and high school teacher has relatively few career paths to select. Of course some become department

FIGURE 5.6 ▨ Blanche LaMont and her students in Hecla, Montana, October 1893. Courtesy of the Library of Congress. It is interesting to note that this is perhaps the most famous photograph of a teacher in a nineteenth-century U.S. frontier community. Few people know that Miss LaMont came to a tragic end shortly after this photograph was taken. Her mutilated, nude body, and that of a female friend, were found in the belfry of the Emanuel Baptist Church in San Francisco on Easter Sunday, 1895. A mutual friend of the two women, assistant Sunday school Superintendent Theodore Durrant, was eventually arrested and convicted of their murders— a crime for which he was executed by hanging.

chairpersons, work as administrators, or curriculum developers, but in general only a small proportion of teachers can pursue these kinds of positions.

EDUCATION AND LITERATURE

The Rural Schoolteacher

In the country the repository of art and science was the school, and the schoolteacher shielded and carried the torch of learning and of beauty. . . . It was far from an easy job, and it had duties and obligations beyond belief. The teacher had no private life. She was watched jealously for any weakness of character. She could not board with one family for more than one term, for that would cause jealousy—a family gained social ascendancy by boarding a teacher. If a marriageable son belonged to the family where she boarded a proposal was automatic. . . . Teachers rarely lasted very long in the country schools.

—John Steinbeck, *East of Eden* (1952)

The educational sociologist Dan Lortie has argued that teaching suffers from several anomalies of status, that it is

> . . . honored and disdained, praised as "dedicated service" and lampooned as "easy work." It is permeated with the rhetoric of professionalism, yet features incomes below those earned by workers and considerably less education. It is middle-class work in which more and more participants use bargaining strategies developed by wage-earners in factories. (Lortie 1975, 10)

Lortie argues that teaching has traditionally been afforded a special respect; teachers are seen as fulfilling a special role or mission. Yet despite the rhetoric declaring teachers a specially honored and respected group of professionals, the reality has been that teachers are held in lower regard than those in the learned professions or the upper levels of government and business.

? WHAT DO YOU THINK?

Should Teachers Have Tenure?

Nearly every one of the fifty states and the District of Columbia have tenure laws that protect teachers' rights. These laws provide teachers the freedom to teach without fear of coercion and guarantee the community a permanent and experienced teaching staff. Typically, tenure is awarded after a two- to five-year probationary period. Under a tenure system teachers can, in most instances, be dismissed only for inefficiency or incompetence, gross insubordination, moral misconduct, a major physical disability that seriously interferes with their ability to do their work, or elimination of the position held by the teacher as a result of a cause such as financial exigency. Tenure also protects teachers' rights in terms of due process of law. In other words, to be dismissed teachers must be shown cause and school boards must follow normal procedures.

Many administrators maintain that tenure laws are so complex and procedures so time consuming that it is virtually impossible for them to remove incompetent teachers from the schools. They argue that other professionals do not have tenure, so why should teachers? On the other hand, those supporting tenure argue that teachers work in a virtually monopolistic system. If they are dismissed by one school system, it is almost impossible for them to get rehired. As a result, dismissal becomes a much more serious issue. Because teachers are vulnerable to outside criticism and manipulation, it is important they are provided special job protection.

What arguments can you make in favor of supporting tenure? What possible abuses can result from this system? Is there an answer to the tenure problem? What do you think?

■ WHY DO PEOPLE BECOME TEACHERS?

People become teachers for many reasons. Dan Lortie has identified five major themes in *Schoolteacher*: (1) the service theme, (2) the interpersonal theme, (3) the continuation theme, (4) the time compatibility theme, and (5) the materials benefit theme (Lortie 1975).

The Service Theme

According to Lortie, people who are attracted to teaching are service oriented. This concept of teaching is like missionary work—a type of work that allows you to give back to the society. As Lortie (1975, 28) explained, "teachers have been perceived as performing a special mission in our society". It is one expressed by teachers in Lortie's interviews with them for *Schoolteacher* as providing "a valuable service of special moral worth" (Lortie 1975, 28).

One can see this theme at work in essays by student teachers at the University of Miami. Gloria Segura, for example, explains that she wants to pursue a career in teaching " . . . because I like kids and I want to

have the opportunity to teach them new things they can take with them."
Katie Dalgaard explains: "For me, becoming a teacher is not about
money or advancement. It is about being content in life, knowing that
you make a difference, . . . I am happy and content when I am with
kids. . . . I want to know that I am doing my part to help out society. I
want to know that when I leave this world I will have left something
behind."

The Interpersonal Theme

According to Lortie, teaching is a people-oriented profession. Teachers
spend most of their time interacting with other people—particularly children or adolescents. Teachers, more than most professionals, are attracted to working with people and ideally making a difference in their
lives. According to Haylie Hoffman:

> For me, it always took extra time to grasp the initial aspect of a con-
> cept. When I had a teacher that was patient and supportive of this, I
> eventually had great success. When I had teachers that understood this
> about me, I eventually had great success. When I had teachers that un-
> derstood this about me, I remained motivated to try my hardest. Such
> a teacher conveys that he or she believes in the students and this is very
> meaningful.

The interpersonal theme also can be seen in motion with Danielle
Schaaf:

> I am truly a teacher by nature. As a young child, I loved to learn and
> share my knowledge with others. When I was in third grade I returned
> to my kindergarten classroom and did a presentation on seashells for the
> class. I loved the experience and the children in the class enjoyed my
> visit. The teacher asked me to return until I graduated from the school.
> When I was barely out of elementary school, I would beg my mother to
> let me come to her classroom to help. Almost instinctively, I would as-
> sume a leadership role in her classroom. When I was twelve years old, I
> took my first job as a babysitter. I watched a nine-month-old and a two-
> year-old for hours on end. I enjoyed the job so much that I could hardly
> believe that I was being paid. As the boys grew older, I would teach
> them how to write letters and numbers and even taught them colors.
> Working at the YMCA, my swim lessons became a way of life. As soon
> as I went away to college and no longer [was] working with the children,
> I began to miss it. It became obvious to me that my natural gift was
> working with children.

The Continuation Theme

The continuation theme involves people being attracted to teaching because it allows them to continue to do something they enjoyed or cared about in their schooling. A star athlete might want to continue being involved in a sport by being a coach. A secondary English teacher might continue a passion or interest in literature by teaching it. According to Elaine Schwartz:

> Teaching is a profession I have been interested in since I was a little girl. I really enjoy working with little kids and am fascinated by their everyday conversations and actions. I think I first became interested in young children by playing with my little cousins at family reunions and such. I would either listen to them tell me stories or just play with them around the house. Furthermore, I went to one of my aunt's classes that she taught one day and knew that teaching was what I wanted to do just by watching her teach and looking at the children's reactions.

This interest in teaching at a very young age can be seen also in the case of Suzanne Cohn, who recalled the following:

> Ever since I was a little girl I have always wanted to be a teacher. I would line up my dolls in my room, get my blackboard out, and start teaching. Each day we would start off with spelling and end with a math problem. I would get so caught up that the hours seemed like minutes. When my sisters would play with me, I would beg and plead to be the teacher, and of course they let me.

Similarly, Jenny Weirich remembers how

> Sitting in my assigned blue plastic chair, with strands of my hair from my pigtails caught in the shiny silver screws, I twiddled my thumbs in my messy desk, while the teacher whom I admired greatly talked to each student individually, pointing out his strengths and his areas for improvement. I was supposed to be starting my homework, but all I could do was daydream. My mind was distracted by the many options that faced me as soon as the bell rang. My friend Stephanie was coming over to my house and we were going to play school. Would I be the teacher, I hoped? Would we be in high school, preschool, or maybe even college? If I am the student, would I be a bad student or a good student? Every day I would sit in my blue plastic chair with its shiny silver screws and I would observe my teacher and her teaching strategies for disciplining

us, educating us, and keeping our interests. Then . . . I would begin to think of how I was going to accomplish the same tasks when I became a teacher.

The Time Compatibility Theme

Many people are attracted to teaching because it makes it possible for them to do others things. Being a teacher creates a schedule that makes it easier to raise children and be part of a family than other professions. Long vacations make it possible for people to travel or to work in settings like summer camps.

The Material Benefits Theme

Teaching provides people with very specific benefits. Besides a salary and benefits such as retirement and health care, teaching provides a great deal of job security compared to most professions.

Why Do I Want to Teach?

My greatest desire in the life is to sit on the floor of my own classroom reading James and the Giant Peach *to a bunch of third-graders, who are sitting around me, totally captivated by my words. I simply cannot wait to give my students the feeling that they are actually in the story they are hearing. I had a teacher who did this to her students. Her dramatic voice produced such vivid pictures in our minds that every day she would have students rush through their lunch just so they could hurry back to the classroom and hear more of the story that Miss Sauro was reading that week.*

—Susana Ortiz, undergraduate teacher
education student, University of Miami

Have you thought carefully about why you want to teach? Have you tried to define what teaching means to you? Examining your reasons for wanting to be a teacher is among the most useful activities you can participate in as part of your studies in Education. While at first it may seem a bit corny to write such an essay, it will force you to carefully examine your values and your beliefs, what it is you most care about.

Look carefully at Lortie's five themes. How do they fit you? Do they match up with the goals you have for yourself and your personal and professional life?

---

feminized profession
A profession dominated by women such as teaching or nursing.

■ THE TYPICAL U.S. TEACHER

What is the typical U.S. teacher like? She is a woman more often than a man. She is white. She is forty-two years old. Typically she has taught for twelve years. She has a master's degree. She does not switch jobs very often. She teaches approximately twenty-three students. She is a member of the Democratic Party. Most often she teaches in a suburban setting. Counting her after-school responsibilities (grading papers, etc.), she puts in a longer workweek than most blue-collar workers (Feistritzer 1983, 24–26). When school is in session, for example, she works approximately forty-six hours per week compared to thirty-five hours per week for nonagricultural workers. If she is a high school English teacher with a heavy load of papers to grade, her hours are even longer (Sykes 1984, 74).

Many stereotypes of teachers exist in the United States. One is the classic portrait of the teacher as the gray-haired spinster: sexless, a little awkward with adults, maternal and caring but not too loving (a little rigid), perhaps even bordering on being a bit of a prude. This stereotype of the teacher is frequently described in literature. She is the character of Miss Dove, for example, created by the novelist Frances Gray Patton more than half a century ago:

> Miss Dove was a certainty. She would be today what she had been yesterday and would be tomorrow. . . . Miss Dove's rules were fixed as the signs of the zodiac. And, they were known, Miss Dove rehearsed them at the beginning of the school year, stating as calmly and dispassionately as if she were describing the atmospheric effects of the Gulf Stream. (Patton 1954, 9–10, 20)

This stereotype of the teacher is a bit dated. More recent stereotypes include the with-it urban teacher, such as Abe Kotter in the television program *Welcome Back Kotter*, and the attractive middle-class teacher, such as the Michelle Pfeiffer character in the movie *Dangerous Minds* who brings "civilization" to her inner-city students. One stereotype of teaching that does hold up to scrutiny, however, is the idea that women dominate teaching.

■ TEACHING AS A FEMINIZED PROFESSION

INTASC Standards
Principle #9

Teaching is a **feminized profession,** but this has not always been the case. At the beginning of the nineteenth century teachers were men more often than women. With industrialization and the increasing spread of public education throughout the nineteenth century, women increasingly entered teaching—particularly in elementary schools.

Women represented a majority of public school teachers by the time of the Civil War, and about 90 percent of the total teaching population by the year 1900 (Allison 1995). A number of reasons explain why women came to dominate the teaching profession by the end of the nineteenth century. One explanation is that as business and industry expanded men were drawn away from teaching to work in other sectors of the economy. Women were a cheap and readily available substitute. In addition, women—particularly young unmarried women—were generally believed to have natural maternal tendencies that made them particularly well suited to work with children (Allison 1995).

Teacher salaries have historically been low because of the fact that the profession has been dominated by women. In general, a fairly strong relationship exists between the entry of large numbers of women into a particular profession and its status. When this occurs, pay is often lowered and control from the outside is increased (Apple 1986). As part of a patriarchal tradition in U.S. society, women teachers were discriminated against in terms of salary and status. Yet at the same time, teaching, like nursing, provided women with access to jobs and personal independence in a society that provided few opportunities for women.

In our own era, a residual prejudice against the teaching profession because of its historical feminization almost certainly exists. As greater gender equity has been achieved over the course of the past thirty or forty years, and as teachers have negotiated for better salaries and working conditions, this has become less of a problem.

■ THE PROFESSIONAL SOCIALIZATION OF TEACHERS

In recent years teaching has become increasingly complex and difficult. Desegregation, immigration, and mainstreaming have radically changed the composition and makeup of most elementary and secondary classrooms. Unionization has redefined the power of the profession and the way it is perceived by the public. Postmodern pressures reflected in changes in traditional family structures, work patterns, and new and emerging technologies make the job of being a teacher a particularly challenging task.

Most people enter the teaching profession as idealists. Gary Cornog's description of this idealism in *Don't Smile Until Christmas* is typical:

> A year or so before I began facing a classroom on a daily basis, I had the idea that teaching English would be a series of Socratic dialogues between me and my students . . . I would lead forth my eager, responsive . . . idealistic students from the cave of adolescent mental wistfulness into the clear light of Truth upon the verdant and lush fields of literature. (Cornog quoted by Sykes 1984, 59)

Rarely is teaching such a simple, straightforward process. Apathy on the part of parents and students, distractions in the form of television and the popular culture, pressures from the economy, and a general confusion about the role and purpose of education make the work of teachers unique.

But contrary to popular opinion, teaching is not easy. True, teaching involves a great deal of flexibility and freedom within the classroom, but subtle pressure and tension make teaching stressful work. A student having a difficult time with a parent or friend, experiencing economic problems, or contending with a disability or an extended illness can change the social and learning environment of an entire classroom. Teachers must also deal with the demands and pressures of the local school board, parents, administrators, and of course the students themselves. When things work well, few professions are more satisfying. When things go wrong, few jobs are more demanding.

INTERNET @ CONNECTIONS

Online Information about Teachers

Information about teachers and their work can be found on many different sources on the Internet. If you are interested in statistics about the teaching profession (who teaches, average salary, availability of jobs, and so on), a good place to look for information is on the website for the National Center for Education Statistics, at http://nces.ed.gov/. In particular, use the main search engine on their site to find reports on teacher salaries, job availability, and demographics. Projections on teacher retirements, and thus the availability of new jobs, for example, can be found by typing into the search engine the descriptor *teachers and retirement*. This leads you to a number of different reports, including "Teacher Trends," *Fast Facts* (http://nces.ed.gov/fastfacts/).

Professional organizations provide invaluable resources on teachers and their work. If you are interested in information about accreditation and requirements for entering the profession, a good place to start is the National Council for the Accreditation of Teachers, at http://ncate.org. If you would like to listen in to teachers actually talking about their work, a number of websites provide forums for teachers: Teacher Talk, at http://www.mightymedia.com/talk/working.htm, and Teachers Helping Teachers, at http://www.pacificnet.net/~mandel/.

■ TEACHER SALARIES

Teaching, as argued by Dan Lortie, is basically middle-class work. In 1999, the average starting salary for a public schoolteacher in the United States was $25,735. Geographical variations in salary were significant, ranging from $19,146 in South Dakota to $33,162 in Alaska. Although some of the country's most experienced teachers in wealthy suburbs receive salaries approaching $100,000 per year, the average salary is $39,347 (Greenhouse 1999, 16).

What is the average teacher's salary in your part of the country? Look at the figures in Table 5.2 from the National Education Association. Remember that even at the state level, teachers' salaries significantly differ based on whether they teach in urban, suburban, or rural areas. To find out what the salaries are in your area, contact your local teachers' union or school personnel office.

How does the average teacher's salary of approximately $40,000 per year compare with other professions? In 1999 the average salary for attorneys was $71,530; the average salary for engineers was $64,489; and the average salary for systems analysts was $63,072. Compared to professionals in other areas, teachers receive very good benefits, normally including health care, retirement, and sometimes even legal assistance. Extended periods of free time, provided by summer and holiday breaks, differentiate it from other professions, although it should be emphasized that the total number of hours worked per year is actually more than that of most industrial workers and comparable with most other professions.

According to the National Center for Education Statistics, public schoolteachers earn between about 25 to 119 percent more than private schoolteachers earn. In 1993–1994, the most recent date for which we have salary comparisons, the average salary of public schoolteachers was $36,498 and for private schoolteachers, $24,053 (National Center for Education Statistics, "Teacher Trends").

TABLE 5.2 ■ State Rankings of Average Teacher Salary in 1997–1998

Rank	State	Average Salary	Percent of U.S. Average
1	Connecticut	$51,727	131.5
2	New Jersey	50,284	127.8
3	New York	48,712	123.8
4	Michigan	48,361	122.9
5	Alaska	48,275	122.7
6	Pennsylvania	47,542	120.8
7	District of Columbia	44,746	113.7
8	California	44,585	113.3
9	Rhode Island	44,506	113.1
10	Massachusetts	44,285	112.5
11	Illinois	43,707	111.1
12	Delaware	42,439	107.9
13	Oregon	42,301	107.5
14	Maryland	41,404	105.2
15	Nevada	40,572	103.1
16	Indiana	39,752	101.0
17	Minnesota	39,104	99.4
18	Ohio	39,099	99.4
19	Washington	38,755	98.5
20	Wisconsin	38,179	97.0
21	Georgia	37,412	95.1
22	Colorado	37,240	94.6
23	Virginia	37,024	94.1
24	New Hampshire	36,663	93.2
25	Hawaii	36,598	93.0
26	Vermont	36,299	92.3
27	Tennessee	34,584	87.9
28	Florida	34,473	87.6
29	Kentucky	34,453	87.6
30	Maine	34,349	87.3
31	Iowa	34,084	86.6
32	Arizona	34,071	86.6
33	Missouri	34,001	86.4
34	Kansas	33,800	85.9
35	South Carolina	33,608	85.4
36	Texas	33,537	85.2
37	West Virginia	33,396	84.9
38	North Carolina	33,123	84.2
39	Utah	32,981	83.8
40	Idaho	32,834	83.4
41	Alabama	32,799	83.4

TABLE 5.2 ■ Continued

Rank	State	Average Salary	Percent of U.S. Average
42	Nebraska	32,668	83.0
43	Arkansas	32,119	81.6
44	Wyoming	32,022	81.4
45	Oklahoma	30,940	78.6
46	Montana	30,617	77.8
47	New Mexico	30,309	77.0
48	Louisiana	30,090	76.5
49	Mississippi	28,691	72.9
50	North Dakota	28,231	71.7
51	South Dakota	27,839	70.8
U.S. Average		**$39,347**	100.0
	Guam	$27,827	70.7
	Puerto Rico	$24,000	61.0
	Virgin Islands	$33,311	84.7

Source: American Federation of Teachers, "Annual Survey of State Departments of Education." (Available online at http://www.aft.org/research/survey/tables/tablel-1.html)

Salaries for teachers have remained relatively constant in real dollars since the late 1960s, declining only for a brief period during the late 1970s and early 1980s. Salaries are at their highest level in the last three decades. As teacher shortages increase in the next decade, it is almost certain that salaries will continue to increase.

WHAT DO YOU THINK?
Merit Pay for Teachers

Many people believe the best way to improve the quality of education is to improve the quality of teachers. Merit pay—a system drawn from industry—has been widely promoted as a means of rewarding our best teachers and encouraging them to stay in the profession. Merit-based systems are once again being promoted by many public officials as a way of rewarding outstanding performance on the part of teachers.

Merit pay schemes are not new. Merit pay programs were proposed for U.S. schools in the 1950s and the 1980s. In a speech given at Seton Hall University in May 1983, President Reagan argued, for example, that "teachers should be paid and promoted on the basis of their merit and competence. Hard-earned tax dollars should encourage the best. They have no business rewarding incompetence and mediocrity." Polls of the general public indicate that there is widespread support for merit pay.

Awarding merit pay raises a number of questions: What makes a teacher meritorious? What constitutes good teaching? Is a teacher who gets bright children to perform well academically necessarily as good as another teacher who gets slower children to perform moderately well? Is a teacher who helps students understand themselves as good as a teacher who helps students academically? How do we compare the performances of a physical education teacher with a high school social studies teacher, or a home economics teacher with a kindergarten teacher?

Merit pay can destroy the spirit and enthusiasm of those who do not receive it. Their peers may ostracize those who do receive merit pay. Merit pay may hinder teachers' creativity by making them feel they must adhere strictly to curriculum guidelines set forth by administrators instead of following what they think is best.

What other arguments can be made against merit pay? What arguments can be made in favor of it? Is this concept practical at all in a profession such as teaching? What do you think?

■ TEACHER DEMAND

On average during the mid-1990s, when data was last collected, less than 1 percent of teaching positions were vacant or temporarily filled by substitute teachers because suitable candidates could not be found. In public schools, the attrition rate for teachers for the school years 1993–1994 and 1994–1995 was 7 percent and 12 percent in private schools. Teacher turnover varied by teacher's age. The rate for teachers in the twenty-five- to twenty-nine-year-old age category was 10 percent for public schoolteachers and 13 percent for private schoolteachers; the rate for the sixty- to sixty-four-year-old age category was 30 percent and 13 percent for public and private schoolteachers, respectively.

Teachers left the classroom during the mid-1990s for two main reasons: (1) retirement and (2) pregnancy/childrearing. For the 1994–1995 school year, the figure for retirement was 27.4 percent and for pregnancy/childrearing, 14.3 percent. For private schoolteachers, the two main reasons teachers left the profession were to pursue another career (16.3 percent) and for family or personal reasons (16.2 percent) (National Center for Education Statistics, "Teacher Trends").

Current demographic and population projections indicate a major teacher shortage beginning in the early part of the twenty-first century. According to the U.S. Department of Education, serious teacher shortages will develop by the end of the first decade of the century as large numbers of teachers are expected to retire and enrollments to increase. By 2008–2009, the number of new teachers that will have to be hired is estimated to be between 1.7 and 2.7 million people (Hussar 1999).

Currently, teachers are significantly older than the general labor force. In 1993–1994, the average age of a teacher in the United States was forty-four, compared to thirty-eight for the general working population (Hussar 1999, 9). As a result, the general teaching population is approaching retirement much more rapidly than other sectors of the population. The resulting shortage of qualified teachers is further contributed to by the fact that we are entering a period in which the student population is rapidly expanding as well. To replace the current teaching population, it is estimated that approximately 220,000 teachers will have to be hired each year through the year 2008–2009. High estimates suggest that the total number of replacement teachers needed in the eleven-year period between 1998–1999 and 2008–2009 will be as many as 2,693,000 and even at the lowest, 2,259,000 (Hussar 1999, 43).

Projected demographic needs of this sort represent a major challenge for U.S. society, as well as an unprecedented opportunity for those wanting to enter the profession to get good jobs and to be able to

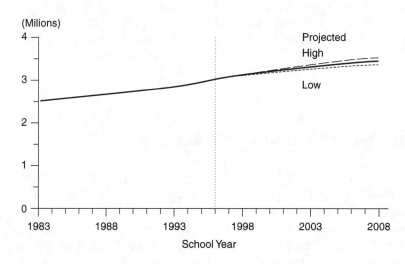

FIGURE 5.7 ■ Elementary and secondary classroom teachers, with alternative projections: Fall 1983 to Fall 2008.

Source: National Center for Education Statistics, *Projection of Education Statistics to 2008.* (Available online at http://nces.ed.gov/pubs98/pj2008/p98f43.html)

demand decent salaries and benefits. Of course, the question is, Will we be able to attract enough good people to the profession and train them well enough to meet its increasing demands?

Teacher Timeline

1857   National Education Association is founded.
1912   America Federation of Teachers is founded.
1940   First National Teacher Exam licensing test is required.
1946   Teachers go on strike in Connecticut, Minnesota, and New York.
1954   National Council for the Accreditation of Teacher Education is begun.
1966   National Education Association is merged with the Black American Teacher's Association.
1972   National Education Association endorses political candidates in the U.S. House and Senate.
1973   Merger talks between the American Federation of Teachers and the National Education Association break off.
1975   Dan Lortie publishes his classic study of teachers, *Schoolteachers: A Sociological Study.*
1976   The National Education Association endorses its first presidential candidate, Jimmy Carter.
1990   Teach for America is launched as an alternative means by which liberal arts majors can enter the teaching profession.
1998   Delegates to the National Education Association meeting reject a merger with the American Federation of Teachers.

■ RECRUITMENT OF MINORITY TEACHERS

The number of minority teachers lags far behind that of minority students. For example, in 1993–1994, African American, non-Hispanic students comprised 16 percent of public school students, whereas African American, non-Hispanic teachers comprised 9 percent of the teaching population (National Center for Education Statistics, "Teacher Trends"). In the case of teachers from more general minority backgrounds (African American, Latino/Hispanic, etc.), underrepresentation is similar. Approximately 13 percent of all teachers are designated as minorities whereas minority students represent approximately a third of the total school population.

INTASC Standards

Principle #10

These demographics are important for a number of reasons. To begin with, they mean that large numbers of minority students will be taught by people who are culturally different from them. Unless people teaching in these positions are culturally sensitive, the potential for cross-cultural conflict will be significant. Coming back to the theme of educators as border crossers, discussed earlier in this book, teachers working in cross-cultural settings, whether they are minority teachers working with majority populations or majority teachers working with minorities, have the potential to reach out and expand their knowledge of others and to act as links between historically segregated cultural groups.

■ TEACHER UNIONS

Since the 1960s, teachers' unions have become more important. Nearly all teachers now belong to one of the two major unions: the National Education Association (NEA) or the American Federation of Teachers (AFT). Although the NEA was originally founded as a teachers' association in 1857 and the AFT as a union in 1912, it has been only in the last two decades that they have emerged as powerful national collective bargaining agents for teachers.

At first glance, the goals and objectives of the AFT and the NEA look similar. Both aspire to improve working conditions, salaries, and benefits. Both want the best education possible in our schools. Both represent teachers, but also janitors, cafeteria workers, technical staff, and various other school employees. But how they achieve their goals reflects significantly different points of view. The AFT, unlike the NEA, is affiliated with an organized labor group—the AFL-CIO. The AFT (580,000 members) has been more militant and represents urban teachers more than suburban or rural teachers. By comparison, the NEA, which has its origins as an administrator and teachers' organization, is more conservative. It has about 1.76 million members (Sykes 1984).

Probably the most important function of a teachers' union is negotiating a labor contract. Highly complex documents, contracts involve considerable bargaining and constant give and take between the union and the local school system. In a large urban area such as Miami-Dade County (Miami, Florida), the fourth largest school system in the United States, the union contract for 1999–2000 numbered over two hundred pages, covered close to 30,000 teachers and school employees, and involved the school system's financial commitment of approximately $2.6 billion.

INTERNET @ CONNECTIONS

Union Websites

Both the main teacher unions, the American Federation of Teachers and the National Education Association, maintain extremely useful websites with a variety of information on teachers and their work. The American Federation of Teachers website is located at http://www.aft.org/index.html. The National Education Association website is located at http://www.nea.org/. Besides information on the unions and their activities, both sources provide extensive information on current issues in education, as well as statistics about U.S. teachers and the conditions of their work.

Initially, unions tried to improve salaries and benefits for teachers. In fact, the AFT owes it origins to the efforts of two teachers, Catherine Goggin and Margaret Haley, who at the beginning of the twentieth century worked to obtain pensions and to increase the salaries of teachers in Chicago (Spring 1978, 179). As salary and benefits have become less important issues, the teachers' unions have focused on conditions of work, hours, and types of employment. Whether teachers should have lunch periods free from having to supervise students, whether teachers should be paid for doing work with students after school, and whether they should be responsible for the physical maintenance of their classrooms, are all issues that have been negotiated in recent years. Collective bargaining often addresses the question of what teaching is all about. When a union says its members should not have to supervise student lunch periods, chaperon athletic events, or have faculty meetings after the school year has ended, then it is clearly defining the proper role of a teacher.

The union movement has been criticized as representing a set of goals and perspectives unsuitable to a professional group such as teachers. Many people feel that teachers, as public employees, should not be able to strike. Many teachers themselves argue that if teaching is indeed a profession, then acting according to the rules of a labor organization demeans the profession. But without unions teachers were unable to obtain the salaries, benefits, and working conditions that make teaching a practical profession. Only through collective action have teachers acquired the means to force communities and school systems to address the crucial issues of wages and benefits.

Unions obtain their strength through numbers. Frequently they can protect teachers' rights and freedoms better than individuals can. Sometimes unions are criticized for protecting incompetent workers. However, unions must represent all their members—both good and bad. As long as what represents competence is open to question and debate, it is inevitable that unions will defend the rights of members who are marginal. Ideally, when unions work best, they monitor the standards and quality of their members' work.

Teachers' unions are powerful, socially and politically. Recently they have influenced government at the highest levels. For example, in 1976 both the AFT and the NEA endorsed Jimmy Carter as the Democratic presidential candidate. Hundreds of teachers served as delegates at the Democratic National Convention. In exchange for the support of the teachers' unions, Carter promised to establish a Department of Education independent from the Office of Health, Education, and Welfare. Teachers' unions play an equally important function in local politics by being able to deliver large numbers of educated voters to a particular candidate.

Some would say that teachers have no business getting involved in politics, that because teachers are public servants who shape and influence students, they should remain essentially neutral on political questions. On the contrary, although teachers do not have the right to force their beliefs on the students they teach, as a professional and social group they represent certain shared interests and concerns. Teachers have the right as members of a democracy to organize themselves and pursue specific social and political goals as they see fit.

■ REWARDS AND SATISFACTION FOR TEACHERS

Teaching is a profession that is in many regards extremely conservative but is also subject to the profound forces and changes at work in society. This is particularly clear in the changes that have taken place in the profession during the last forty or fifty years as we have emerged into a postmodern culture and society.

Historically, why people are attracted to teaching seems fairly consistent. Comparative data collected in Dade County in 1964 and 1984 suggests that the sources of satisfaction teachers get from their work are remarkably stable. In 1964, for example, Dan Lortie surveyed teachers and found that when given six or seven items to choose from (monetary rewards, free time, etc.), 86.2 percent reported that the experience they found most satisfying in their work was "The times I know I have 'reached' a student or a group of students and they have learned" (Lortie 1975, 105). When a similar group of teachers was asked the same question in 1984 in surveys conducted by Robert Kottkamp, Eugene F. Provenzo, Jr., and Marilyn M. Cohn, this figure was 86.7 percent (see Table 5.3).

TABLE 5.3 ■ Intrinsic Rewards That Are Most Satisfying to Dade County Teachers

	1964 %	1984 %
The opportunity that teaching gives me to study, read, and plan for classes	3.4	1.9
The chance that teaching offers to develop mastery of discipline and classroom management	1.1	1.4
The time I know I have "reached" a student or group of students and that they have learned	86.2	86.7
The chance to associate with children or young people and to develop relationships with them	7.9	7.6
The chance that teaching gives me to associate with other teachers and educators	1.0	.7
I have received no satisfaction from these	.3	1.6

Source: Robert B. Kottkamp, Eugene F. Provenzo, Jr., and Marilyn M. Cohn, "Stability and Change in a Profession: Two Decades of Teacher Attitudes, 1964–1984," *Phi Delta Kappan* 67(8): 565. Used with permission.

In 1964, 76.3 percent of the teachers surveyed by Lortie reported that the most important sources of reward for them were "the opportunities to study, plan, master classroom management, 'reach' students and associates with colleagues and children" (Lortie 1975, 105). Although this figure had declined slightly to 70.2 percent in 1984, its overwhelming importance to teachers is noteworthy (Kottkamp et al. 1986) (see Table 5.4).

Teachers were less satisfied with their work in 1984 versus 1964 (see Table 5.5). In 1964, for example, 80 percent indicated some level of satisfaction with their jobs. By 1984, this figure had declined to 68 percent. Profound changes took place in the schools in the twenty years between the two surveys—many of them indicative of the shift from a modern to a postmodern culture.

In *Schoolteachers and Schooling: Ethoses in Conflict,* Eugene F. Provenzo, Jr. and Gary N. McCloskey argue that the *climate* or the *ethos* of schools—and therefore the experience of teachers in their work—underwent a profound set of changes in the years between 1964 and 1984. Most of these changes can be linked to forces associated with postmodern culture. They are as diverse as technologies (such as television and computing) and social forces (such as changes in the economy, the nature of work, and the civil rights movement). The historian

TABLE 5.4 ■ Most Important Category of Rewards to Dade County Teachers

	1964 %	1984 %
The salary and respect received and the position of influence	11.9	11.3
The opportunities to study, plan, master classroom management, "reach" students, and associate with colleagues and children	76.3	70.2
The economic security, time, freedom from competition, and appropriateness for persons like me	11.8	18.4

Source: Robert B. Kottkamp, Eugene F. Provenzo, Jr., and Marilyn M. Cohn, 1986, "Stability and Change in a Profession: Two Decades of Teacher Attitudes, 1964–1984," *Phi Delta Kappan* 67(8): 565. Used with permission.

Lawrence Cremin identified many of these forces as early as the mid-1970s. According to him, their influence on U.S. culture and education was possibly as profound as the development of public schools in the mid-nineteenth century. As he explained, a revolution was at work that included:

> . . . the rapid expansion of higher education to a point where one out of every two high-school graduates has been going on to college; the

TABLE 5.5 ■ Teachers' Feelings about Job and Workplace

	Feelings about My Job		Feelings about My School	
Very satisfied	31.9	27.4	30.4	23.6
Satisfied	26.5	29.1	26.4	25.3
More satisfied than not	22.6	19.7	23.7	18.6
Equally satisfied and dissatisfied	10.0	10.7	11.6	12.4
More dissatisfied than satisfied	6.0	7.6	5.4	9.9
Dissatisfied	1.9	3.5	1.6	5.6
Very dissatisfied	1.0	2.0	.9	4.6

Source: Robert B. Kottkamp, Eugene F. Provenzo, Jr., and Marilyn M. Cohn, 1986, "Stability and Change in a Profession: Two Decades of Teacher Attitudes, 1964–1984," *Phi Delta Kappan* 67(8): 561. Used with permission.

massive shifts in population from east to west, from south to north, from country to city, and from city to suburb, which have created new and extraordinary clienteles to educate; the movement of women into the labor force in unprecedented numbers, with prodigious consequences for the family; the changing character of work associated with the emergence of postindustrial society, and in particular the rapid growth of the so-called knowledge industries; the various civil rights and libertarian movements of the 1960s, which so radically changed the management and politics of education. (Cremin 1976, ix)

Cremin adds television to this list. More recently we could add AIDS, micro and personal computing, the Internet and World Wide Web, cable television, and the development of multimedia technology including video and digital recording.

INTASC Standards
Principle #9

Think about how much schools, and therefore the work of teachers, has changed since the late 1960s. The author of this book, who graduated from high school in 1968, went to a segregated high school. I only heard about drugs, but never actually saw them being used or even talked about in school. When I began working in public schools in 1972, security issues were minimal. Violence of the type found in the recent spate of school shootings was unheard of. Divorce, discussed in Chapter 9, was less frequent. There were fewer single-parent and complex families. Women of childbearing age were less actively engaged in the workforce. AIDS would not even be identified as a disease for nearly a decade. Micro or personal computers would not be available commercially until the late 1970s, and would take several more years to begin to circulate into the schools. The Internet was an experimental military project that would not begin to be used on a widescale basis until the mid-1980s. The World Wide Web would not be invented for another twenty years.

What I am trying to suggest is that whereas the attractions to teaching have probably always remained constant, the forces at work in the teaching profession and the schools in general have changed profoundly in recent years. Postmodernism and the changes it has brought with it represent a profound redefinition of U.S. culture. If U.S. culture has changed, so too has the work of the schools and in turn the work of teachers. Subsequent chapters continue to return to the theme of postmodernism and its influence on contemporary education and culture. Our analysis comes to include not only changing models of the family, gender, and race, but the influence of media such as television and computers.

■ TEACHERS' RIGHTS

As a result of the civil rights movement of the 1950s and 1960s, our society has become more aware of the rights of individuals. Teachers, as
well as the general public, have been affected by this growing awareness
and have increasingly litigated their concerns.

Court cases involving teachers' rights go back to the beginning of this
century. Among the most famous was the 1925 Scopes Monkey Trial.
The Scopes trial involved laws passed in 1923 in several Southern states
that opposed teaching evolutionary, or Darwinian, theory in schools.
The most important of these laws, passed by Tennessee in 1925, banned
teaching the theory in any public school. John Scopes, a young biology
teacher from Dayton, Tennessee, immediately challenged it with legal
support from the American Civil Liberties Union. Although Scopes lost
the case and was found guilty of teaching evolutionary theory, his case
provided an interesting and successful defense of the proevolutionary
point of view (Marsden 1980, 185). (Teaching evolution in Tennessee
has been legal only in recent years.)

Profound questions about teaching arose at this trial. Did Scopes
have a right to teach what he thought, despite the community standards?
Did the community have a right to teach traditional religious explanations of human development? To what extent should teachers decide
what is to be taught? Should a teacher be allowed to support an unpop-
ular viewpoint? Related issues include: Is a teacher's lifestyle germane to
his job? Should homosexuals be teachers? Should a teacher be required
to take a loyalty oath to the federal government? Should a teacher be
able to publicly criticize the school and still expect to keep her job? Obviously these questions are highly sensitive and not easily answered.

INTASC Standards
Principle #9

The courts have addressed some of these questions in rulings on
cases concerned with teaching evolution in the public schools. Under a
1928 Arkansas law it was illegal for any teacher to maintain mankind
evolved from a lower order of animals such as monkeys or apes. In *Eperson v. Arkansas* (393 U.W. 97, 1968) that law was struck down as a violation of the First Amendment (separation of church and state).
Essentially, it was argued that a religious philosophy was determining the
school curriculum. The Supreme Court ruled that the law violated the
rights not only of the teachers but also of the students.

In a complex, multicultural society such as the United States where
various groups hold many different values and beliefs, the question of
teachers' rights becomes extremely difficult. When are the rights of the
community violated and when are the rights of the teacher violated?

INTASC Standards
Principle #9

Should one take precedence over the other? Is compromise possible or even desirable?

? WHAT DO YOU THINK?

He? She?

During the summer of 1999 David Warfield, a popular journalism teacher, baseball coach, and football announcer, returned to his job at Center High School in Sacramento, California. The award-winning forty-four-year-old teacher no longer called himself David but instead Dana and had changed his last name to Rivers. He had also changed his sex.

During the previous January Warfield started taking hormones and in May told school officials that he was suffering from gender dysphoria—a medical condition in which an individual believes him- or herself to be psychologically of the opposite sex. Warfield explained that he would return to class in the fall dressed as a woman in anticipation of a sex-change operation that would make him into a female. In June, the school board let parents know that Warfield would be returning to the school in September as a woman. Warfield was instructed that if students asked him about his sex change in class, he should "tell them to go home and talk to their parents" (Hornblower 1999, 76).

Warfield/Rivers did not follow the directives of the board and took a number of her students aside and explained her transition from being a man to being a woman. Four parents filed formal complaints against the school system, arguing that the religious and moral standards they held for their children were being violated by Warfield/Rivers. Were the First Amendment rights of Warfield/Rivers violated by not being able to discuss her sex change with her students? Were the rights of the students and their parents violated? Should Warfield/Rivers be disciplined for his/her actions? What do you think?

■ THE TEACHER AS A SOCIAL FORCE

Teachers, as these various court cases suggest, are particularly subject to community standards. The schools and the connections they have to other powerful social agencies generate "the dominant rules and practices of educators' lives" (Apple 1982a, 23). Many restrictions placed on teachers, both in the past and in our own era, are a result of recognizing that teachers are agents of socialization; we all recognize education is far from a neutral process. As a consequence of their work, teachers are agents in this systematic process.

Certainly teachers must inevitably function as guardians of traditional culture; by the very act of teaching they perpetuate the existing social system. In doing so, however, teachers must be "aware of the hidden assumptions that underlie the nature of the knowledge that they use and the pedagogical practices that they implement" (Giroux 1982, 55). Our earlier discussion demonstrates how teachers transmit values to their students that they may not even be aware of themselves. If teachers are to educate students and if they are to better society as a whole, they must be critically aware of the social, political, and economic values they are communicating.

We are at a crucial point in the development not only of our educational system, but also of our culture. We cannot simply be sleepwalkers or automatons in the classroom. We must look carefully at the institutions in which we work, the forces that shape them, and the possibilities for creative action within them. As Henry Giroux points out:

> Teachers at all levels of schooling represent a potentially powerful force for social change. But one thing should be clear: the present crisis in history, in essence, is not an academic problem but a political problem. . . . What classroom teachers can and must do is work in their respective roles to develop pedagogical theories and methods that link self-reflection and understanding with a commitment to change the nature of the larger society. There are a number of strategies that teachers at all levels of schooling can use in their classrooms. In general terms they can question the common sense assumptions that shape their own lives as well as those assumptions that influence and legitimize existing forms of public school classroom knowledge, teaching style, and evaluation. (Giroux 1982, 58)

Teachers need to understand their role as **cultural agents** and as **cultural workers.** Few jobs are as complex, as interesting, or as important for the future of our society.

■ SUMMARY

Many different factors coming together in the postmodern era have the potential to shape profoundly the experience and work of teachers. Many of these have already been referred to in the first chapters

INTASC Standards

Principle #9

cultural agents
Individuals whose work defines the direction and meaning of a culture or a society.

cultural workers
People who work in jobs that define and shape a culture or society.

INTASC Standards

Principle #9

of this book. Many others are discussed in more detail in subsequent chapters.

In general, teachers in the future will have to learn to work in increasingly complex and demanding settings. The ethos of schools (i.e., the fundamental character or spirit of the schools) is clearly different than it was forty or fifty years ago. Think about how much U.S. culture has changed since the mid-1950s. Consider how the work of teachers has been affected by social and cultural movements such as racial desegregation, gender equity, gay rights, and rights for the physically challenged. Think about how changes in the economy and in families, the impact of electronic media such as television and computers—just to name a few factors—affect the schools and the work that teachers do. Postmodern trends demand that people going into the field be much more capable of dealing with difference, as well as with ambiguity and change. In dealing with the demands of an ever-changing and protean culture, they will have to be able to reflect upon and contextualize their work.

Subsequent chapters focus on issues of ethnicity, race, gender, and technology. We deal with each one of these topics in a postmodern context. Our purpose is to provide you with some of the background essential to becoming border crossers of the type described in Chapter 1 of this book. In doing so, we believe you will be better prepared to deal with the social and cultural complexity of contemporary schools.

■ DISCUSSION QUESTIONS ■

1. Traditionally, teaching has been a female profession. How has this fact affected cultural attitudes toward teaching and teachers?
2. What are the rewards and incentives for being a teacher today? What are the disincentives?
3. What are the advantages and disadvantages of a merit pay system?
4. What are the positive benefits provided to teachers by a union? What are some of the problems created by teachers joining unions? Is being a professional consistent with being a member of a union?
5. What is acceptable behavior for a teacher? Who should define standards of behavior? What are the rights of the community? What are the rights of the teachers?
6. Is teaching a profession? Can you make arguments for and against the idea that teachers are professionals?

■ SOURCES CITED ■

Apple, Michael, ed. 1982a. *Cultural and economic reproduction in education: Essays on class, ideology and the state.* London: Routledge and Kegan Paul.

———. 1982b. *Education and power.* Boston: Routledge and Kegan Paul.

———. 1986. *Teachers and texts: A political economy of class and gender in education.* New York: Routledge and Kegan Paul.

Campbell, Roald F., Luvern L. Cunningham, Raphael O. Nystrand, and Michael Usdan. 1980. *The organization and control of American schools.* Columbus, Ohio: Charles E. Merrill.

Carnoy, Martin. 1974. *Education as cultural imperialism.* New York: David McKay.

Doyle, Denis P. 1984. Window of opportunity. *The Wilson Quarterly* 8(1): 91–101.

Duke, Daniel. 1984. *Teaching: The imperiled profession.* Albany: State University of New York.

Eperson v. Arkansas. 393 U.S. 97, 1968.

Evans, David R. 1971. Decolonization: Does the teacher have a role? *Comparative Education Review* 15: 276–287.

Fanon, Frantz. 1968. *The wretched earth.* Trans. by Constance Farrington with a preface by Jean-Paul Sartre. New York: Grove Press.

Feistritzer, C. Emily. 1983. *The condition of teaching: A state by state analysis.* Princeton: Princeton University Press.

Frankel, Martin M., and Debra E. Gerald. 1982. *Projections of education statistics to 1990–91. Analytical report.* Vol. 1. Washington, D.C.: U.S. Government Printing Office.

Freire, Paulo. 1970. *Cultural action for freedom.* Cambridge: Harvard Educational Review.

———. 1973. *Education for critical consciousness.* New York: Seabury Press.

Gartner, Alan, Colin Greer, and Frank Riessman, eds. 1973. *After deschooling what? Ivan Illich, et al.* New York: Perennial Library.

Giroux, Henry. 1981. *Ideology, culture and the process of schooling.* Philadelphia: Temple University Press.

Greene, Maxine. 1973a. And it still is news. In *After deschooling what? Ivan Illich, et al.,* edited by A. Gartner, C. Greer, and F. Riessman, 129–136. New York: Perennial Library.

———. 1973b. *Teacher as stranger.* Belmont, Calif.: Wadsworth.

Greenhouse, Steven. 1999. Adding Up the Impact of Raising Salaries. *The New York Times,* 8 August, Week in Review, 16.

Hansen, David T. 1995. *The call to teach.* Foreword by Larry Cuban. New York: Teachers College Press.

Henry, Jules. 1965. *Culture against man.* New York: Vintage.

———. 1972. *On education.* New York: Vintage.

———. 1973. *On sham, vulnerability and other forms of self-destruction.* New York: Vintage.

Hornblower, Margot, "He? She? Whatever!" *Time,* October 11, 1999, 76.

Husser, William J. 1999. *Predicting the need for newly hired teachers in the United States 2008–09.* Washington, D.C.: National Center for Education Statistics. Available online at http://nces.ed.gov/pubsearch/pubsinfo.asp?pubid=1999026.

Illich, Ivan. 1970. *Deschooling society.* New York: Harper and Row.

———. 1971. *Celebration of awareness.* New York: Anchor.

Johnson, Susan Moore. 1990. *Teachers at work: Achieving success in our schools.* New York: Basic Books.

Kottkamp, Robert, Eugene F. Provenzo, Jr., and Marilyn M. Cohn. 1986. Stability and change in a profession: Two decades of teacher attitudes, 1964–1984. *Phi Delta Kappan* 67(8): 559–567.

Kozol, Jonathan. 1981. *On being a teacher.* New York: Continuum.

Kelly, Gail P., and Phillip Altbach. 1978. *Education and colonialism.* New York: Longman.

Lortie, Dan C. 1975. *Schoolteacher: A sociological study.* Chicago: University of Chicago.

Marsden, George M. 1980. *Fundamentalism and American culture: The shaping of twentieth century evangelicalism, 1870–1925.* New York: Oxford.

Mini Digest of Education Statistics 1995. Numbers of Teachers. Washington, D.C.: U.S. Government Printing Office.

National Center for Education Statistics (NCES). 1982. *The condition of education.* Washington, D.C.: U.S. Government Printing Office.

———. 1984. *The condition of education.* Washington, D.C.: U.S. Government Printing Office.

———. 1993–1994. Teacher Trends. *Fast Facts.* Available online at http://necs.ed.gov/fastfacts/. Accessed May 21, 2001.

National Education Association. 1981. *Status of the American public school teacher: 1980–1981.* Washington, D.C.: Author.

Nyberg, David. 1981a. A concept of power for education. *Teachers College Record* 82(4): 535–551.

———. 1981b. *Power over power.* Cornell, N.Y.: Cornell University Press.

Patton, Frances Gray. 1954. *Goodmorning Miss Dove.* New York: Dodd, Mead.

Provenzo, Eugene F., Jr., and Gary N. McCloskey, O.S.A. 1996. *Schooling and schoolteachers: Ethoses in conflict.* Norword, N.J.: Ablex.

Rousseau, Jean-Jacques. 1970. *The social contract.* Trans. by Maurice Cranston. Baltimore: Penguin Books.

Sarason, Seymour. 1971. *The culture of school and the problem of change.* Boston: Allyn and Bacon.

Scopes v. State of Tennessee. 154 Tenn. 105, 289 S.W. 363, 1927.

Seybolt, Robert. 1935. *The private schools of colonial Boston.* Cambridge: Harvard University Press.

Spring, Joel. 1978. *American education: An introduction to social and political aspects*. New York: Longman.

Sykes, Gary. 1984.The deal. *The Wilson Quarterly* 8(1): 59–77.

Weber, Margaret B. 1982. Teacher supply and demand. In *Encyclopedia of Educational Research*. Vol. 4: *1918–1926*. New York: Macmillan and the Free Press.

Weiner, Lois. 1993. *Preparing teachers for urban schools: Lessons from thirty years of school reform*. Foreword by Larry Cuban. New York: Teachers College Press.

CHAPTER 6

Local and State Involvement in U.S. Education

Although local, state, and federal governments share the responsibility for public education, the states, under the **Constitution,** assume the primary burden. This chapter begins with an overview of local and state involvement in education and then moves on to an examination of the federal government's involvement with public schools.

INTASC Standards

Principle #10

■ SCHOOLS AS BUREAUCRACIES

Schools and the educational systems in which they are located are by definition bureaucracies. A *bureaucracy* is a complex, highly structured social organization designed to carry out a specific task. In the case of a school system, it includes all the people and the administrative units that are involved:

bu·reau·cra·cy (pronounced: byu-'rä-krə-sE). *noun.* Etymology: French *bureaucratie,* from *bureau* + *-cratie* –cracy, 1818. 1 a : a body of nonelective government officials   b : an administrative policy-making group   2 : government characterized by specialization of functions, adherence to fixed rules, and a hierarchy of authority   3 : a system of administration marked by officialism, red tape, and proliferation.
—(*Merriam-Webster Dictionary,* 1994)

Constitution
The primary political document of the United States that outlines the rules of our government and the fundamental laws of the nation.

Bureaucracies are typically perceived as being negative—entangled with "red tape" (a term associated with the eighteenth-century British colonial government in India, which would wrap its documents in red string or "tape") and inefficiency. In fact, bureaucracies are essential to the effective running of large and complex social systems. Without them, despite all their limitations, modern society could not function.

The great German sociologist Max Weber (1864–1920) described the six essential characteristics of a bureaucracy as follows:

1. A bureaucracy is a structure of offices each having specific responsibilities and duties.
2. In a bureaucracy authority rests with the office rather than the person.
3. Bureaucracy tends to encourage specialization.
4. The organization of a bureaucracy is governed by rules of procedure that tend to routinize and categorize activities.
5. The functions and procedures of bureaucracies tend to be formal and impersonal.
6. Bureaucratic organizations are stratified and hierarchical. (Weber 1909–1920, 104–106)

INTASC Standards

Principle #9

As bureaucracies, most public school systems include each of these six characteristics. Think about the schools you might have gone to, or the schools in the community where you live. Can you identify in them some of the elements described by Weber? How does a large urban school district fit Weber's model? A school district like Dade County Public Schools (Miami, Florida) can serve for an analysis.

Dade County Public Schools is the fourth largest school district in the United States. It has an annual budget of just under $3.5 billion and a total student population in the 1997–1998 school year of 345,861 students. Median cost per pupil is $5,815. Administrative staff includes approximately 350 administrators working in the central office and on special projects, 325 principals, 640 assistant principals, 8,096 elementary teachers, 5,805 secondary teachers, 2,906 exceptional education teachers, and 1,359 vocational and adult teachers. The total number of teachers is 18,166. Full- and part-time employees in the entire district number approximately 44,500 (Miami-Dade County Public Schools, *Statistical Highlights 1998–99*).

Dade County public schools are divided into nine separate regions, each with an elected school board member. The board is responsible for hiring a **superintendent** of the school system. The superintendent serves at the pleasure of the school board. A very general administrative flow chart for the school system is illustrated in Figure 6.1. Each box includes

superintendent
The lead or highest-level administrator in a school district.

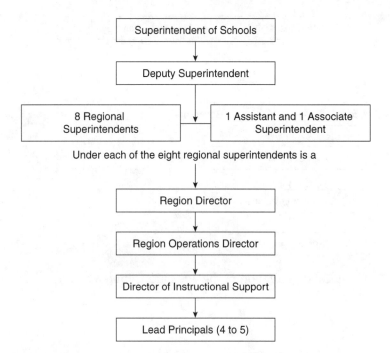

FIGURE 6.1 ■ Organization of the Dade County public schools.

its own bureaucracy underneath it. Under each of the eight Regional Superintendents, for example, is included a Region Director, a Region Operations Director, a Director of Instructional Support, and a group of Lead Principals. Each of these individuals, in turn, have their own groups of people reporting to them. The structure outlined in Figure 6.1 does not even reach the individual school level, which includes the familiar structure of a principal, assistant principals, teachers, staff, and students.

Weber's six characteristic of a bureaucracy can clearly be seen to be operational in the Dade County system. Different positions and different regions are given separate responsibilities—a bureaucracy is a structure of offices each having specific responsibilities and duties. Authority is specific to an area not to a person—in a bureaucracy authority rests with the office rather than with the person. Many different units have their own special responsibilities—bureaucracy tends to encourage specialization. Procedures in the system are routine—the organization of a bureaucracy is governed by rules of procedure that tend to routinize and categorize activities. The bureaucratic structure of the system has a set

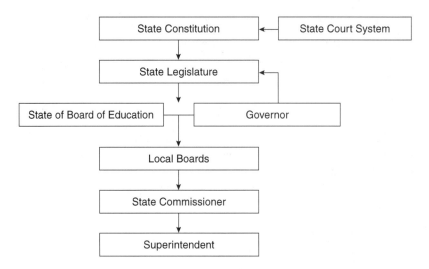

FIGURE 6.2 ■ Typical organization of the educational bureaucracy at the state level.

stratified
In layers or levels.

hierarchical
Involving different levels of authority and responsibility.

of fairly formal and rigid rules—the functions and procedures of bureaucracies tend to be formal and impersonal. Finally, the bureaucracy has a clearly definable hierarchy—bureaucratic organizations are **stratified** and **hierarchical**. The bureaucracy of the school system is part of a larger state educational bureaucracy, which is shown in Figure 6.2.

INTERNET @ CONNECTIONS
School System Websites

Nearly every major school system in the country has a website. Visiting the website for your local district can provide you with invaluable information of all sorts. You may also like to investigate other school districts across the country. A list of addresses for the five largest school districts in the United States follows.

New York City Public Schools
http://www.nyecenet.edu/

Los Angeles Public Schools
http://www.lausd.k12.ca.us/

Chicago Public Schools
http://www.cps.k12.il.us/

Miami-Dade County Public Schools
http://dcps.dade.k12.fl.us/

Broward County Public Schools
http://www.browardschools.com/main.htm

■ SCHOOL DISTRICTS AND SCHOOL BOARDS

The local school district is the basic unit in the organization and operation of U.S. public schools. Under the control and governance of a board of local citizens, school districts are an important part of both the educational and the political system.

INTASC Standards
Principle #10

In most districts school board members are elected. At their best, they embody the democratic ideal of elected officials pursuing the will of the electorate. Ninety thousand men and women serve as school board members in sixteen thousand school districts across the country. The economic power and influence of school boards is reflected in the fact that they are responsible for the disbursement of hundreds of billions of dollars per year in public funds (Brodinsky 1977, 8).

Ben Brodinsky has described the school board as

> . . . a body of laypersons, ever-changing in its make-up, its individuals seldom becoming entrenched; a creature of the state, yet responsible to local voters; weak in many respects, yet endowed with power to legislate, to administer its acts, and function as a semijudicial agency. (Brodinsky 1977, 8–9)

The school board formulates policy for the school district; it drafts budgets; enters into contractual agreements; hires and fires the school system's superintendent; builds new buildings; handles investments; and employs teachers, psychologists, janitors, librarians, and the many other people who serve the system. The board is also responsible, along with the superintendent, for defining educational standards and determining the general educational goals and ideals the school district pursues (Brodinsky 1977, 9).

INTASC Standards
Principle #7

In a large urban school district such as Dade County, the members of the school board represent different parts of the county and different political constituents. In this context they play an important part in the democratic process. They also are responsible for enormous numbers of people and huge budgets. Think about the logistics involved in providing

FIGURE 6.3 ■ Photograph of contemporary school board members.

lunches for 345,000 students or in maintaining more than four hundred different school buildings and special facilities throughout the district. All this is overseen by nine elected officials who technically work on a part-time basis for little or no salary.

■ HISTORICAL FOUNDATIONS OF SCHOOL BOARDS

The school board is a U.S. invention having its origins in seventeenth-century colonial New England. The Massachusetts General Court passed a school act on November 11, 1647, requiring each town with fifty or more families to establish public elementary schools; towns with one hundred or more families were also required to establish a Latin grammar school (Cremin 1970, 181).

The education act of 1647 placed the responsibility for educating children in the Massachusetts Bay Colony in the hands of the local townships and their citizens. Originally, school matters were dealt with at town meetings. Eventually, committees of citizens took over the responsibility of running the local schools. A permanent school board was set up in Boston in 1721. Later designated the School Committee, it began the practice of separating the operation of local schools from other city and government affairs (Cistone 1982, 1637).

In 1789, the Massachusetts legislature authorized local townships to establish special committees devoted only to school affairs. By 1826, the state legislature had made it mandatory that each township have a school committee. The concept of the school committee soon gathered wide acceptance throughout New England and eventually spread across the nation.

■ CONTEMPORARY SCHOOL BOARDS

In our own era the regulation and control of school boards varies widely from one part of the country to the other. The size of the board, the length of time members serve, procedures for filling vacancies, and so on differ in every area (Campbell et al. 1980, 188). Approximately 25 percent of all school board members are appointed; the remaining 75 percent are elected (Campbell et al. 1980, 193).

School board members usually work without salary because they want to serve the community or because they see service on the school board as a vehicle for entering politics. In most communities, the school board is the lowest level of elected office. As elected and appointed officials, school board members are expected to reflect the beliefs and values of their communities. But as a rule, school board members are not typical citizens; most often they are white, middle-aged, married, professionals; their children attend public schools (Cistone 1982, 1641).

Men dominate school boards although more women have acquired membership in recent years. In 1927 a study of U.S. school boards showed that 10.2 percent of all school board members were women (Counts 1927). By 1977 this figure had risen to 15 percent. A 1978 study of Ohio school boards indicated that nearly 19 percent of all school board members were women (Campbell et al. 1980, 198).

Minority membership on school boards is limited because, historically, school boards have had a tendency to perpetuate themselves. School board members frequently promote new candidates, informally acting as their sponsors. Therefore, like-minded people tend to serve on the boards. Because of their strong feelings about specific issues, minority candidates tend to be less popular. With important exceptions, school boards tend to be relatively conservative, reflecting the status quo and the power blocks in their communities.

Typically, school board members are reimbursed only for the expenses of their work for the board. General board meetings, special committee meetings, emergency sessions, and discussions with administrators, contractors, and special interest groups demand an enormous amount of time. Individuals with lower incomes and young people starting their careers frequently find it difficult, if not impossible, to make the sacrifices of time and money necessary to be involved with the activities of a school board.

Of course the time and duties involved in being a member of a school board depend in large part on the size of the school district. Being a member of the school board in a large urban area such as Dade County, Florida, or New York City is very different from serving on the local school board in a small suburban or rural school district. In the case of the Dade County school system, for example, the board is responsible for administering a budget of more than $3.5 billion each year; a small suburban school board might administer only several million dollars a year.

School board members work in different ways and often with widely different objectives and purposes. Board members may be described as ratifiers who legitimatize the recommendations of administrators (policy initiators); as negotiators who mediate conflicts; as educational advocates who want to improve specific programs within the schools; as judges who pass judgment on teachers and administrators; as administrators and budget analysts who scrutinize how every penny is spent and how the superintendent makes decisions; as gossipers who keep an eye on everything going on inside the school district; and finally as status seekers who use their positions on the board to gain recognition and attention (Brodinsky 1977, 9–10).

Schools and school boards are under local control, but since the 1950s their power has been significantly reduced by court decisions and increasing federal involvement in education. The imposition of laws requiring racial integration of schools exemplifies how federal involvement has increasingly taken control of the schools out of the hands of local officials.

Many critics of U.S. schooling have argued that in reality local officials have not controlled education for some time. The rapid growth of large urban and suburban school districts has seriously diminished the power and influence of the local school board. As school systems became larger and more complex, professional educators assumed greater control over day-to-day administration.

■ PRINCIPALS

The principal is the administrative officer of most schools. In general, being a principal is a full-time administrative job; relatively few principals teach, even part time. In both elementary and secondary schools the principal often has additional staff under her control, most often a vice- or assistant principal. At the secondary level, principals usually have a director of guidance and a registrar or attendance officer assigned to them as well.

About 100,000 private and public schools operate in the United States; fewer than a third are secondary schools, and the remainder are elementary schools. The number of administrators (including central office administrators and supervisors as well as principals) totals approximately 165,000.

The principal and her staff are most closely associated with what goes on in the schools on a day-to-day basis. They have the most immediate contact with students and parents, they are responsible for discipline and the physical operation of the schools, and they carry out the directives of the local school board and superintendent's office. As Lloyd E. McCleary and Scott D. Thomason have explained:

> The principal occupies the key position in school organization. The school is a social system with belief patterns, authority structures, formal and informal communication systems, special interest groups, etc.: and the influence of the principal reaches into each of these elements. (McCleary and Thomson 1979, 5)

Principals are predominately men. Although women make up approximately 50 percent of the high school teaching population, they

FIGURE 6.4 ■ Photograph of school principal.

represent only 7 percent of high school principals; this represents a decline from 10 percent in 1965 (Byrne 1979, 1). Ninety-six percent of all high school principals are white, 3 percent are African American, and the remaining 1 percent are Chicanos, Native Americans, Asian Americans, and others (Byrne 1979, 2).

INTASC Standards

Principle #9

What the principal's role should be is of interest to both educational practitioners and theorists. Principals provide leadership, but how that leadership is defined is open to debate. Lipham and Hoeh have distinguished five basic tasks for most principals: the instructional program, the staff, student personnel, financial and physical resources, and school–community relations (1974, 10). What does each responsibility involve? Most principals leave curricular development (the instructional area) almost completely in the hands of their staff. Nonetheless, they play a crucial role in "assessing the context for the educational program" (Lipham and Hoeh 1974, 11). It is the principal who ultimately determines the educational needs of the students in her school and what is most appropriate to the values of the community. This can be a difficult task. Acceptable goals and objectives for the curriculum in one community may not be acceptable in another; what pleases one group of parents or taxpayers may infuriate another.

Dealing with staff has become more difficult in recent years. With the growth of teachers' unions many principals have had their traditional power and influence reduced. Yet even with the growing power of teachers' groups, the principal is responsible in the end for evaluating staff performance, reassigning or dismissing staff members, and setting general objectives for the curriculum (Lipham and Hoeh 1974, 12).

Principals must also deal with the students. Recently students have become more active in influencing the content and purpose of what they are taught, as well as how their daily routines in the schools are regulated and controlled. Besides providing leadership and guidance to the students, the principal sets disciplinary policy and addresses questions of free expression and due process (Lipham and Hoeh 1974, 13).

Most principals face considerable responsibility for how money and resources are allocated and used in their schools. Typical responsibilities include requisitioning and purchasing supplies, accounting for monies, maintaining an inventory or property, and supervising construction and maintenance (Lipham and Hoeh 1974, 14).

Finally, through Parent Teachers Association (PTA) meetings, conferences with individual parents, and news releases to the community about the school and its programs, the typical principal tries to foster harmony between the school and the community. To achieve this end the principal must often work with community leaders and agencies, responding to their needs and desires as well as the needs and desires of individual parents and citizens (Lipham and Hoeh 1974, 14).

■ THE SUPERINTENDENT OF SCHOOLS

Still, no matter how much control or influence principals may have within their own schools, they ultimately answer to a central administration headed by a superintendent. It is the superintendent who acts in the service of the local school board and oversees the day-to-day operation of the school system. More than any other person within a school district, the superintendent has the potential to set the tone for teaching and learning in the schools under his or her supervision (Callahan 1966, 1).

INTASC Standards
Principle #10

Although in many respects the superintendent is the most powerful figure within the school district, his influence is by no means complete or unrestricted. Traditional structures of power and authority have been redefined in recent years; the power of most school boards and in turn of school superintendents has eroded steadily since the 1950s. Minority groups representing liberal and conservative points of view have become more powerful. In addition, state and federal agencies have assumed authority traditionally assigned to the superintendent (Hansen 1976, 90–94).

As Raymond Callahan, David Tyack, Elizabeth Hansot, and others have pointed out, the superintendent is extremely vulnerable. He is hired and fired by the school board, and subject to the pressure of parents, local interest groups, and teachers. Superintendents were first appointed to head school districts during the 1840s and 1850s. The importance of the superintendency during the latter part of the nineteenth century was noted by the physician and educational researcher Joseph Mayer Rice. After completing an extensive survey of U.S. schools during the first half of 1892, he wrote:

> The office of the superintendent is, in my opinion, one the importance of which cannot be overestimated. Indeed, in the study of the educational conditions in any given locality, the superintendent may be regarded as the central figure, . . . (Rice 1893, 11)

Rice enumerated four elements that determine the superintendent's success: his educational qualifications, his concept of the superintendent's role, his relationship with the board of education, and his longevity as an administrator within a school district.

How well a superintendent functions often depends on personal aspirations. In *The Politics of Educational Innovation*, Ernest House has pointed out two basic types of school superintendents. Some are deliberately place bound; they hope to remain in their positions until they retire. They are careful about the relationships they develop with the community and are often deliberately conservative. Over a long period of time they are given a large degree of latitude and freedom, as long as their decisions and activities agree with those in power within the community.

Other superintendents are career bound; they see their jobs as stepping stones to other positions. They often initiate rapid and visible changes to attract regional or national attention and encourage job offers. Career-bound superintendents pay less attention to developing a strong base of local support than do place-bound superintendents (House 1974, 44). Whether place bound or career bound, most superintendents share similar responsibilities and work hard. The average superintendent works approximately fifty to sixty hours a week. The overwhelming number of superintendents are men.

FIGURE 6.5 ■ Photograph of
school superintendent.

Superintendents draw most of their power and influence from the
board of education to whom they report. Whereas their power is often
limited, their influence operates in various ways.

1. The superintendent can influence salaries, promotions, and assignments within the school district.
2. The superintendent can determine what types of problems need
   study within a school district and can assign resources so that an examination of them can be undertaken.
3. The superintendent can analyze problems within the school district
   and determine ways in which these problems can be addressed.
4. The superintendent can develop plans and long-term goals for the
   school district and implement them.
5. Finally, the superintendent can act as a mediator between various
   groups concerned with education in the community, whether it is the
   school board, teachers, parents, or others. (Campbell et al. 1980,
   245–246)

KEY SUPREME COURT CASES

Pierce v. Society of Sisters (1925)

> *The fundamental liberty under which all governments in this Union repose excludes any general power of the State to standardize its children by forcing them to accept instruction from public teachers only. The child is not the mere creature of the State; those who nurture him and direct his destiny have the right coupled with the high duty, to recognize and prepare him for additional obligations.*
>
> —*Pierce v. Society of Sisters*, 268 U.S. 510 (1925)

Taken from a 1925 U.S. Supreme Court decision that defended the right of parents to send their children to a private religious school, the preceding quotation raises some important questions. Does the state have a right to participate in the education of the children who will be its future citizens? Or does it have the right only to make sure that schools meet certain minimum standards? Should it even have the right to maintain minimum standards? To what extent is any public schoolteacher an agent of the state or social system? What do you think?

■ FINANCING THE SCHOOLS

INTASC Standards

Principle #10

Paying for public education costs the U.S. taxpayers hundreds of billions of dollars each year; next to defense, education was our country's largest single expenditure. Funding plays a critical role in how schools function. Because most funds for local school districts come from local taxes, a district's wealth determines to a large degree the services its schools provide. Inadequate funding often means larger classes, smaller libraries, and poorer instructional equipment (Campbell 1980, 386).

The tax base for any school system is based on the number of people paying taxes and the rate at which the local school tax is set, but the amount of funding available from taxes for the support of schools is determined by many different factors. A small suburban school district, for example, might have a downtown area with a large number of office buildings. The largest single source of revenue for the school district comes from the real estate taxes on these buildings. Because the school district itself is relatively small, the funding level for the school system is extremely high. Individuals living in the school district have lower school taxes than residents in districts that do not have a similarly strong tax base.

Rural school districts and poor urban areas with limited tax revenues are at an obvious disadvantage in raising monies to support their public schools. Coons, Clune, and Sugarman (1970) have argued that existing arrangements for financing schools often violate the constitutional rights of students to receive an equal education. The U.S. Supreme Court eventually rejected this argument in *San Antonio v. Rodriguez* (1973) which asserted that equal education is not guaranteed by the Constitution.

The inherent inequity of resources in different school districts can be overcome to some extent by providing state and federal aid to poorer school districts. But with state or federal aid taxpayers and school officials lose a great deal of control over the local school district. The federal government's ability since the late 1960s to implement civil rights legislation has in large part depended on its ability to withdraw funding from local school districts and communities that have failed to comply with the law.

Federal support for local school districts includes three categories of direct aid: aid for children of economically disadvantaged families awarded by the provisions of Title I of the Elementary and Secondary Education Act (ESEA) of 1965; aid for schools in districts with military bases or other government installations; and categorical aid such as vocational support mandated by the Vocational Education Act of 1963 (Cohn 1980, 697).

Federal aid is also funneled through state agencies and then passed on to local school districts. In 1983 federal funding for elementary and secondary schools amounted to $9.4 billion or approximately 7.4 percent of all school expenditures (U.S. Department of Commerce 1985, 129). By comparison federal contributions represented only 3.9 percent of the total spent on education throughout the nation in 1955–1956 (Cohn 1982, 697).

State responsibility for funding local schools has increased in recent years. In California, the passage of Proposition 13 mandated a significant reduction in local taxes and resulted in increased state support of the schools. Local efforts to restrict the increase of property taxes have probably been popular, because they are one of the few taxes that individual citizens can successfully oppose. Opposition to local school taxes has forced many school districts to restrict services when funds have run short. Increasingly, school districts have drawn on support from state and federal sources, thus shifting the control of the schools away from the community.

INTERNET @ CONNECTIONS

The Parent Teachers Association

The National Parent Teachers Association was founded in 1897 as the National Congress of Mothers. It is the oldest and largest volunteer association in the United

States concerned with education and the needs of children. Throughout its history, the PTA has consistently been concerned with the improvement of local schools and the welfare and health of children. It serves an important role in local and national politics, while promoting projects that encourage parents to participate actively in their children's education. You can visit the National Parent Teachers Association online at http://www.pta.org/index.stm.

■ STATE INVOLVEMENT IN EDUCATION

State control of education varies widely from one part of the country to another. Most state constitutions make education a legal responsibility of the state, but as an old aphorism states, "education is a state authority locally administered" (Kirst and Wirt 1982, 1771). State governments have general educational guidelines to ensure that local officials carry out state policies. Thus, the state certifies teachers, but local officials review their credentials. Similarly, the state usually reviews and adopts textbooks but local boards of education buy and use them.

In recent decades state boards of education have become more involved in regulating and controlling the schools. These departments exercise influence by disseminating statistical and technical information about the schools, providing technical services, regulating standards for textbooks and curricula, allocating funds to local school districts, certifying school personnel, establishing coalitions to promote education, making sure programs are properly implemented and administered, implementing laws relating to compulsory attendance and teacher fitness, and allocating funds for the federal government (Campbell et al. 1980, 85–86).

State education departments are really regulatory agencies. Ideally, through cooperation with local communities and the federal government, state education departments set policies and standards. Campbell, Cunningham, Nystrand, and Usdan have argued that state departments of education could provide a particularly useful function if they were to expand their role in research and evaluation and leave the operation of the schools as much as possible to local school districts. State departments of education should help people do better what they are already doing and see new and worthwhile things to do (Campbell et al. 1980, 84).

INTERNET @ CONNECTIONS

State Department of Education Web Sites

Nearly every state department of education has a website with resources. Often these sites are excellent places to find out about certification, grants, or a specialized curriculum area (e.g., state history). A list of addresses follows.

Alabama
http://www.alsde.edu

Alaska
http://www.educ.state.ak.us/

Arizona
http://ade.state.az.us/

Arkansas
http://arkedu.k12.ar.us

California
http://goldmine.cde.ca.gov.

Colorado
http://cde.state.co.us/

Delaware
http://www.dpi.state.de.us/dpi/index.html

Florida
http://www.firn.edu/doe/index.html

Georgia
http://gadoe.gac.peachnet.edu/

Hawaii
http://www.K12.hi.us/

Idaho
http://www.state.id.us/

Illinois
http://www.isbe.state.il.us/homepage.html

Kansas
http://www.ksbe.state.ks.us/

Kentucky
http://www.kde.state.ky.us/

Louisiana
http://www.doe.state.la.us/

Maryland
http://www.mec.state.md.us/mec/

Massachusetts
http://info.doe.mass.edu/

Michigan
http://www.mde.state.mi.us/

Minnesota
http://www.educ.state.mn.us/

Mississippi
http://mdek12.state.ms.us/

Missouri
http://services.dese.state.mo.us/

Nebraska
ttp://www.nde.state.ne.us/

New Hampshire
http://www.state.nh.us/doe/education.html

New Jersey
http://www.state.nj.us/education/

New Mexico
http://www.nmche.org/

New York
http://www.nysed.gov/

North Dakota
http://www.sendit.nodak.edu/dpi/

Ohio
http://www.ode.ohio.gov/

Oklahoma
http://www.osrhe.edu/

Pennsylvania
http://www.state.pa.us/

Rhode Island
http://www.ri.net/RIDE/

South Dakota
http://www.state.sd.us/state/executive/deca/

Tennessee
http://www.state.tn.us/other/sde/homepage.htm

Texas
http://www.tenet.edu/

Utah
http://www.usoe.k12.ut.us/

Vermont
http://www.state.vt.us/educ.htm

Virginia
http://pen.k12.va.us/Anthology/VDOE/

Washington
http://www.ospi.wednet.edu/

West Virginia
http://access.k12.wv.us/

Wisconsin
http://www.state.wi.us/agencies/dpi/

■ CONTROLS AND INFLUENCES

Influences shaping the schools fall into seven different categories: demographic, legal, structural, ideational, knowledge, financial, and network (Campbell et al. 1980, 469–488). Demographic influences include the number and character of adults and students in a school district. The population's cultural traditions and values and the mix of individuals play a critical role in shaping schools. A midwestern rural school system is likely to have a relatively uniform population with similar values. Large urban school districts such as New York City, Los Angeles, Miami, or Houston comprise different groups with different goals, ideals, and values as well as a greater range of incomes, a greater range of educational backgrounds, and almost always a greater potential for conflict.

INTASC Standards

Principle #7

WHAT DO YOU THINK?
Deschooling Society

The radical educational theorist Ivan Illich has argued in *Deschooling Society* that the teaching profession holds a monopoly on the educational system. According to him, we have developed a system in which only those who have been trained and "certified" as part of the system are allowed to teach in the public schools. But do all teachers need to be formally trained and certified? Clearly, some teachers have gained an important understanding of the world that they did not receive as part of a formal education. What are the benefits of a system in which all teachers must comply with a relatively uniform and rigid standard? What are the disadvantages? Can some sort of compromise be achieved by which basic certification requirements are waived under certain conditions? What do you think?

Legal controls include local, state, and federal laws that affect what can or cannot go on in schools. Legal controls vary widely and impinge on local school districts in different ways. Local laws typically deal with school boundaries and taxation. State laws ordinarily deal with issues such as fire codes and certification. Federal laws address constitutional issues such as providing students with equal educational opportunities. These legal controls combine to create unique conditions for each school district and system.

Structural influences encompass official and unofficial bodies such as local school boards, teacher unions, parent–teacher associations, and groups of concerned parents or business leaders. All combine to shape and define the structures that control a local school district.

Ideational elements are outgrowths of the values, beliefs, and attitudes people hold. Depending on the demographic character of a local school district, ideational elements can critically shape the local school system, and in a multicultural society such as ours questions of ideational control are complex and significant. In a rural southern community with a strong conservative Christian element, the selection of textbooks may be a major source of controversy. In places such as Miami and Los Angeles, conflicting factions may dispute the value of bilingual education, but whether schools should support bilingual education is largely an ideological question. Different positions reflect different ideas about the nature of U.S. society.

Francis Bacon suggested more than four centuries ago that knowledge is power. Knowledge control involves the organization and distribution of information within a school system. Who has access to information about the schools and their students? How is information generated and used? What is the role of the expert, and what is the role of the layman? Financial control involves the sources and distribution of funds. Local taxpayers influence the distribution of funds as do teachers' organizations and other groups. The federal government can effect changes within schools by withholding or granting funds based on a lo-

---

? WHAT DO YOU THINK?
Edison Schools

Chris Whittle is a media entrepreneur who launched the Edison project in 1991. His idea was to open a nationwide chain of public schools. The company mission changed over time, evolving into a school management group concerned with running traditional public schools and publicly funded chartered schools. The Edison project now includes fifty-three schools under contract with local school districts and twenty-six independent charter schools.

Edison claims that it can run public schools more efficiently than local school boards. It is a publicly traded company and its purpose is to make money for stockholders. Teachers working in the Edison schools are provided stock options in much the same way that people are offered stock options in more traditional businesses.

Edison claims it will lobby for greater funding in education and, through the efficient use of new technologies such as computers, both bring down the cost and improve the quality of schooling.

The United States is a capitalist culture whose economy is based on the profit motive. Should its schools be run as for-profit businesses? What do you think?

---

cal school system's compliance with state or federal statutes. What is the actual relationship between local and state systems of education and the federal government?

■ FEDERAL INVOLVEMENT IN U.S. EDUCATION

The Tenth Amendment to the Constitution states, "the powers not delegated to the United States by the Constitution, nor prohibited by it to the States, are reserved to the States respectively, or to the people." Not having been delegated to the federal government, the administration and control of public education became a local responsibility. Of course when the Constitution was adopted in 1788 a public school system did not exist in the United States. Public education was provided by some local townships throughout many northern states, but was less common in the South. Until well into the nineteenth century, private and religious schools predominated over public tax-supported schools.

Despite constitutional restrictions on its involvement, the federal government has played an important role in promoting education throughout U.S. history. Under the Northwest Ordinance of 1785,

INTASC Standards
Principle #10

Congress declared that newly acquired territory (later Indiana, Illinois, Michigan, Ohio, Wisconsin, and part of Minnesota) would be divided into Congressional townships of thirty-six square miles and subdivided into sections of one square mile (640 acres). The sixteenth section in each township was reserved for the use of the public schools (Commanger 1958, 123–124). Two years later the Northwest Ordinance of 1787 laid out the details of territorial organization and the requirements for statehood. Article III of that ordinance specifically stated: "Religion, morality, and knowledge, being necessary to good government and the happiness of mankind, schools and the means of education shall forever be encouraged" (Commanger 1958, 128–132). The immediate result of the passage of the ordinances of 1785 and 1787 was that funds from the sale of the designated lands in each township intended by the federal government for the schools was actually diverted to other purposes such as the development of canals and roads.

The significance of the grants provided in the land ordinances of 1785 and 1787 lay primarily in the precedent they set for federal funding with the passage of the Morrill Act or, as it is more commonly known, the Land Grant College Act.

■ THE LAND GRANT COLLEGE ACT OF 1862

The Land Grant College Act was signed into law on July 2, 1862, by President Abraham Lincoln. The act made available to each state the profits from the sale of thirty thousand acres of land on the western frontier for each state's senators and congressmen. Thus each state received the profits from the sale of no less than ninety thousand acres of land. Specifically the money was to be used to develop state colleges and universities emphasizing technical subjects such as engineering and agriculture. It is significant to note that although the federal government provided the funds, the individual states retained control of the schools.

In general, major federal legislation has set new directions and priorities for the educational system closely linked to major technological and social changes. For example, in the case of the passage of the Land Grant College Act of 1862, it was clear that as the country became industrialized, it would have to develop ways of training highly skilled mechanics and engineers. The new land grant colleges and universities fulfilled this need. In 1917 the passage of the Smith-Hughes Act, which provided federal support for vocational educational programs, fulfilled many of the same objectives, only this time for students in secondary schools.

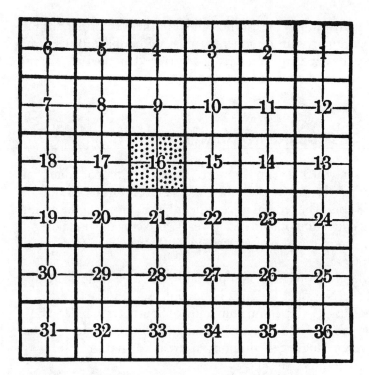

FIGURE 6.6 ■ Division of congressional townships according to the Northwest Ordinance of 1785.

■ THE U.S. OFFICE OF EDUCATION

The federal government's involvement with education in the nineteenth century was by no means restricted to granting funds for special programs like the Land Grant College Act. In 1867, for example, the U.S. Office of Education was established as a special division of the Department of the Interior. Known originally as the Department of Education, the Office of Education was first headed by the common school reformer Henry Barnard. The Office of Education had very little power or influence during its early years, functioning almost exclusively as a tool for collecting and disseminating educational data and statistics.

In 1939 the Office of Education was transferred to the Federal Security Agency, and then in 1953 it became part of the Department of Health, Education, and Welfare. Only in the late 1970s under the Carter administration was a separate Department of Education established for the first time. Opposition to the establishment of the Department of Education has been bipartisan; opponents (mostly Republican) maintain that establishing the department in fact has infringed on the rights of the states to administer and control the schools.

■ PATTERNS OF FEDERAL INFLUENCE

Unlike countries in which a central ministry is responsible for education (Great Britain, France, and Russia), the United States runs its schools on a decentralized basis. The federal government has in fact become an important force in education only in recent years, and constitutional, legal, ideologial, and programmatic interests have influenced its involvement (Mosher 1982, 671).

Modern federal involvement can probably be dated from 1958 and the passage of the National Defense Education Act. In reaction to the fear inspired by Russia's successful launching of Sputnik, the federal government designated special funds for training people in science, mathematics, and foreign languages—important areas for national security. The opening paragraph of the act stated:

> The congress hereby finds and declares that the security of the Nation requires the fullest development of the mental resources and technical skills of its young men and women. The present emergency demands that additional and more adequate educational opportunities be made available. The defense of this nation depends upon the mastery of modern techniques developed from complex scientific principles. (National Defense Education Act of 1958)

Loans and fellowships helped students to receive advanced training in designated fields. Financial support encouraged the states to develop educational programs in areas such as science and foreign languages.

Although many groups welcomed the additional support for education provided by the NDEA, others feared that federal funding for special programs would interfere with the rights of state and local governments. Clearly the federal government did come to play a role in shaping local school policy; for example, money was provided to local school districts to train students in mathematics and science but not the arts. Those programs that would receive special federal support were emphasized by local school districts.

Federal government assistance to local school districts, colleges, and universities was justified under its constitutional power to advance the general welfare of the country and as a means of coping with a crisis (Mosher 1982, 675). This rationalization provided the basis for passing federal legislation to support the schools during the Great Society legislation undertaken at the initiative of President Lyndon B. Johnson between 1963 and 1968. Numerous legislative acts such as the 1963 Higher Education Facilities Act and the Vocational Education Amendments of 1968 provided federal funding for educational programs. Other legislation included the Elementary and Secondary Education Act (1965) and the Bilingual Education Act (Title VII of the Elementary and Secondary Education Act of 1968). Federally funded groups such as the National Institute of Education (the research arm of the Department of Education) were also established.

All these programs, as well as more recent legislation, represent increased federal involvement in local educational policy. Under legislation passed since the 1960s the federal government can withhold financial support to organizations in violation of federal statutes. In many instances the threat of withdrawing federal assistance for programs prompted important changes and reforms at the local level. This can be most clearly seen in the case of civil rights legislation.

Title IX (Public Law 92-318), for example, an amendment to the 1964 Civil Rights Act, was passed to insure the end of sex discrimination in the schools. Complaints about sex discrimination can be directed to the Secretary of the Department of Education or taken directly to the courts (Campbell et al. 1980, 48), and organizations found in violation of the law can have their federal funding withdrawn. Thus a private university, found to discriminate on the basis of sex by not providing equal athletic facilities for men and women, could have its total federal funding withdrawn if it did not show an effort to comply with the law.

Such actions clearly represent a new and important kind of federal control over state and local agencies and pose a difficult dilemma. On the other hand, it can be fairly argued that the federal government has an obligation and duty to take whatever reasonable action necessary to enforce its laws and to protect its citizen's civil rights.

KEY SUPREME COURT CASES

Desegregating Contact Sports

With the passage of Title IX women have begun to participate in many organized sports for the first time (track, golf, cross country, swimming, baseball, and tennis, to name a few). Traditionally men and women have been segregated from one another in sports and particularly in contact sports such as football and soccer. The case of the *Yellow Springs Board of Education v. The Ohio Athletic Association* (1978) successfully challenged the traditional separation of men and women in contact sports. What arguments can be made for or against the decision? Examine the reasons for your position. Should the federal government have the right to withold funds from schools that refuse to comply with the Court's decision? What about the rights of communities and parents? What do you think?

■ CONCLUSIONS OF FEDERAL CONTROL OF EDUCATION

INTASC Standards

Principle #10

The nature of the federal government's control and authority over state and local government can be outlined in detail (Campbell et al. 1980, 56–57).

1. **The law.** The federal government can enact and enforce law related to its constitutional mandate such as civil rights.
2. **The courts.** Federal courts have come to have an increasing influence in such matters as sexual and racial discrimination; this influence is exemplified in recent cases involving court ordered desegregation.
3. **Money.** Allocating federal funds to selected educational programs represents a reduction of state and local control. By emphasizing one subject or program over another the federal government is in fact imposing specific curricular objectives upon local school districts.
4. **State federal offices.** By establishing specific offices and divisions with federal support in state departments of education the federal government extends its control. These offices typically deal with the enforcement of civil rights legislation related to education.
5. **Regional resource centers.** Regional resource centers are supposed to provide support for federal educational programs on a local level. For example, the National Institute of Education's research laboratories and centers are placed strategically throughout the United States. Those laboratories and centers have activities as varied as developing curricular materials, conducting research, and collecting and disseminating different educational information.
6. **Teacher training.** Federal legislation provides training and support for teachers. For example, teachers and teacher's aides working in a bilingual community might get specific instruction at a local university in cross cultural education.
7. **Professional interest groups.** The federal government pays the salaries of teachers in special subjects to promote and encourage the

development of particular disciplines. Thus in a multicultural community, the federal government rather than the local school districts might pay the salary of a bilingual educational coordinator.

8. **Special interest groups.** The federal government has played an active role over the years in promoting selected special interest groups within the community. Special citizen advisory panels on everything from the education of the handicapped to civil rights have come to play an influencial and important role in the school district.

Clearly all these controls represent a powerful influence on the public schools. Since the end of the Second World War, this influence has consistently increased. Federal aid for education, for example, has increased from 1.4 percent of elementary and secondary school budgets in 1946 to roughly 7 percent in the year 2000. State and local governments contribute almost equally to the remaining costs (Viadero 2000, 238).

WHAT DO YOU THINK?

Fighting the System

Rebecca Buseth is a middle school student who has a fashion sense that goes against those held by her local school. In sixth grade, she colored her hair blue with magic markers. In seventh grade, she wore her shirts out even though her school had a tuck-in rule. As an eighth grader at Lehigh Acres Middle School near Fort Myers, Florida, she become embroiled in a major conflict with school officials as to whether her pierced tongue violated the school dress code.

According to her principal, Mary Ann Moats, her tongue stud violated the school board's dress policy, which prohibited "the piercing of exposed body parts other than the ears." Rebecca, who was suspended for three days for not removing her tongue stud, which she maintained was not visible, sued the school board for its action against her. Should students lose their rights to wear what they want when they enter the schoolroom? What does the law say? What do you think?

■ POSTMODERN TRENDS AND THEIR IMPLICATIONS FOR THE LOCAL, STATE, AND FEDERAL CONTROL OF SCHOOLS

Many different factors coming together in the postmodern era have the potential to shape profoundly the experience and work of teachers.

Many of these have already been referred to in the first chapters of this book. Many others are discussed in more detail in subsequent chapters.

In general, teachers in the future will have to learn to work in increasingly complex and demanding settings. The ethos of schools, that is, the fundamental character or spirit of the schools, is clearly different than it was forty or fifty years ago. Think about how much U.S. culture has changed since the mid-1950s. Consider how the work of teachers has been affected by social and cultural movements such as racial desegregation, gender equity, gay rights, and rights for the physically challenged. Think about how changes in the economy and in families, the impact of electronic media such as television and computers—just to name a few factors—affect the schools and the work that teachers do.

Postmodern trends demand that people going into the field be much more capable of dealing with difference, as well as ambiguity and change. In dealing with the demands of an ever-changing and protean culture, they will increasingly have to be able to reflect on and contextualize their work.

Subsequent chapters focus on issues of ethnicity, race, gender, and technology. We deal with each one of these topics in a postmodern context. Our purpose is to provide you with some of the background essential to becoming border crossers of the type described in Chapter 1 of this book. In doing so, we believe you will be better prepared to deal with the social and cultural complexity of contemporary schools.

■ SUMMARY

Whether the federal government should play an increasing role in establishing educational policy across the country is debatable. On the one hand, the federal government can act as a powerful force for educational reform and innovation, and as a watchdog for the rights of individuals and minorities. On the other hand, federal control and influence can reduce the initiative to improve and reform the schools through state and local governments and the general public. What the federal government deems as being best for the nation may in many instances not be best for a community. Since our Constitution and government are based on principles of compromise and accommodation, it may be that the tension between local, state, and federal government in matters of education is part of the larger political process that is uniquely American.

■ DISCUSSION QUESTIONS ■

1. What are the advantages and disadvantages of local school boards controlling the schools?
2. What are the advantages and disadvantages of local school board members being appointed? Elected?
3. How can a principal or superintendent influence what goes on in schools?
4. In what situations should state education departments and agencies have precedence over the authority of local school officials? Why?
5. Think about the various controls that affect education. How might these elements function in the community in which you live?
6. How should the federal government be involved in education in the United States?
7. Should the federal government intervene to help equalize the amount of money spent by individual states and local communities on education (i.e., help poorer parts of the country finance their schools)?
8. Could schools in the United States be run more effectively if they were under the centralized control of the federal government?
9. What are the advantages of local control of the schools?
10. In what areas does the federal government have the greatest influence over schools? What are the implications of this influence?
11. Was the federal government justified in pouring money into schools after the passage of the National Defense Education Act of 1958? Or did it supersede its authority and wrongly interfere in local and state domains? To what extent is education a federal concern?

■ SOURCES CITED ■

An Act to Amend and Extend the National Defense Act of 1958, Public Law 88–665.

Berke, Joel S., and Michael W. Kirst. 1972. *Federal aid to education—Who benefits, who governs?* Lexington, Mass.: Heath.

Bidwell, Charles E. 1965. The school as a formal organization. In *Handbook of organizations*, ed. James G. March. Chicago: Rand McNally.

Boyd, L. 1976. The public, the professionals, and educational policy making: Who governs? *Teachers College Record* 77: 539–577.

Brodinsky, Ben. 1977. *How a school board operates.* Bloomington, Ind.: Phi Delta Kappa.

Byrne, David R., and Susan A. Hines. 1979. *The senior high school principalship. The National Survey.* Reston, Va.: The National Association of Secondary School Principals.

Callahan, Raymond E. 1966. *the superintendent of schools: An historical analysis*. Final Report of Project S-212, Cooperative Research Branch. Washington, D.C.: U.S. Office of Education.

Campbell, Roald F., Luvern L. Cunningham, Raphael O. Nystrand, and Michael D. Usdan. 1980. *The organization and control of American schools*. 4th ed. Columbus, Ohio: Charles E. Merrill.

Cistone, Peter J. ed. 1975. *Understand school boards*. Lexington, Mass.: Heath.

Cistone, Peter J. 1977. The socialization of school board members. *Educational Administration Quarterly* 13: 19–33.

———. 1982. School boards. *The encyclopedia of educational research*. Vol. 4, 1637–1645. New York: Macmillan and the Free Press.

Cohn, Elechanan. 1982. Financing schools. *The encyclopedia of educational research*. Vol. 2, 695–702. New York: Macmillan and the Free Press.

Coons, J. E., W. H. Clune, III, and S. D. Sugarman. 1970. *Private wealth and public education*. Cambridge: Harvard University Press.

Counts, George S. 1927. *The social composition of boards of education*. Supplementary Educational Monographs 33. Chicago: University of Chicago Press.

Cremin, Lawrence. 1970. *American education: The colonial experience, 1697–1783*. New York: Harper and Row.

Cronin, J. M. 1973. *The control of urban schools*. New York: Free Press.

Datta, L. E. 1982. Changing times: The study of federal program supporting educational changes and the case for local problem solving. *Teachers College Record* 82: 101–116.

Elementary and Secondary Education Act of 1965, Public Law 89-10.

The Elementary and Secondary Education Act of 1965, Public Law 89-10.

Florio, David H. 1982. U.S. Department of Education. In *Encyclopedia of educational research*. Vol. 4: *1980–1989*. New York: Macmillan and the Free Press.

Goldhammer, K. 1964. *The school board*. New York: Center for Applied Research in Education.

Gorton, Richard A., and Kenneth E. McIntyre. 1979. *The senior high school principalship*. Vol. 2, *The effective principal*. Reston, Va.: The National Association of Secondary School Principals.

The Higher Education Facilities Act of 1963, Public Law 88–204.

Hansen, Lee. 1976. Political reformation in local districts. *Educational Leadership* 34(2): 90–94.

House, Ernest. 1974. *The politics of educational innovation*. Berkeley, Calif.: McCuthchan.

Kirst, Michael, and Frederick Wirt. 1982. State influences on education. In *Encyclopedia of educational research*. Vol. 4: 1770–1780. New York: MacMillan and the Free Press.

Land Ordinance Act of May 20, 1785.

Lipham, James M., and James A. Hoeh, Jr. 1974. *The principalship: Foundations and functions*. New York: Harper & Row.

Lutz, Frank W., and Lawrence Iannaccone, eds. 1978. *Public participation in school districts*. Lexington, Mass.: Heath.

McCleary, Lloyd E., and Scott D. Thomson. 1979. *The senior high school principalship*. Vol. 3, *The summary report*. Reston, Va.: The National Association of Secondary School Principals.

McGivney, J. H., and W. Moynihan. 1972. School and community. *Teachers College Record* 74: 209–224.

Miami-Dade County Public Schools. *Statistical Highlights 1998–99*.

Morrill Act, 1862 (The Land Grant College Act).

National Center for Education Statistics. 1980. *The condition of education*. Washington, D.C.: U.S. Government Printing Office.

National Education Association Research Division. 1977. *Status of the American school teacher, 1975–76*. Washington, D.C.: The National Education Association.

Rice, Joseph Mayer. 1893. *The public school system of the United States*. New York: Century.

Rozsa, Lori. 1997. Fighting the system: Piercing gets student in trouble at school. *The Miami Herald*, 30 November, 6b.

San Antonio Independent School District v. Rodriguez. Supreme Court of the United States, 1973. 411 U.S. 1, 93 S. Ct. 1278, reb. denied 411 U.S. 959, 93 S. Ct. 1919.

Seybolt, Robert. 1935. *The private schools of colonial Boston*. Cambridge: Harvard University Press.

Tyack, David B. 1976. 'Pilgrim's progress,' Toward a social history of the school superintendency, 1860–1960. *History of Education Quarterly* 16(Fall): 257–300.

United States Department of Commerce. 1985. *Statistical abstracts of the United States*. Washington, D.C.: U.S. Government Printing Office.

Viadero, Debra. 2000. Financial burden shifts. In *Lessons of a century: A nation's schools come of age*, p. 238. Bethesda, Maryland: Editorial Projects in Education.

Vocational Education Act of 1963, Public Law 88-210.

The Vocational Education Amendments of 1968, Public Law 88–210.

Walsh, Mark. 1999. All eyes on Edison schools as company goes public. *Education Week*, 24 November, 17.

Warren, Donald R. 1974. *To enforce education*. Detroit, Mich.: Wayne State University.

Weber, Max. 1909–1920. The bureaucratic machine. In *Social theory: The multicultural and classic readings*, 104–110.

Yellow Springs Exempted Village School District Board of Education v. Ohio High School Athletic Association. 443 F. Supp. 753 (S.D. Ohio 1978).

CHAPTER 7

Private Education and Religion in the United States

When most people think of schools in the United States, they think of public schools. Yet *private* or *independent* schools are an important part of the contemporary educational scene. Approximately 10 percent of the elementary and secondary schools in the United States are private or independent.

In a democratic and pluralistic society such as the United States, private education offers an important alternative for parents and students. Private schools represent an exceptional range of interests and traditions. Church-affiliated or **parochial** schools (Catholic, Jewish, Lutheran, etc.) provide ethnic and minority groups with religious instruction in an environment that supports their values and beliefs. Elite private schools have often been centers for academic excellence and innovation.

Private schools are numerous and diverse, and the reasons people support them are complex. Besides educating children in specific values and beliefs, private schools present an alternative to public schools. In recent years support for private schools in the United States has stemmed from the belief that public schools are not as productive or efficient as they should be, that they are not meeting the needs of their clients, and that they are too bureaucratic.

INTASC Standards
Principle #3

parochial
Referring to a religious parish—a parochial school being a religious school.

TABLE 7.1 ■ Number of Private Schools and Percentage Serving Each Grade Level, By Affiliation: 1993–1994

	Total	Elementary	Secondary	Combined
Total Private	26,093	59.5	9.8	30.7
Total Public	80,740	71.9	24.3	3.8
18 Affiliation Categories				
Catholic	8,351	82.9	13.9	3.2
Episcopal	349	64.3	10.8	24.9
Friends	75	69.7	9.2	21.2
Seventh-Day Adventist	1,071	70.8	5.8	23.4
Hebrew Day	201	59.9	25.4	14.7
Solomon Schechter	56	95.1	4.9	0.0
Other Jewish	398	54.0	27.6	18.4
Christian Schools International	355	61.7	9.8	28.5
Association of Christian				
Schools International	2,472	49.4	3.9	46.8
Lutheran, Missouri Synod	1,042	92.3	6.3	1.5
Lutheran, Wisconsin Synod	373	94.0	5.4	0.6
Evangelical Lutheran	107	97.3	0.8	1.9
Other Lutheran	57	83.0	4.2	12.7
Montessori	732	82.3	0.2	17.5
Schools for Exceptional Children	284	8.4	22.3	69.3
National Association of				
Independent Schools (only)	893	32.5	20.8	46.7
Military	—	0.0	74.0	—
Other Private Schools	9,247	36.4	6.8	56.8

Source: Adapted from *Private Schools in the United States: A Statistical Profile, 1993–94,* Table 1.1.

■ ORIGINS OF PRIVATE EDUCATION

Private schools have been part of the educational scene in the United States since colonial times. Except in areas such as New England where support for public schools was relatively strong from the earliest period, private education predominated well into the nineteenth century. Education during the colonial period was almost exclusively religious and therefore a private undertaking (Bailyn 1960, 3–49).

Private elementary schools of every kind, from religious to nonsectarian, were to be found during the colonial period. **Dame schools, petty schools, writing schools,** and **grammar schools** were just a few of the names that described the activities of the schools and the people who taught or studied in them. By the end of the colonial period, a new type of secondary school known as the **academy** had emerged.

The academy had its origins in seventeenth-century England. In the 1640s, the English poet John Milton (1608–1674) suggested the outlines of academy organization and curriculum in his *Tractate on Education.* Unlike existing secondary schools of the period (the Latin grammar schools) that emphasized the study of Latin and Greek, Milton's academy included modern subjects. In 1751, more than a century after Milton proposed his academy, Benjamin Franklin described the many subjects taught in the academy he founded in Philadelphia:

> . . . the Latin and Greek languages, the English tongue, grammatically and as a language, . . . French, German, and Spanish . . . history, geography, chronology, logic and rhetoric, writing, arithmetic, algebra . . . natural and mechanic philosophy (science), drawing . . . and every other useful part of learning. (Franklin, quoted in Button and Provenzo 1983, 39)

Many early U.S. academies were associated with churches whereas others were open to anyone willing to pay the tuition to attend them. Most academies offered a broad range of studies with an emphasis on practical subjects (e.g., English, modern languages, history) rather than traditional **classical studies** found in the **Latin grammar schools** of the period.

By the beginning of the nineteenth century the academies were the principal type of **secondary school** in the United States. Significantly, the content and difficulty of their curricula varied greatly from one school to another. Some schools functioned at what was essentially a beginning collegiate level whereas others were much more limited. If public high schools had not been introduced during the 1820s, and had not experienced widespread development and growth by the end of the nineteenth century, considerable evidence suggests that the private academy would have become the model for secondary education.

The private academies laid the foundation for many of today's elite private schools. Deerfield Academy and Phillip's Academy, for example, can trace their origins and traditions back to the eighteenth and nineteenth centuries. Such schools have provided highly structured college preparatory programs for select groups of students. Often accused of

dame schools
Early elementary private schools run by women.

petty schools
Early private schools for younger children.

writing schools
Early schools that emphasized writing.

grammar schools
Early schools that emphasized grammar and the fundamentals of reading and writing.

academy
An early type of secondary school.

classical studies
Studies emphasizing ancient Greek and Roman sources.

Latin grammar schools
Early schools that focused on the teaching of Latin.

secondary school
Schooling at the high school level or junior high school level.

progressive education movement
A movement in education, based originally on the ideas of the philosopher John Dewey (1859–1952), which emphasized the idea of children being part of a community and of "learning by doing."

elitism, they provide an example of the varieties of education available to people in the United States. Similarly, experimental schools have undertaken some of the most innovative and influential experimental education programs in the United States. Examples include the Laboratory School of the University of Chicago, the Park School of Buffalo, and the Shady Hill School in Massachusetts, which originated in the late nineteenth and early twentieth centuries and reflected the philosophy of the **progressive education movement.**

? WHAT DO YOU THINK?
Issues in Private Education

The educational sociologist Donald Erickson has outlined four questions that reflect the major controversies over private schooling in the United States:

1. Are private schools divisive along religious, ethnic, racial, socioeconomic, or other lines, thus posing a threat to national unity?
2. Do private schools compromise the equality of educational opportunity?
3. Need private schools be regulated to ensure that their students will not be deprived of educational experiences needed to reach their full potential?
4. Should private schools or their patrons be given some form of direct or indirect financial assistance or relief? (Erickson 1980, 1452–1453)

   None of these questions has an easy answer. In terms of question 1, "Are private schools divisive along religious, ethnic, racial, socioeconomic, or other lines, thus posing a threat to national unity?" it can be argued that private schools can provide an alternative to individuals with nonmainstream interests, and that they can also isolate these individuals in ways that ultimately threaten the community. Carefully consider each of these questions. What do you think about the issues they raise?

■ CATHOLIC EDUCATION

INTASC Standards

Principle #7

Catholic schools provide instruction for approximately 11 percent of the schoolchildren in the United States. Approximately 8,500 schools serve roughly two and one-half million students. Studies by the sociologist James Coleman and his colleagues suggest that the sense of community, the tradition of discipline, and the emphasis on academic learning have led to an increased interest in Catholic education on the part of many

FIGURE 7.1 ■ Catholic school.

parents (Coleman et al. 1981). Approximately 18 percent of the students attending Catholic schools are disadvantaged minority students. Many minority parents seeking upward social and economic mobility for their children, particularly in urban areas, think that Catholic schools provide a decided advantage for their children over public schools (McInnes 1982, 244).

In the past few years, Catholic educators have attempted to obtain greater public funding and support for their schools. Efforts to obtain financial relief in the form of tuition tax credits and vouchers for Catholic parents sending their children to church schools have grown in recent years, as have efforts to increase the provision of special, federally funded services and programs for children attending their schools.

Besides the academy movement, other powerful forces promoted private education in the nineteenth-century United States. Catholic education can trace its roots to the colonial period, but the real impetus for its growth and development came in the 1830s and 1840s. Massive waves of Catholic immigrants came to settle in urban areas such as New York City, Boston, and Philadelphia during the first half of the nineteenth century. In many instances, they faced great prejudice because of their religious beliefs.

Anti-Catholic sentiments, often synonymous with anti-immigrant sentiments, were widespread. Many native-born U.S. citizens feared Catholic immigrants would be loyal not to the U.S. government, but to the Pope. Equally important, the new immigrants provided competition to established workers because they would work for lower wages. Anti-Catholic newspapers and propaganda pamphlets warned of the Catholic threat and the need to counter it.

Many saw the new Catholic schools as a deliberate attempt by Catholic leaders to indoctrinate Catholic children with antidemocratic values. Opposition to those schools often became violent. In August of 1834, for example, an angry mob of Protestants burned down the Ursuline convent in Charleston, Massachusetts. The burning of the convent in Charleston focused attention on the anti-Catholic movement. This was the same period that saw the rapid development and growth of the common school movement.

As the common schools became more and more widespread, Catholic parents grew concerned about their children's education. Although the First Amendment stipulated a separation of church and state, nonetheless the early common schools had strongly Protestant overtones. In most instances teachers were Protestant and the textbooks were written almost exclusively by Protestant authors. In addition, curricula frequently included selections from the King James version of the Bible, as well as Protestant prayers and hymns. Catholic parents protested that their children were being subjected to instruction that was prejudicial to their religious faith. During the late 1830s, Catholic religious leaders in New York City began to set up an extensive system of church-supported private schools. Within a short period a massive system of private Catholic schools was providing an alternative to the public schools.

EDUCATION AND LITERATURE

Remembering a Catholic Education

It was the religious calendar that governed my school year. In early September there was a nine o'clock mass on the Friday of the first week of school to pray for academic success. (Students were grouped according to class; behind my class would be my new teacher's face, a face I still wasn't used to.) In June, there was a mass of graduation for the eighth-graders. Between those events, school often stopped or flowered as routine bowed to the sacred. In the middle of a geography or an arithmetic lesson, the nuns would lead us out of our classrooms and we would walk—four hundred students in double lines—down a block to church, stopping traffic (We were Catholics!) to attend a First Friday mass or a

rosary to Mary. In Lent there were Friday Stations of the Cross. (Fourteen meditations on the passion of Christ—He stumbled, He fell—fourteen times the priest intoning, 'We adore Thee, O Christ. . . .') Benediction, the adoration of the Host, followed. The lovely hymn, the Tantum Ergo sounded as smoke of incense rose like vine. Upon the high altar stood a golden monstrance in the shape of a sunburst, at the center of which— exposed through a tiny window—was the round wafer of bread. We re- turned to the classroom, came back to the same paragraph in a still-opened book. Routine resumed. Sacred dramas of Church thus fitted into a day, never became the routine; rather they redeemed the routine.
—Richard Rodriguez, *Hunger of Memory* (1982)

Private Catholic education began primarily as a means of coping with religious prejudice and discrimination. Soon, however, schools be- came an important way to hold the Catholic community together and es- tablish shared norms and beliefs. As various Catholic ethnic groups became established, and more powerful, they began to assert their rights. Throughout the second half of the nineteenth century, for example, Catholics in New York consistently protested that their taxes were fi- nancing a largely Protestant public school system.

The Catholics' argument was simple. Money collected through tax- ation for the support of the schools should be available to private as well as public schools. Although Catholics in New York did receive public funds for their schools for a short period in the 1870s, they were denied public funding for most of the nineteenth and early twentieth centuries on the principle of separation of church and state (Provenzo 1981–1982, 359–379).

■ SEPARATION OF CHURCH AND STATE

As a democracy that guarantees equal rights to all citizens, the United States has had to reconcile the problem of competing, and sometimes contradictory, religious traditions. Education and the public schools have often provided the focus for the debate over religion, and in most instances this debate has manifested itself in questions related to the sep- aration of church and state.

The principle of **separation of church and state** is among the most firmly established principles of the Constitution. Under the First Am- endment, every individual is guaranteed the right to practice whatever

separation of church and state
Policy involving the sepa- ration of religion from governmental affairs and actions.

denominational
Referring to a specific religious group or denomination.

religion he wishes: "Congress shall make no law respecting an establishment of religion, or prohibiting the free exercise thereof." To ensure that right, our government has made a conscious attempt to separate secular and political activities from religious and **denominational** activities as much as possible.

The idea of the separation of church and state logically evolved out of our historical development. Many of our earliest colonists and later immigrants came to the United States to escape religious persecution. With the coming of the Reformation, various Protestant religious groups waged battle with the Catholic Church to achieve recognition for their religious and political points of view. Crucial to the success of the Reformation was the alignment of religious groups with the civil powers in many states. Thus in Germany religious leaders such as Martin Luther became closely associated with key German political leaders whereas in England, beginning with the reign of Henry VIII, the Church of England was actually headed by the British Crown. Church and state were partners working to promote the public welfare and maintain what was believed to be the true religion (Butts 1974, 12–13).

Unfortunately, individuals not associated with the state church were subject to religious prejudice and persecution. The English Pilgrims and Puritans in the seventeenth century and the Amish (a Swiss Anabaptist group) in the eighteenth century came to the New World to practice their religions without state interference. Gradually a tradition of religious toleration and accommodation developed. No single church or denomination officially dominated the culture, although a generalized Protestant Christianity has often been subtly emphasized to the exclusion of other competing religious traditions.

FIGURE 7.2 ■ Should the phrase "In God We Trust" be included on money such as a dollar bill?

Examples illustrate how a generalized Protestant Christianity has sometimes contradicted a literal enforcement of the separation of church and state. Religious statements are engraved on our coinage and printed on our paper money. If church and state were strictly separated, the statement *In God We Trust* would have to be removed. Chaplains representing various religious denominations are assigned to the Senate. Prayers and blessings are often invoked as part of our public ceremonies. A direct appeal to the "Laws of Nature and Nature's God" is included in the Declaration of Independence. Although in theory the United States strictly prohibits religious involvement in the public schools, a series of accommodations and compromises have also been made to those with strong religious beliefs. When conflicts have been irreconcilable, the courts have decided policy.

? WHAT DO YOU THINK?
"In God We Trust"

We make explicit references to God in many public documents. *In God We Trust* is inscribed on our money; the eye of God appears on the dollar bill. When we pledge allegiance to the flag, we refer to the U.S. republic as "one nation under God." Both the Declaration of Independence and the Constitution make specific references to the existence of God. To what extent do these references violate the principal of the separation of church and state? Does an atheist have the right to object to these references to God? What do you think?

■ JUDICIAL DECISIONS

Public schools in the United States are generally obligated by local laws and the Constitution to eliminate sectarian religious instruction from the curriculum, and local, state, and federal courts have been repeatedly called on to make rulings on religion in the schools. The first major United States Supreme Court case testing religious freedom and the educational system was *Pierce v. The Society of Sisters* (1925). In 1922 Oregon passed a Compulsory Education Act that required children between eight and sixteen years of age to attend public schools. The law was intended to provide children in Oregon with a uniform education under state control; in large part it was a response to fears in the postwar period that foreign children would not be sufficiently integrated into U.S. society if they were educated in private schools.

The most immediate effect of the law was that it closed down the Catholic school system in Oregon and eliminated the possibility of choice for parents who did not want their children to attend public schools. Eventually, in *Pierce v. The Society of Sisters*, the Supreme Court ruled in favor of the Society of Sisters, maintaining that the establishment of an exclusively public system of schooling unreasonably interfered with the freedom of "parents and guardians to direct the upbringing and education of children under their control." Significantly, this decision did not in any way interfere with the state's right to certify teachers or regulate the basic curricular requirements of the school. Thus the state had the right to regulate what goes on in the schools in terms of certain minimal requirements, but could not stop the teaching of selected subjects or exclude properly qualified individuals from running schools that functioned independently of the state.

In more recent years, considerable debate has been raised over the extent to which religious instruction should be permitted or included within the public school system. In 1948 the case of *McCollum v. Board of Education* raised the question of whether religious teachers employed by private religious groups should be allowed to provide instruction in the public schools for children whose parents requested they be able to attend special classes. Essentially the case debated whether a church group should have access to a public building for the purpose of conducting religious instruction. The Court ruled against such practices, arguing that by providing a place for religious instruction, the schools were in effect supporting a religious group and violating the principle of separation of church and state. Four years later in *Zorach v. Clauson* (1952), the Court argued that children could be released during the school day to attend religious instruction provided the instruction took place at a separate facility run by the religious group providing the instruction. In this way, the conflict over the use of public buildings in support of religious instruction was avoided.

In 1962 the Court decided perhaps the most controversial issue concerning the separation of church and state. In *Engle v. Vitale* the question was raised as to whether prayer services should be permitted in school buildings during regular school hours. A local school district in New York had been granted the right by the New York Board of Regents to include a brief prayer at the beginning of each school day. The prayer was not associated with any religious denomination and was in fact prepared by the school system. It simply read: "Almighty God, we acknowledge our dependence upon Thee, and we beg Thy blessings upon us, our parents, our teachers, and our country." Students were not required to say the prayer if they did not want to. In *Engel v. Vitale*, the Court ruled against the decision to include prayer in the school on the grounds that it was inappropriate for the school system to be writing any type of prayer because this involved the government (i.e., the school system) in promoting specific religious beliefs. That these religious beliefs were largely neutral and nondenominational did not matter.

The same logic used in *Engel v. Vitale* was applied a year later in the case of *School District of Abington Township v. Schempp* (1963). In this case, the question was raised as to whether the schools could include the reading of brief passages from the Bible at the beginning of each school day. Students could be excused from these activities, maintaining that they represented a direct involvement on the part of government-sponsored schools in the promotion and support of religious activities. The Court made it clear that the Bible could be used in the schools as part of the study of comparative religions or as part of a course on literature but not as a religious exercise.

The decisions of the Supreme Court have been particularly upsetting to those who believe that religious instruction should be included in public school curricula. In particular, this failure to include religious materials has been a problem for those loosely described as Protestant or Christian fundamentalists.

KEY SUPREME COURT CASES

A Moment of Silence

The 1962 Supreme Court case of *Engle v. Vitale* prohibited schools and teachers from organizing formal prayer sessions. Since that decision those who want to promote prayer within the schools have been trying to find ways to introduce it without establishing laws requiring it. One way of getting around the issue has been to have students participate in a moment of silent contemplation or meditation. Those interested in praying may do so silently; those who do not want to pray can remain quiet and think about whatever they like.

As of 1984 nineteen states had passed laws that permitted moments of silent meditation in the schools. Is a moment of silent meditation a reasonable compromise to a difficult problem? Can it be argued that it is inadequate to meet the religious needs of students in school? Can it also be argued that it represents an infringement on the time and rights of nonreligious students?

■ CHRISTIAN FUNDAMENTALISM AND THE SCHOOLS

INTASC Standards

Principle #10

Christian **fundamentalism** began as a religious movement in the United States during the middle of the nineteenth century. Part of the larger Christian evangelical movement, fundamentalists are highly traditional; they profess a belief in the literal interpretation of the Bible. In the late 1970s, the fundamentalist movement emerged as an increasingly powerful social and political force. Sometimes called the "New Christian Right," the fundamentalists focused attention on public schools.

On a national level the fundamentalists led the forces supporting the passage of federal legislation for school prayer and tuition tax credits for private schools. On a local level, fundamentalist groups began to pressure schools across the country to adopt scientific creationism (a Biblically based explanation of biology in sharp contrast to Darwinian or evolutionary theory) in high school biology courses, to censure textbooks they considered inappropriate, to eliminate values education, to ban homosexuals from teaching, to eliminate sex education from the curriculum, and to remove what they considered objectionable reading materials from the libraries. Essentially the fundamentalists called for a return to traditional Christian values in the schools. In doing so, they articulated a very specific concept of education and humanity.

Fundamentalists represent a significant sector of U.S. society—probably as large as 10 percent to 15 percent of the population. They are heavily concentrated in certain regions of the country, such as the Southeast. In questioning the content of the curriculum of the public schools, or whether prayer and religious instruction should be included as part of the curriculum, fundamentalists are in fact asking much larger questions about the role and function of schools. What is the nature and purpose of our educational system? Does the educational system meet the needs not only of the majority but also of the minority? What are the values and assumptions underlying our educational system?

fundamentalism
A conservative movement in U.S. Protestantism that emphasizes the literal interpretation of the Bible.

humanistic
Referring to a philosophy emphasizing humankind's capacity to live ethically and productively, using human reason.

Many objections of the fundamentalists reflect deeply rooted beliefs and value systems and bring up important issues. Many fundamentalists, for example, believe that a large number of tax-supported activities contradict conservative Christian beliefs. Carl Sagan's public television series *Cosmos*, for example, maintained, "The cosmos is all that ever is or ever was or ever will be." Francis Schaeffer, among the most prominent of the fundamentalist writers, argued that such an opinion clearly implied a denial of God and a specifically **humanistic** outlook (Schaeffer 1981, 53). For the same reason, Schaeffer objected to documentaries on controversial issues such as abortion being funded by tax-supported groups, such as public television (Schaeffer 1981, 57–58).

Christian fundamentalists raise important questions about the separation of church and state. They see contemporary culture as becoming increasingly **secular;** they fear the loss of traditional values and the dehumanization of the individual. Much of the curriculum found in public schools contradicts their fundamental religious beliefs. In light of problems such as AIDS and the high teenage pregnancy rate, it might seem reasonable for public schools to promote sex education. Doing so, however, may fly in the face of deeply held religious beliefs of conservative Christian families. In this context, what are the rights of parents? Who should control the curriculum? What should or should not be learned in the schools? As James Carper, one of the country's leading authorities on religion and education argues:

INTASC Standards

Principle #9

> Education is inevitably a value-laden enterprise. It deals with questions of the nature of the cosmos, the moral foundations of right and wrong, and of the appropriate roles of men and women. People of goodwill differ radically in their answers to those questions, and so it's extremely difficult for a government institution to package a particular set of values and beliefs to suit everyone. (Archer 2000, 206)

Private education provides individuals with alternative perspectives, such as those held by the Christian fundamentalists, the opportunity to have their children educated in schools whose values conform to their own beliefs. Yet, if these same parents are paying taxes, is it unfair to have them pay tuition for their children to go to private schools?

■ EDUCATIONAL VOUCHERS AND TUITION TAX CREDITS

Since the late 1970s a vocal movement has sprung up among parents, educators, and politicians supporting **tuition vouchers** and **tuition tax credits.** Under the voucher system parents would receive tuition vouchers to use at any eligible school. Schools would compete for students on a free-market basis; those providing the best product (i.e., instruction and training) would be able to attract the most students. Tuition vouchers would operate locally, distributing property taxes normally used only for public schools to private schools as well. Tuition tax credits would allow parents to claim a tax deduction on their federal income tax for part of the tuition they pay to send their children to private schools.

secular
Nonreligious.

tuition vouchers
Monetary credits that can be used toward paying for private school tuition.

tuition tax credits
Monetary credits, assigned to parents wanting to send their children to private schools, which are based on the taxes they have to pay.

Advocates of tuition vouchers and tuition tax credits maintain that excluding private schoolchildren from public support is unfair because some parents must then pay twice for education, once through taxes and again through tuition. They also maintain that tuition vouchers and tax credits would force public schools to be more competitive. Opponents maintain that parents who send their children to private schools are not being denied access to the public school system, but instead have chosen private education an alternative. In addition, critics argue that tuition vouchers would seriously undermine the existing public school system. Public schools would be responsible for students no one else wanted to teach: slower students, students with physical disabilities, and students with behavior disorders would be relegated to the public system. The brightest and most easily taught children would be attracted to private schools. How would subsidies be determined equitably for each child? How would religious and racial discrimination be avoided?

Voucher plans in Cleveland, Milwaukee, and Florida have provoked a great deal of controversy in recent years. Advocates maintain that vouchers provide citizens and taxpayers with important opportunities for choice. Opponents maintain that when vouchers are used for religious schools, they violate the First Amendment of the Constitution and our commitment to separation of church and state. When they are used in elite private schools, they are perceived as unfairly benefiting the rich and financially privileged.

WHAT DO YOU THINK?

Public Funding for Private Schools

Whether public funds should be used to support Catholic and other private schools is an issue hotly debated since the middle of the nineteenth century. In general, public support for private religious schools has been opposed as a violation of the separation of church and state. Yet as early as the 1840s, groups of Catholics have argued that separate school systems were necessary because of the overtly Protestant character of the public school system. The public schools had not been set up with Catholic children in mind, and Protestant books, hymns, prayers, and Bibles offended Catholic beliefs. It is not surprising that having been forced to set up a private school system of their own, Catholics objected to paying taxes that supported public schools—schools where they could not, in good conscience, send their own children.

In our own day other groups also object to paying taxes for the support of public schools. Parents sending their children to independent private schools, parents with children in Christian fundamentalist schools, and others are demanding that they be given a greater choice in determining how their school tax dollar is spent. Plans for tuition tax credits and educational vouchers for parents sending their children to private schools are hotly debated.

What are the arguments for and against the major part of school taxes being spent to support the public schools? Is the public school system in danger of not being able to survive without a virtual monopoly on school tax dollars? Is this monopoly fair? What do you think?

■ SUMMARY

Private education represents an important tradition in U.S. education. Historically, private schools have provided parents a means to cultivate and develop specific values and beliefs in their children, to avoid discrimination, and to encourage alternative models of learning. Private education also represents intersecting and sometimes conflicting rights. Nowhere is this as clear as in the case of issues involving religion and the separation of church and state.

Private education is a particularly important issue in this context. In an increasingly complex and diverse society such as that of the United States, questions involving private schooling and religion are likely to continue to surface. In years to come, we are likely to see test cases in the Supreme Court about school vouchers and issues related to the separation of church and state.

■ DISCUSSION QUESTIONS ■

1. What are the arguments for and against private schools receiving some share of public funds for their support?
2. What are the potential advantages and disadvantages for students in private schools versus public schools?
3. Should local, state, and federal officials have the right to regulate the qualifications of teachers and the content of curricula in private schools?
4. What are the arguments for and against tuition vouchers?
5. Do private schools have the potential to diminish or improve the quality of public schools? If yes, how might this be the case?
6. Why is the concept of the separation of church and state more important for a country such as the United States than for countries such as Italy or France?

7. Should state officials have the right to regulate instruction in private religious schools? If so, what should be the scope of their jurisdiction?
8. What are the arguments for and against prayer in public schools?
9. What rights do Christian fundamentalists and other parents have in determining what should or should not be taught to their children in the schools?

■ SOURCES CITED ■

Abramowitz, Susan, and E. Ann Stackhouse, with Denis P. Doyle, William T. Garner, Jana Hannaway, Robert R. Newton, and Arthur G. Powell. 1980. *The private high school today.* Washington, D.C.: U.S. Department of Education.

Archer, Jeffrey. 2000. Uncommon values. In *Lessons of a century: A nation's schools come of age,* 206–213. Bethesda, Maryland: Editorial Projects in Education.

Bailyn, Bernard. 1960. *Education in the forming of American society.* New York: W. W. Norton.

Baird, Leonard L. 1977. *The elite schools: A profile of prestigious independent schools.* Lexington, Mass.: Lexington Books.

Button, H. Warren, and Eugene F. Provenzo, Jr. 1989. *History of education and culture in America.* Englewood Cliffs, N.J.: Prentice-Hall.

Butts, R. Freeman. 1974. *The American tradition in religion and education.* Westport, Conn.: Greenwood Press.

Coleman, J., T. Hoffer, and S. Kilgore. 1981. *Public and private schools.* Report to the National Center for Educational Statistics, National Opinion Research Center. Chicago: University of Chicago Press.

Engel v. Vitale. Supreme Court of the United States, 1962. 370 U.S. 421, 82 S. Ct. 1261.

Erickson, Donald A., and Richard L. Nault. 1978. Recent trends in U.S. non-public schools. In *Declining enrollments: The challenge of the coming decade,* edited by Susan Abramowitz and Stuart Rosenfield. Washington, D.C.: U.S. Government Printing Office.

Erickson, Donald A. 1982. Private schools. In *Encyclopedia of educational research.* Vol. 3, 1443–1454. New York: Macmillan and the Free Press.

Kraushaar, Otto F. 1972. *American non-public schools: Patterns of diversity.* Baltimore: Johns Hopkins.

_____. 1976. *Private schools from the Puritans to the present.* Bloomington, Ind.: Phi Delta Kappa Educational Foundation.

Lahaye, Tim. 1980. *The battle for the mind.* Old Tappen, N.J.: Fleming H. Revell.

_____. 1983. *The battle for the public schools. Humanism's threat to our children.* Old Tappen, N.J.: Fleming H. Revell.

National Center for Education Statistics. 1997. *Private schools in the United States: A statistical profile, 1993–1994.* Washington, D.C.: U.S. Government Printing Office.

People of State of Illinois Ex Rel. McCollum v. Board of Education of School District Number 71, Champaign County, Illinois. Supreme Court of the United States, 1948. 333 U.S 203, 68 S. Ct. 461.

Pierce v. Society of the Sisters of the Holy Names of Jesus and Mary. Supreme Court of the United States, 1925. 268 U.S. 510, 45 S. Ct. 571.

Provenzo, Eugene F., Jr. 1981–1982. Thomas Nast and the church/state controversy in education (1870–1876). *Educational Studies* 12(4): 359–379.

_____. 1990. *Religious fundamentalism and public education in the United States: The battle for the public schools.* Albany, New York: State University of New York Press.

School District of Abington Township v. Schempp and Murray v. Curlett. Supreme Court of the United States, 1963. 374 U.S. 203, 83 S. Ct. 1560.

Schaeffer, Francis. 1981. *A Christian manifesto.* Westchester, Ill.: Crossway Books.

Zorach v. Clauson. Supreme Court of the United States, 1952. 343 U.S. 306, 72 S. Ct. 679.

CHAPTER 8

Immigration, Education, and Multiculturalism

Give me your tired, your poor,
Your huddled masses yearning to breathe free,
The wretched refuse of your teeming shore.
Send these, the homeless, tempest-tost to me.

—Emma Lazarus, "The New Colossus" (1883)

The United States has been described by the poet Walt Whitman in his poem "Leaves of Grass" "as a nation of nations, a people of peoples." More than any other country, it has brought together people from diverse cultural backgrounds and joined them to form a single society. Excepting the Chinese, most people who emigrated to the United States prior to 1890 were from northern Europe. Most, with the exception of the Irish, were Protestant. U.S. culture at that time largely reflected the traditions and beliefs of northern Europe and particularly Great Britain. Despite this fact, conflicts between old and new immigrant groups were common. The groups that had come earlier considered themselves legitimate U.S. citizens and viewed the new immigrants, arriving during the 1890s from countries such as Italy, Russia, and Poland, as interlopers.

The tradition of distrusting recently arrived immigrants became particularly marked by the middle of the nineteenth century. Opposition to new immigrants grew throughout the 1830s and 1840s. Known as the **Nativist Movement,** antiforeign groups saw the massive waves of

INTASC Standards

Principle #9

nativism
A social and political movement favoring the interests of established inhabitants over those of immigrants. During the mid-nineteenth century in the United States this movement was also associated with anti-Catholicism.

FIGURE 8.1 ■ The Statue of Liberty seen from the SS *Coamo* leaving New York.

Source: Photograph by Jack Delano. Courtesy of the Library of Congress.

immigrants entering the country as a potential threat to the U.S. political system. Arguing that the new immigrants came from nations ruled by tyrants and monarchs, the nativists believed they would subvert democratic values. More subtle, but very much a part of the opposition to new immigration, was the prejudice of many U.S. citizens against Catholicism.

Until the first half of the nineteenth century, most immigrants were Protestant. With the arrival of successive waves of Catholic immigrants in the middle of the nineteenth century, many U.S. Protestants feared that the newly arrived Catholic immigrants would give their political allegiance to the Pope and the Catholic Church instead of to the U.S. government.

Other more immediate problems contributed to the antiforeign and anti-immigrant feelings so widespread throughout the period. New immigrants competed for jobs. Willing to work for low wages to get a start in this country, they threatened the job security and financial well-being of more established groups. The extent to which the United States was a nation of immigrants during the nineteenth century is indicated by population figures. Between 1860 and 1890 the population more than doubled, from thirty-one million to sixty-three million. Approximately

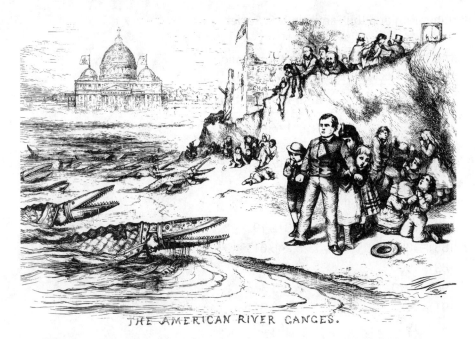

THE AMERICAN RIVER GANGES.

FIGURE 8.2 ■ Thomas Nast's editorial cartoon "The American River Ganges." Note the "crocodiles" who are bishops and "Tammany Hall" rising from the water. St. Peter's Basilica is in the distance.

Source: Harper's Weekly, September 30, 1871.

FIGURE 8.3 ■ German emigrants embarking for the United States.

Source: Harper's Weekly, November 7, 1874.

TABLE 8.1 ■ United States Immigration Levels by Decade (1821–1997)

Time Period	Total Immigration
1821–1830	143,439
1831–1840	599,125
1841–1850	1,713,251
1851–1860	2,598,214
1861–1870	2,314,824
1871–1880	2,812,191
1881–1890	5,246,613
1891–1900	3,687,564
1901–1910	8,795,386
1911–1920	5,735,811
1921–1930	4,107,209
1931–1940	528,431
1941–1950	1,035,039
1951–1960	2,515,479
1961–1970	3,321,677
1971–1980	4,493,314
1981–1990	7,338,062
1991–1997	6,944,591

Source: Statistical Yearbook for the Immigration and Naturalization Services, 1994. Updated 1997.

fourteen million of these new citizens were immigrants—mostly from Great Britain, Ireland, Germany, and Scandinavia.

Beginning in the 1880s, increasing numbers of immigrants began to come from southern and eastern European countries, including Austria, Hungary, Bohemia, Serbia, Italy, Poland, and Russia. Legislation restricting immigration from certain countries (China, for example) was enacted for the first time in 1882. Yet despite various restrictions, the flood of new immigrants continued until about the time of the First World War. In 1905, 1,026,000 immigrants were admitted into the United States. This figure is quite remarkable when we consider that in 1900 the population of the United States was only about 76,000,000 (Marzio 1976, 301).

■ RESTRICTIONS ON IMMIGRATION

Significant restrictions on immigration were put in place by the end of the nineteenth century. Immigration from China, for example, had been widely encouraged during in the late 1840s to overcome labor shortages in the West. By the early 1880s, however, settlement in states such as California was sufficient to make the need for the importation of Chinese workers no longer necessary. Congressional legislation, known as the Chinese Exclusion Act, was passed in 1882 and prevented Chinese workers from coming into the country (Lai 1980, 218).

FIGURE 8.4 ■ "The Great Fear of the Period: That Uncle Sam May Be Swallowed by Foreigners."

Source: Published by White and Bowar, circa 1860. Courtesy of the Library of Congress.

Extreme U.S. nationalism at the time of the First World War also saw the fostering of restrictions on immigration. In 1917, Congress required all immigrants to pass a literacy test before they would be allowed to settle in the United States. The same legislation excluded people from such geographic areas as Asia and the Pacific islands. The Johnson Act of 1921 limited the number of immigrants allowed to enter the United States to about 350,000 each year—approximately 200,000 from northern Europe and 155,000 from southern and eastern Europe. Further restrictions in 1924 allowed only 130,000 northern Europeans and 20,000 southern and eastern Europeans. Immigrants from non-European countries were negligible (Marzio 1976, 301).

Restrictions on immigration remained in effect until the Second World War. At that time, the United States resumed its tradition of providing refuge to the persecuted. But during the cold war of the late 1940s and 1950s, restrictions were once again placed on immigration. By 1965 legislation was passed that permitted approximately 170,000 people to

THE ONLY WAY TO HANDLE IT.

FIGURE 8.5 ■ "The Only Way to Handle It."

Source: The Literary Digest, May 7, 1921.

enter the country each year. For the first time, the number of immigrants from any one country was limited; quotas not used by one country were redistributed to other countries (Marzio 1976, 301).

WHAT DO YOU THINK?

Should We Limit Immigration?

Bob Dole, 1996 Republican Nominee for President
A family from Mexico who arrived here this morning, legally, has as much right to the American dream as the direct descendants of the founding fathers. . . . when the blood of the sons of immigrants and the grandsons of slaves fell on foreign fields, it was American blood. In it you could not read the ethnic particulars of the soldier who died next to you. He was an American. And when I think of how we learned this lesson, I wonder [how] we could have unlearned it. (Republican National Convention acceptance speech as quoted in *The San Diego Union-Tribune*, August 16, 1996)

Representative Dick Armey (Republican—Texas)
In my view, immigrants today aren't any different from immigrants who have come to America throughout our nation's history. They bring new ideas, an entrepreneurial spirit and close family ties. They place a high value on education. And they are eager to achieve the American Dream. . . . It's to our benefit to keep our doors open, and to keep enriching our economy and culture. I'd like to see America continue to do so. (Letter to a constituent, September 22, 1995)

Senator Spencer Abraham (Republican—Michigan)
By balancing the needs of families and employers, and by extending a safe haven to those fleeing persecution, our immigration policy serves its historic purpose. Freedom and opportunity is the cornerstone of American society, and immigrants continue to embody that freedom. (*The Christian Science Monitor*, December 3, 1996)

Mayor Rudolph W. Guiliani (Republican—New York City)
Immigrants are exactly what America needs. They're what we need economically, and I think they're what we need morally . . . [they] revitalize America and get it back to its sense of confidence . . . All of these immigrants that come here help us with the work they do, they challenge us with new ideas and new perspectives, and they give us perspective . . . (*The New York Times*, October 1, 1996)

Stuart Anderson, Director of Trade and Immigration Studies at the Cato Institute
Throughout our history, immigrants have come to America, established themselves and been joined by other members of their families. That process has

brought us energetic individuals and strong families who have enriched our economy and way of life. (*The Los Angeles Times,* February 1996)

George Soros, Billionaire Wall Street Financier and Philanthropist
Legal immigrants—refugees fleeing religious and political persecution, family members wanting to be reunited with loved ones, young entrepreneurs with talent and drive—have long come to America seeking a fair chance to contribute and, in the process, have enriched our culture and strengthened the nation.... Immigrants have always pulled their weight. (*The New York Times,* "Immigrants' Burden," October 2, 1996)

Think about the preceding quotes. They present positive views on whether the United States should continue to encourage immigration. What do you think?

■ THE AMERICANIZATION OF IMMIGRANTS

Education was seen as the primary means to Americanize and assimilate newly arrived immigrants. The school system could impose a uniform set of political values upon the immigrant child—values consistent with a democratic and capitalistic society. Common school leader Horace Mann argued: " . . . if we do not prepare children to become good citizens, if we do not enrich their minds with knowledge—then our republic must go down to destruction as others before it" (quoted by Marzio 1976, 307). The school was to act as a homogenizing agent to break down immigrant cultures and traditions and create uniform Americans.

? WHAT DO YOU THINK?
Americanizing Immigrants

In 1903, Richard Watson Gilder wrote that kindergarten provided the "earliest opportunity to catch the little Russian, the little Italian, the little German, Pole, Syrian, and the rest and begin to make good American citizens of them." Throughout the nineteenth and twentieth centuries, schools have been given the task of molding immigrant children into loyal U.S. citizens and workers.

To what extent should the schools inculcate U.S. values and cultural traditions in these "newest of Americans"? Was it, and is it, important that the traditions and cultural values held by these immigrant groups be erased as part of the educational process? Can schools and the educational system support immigrant traditions and U.S. values simultaneously? What do you think?

In describing the immigrant experience in the United States, the analogy of a melting pot has frequently been used. First introduced in 1909 by the Jewish playwright Israel Zangwill in a play called *The Melting Pot,* the term suggested how newly arrived immigrants would be assimilated into the culture through education and acculturation. Diverse elements would be melted or fused together to form a single U.S. identity. A character in the play explains:

> America is God's Crucible, the great Melting Pot where all races of Europe are melting and reforming! Here you stand good folk, think I, when I see them at Ellis Island, here you stand in your filthy hatreds and rivalries, but you won't be long like that, brothers, for these are the fires of God. A fig for your feuds and vendettas! Germans and Frenchmen, Irishmen and Englishmen, Jews and Russians—into the Crucible with you all. God is making the American . . . The real American has not yet arrived. He is only in the Crucible. I tell you—he will be the fusion of the races, the coming superman. (Zangwill 1909, 37)

In many respects the notion of a melting pot does not correspond with the reality of the U.S. experience. Many immigrant groups maintained their ethnic identity and traditions despite attempts to assimilate them. In addition, the idea of the melting pot did not take into account immigrants and ethnic groups who did not easily blend into the culture. Thus Asians, African Americans, Native Americans, and others were excluded from this process of fusion and amalgamation (Gollnick et al. 1983, 24).

Educational and social theorists from the period immediately before the First World War clearly associated the idea of **assimilating** and **Americanizing** the immigrant groups with anglicizing them. They argued that our educational system, our laws, and our business system were largely **Anglo-Saxon** in origin. Prominent educational leaders such as Ellwood P. Cubberley maintained that the new immigrants from southern and eastern Europe were different from other immigrant groups. "Illiterate, docile, lacking in self-reliance and initiative, and not possessing the **Anglo-Teutonic** conceptions of law, order, and government, their coming has served to dilute tremendously our national stock, and to corrupt our civic life" (quoted in Cremin 1964, 67–68). For Cubberley the primary purpose of education was to assimilate and Americanize foreign groups as quickly as possible, and to impart to them "Anglo-Saxon conceptions of righteousness, law, and order" (Cremin 1964, 68).

The assimilationists were only partially successful in their attempts to anglicize immigrant groups. To begin with, although many immigrants

assimilation
The process of becoming like another group or being absorbed in another cultural group.

Americanize
To acculturate one to hold mainstream American values—that is, those of a largely northern European, and particularly English, origin.

Anglo-Saxon
English in origin.

Anglo-Teutonic
Literally meaning English and German in origin.

INTASC Standards
Principle #3

embraced the English language, they did not abandon their religious beliefs or the traditions and values derived from their family life—despite attempts to get the immigrant to adopt the clothes, foods, and beliefs of the mainstream culture.

The strength of immigrant traditions is reflected in the fact that much of the identity of the American people is drawn from its recent immigrant cultures. American food provides an obvious case. Whereas early American cooking may have been associated with apple pie, roast beef, and ice cream, modern cuisine is clearly rooted in immigrant cultures. What could be more American, for example, than hot dogs or hamburgers, except that they are of German origin; or French fries, although American by adoption, reveal in their name their Gallic origins.

Perhaps more accurate than the notion of the United States being a melting pot is the idea of it being a tossed salad of cultures or even, possibly, a stir-fry in which different groups are combined as in a Chinese wok but not completely blended, giving the nation its ultimate strength and vitality. This idea has been most clearly expressed by terms such as **cultural pluralism** and **multiculturalism.**

INTASC Standards

Principle #3

Principle #9

IMMIGRANT VOICES

Teaching Immigrant Students: Alice Boardman, Barre, Vermont

Alice Boardman was an elementary schoolteacher in Barre, Vermont. The following interview is excerpted from an oral history conducted after she retired sometime between 1936 and 1940 as part of the federal government's *American Life Histories.* It is included in the Library of Congress, Manuscript Division, WPA Federal Writers' Project Collection. To read the interview in its entirety, go online to American Life Histories at http://memory.loc.gov/ammem/wpaintro/wpahome.html and, using the search engine, type in the name of the interviewee.

cultural pluralism
Many cultures.

multiculturalism
The idea of a state or society, such as the United States, being represented by diverse cultural groups and belief systems.

Through the fifteen years that I've taught in Barre I'd say that on an average half of my pupils' parents were foreign born. Most of them European born, except for the French. The French who came to the Barre sheds and quarries were mostly Canadian born. Today you're hardly able to distinguish one nationality from the other. When I first came here to teach, some of the children dressed old-country style. Some of the little Spanish and Italian girls wore gold earrings. Today only a few do. I remember a little Italian girl, Monica was her name. She teaches school in Burlington now. She was shy, very sensitive; at the recess period she kept to herself in a corner. One winter there was a whole week she didn't appear at school. Her parents sent me no news of her. One of the pupils from her neighborhood told me she'd seen Monica making a snowman in the backyard that morning and ended with, "she wouldn't be doing that if she had a cold, would she?"

That evening I called on Monica's mother. Before I was inside the door I heard a scampering of feet on bare, wooden steps, and I had a hunch that Monica had recognized my voice and had gone upstairs in hiding.

No, Monica's mother assured me, Monica did *not* have a cold; it was the earrings that kept her from school. She came home one afternoon crying that two classmates had laughed and made fun of them, and she begged her mother to let her take them off. Monica's mother would *not* take them off. They were sent from [Brieso?], Italy, by her husband's mother. The father had pierced Monica's ears and put the rings there himself. He'd been away all week. Monday he was coming back. Monica's mother shrugged her shoulders. If he wanted to remove them when he came back, all right. If not, well they stayed there. As for the days Monica had missed at school, well, she demanded of me, Monica got good marks didn't she? Besides, the two younger children were having colds and Monica could help with them.

I asked her: suppose your husband insists that she wear them? She'll have to go to school, you know.

Yes, Monica's mother understood that, and she smiled gratefully when I promised there would be no more fun poked at Monica's earrings.

Monica came to school Monday morning minus the gold earrings. In Monica's young mind the discarding of these earrings must have been the final step towards Americanization. She lost her shyness and self-consciousness. At recess she left her corner and played with the rest of the children. Speaking of Americanization, for two years Americanization classes were held in the *Casa Italiana* of our Community House, for adult Italians. The granite-cutting Barre Italians come from northern Italy; they're a higher class than the southerners who flock to Massachusetts and New York. They adapt themselves more easily to their new home, and American customs.

■ DEFINING CULTURAL PLURALISM AND MULTICULTURALISM

The United States is typically defined as a multicultural society. Multiculturalism refers to the idea of many cultures coming together to create a single culture—an idea implicit in the motto "E Pluribus Unum" (one from many). Multiculturalism is often associated with the idea of cultural pluralism.

INTASC Standards
Principle #3
Principle #9

The concept of cultural pluralism was first introduced in the early decades of this century. Theorists such as Israel Friedlaender in his work *Past and Present* (1919) and Horace Kallen in *Culture and Democracy in the United States* (1924) formulated a concept that would make it possible for immigrants to preserve the best of their old-world cultures while gradually assuming U.S. customs and beliefs. Under this system ethnic minorities would be encouraged to preserve their own traditions while taking an active part in the economic and social life of the United States (Cremin 1961, 69).

Cultural pluralism assumes that cultural diversity contributes to the richness of U.S. society, that our strength as a nation derives in large part from the diversity of its ethnic cultures. Instead of supposing ethnic membership to be of marginal value, cultural pluralism maintains that it provides the individual with a positive means of achieving social identity (Pratte 1982, 395). In our depersonalized and complex society the ability to draw on ethnic and cultural traditions intimately connected with our family history may be valuable. Ethnic traditions can provide us with shared experiences, insights, and a sense of security that comes from having a common heritage.

Cultural pluralism embraces all people, no matter what their backgrounds or beliefs. Although the white Anglo-Saxon Protestant may be seen as representing the dominant cultural model in the United States, the WASP remains only one of many groups within the culture. Native Americans, African Americans, Asian Americans, and those of other foreign origins can also identify with a society based on the principle of cultural pluralism.

The National Coalition provides a more specific definition of the concept of cultural pluralism (1973). They argue that cultural pluralism represents

> a state of equal coexistence in a mutually supportive relationship within the boundaries or framework of one nation of people of diverse cultures with significantly different patterns of beliefs, behaviors, colors, and in many cases with different languages. To achieve cultural pluralism, there must be unity with diversity. Each person must be aware and secure in his [her] own identity, and be willing to extend to others the same respect and rights that he [she] expects to enjoy himself [herself]. (Cited by Sleeter and Grant 1999, 153)

Implicit in the recognition that the United States is a pluralistic and multicultural society is an understanding of the importance of race and ethnicity in defining who Americans are as a people. In fact, many people understand multiculturalism in different ways. Kincheloe and Steinberg have developed a very useful model, in which they define five types of multiculturalism: (1) monoculturalism, (2) liberal multiculuralism, (3) pluralist multiculturalism, (4) left-essentialist multiculturalism, and (5) critical multiculturalism.

▪ MULTICULTURAL MODELS AS CONTINUUMS

INTASC Standards
Principle #9

Kincheloe and Steinberg's contribution lies in the fact that they recognize the political and ideological assumptions underlying different models of multiculturalism, and that these different approaches represent a continuum in terms of actions, thoughts, and beliefs. **Monoculturalism** is the most conservative of the multicultural models. In fact, it is actually a rejection of the idea of multiculturalism, and argues that diverse ethnic and racial groups need to become like the traditional mainstream culture as much as possible. This argument assumes that Western society is superior in virtually all its characteristics and that individuals who do not conform to its values are somehow deficient.

The monoculturalist model is insular. It does not examine its assumptions. It tends not to ask questions about who possesses power in U.S. society, what is the nature of discrimination, and so on. In doing so, it insulates itself from significant criticism and creates a largely self-serving system. A figure like E. D. Hirsch, introduced in Chapter 2 of this book, is an example of someone who holds this position.

Liberal multiculturalism assumes "that individuals from diverse race, class and gender groups share a natural equality and common humanity" (Kincheloe and Steinberg 1997, 10). This position assumes that we as a culture should be working toward a universal equality, and that differences should not be based on race, gender, or ethnicity. This model is based on a generalized ideal of culture made up almost exclusively of Western and white middle-class assumptions.

In the liberal multicultural model minority groups such as African Americans are assimilated into the mainstream culture. This process of **normalization** can be seen in a television program such as *The Cosby Show*, which assumes unity sameness across diverse populations. Whereas such an approach is comforting, it does not take into account the dynamics of power and competition that exist in any culture. As Kincheloe and Steinberg explain, liberal multiculturalism is "reluctant to address racism, sexism and class bias or to engage in a critical analysis of power asymetrics" (Kincheloe and Steinberg 1997, 12).

Thus in *The Cosby Show* the characters are African American, but the specific experience of being so—that is, issues of historical oppression, cultural and linguistic difference, and so on—are never addressed. Dr. Huxtable (the Bill Cosby character) is a successful middle-class doctor. He is pleasant, affable, and amusing, but never "black." Race and ethnicity are attributes to rise above rather than to embrace and identify with. Neither a sense of struggle nor a recognition of power or power-related issues is evident.

monoculturalism
A model of culture in which a single culture is emphasized to the exclusion of all others.

liberal multiculturalism
Generalized model of multiculturalism that assumes universal equity and common humanity.

normalization
The process of conforming to the status quo, or assimilating into the dominant culture.

pluralist multiculturalism
Model of multiculturalism that recognizes the differences between various ethnic and cultural groups.

left-essentialist multiculturalism
Model of multiculturalism that sees people united by their experience and background in the culture.

critical multiculturalism
Model of multiculturalism that draws heavily on critical theory. It sees humans as being shaped by a wide range of social, economic, and cultural forces.

critical theory
Philosophical model that sees individuals and their behavior as being shaped by a wide range of social, political, and economic forces.

cultural studies
An interdisciplinary approach to studying social issues that focuses on culture and identity.

Pluralist multiculturalism is the most widely accepted model of multiculturalism. Unlike liberal multiculturalism, the pluralist model emphasizes the difference between various ethnic and cultural groups rather than focusing on their sameness. Pluralist multiculturalism celebrates our differences and diversity. This position, according to Kincheloe and Steinberg, fails to sufficiently take into account the actual experience of falling outside of white, male, European, and middle-class norms—specifically the experience of powerlessness, violence, and poverty. Whereas no harm comes from celebrating our diversity as a culture, problems arise from not understanding our essential differences within the context of larger social, cultural, and economic forces. This failure to understand multiculturalism in the context of power is the main limitation of the pluralistic multicultural perspective.

Left-essentialist multiculturalism argues that essential and unchanging characteristics define the construction of multiculturalism. In this model, exclusiveness and solidarity preclude outside involvement and perspectives. A group of radical feminists, for example, argue that no men, no matter how morally or socially committed they are, can really understand their position because they have not had the experience of being a woman in U.S. society. This model can apply to other groups as well, including gays and lesbians, and African Americans.

The left-essentialist model has many problems in a democratic culture. It is exclusive and isolating. It tends to discourage coalitions between groups with different backgrounds but similar purposes (in terms of social justice), such as gay rights and disability rights organizations (Kincheloe and Steinberg 1997, 23).

The fifth and final category of multiculturalism posited by Kincheloe and Steinberg is **critical multiculturalism.** This model draws heavily on **critical theory,** which in turn is based on the work of the Frankfurt School of Social Research that emerged in the 1920s in Germany. Critical theory recognizes humans as social beings who are shaped by a wide range of economic, political, and cultural forces. Understanding power and power relationships is essential in this model.

Critical multiculturalism draws on critical theory and the more general field of **cultural studies** by trying to understand multiculturalism not just as an issue of diversity, but as one involving the complex interrelationship of race, gender, and social class. According to Kincheloe and Steinberg, this model "refuses to posit the mere establishment of diversity as its final objective; instead it seeks a diversity that understands the power of difference when it is conceptualized with a larger concern with social justice" (Kincheloe and Steinberg 1997, 26).

Kincheloe and Steinberg's idea of a critical multiculturalism is very similar to what Giroux describes in his work as "**insurgent multiculturalism.**" According to Giroux, "this is not a multiculturalism that is limited to a fascination with the construction of identities, communicative competence, and the celebration of tolerance" (Giroux in Duarte 2000, 196). Instead, he is interested in a model of multiculturalism in which "relations of power and racialized identities become paramount as part of a language of critique and possibility" (Giroux in Duarte 2000, 196).

In the case of Kincheloe and Steinberg's five models of multiculturalism, one is provided with a spectrum or continuum along which the multicultural experience can be interpreted. Although they include a number of difficult concepts, they also provide educators with models that can be used to delineate the meaning of multiculturalism in their own schools and communities. In doing so, a critically important task is accomplished—one that should make the problem of being a border crosser easier for those entering the teaching profession.

■ ETHNICITY AND MULTICULTURALISM

Ethnicity is among the most important elements of multiculturalism. The word *ethnic* is Latin in origin. Its roots can be traced back to the Greek word *ethnikos*—a nation or race (Peterson 1980, 234). In the United States, ethnicity is an extraordinarily complex phenomena. It has been defined as a sense of peoplehood developed through language and traditions (Gollnick and Chinn 1983, 35). Schermerhorn has defined ethnicity as ". . . a collectivity, within a larger society having real or putative common ancestry, memories of a shared historical past, and a cultural focus on one or more symbolic elements defined as the epitome of their peoplehood" (Schermerhorn 1970, 123).

Common languages or dialects define ethnicity. Polish Americans in Chicago or Buffalo speak Polish; black or African Americans in New York or Philadelphia speak a black dialect; German and Russian Jews in Miami Beach and Brooklyn speak Yiddish; rural white Anglo-Saxon Protestants in Georgia or northern Florida speak with a regional dialect and accent; and Mexican Americans in San Diego or San Antonio speak Spanish. Religious traditions define ethnicity. Jews celebrate Passover; Christians celebrate Christmas and Easter. Food, clothing, courting, and the organization of the family define ethnicity too. Ethnicity is all these things and more.

insurgent multiculturalism
A model of multiculturalism similar to critical multiculturalism in which the relationships of power and racialized identities are emphasized.

ethnicity
Refers to one's cultural affinity or origins based on common racial, national, tribal, or linguistic origins.

ethnic
Referring to groups of people classed according to common racial, national, tribal, religious, linguistic, or cultural origins or background.

INTASC Standards
Principle #3

A popular aphorism based on the work of the eighteenth-century French writer and gourmet Brillante Saverin says, "You are what you eat." Similarly, the collective experience of past generations and present cultures lives on in us. Think for a moment about the first names in your family. How many of them are of foreign origin? How many are based on the name of a grandparent, or great grandparent, or some other relative? How much are the traditions, celebrations, cuisine, and special events in your life a reflection of your ethnic origins and traditions?

IMMIGRANT VOICES

Steve Commeau, French Canadian Immigrant

Steve Commeau was a French Canadian who immigrated to Maine in 1896. The following interview is excerpted from an oral history conducted in 1938 as part of the federal government's *American Life Histories.* It is included in the Library of Congress, Manuscript Division, WPA Federal Writers' Project Collection. To read the interview in its entirety, go online to American Life Histories at http://memory. loc.gov/ammem/wpaintro/wpahome.html and, using the page's search engine, type in the name of the interviewee.

I was born in Kouchidoudouc [Canada], in 1876. That would make me sixty-two years old. That was just a little settlement—maybe two hundred people lived there. My father owned a farm of about 150 acres. Most of the people there owned farms, and they run from 50 to 200 acres. Some of the folks up that way run trap lines, and some of them worked in the woods in the winter and on the drives in the spring. It was pretty much the same up there then as it was in Maine about that time. Some times people up there would go across the line to work in the Maine woods in the winter, and go back to work their farms in the spring. There was practically no business or industry of any kind in the place I was brought up in. It was just a village of farms. There was a small Catholic church there. All the folks were French Catholics.

The school I went to had only one room and one teacher. I guess they had a grade system in the bigger places about like they have here. They always called the high schools "academies." I started going to school when I was about five or six and kept it up until I was twelve years old. I never had to carry any lunch because our farm was only about fifteen minutes walk from the school. The teacher was always a girl that boarded at one of the farmhouses. A few of the pupils that lived farther out had to carry lunches. I can't remember exactly what they had, but I imagine it was something like a couple of sandwiches made of homemade bread and some fish, meat, or cottage cheese. It wouldn't always be the same, of course. They might have cake, cookies, or a doughnut to add to that. There were a lot of things they could carry such as a tomato, a piece of pie, or an apple. They carried tea or milk to drink and unless there was a fire in the stove they had to drink it cold for nobody had any vacuum bottles then.

Living conditions up there when I was a boy were a lot different than they are now. Of course I'm talking about the small villages like the one I lived in. They didn't have any telephones, bathtubs, washing machines, electric lights, radios, or a lot of things people think they have to have today. We used to have dances and parties, but nobody ever thought of a moving picture show then. I think, though, we enjoyed ourselves just as much as people do now.

The fuel was always wood and there wasn't anything automatic about it. Some people had a pump in the kitchen, but usually it was out in the yard. Instead of raising just one crop the farmers went in for general farming. They raised about what they needed and although they generally had plenty to eat, they never had much money. There were no labor-saving machines on the farms up there then. Nobody sprayed apple trees, and grain was threshed on the barn floors. I don't think farmers worked any harder then than they do now. If you have tractors or machines that do the work faster, you simply go in for farming on a larger scale, so you keep busy anyway. The trouble with farmers nowadays is that they want to get a living without doing any work. If they'd work as long as people do in the factories, they wouldn't be so hard up. When I was a boy on a farm in Canada, I helped as much as I could with the work. Same of the farmers raised flax. The women would spin it into yarn and weave the yarn on hand looms into homespun cloth that was used in suits and overcoats. Winter stockings, winter caps, and mittens were always knit. We always kept enough sheep to provide wool.

I couldn't say much about the cost of living in Canada when I was young. About all we had to raise money for was shoes and clothing that we couldn't make, certain kinds of foods that we couldn't raise, and maybe a doctor's bill if we got sick. A lot of farmers had home remedies that were made from herbs, to use for minor ailments. We never had to get money to pay light bills, water rates, fuel bills, etc. We could generally raise or grow enough extra to pay for what we couldn't produce. The more a farmer can raise the better off he is, for he has to sell his stuff at a wholesale price, and he has to pay a retail price for what he buys. Sometimes when a couple of the young folks got married a lot of the people would get together and help build a home for them. The roads were always pretty bad in the spring, but they were all right at other times. In the winter people had to travel in sleighs or pungs and if the day was real cold they had to dress pretty warm to keep from freezing. Unless you had hot bricks or something like that to keep your feet warm it was like sitting with them on a cake of ice.

The French Canadians that came to Maine about the time I did, didn't come from any special section of Canada: they came from all parts of it. I guess, though, that the most of them came from Quebec. . . .

There were different reason why they left, I suppose. When a person leaves one place and goes to another, the main reason why he leaves is because he wasn't satisfied in the first place, and he thinks he can better himself by going somewhere else. I know a lot of people up there were hard up. They thought times were better in the states, and I guess they were. Some of the farmers thought they could do better farther south (in Maine) where the growing season would be a little longer. Some of the young fellows, like myself, couldn't see much future for themselves on a small village farm where there were a lot of kids growing up. Some of them wanted a change, or they wanted to see a little of the world. The ones that left were generally of the poorer classes, and they thought they could do better across the line.

In early days there were no restrictions whatever on immigration; that is, there were no laws or regulations to prevent any one from coming to the states from Canada. There may have been family objections in a few cases, but they were seldom serious. The greatest obstacle was generally a lack of the necessary cash. Some of those that left were fortunate enough to have relatives here that they could stay with until they found work. I think the first immigration laws were passed soon after the Aroostook War, but for a long time they weren't strictly enforced. The laws have been changed from time to time and a head tax has been added. The laws are strictly enforced now and the quota can't be exceeded . . .

The French Canadians who come to Maine either go to some town where they have relatives, or they start for some place where they think they can get the kind of work they can do. The towns that have large French populations are pretty well known, and they naturally attract the most immigrants. . . .

The average age of people who came over would be hard to say, but I think it would be in the early twenties. More men came over than women. The women were generally unmarried, and they usually found jobs in hotels or in private families, unless they had some special skill.

■ A SURVEY OF ETHNICS

The United States has many ethnic communities and traditions. Many immigrants have established themselves as Americans and yet maintained much of their culture and traditions. A Chinese American in San Francisco, an Irish American in Boston, or a Cuban American living in Miami have been defined by U.S. traditions and experiences, as well as the customs, languages, and religions of the countries where they or their families came from.

Today more people of Italian origin live in New York City than in Venice, Italy. More individuals of Polish origin live in cities such as Detroit, Buffalo, and Chicago than in the major cities of Poland. More people of Jewish origin live in the United States than in Israel. A single ethnic group does not dominate the United States. Those of British or Anglo-Saxon origin make up only 15 percent of the population. German Americans made up approximately 13 percent and African Americans make up 11 percent of the population (Sowell 1981, 4).

Many Americans have an incredible assortment of ethnicities in their background and cannot be associated with any one group. For example, my paternal grandfather was Sicilian, my paternal grandmother Irish English, my maternal grandfather Russian, and my maternal grandmother German. Besides representing different countries of origin, each represented different religious traditions, including Catholicism, Judaism, and Protestantism. Combinations of traditions and cultures such as these will become more common as our nation develops. But ethnic groups have not necessarily cooperated with one another or encouraged each other; in fact, pluralism has often been more a grudging accommodation than a cherished ideal. Undoubtedly the wealth of the land and its varied opportunities for advancement made mutual acceptance more possible than would have been the case in other circumstances.

IMMIGRANT VOICES

Andreas Ueland, Norwegian Immigrant

The following excerpts are taken from Chapters 6, 7, and 40 of the book *Recollections of an Immigrant* (New York: Minton, Balch & Company 1929) in which the Norwegian author, Andreas Ueland, recounts his immigration experience. Son of a farmer and politician, Ueland left for the United States when a teenager in 1871. The full text from which these excerpts are taken is included in the Library of Congress, Manuscript Division, WPA Federal Writers' Project Collection. To access all of Ueland's book, go online to Pioneering the Upper Midwest: Books from Michigan, Minnesota, and Wisconsin, ca. 1820–1920 at http://lcweb2.loc.gov/ammem/umhtml/umhome.html and, using the page's search engine, type in his name.

> Speaking generally, America was not favorably regarded in Norway until many years after the emigration started in 1825. The official class naturally disliked to see people leave the country and were disposed to sneer at almost everything American. Being well educated at the university and holding their offices for life, they were looked up to with great respect by the common country-people. No wonder, therefore, that to the official class many things in America seemed bizarre. Just think, a railsplitter being president and a tailor vice-president! Besides, was not almost everybody in America carrying revolvers, and quick on the trigger on slight provocation? Was not justice administered by mobs or vigilance committees? In addition to that, there was negro slavery and so much humbug— "American humbug!" Why should anyone go to a country like that?
>
> Some had gone, however, following the Sloopers of '25 from 1836 on, but they were mostly tenants or very poor farmers who had barely scraped up enough to pay the passage on sailships and canal boats as far as Chicago or Milwaukee. Of some of the few educated persons leaving it was said they were no longer safe at home and that for them America was a safer and more suitable place. Letters were coming back from the poor emigrants, telling how much land they had acquired for little or nothing, how much stock they had and how they had fared on pork, eggs, and white bread every day, instead of in Norway (as they used to say) "one day on soup and herring and the next day on herring and soup," or "one day mush and milk and the next day milk and mush." But years passed before this changed the attitude toward America of farmers with land owned in the family for

generations, and proud to think themselves better than the poor emigrants. Those proud farmers could not then think of going to America without a feeling of humiliation, and when one of them went he felt half-ashamed.

Father died in January, 1870. That changed abruptly my whole aspect of life. An older brother was to have the farm after Mother; what was I to do? Mother wished to have me educated to teach, but I did not wish to be a teacher. There was left the choice to stay home and wait for something to turn up, go out as a laborer or to learn a trade, or to sea, or to America!

A farmer from Houston County, Minnesota, returned on a visit the winter of '70–'71. He infected half the population in that district with what was called the America fever, and I who was then the most susceptible caught the fever in its most virulent form. No more amusement of any kind, only brooding on how to get away to America. It was like a desperate case of homesickness reversed. Mother was appealed to with all the arguments I could think of, such as that I would escape being drafted as a soldier and would surely soon return. On my solemn promise to be back within five years, she consented, stocked me up. . . .

We were a party of about thirty and left Stavanger for Hull May 6th on an English steamer as deck passengers and slept below on a cargo of hay; were herded on the railroad by an interpreter from Hull to Liverpool, then put into another English boat for New York, driven party by sail and partly by steam. . . .

We had no Ellis Island or other gauntlet to run in New York but were speedily lodged in the old Castle Garden where we slept one night on the floor, and that did not matter to one who travelled with his thoughtful mother's feather quilt.

Then west by train on road and route not known to us. We saw mountains, which must have been the Alleghenies, and felt much depressed. Was that America? Had we been fooled? We expected to see flat ground with no timber or boulders to clear. When we came far enough to see that kind of country our spirits rose again. . . .

Some Forty Years Later
. . . I am again on a railroad train winding its way westward between wooded hills for one hundred and fifty miles and thence in straighter lines four hundred miles further over Minnesota, North Dakota and Montana prairies. I see farms to the right and left with comfortable dwellings and big, red barns, sheltered in groves of planted trees. I see herds of cattle, horses, hogs and sheep browsing on cornstalks left in the fields, or burrowing for food or shelter into huge straw piles left from the fall threshing. The ground is fall-plowed, ready to be seeded again as soon as spring returns. I pass through towns with fine buildings for dwellings and business. I reflect that when there wasn't yet a wagon road where I now ride in Pullman, Norwegian and Swedish immigrants came here in canvas-covered wagons pulled by oxen, and where they found no human trace on the ground they unhitched, built log or sod houses for shelter, and out of the wilderness made what I now see. How proud they well may be of that hard, creative work! They have been given political independence and have earned economic independence of their native countries, and they must, I think, for their own development, and in the interest of their adopted country, attain intellectual and spiritual independence also, without a dual national sentiment.

■ JAPANESE AMERICANS

Japan was almost completely cut off from Europe and the United States until 1854 when Admiral Perry visited the country with a U.S. naval fleet and established the first modern trade agreements between Japan and the West. During the 1860s and 1870s about four hundred Japanese immigrated to the United States. During the 1880s an additional two thousand arrived, and in the 1890s another six thousand entered the country. Japanese immigration peaked between 1900 and 1910 when one hundred thousand Japanese entered the United States (Sowell 1981, 160).

The Japanese were initially welcomed into the United States because of their thrift and industry. Primarily settling in California, they soon came to be perceived as a threat by farmers and businessmen who feared them as competitors when they began purchasing farms and businesses. In 1913, for example, the Alien Land Laws (directed specifically against the Japanese) forbade aliens ineligible for citizenship to own land in California. Japanese immigration into the United States came to a virtual standstill during the 1920s when federal laws established immigration quotas.

As second-generation Japanese were born in the United States, they were able to own land. More discriminatory laws were passed in the 1920s; nonetheless, the Japanese achieved remarkable success as a group. By 1919, Japanese businessmen owned almost half the hotels and one-fourth of the grocery stores in Seattle, Washington. By 1940, Japanese Americans produced one-third of the commercial truck crops in California (Sowell 1981, 166–167). Japanese families were stable, and as an ethnic group the Japanese rarely had difficulties with the law. In the schools Japanese children were noted for their diligence and intelligence. But despite tangible accomplishments, discrimination continued.

Then in 1942, in a violation of civil rights as remarkable for its methodical organization as for its magnitude, the federal government interned more than one hundred thousand Japanese Americans in camps around the country. Authorized by an executive order, the government defended its action by drawing on the fear that Japanese Americans would act as agents for the Japanese government. Farms and businesses were confiscated and families separated from one another. Despite this internment, more than three hundred thousand Japanese Americans served in the armed forces during the Second World War. Most were sent to fight in the European rather than in the Pacific theater. Ironically, the Forty-Second Regimental Combat Unit, a Japanese-American unit, was the most highly decorated combat unit in the Second World War.

INTASC Standards

Principle #3

It is important to realize the extent to which Japanese Americans were singled out for discriminatory treatment during the Second World War. German Americans were not interned even though many had been in the United States no longer than the Japanese. Undoubtedly, Japanese Americans were singled out because of their distinctive racial features. Being visible made them convenient scapegoats.

But despite the discrimination they faced during the Second World War, Japanese Americans quickly advanced socially, educationally, and economically during the postwar period. By 1969, the income of the average Japanese family in the United States was 32 percent above the national average (Sowell 1981, 175). The Japanese Americans born since the early 1940s have been Americanized to a large extent; few speak Japanese or follow traditional Japanese customs. As a group, they are remarkably well educated; 88 percent have attended college and 94 percent intend to become professionals in some field (Sowell 1981, 176).

Today six hundred thousand Japanese Americans live in the United States. About one-third live in Hawaii. They are rapidly being assimilated into mainstream U.S. culture. Approximately 12 percent of married Japanese women had non-Japanese spouses in 1970. About half of all Japanese American marriages in Los Angeles County during the early 1970s were mixed (Sowell 1981, 178–179).

■ GERMAN AMERICANS

INTASC Standards
Principle #3

German Americans number more than twenty-five million. German immigration to the United States has been constant since the colonial period. German settlers were among the Dutch who founded New Amsterdam (New York City) in 1620. William Penn, the founder of Pennsylvania, made a tour of Germany in 1677 to recruit immigrants for his colony. The Pennsylvania Dutch, whose traditional home cooking and crafts are well known to many people in the United States, is a term that refers to the German settlers (*Deutsch* is the German word for German) who came to Pennsylvania during the colonial period. By 1745, their numbers had reached forty-five thousand. They founded influential colleges (Bethlehem and Muhlenberg), established a German language printing industry, and created much of our country's early sacred music (Sowell 1981, 47). In 1683 a group of German Mennonite families founded Germantown in Pennsylvania.

Many early German immigrants, such as the Mennonites, were attracted to Pennsylvania because of the promise of religious freedom.

Other German denominations, including the Amish, Lutherans, and Calvinists, settled there as well. Some, for example the Amish, have kept their religious and cultural beliefs largely intact since their arrival in this country almost three hundred years ago.

Waves of German immigrants continued to come to the United States throughout the nineteenth century. Nearly a million arrived in the United States during the 1850s and a million and a half during the 1880s. In fields as diverse as science, agriculture, and industry, German Americans were remarkably successful. Famous German Americans have included Thomas Nast (the great nineteenth-century political cartoonist), Babe Ruth, and General Dwight D. Eisenhower. The German tradition has given us such cultural originals as apple pie, the Kentucky long rifle, and hamburgers and hot dogs.

U.S. opposition to Germany during the First World War created strong sentiments throughout the country against many German Americans; the same was true to a lesser degree during the Second World War. Yet despite the problems and potentially conflicting allegiances brought on by the two world wars, people of German descent, like Japanese Americans, have consistently placed their allegiance with the United States rather than with the country of their ancestral origin. In 1972 individuals who considered themselves German Americans made up about 13 percent of the population. Like so many other groups, they have been assimilated into mainstream U.S. society to a remarkable degree.

IMMIGRANT VOICES

Hilda Polacheck's Essay Describing the Russian Immigrant Jacob Saranoff and His Family

Hilda Polacheck conducted oral history interviews in Chicago for the federal government as part of its *American Life Histories* during the late 1930s. The following description, written by Polacheck, of the Saranoffs, a Russian-Jewish immigrant family, was titled "Dust." Polacheck describes some of the dreadful living and working conditions many immigrant families faced. To read her essay in its entirety, go online to American Life Histories at http://memory.loc.gov/ammem/wpaitro/wpahome.html and, using the page's search engine, type in the name of the essay, "Dust."

Jacob Saranoff worked in a rag-shop near Hull House. He had come to Chicago from Russia in 1902, bringing his wife and two children with him. The family was met at the train by a relative who helped to find a home for them. They rented four rooms in a rear tenement on Halsted Street. After visiting several second-hand furniture stores, the Saranoffs bought two second-hand beds, a kitchen stove, a kitchen table and four chairs. They unpacked the bedding that they had brought with them from Russia and spent their first night in their first American home.

The next morning the children were enrolled in the public school. The first great ambition of Jacob and Sarah Saranoff had been realized. Their children were in school.

After paying a month's rent and the price of the furniture and the most necessary household utensils, Jacob had two dollars left. It was necessary for Jacob to take the first job that he could find. The job was sorting rags. His wages were eight dollars a week. The rent was six dollars a month. Jacob and Sarah decided that they could get along.

The rag-shop was located in an abandoned barn. There was a small window in the rear of this barn, which had been opened when the horses were housed in it. But since it had become a rag-shop, the window had been nailed up to keep out any possible thieves. Ventilation was not considered.

The floor of the rag-shop was never swept. The dust was allowed to gather day after day, week after week. But Jacob paid no attention to the dust. His children were in school. They could not have gone to school in Russia. There were no schools for Jewish children in the village where he had lived. So why pay attention to dust?

Solomon, or Solly, as he was called, the older of the two children, wanted to learn to play the piano. But how does one get piano lessons and buy a piano on which to practice on eight dollars a week?

"Some day I will learn to play," Solly said. "All sorts of miracles happen in America. Maybe something will happen so that I can learn."

Solly was eight years old. His sister, Rosie, was six. They were learning American games. They now played hide and seek, run-sheep-run and peg, with the American-born children. These American-born children took Solly and Rosie to Hull House.

The children ran up the stairs to a play-room in which there was a piano. It was the first time that Solly had been near a piano. He struck a note and was thrilled with the sound. He looked around, and no one seemed to mind his touching the piano. So he struck a few more notes. This was indeed a miracle! Such miracles could only happen in America, thought Solly. . . .

So Solly started to take piano lessons and he was allowed to come to Hull House to practice. . . .

[Some time later] "For the last number," the piano teacher announced, "Solly will play a piece that he wrote. I am very proud of Solly, for it is not often that a child of his age can compose music. I think Solly will be a great musician."

Solly played his composition. It was a haunting little melody. There was a little of the Russian persecution in it. There was a little of the joy of Hull House. There was a little of the dust of the rag-shop. . . .

The dream of buying a piano now became an obsession with Jacob. He had heard one of the men who worked in the rag-shop say that his two brothers were coming from Russia and that they would be looking for a place to live. The idea came to Jacob that he could rent one of the bedrooms to these two men. He broached the subject to Sarah. She thought it would be a good idea. Sarah had heard that pianos could be bought on easy payments. Perhaps she could get enough from the men to make the payments on a piano.

The boarders moved into one of the two bedrooms. A shiny new piano was moved into the bare parlor. A relative gave the family a discarded cot which was put into the parlor. On this Solly slept. Rosie was moved into the bedroom where her parents slept. Her bed was made up of the four chairs. . . .

[Again, time had passed.] Solly was ready to graduate from high school. He was to play one of his own compositions at the graduation exercises. This graduation was another event in the life of the Saranoff family. Jacob was proud of his tall, dark-haired son, who was loudly applauded by the audience. Solly bowed again and again. Jacob thought: if only the cough did not bother him; he would be the happiest man in the world. But the cough did bother him.

Jacob would have liked to stay in bed the morning after the graduation. But a man had been fired the week before for staying home one day. So he dragged himself out of the bed and went to the rag-shop. Several hours later he was brought home by two men. They said that Jacob had started to cough and had spit large chunks of blood.

"Yes, the dust in the rag-shop is bad," said one of the men.

Sarah was panic stricken. The neighbors called a doctor from the health department. A week later, Jacob was dead.

■ ITALIAN AMERICANS

Since the nineteenth century more than 5 million Italians have migrated to the United States, four-fifths of them arriving between 1880 and 1920. Most were of rural origin and came from the southern provinces, such as Calabria, Aplia, Campania, Abruzzi, and Sicily (Nelli 1980, 545). For many Italians immigration was not a one-way process. Of the approximately 3.8 million Italians who landed in the United States between 1899 and 1924, roughly 48 percent from the northern provinces and 56 percent from the south returned to Italy (Nelli 1980, 547).

Despite their largely rural origins, most Italian immigrants settled in towns such as Boston, Chicago, New York, San Francisco, and St. Louis. By 1910, New York City had a population of 340,765 Italian immigrants, making its Italian population larger than the populations of Genoa, Florence, and Venice combined (Nelli 1980, 548). Most Italians came to the United States to seek a better life. Poverty was particularly widespread in southern Italy, and became even more of a problem with an Italian unification in the middle of the nineteenth century, as northern Italians increasingly exploited those living in southern Italy.

Prejudice against Italian Americans was widespread throughout the first half of the twentieth century. In part, this was based on the rural and

INTASC Standards
Principle #3

socioeconomic background of many Italian immigrants, as well as the fact that the majority of Italians were Catholic. Italian immigration significantly declined during the First World War. In 1914 a total of 283,738 Italians immigrated to the United States. By 1915, these numbers had gone down to 49,688. The Immigration Act of 1924 set a yearly quota of 3,845, essentially bringing an end to Italian immigration to the United States (Nelli 1980, 556).

Italian Americans have become highly assimilated in the United States. Ethnic prejudice is no longer a major problem, although stereotyping still exists to a certain degree. Much of this problem comes from the association of selected Italian immigrant groups with organized crime. Through films such as Francis Ford Coppola's brilliant trilogy *The Godfather*, a narrow segment of the Italian immigrant culture has come to dominate the popular imagination of many people in the United States.

IMMIGRANT VOICES

Roland Damiani, Italian Immigrant

Merton Lovett, a federal researcher, interviewed the Italian immigrant Roland Damiani in 1938 at the latter's home in Beverly, Massachusetts. The interview is included in *American Life Histories,* 1936–1940, Library of Congress, Manuscript Division, WPA Federal Writers' Project Collection. To read the interview in its entirety, go online to American Life Histories at http://memory.loc.gov/ammem/wpaintro/wpahome.html and, using the page's search engine, type in the name of the interviewee.

> I wish you could see, Mr. Lovett, the town where I lived in Italy. It was called Cartoceto. It was builded on the top of a high hill. All around was a stone wall. Once upon a time this wall protected the town from bandits, from pirates and other enemies.
>
> You have heard of Carthage? For many years Carthage and Rome were the great rivals. Sometimes Rome was badly beaten. Sometimes the Romans were successful. Finally Hannibal, he was the great general, was completely defeated. The Africans ran away. At Cartoceto, where I was born, they made their last stand. Behind the walls they fired arrows and spears at the Romans. For months they put up a great fight.
>
> Why should I not know history? In Italy I attended the good schools. In this country I have studied much.
>
> Thank you, Mr. Lovett. If I did not get a good education would I be the officer in your evening schools? And my fellow Italians have elected me to many positions, because they appreciate learning and wish themselves to become true Americans.

You are right. The children of Italian immigrants wish most of all to become Americans. They make haste to adopt the American customs and speech. In fact they worry and grieve their parents, who cannot understand or keep pace with them. It is not a little tragic sometimes—this conflict between the children and their elders.

Yes, that is true. But a price must be paid for progress. In this case it is the parents that pay. They adapt themselves slowly to new and strange conditions. That is why we have emphasized adult education. It prevents misunderstanding. Too often the Italian youth seem cruel and disrespectful. The elders appear tyrants and kill-joys to their children.

We lived first in Portsmouth, N.H. My father worked at the navy yard. The next year we moved to Beverly, where the United Shoe Machinery plant was under construction. Already my uncle, Emilo, was a boss there. He was a graduate from an Italian college and had charge of Shantyville. That was the rough village, where the Italian workmen then lived. . . .

Sure, I was acquainted with Shantyville. My family did not live there. Mostly the residents were single men. The shanties were built of boards. The roof was covered with tarpaper. They were not plastered inside, but they were clean. They were kept neat and they were comfortable. . . .

The people here in Beverly never did understand the Italians of those days. Very, very slowly, their ignorance is being destroyed. In 1905 they imagined that terrible things were done in Shantyville. The police were given orders to watch closely. People thought the Wops or Dagos, as they called them, were dangerous. They thought they were always ready to draw a knife or stick someone with a stiletto. Perhaps they considered the Italians reckless, bloodthirsty and dishonest. If so, it was because they read stories of the American shanty towns in California and the West. Compared to them, the camp in Beverly was like a Sunday School. A child or woman could visit there night or day with perfect safety. It is ignorance that causes suspicion and prejudice. It is still ignorance that makes it hard for Italians to take their proper and natural position in the community. Thank God, conditions are getting better each year.

EDUCATION AND LITERATURE

Mark Twain's Comments about Chinese Immigrants in California

The following excerpt from Mark Twain's 1872 novel *Roughing It* describes his perception of Chinese immigrants in California. The full text from which these excerpts are taken is included in the Library of Congress, Manuscript Division, WPA Federal Writers' Project Collection. To access a complete copy of Twain's book, go online to "California as I Never Saw It": First-Person Narratives of California's Early Years, 1849–1900 at http://lcweb2.loc.gov/ammem/cbhtml/cbhome.html and, using the page's search engine, type in his name.

Of course there was a large Chinese population in Virginia—it is the case with every town and city on the Pacific coast. They are a harmless race when white men either let them alone or treat them no worse than dogs; in fact they are almost entirely harmless anyhow, for they seldom think of resenting the vilest insults or the cruelest injuries. They are quiet, peaceable, tractable, free from drunkenness, and they are as industrious as the day is long. A disorderly Chinaman is rare, and a lazy one does not exist. So long as a Chinaman has strength to use his hands he needs no support from anybody; white men often complain of want of work, but a Chinaman offers no such complaint; he always manages to find something to do. He is a great convenience to everybody—even to the worst class of white men, for he bears the most of their sins, suffering fines for their petty thefts, imprisonment for their robberies, and death for their murders. Any white man can swear a Chinaman's life away in the courts, but no Chinaman can testify against a white man. Ours is the "land of the free"—nobody denies that—nobody challenges it. [Maybe it is because we won't let other people testify.] As I write, news comes that in broad daylight in San Francisco, some boys have stoned an inoffensive Chinaman to death, and that although a large crowd witnessed the shameful deed, no one interfered.

EDUCATION AND LITERATURE

Immigrant Memories

It was when I found out I had to talk that school became a misery, that the silence became a misery. I did not speak and felt bad each time that I did not speak. I read aloud in first grade, though, and heard the barest whisper with little squeaks come out of my throat. "Louder," said the teacher, who scared the voice away again. The other Chinese girls did not talk either, so I knew the silence had to do with being a Chinese girl.
—Maxine Hong Kingston, *The Woman Warrior: Memoirs of a Girlhood among Ghosts* (1976)

■ BILINGUALISM AND U.S. EDUCATION

Most immigrants have had to learn a new language, and as a national language English has acted as a powerful force in their assimilation. This is not to suggest, however, that other languages have not played a part in the development of U.S. society. Native Americans spoke about three hundred different languages when the first European explorers came to the New World. During the colonial period, settlers spoke Spanish, French, German, Russian, Swedish, and Dutch as well as English. Nineteenth- and early twentieth-century immigrant languages included Italian, Polish, and Yiddish.

An important facet of U.S. culture and education from the colonial period, bilingualism remains a controversial and emotional issue. Many groups assert their children must be educated not only in English but also in their "native" language if they are to maintain their cultural traditions and heritages. Critics of bilingualism maintain that a common language (English) provides the most effective means of drawing together the diverse ethnic and cultural groups that constitute the United States.

During the nineteenth century public school instruction was often in languages other than English. In 1837, for example, the Pennsylvania legislature ordered German-English schools to be established on an equal basis with English language schools. German-English public schools could be found in Ohio by 1840. French was the language of instruction in Louisiana schools during this period, and by 1848 Spanish was the language of instruction in New Mexico (Cordasco 1976, 2).

By the end of the nineteenth century opposition to bilingual education had developed and continued to grow until the First World War when bilingual education was virtually eliminated in public schools. Interest in bilingual education revived during the early 1960s as a result of the massive influx of immigrants from countries such as Cuba and because of the civil rights movement. In Miami-Dade County, Florida, a bilingual education program was established in 1963 to meet the needs of the nearly twenty-one thousand Cuban children who had come to the United States with their families as political refugees (Genderson 1982, 203).

Federal support for bilingual education began in 1968 when Title VII, the Bilingual Education Act (1968), amended the Elementary and Secondary Education Act (ESEA) of 1965. Under Title VII, the government acknowledged that children whose native language was not English needed instructional programs different from those offered to English-speaking children (Gunderson 1982, 204). Of course the primary purpose of bilingual education is not to teach language but to allow children to obtain the knowledge and skills they need through the language they know best. At the same time, bilingual programs encourage children to become fluent in English.

Some ethnic groups, such as Hispanic Americans, have held onto their traditional languages longer than others. Part of the reason may be that some Hispanics (Mexican Americans or Hispanics from Central and South America, for example) travel freely back and forth between the

United States and their homelands where Spanish is the national language. Other recent immigrants may find it impossible to return to their countries of origin—a situation that may contribute to their being more quickly assimilated into mainstream U.S. culture.

KEY SUPREME COURT CASES

Bilingualism

Court cases going back to the mid-1970s have had a profound impact on bilingualism and education. In 1974, the landmark case of *Lau v. Nichols* was presented before the Supreme Court. In that case, both the plaintiff and the San Francisco school district agreed that the educational needs of nearly two thousand Chinese-American children were not being met. The plaintiffs argued that because of their linguistic background and lack of familiarity with English, Chinese-American students were being denied an adequate education and their civil rights were being violated. Under the Supreme Court decision, the San Francisco school system was not required to provide those children with training in Chinese, but it did have to provide them with special services and support to help them make the transition to learning in English.

Subsequent Court decisions have reinforced the *Lau v. Nichols* decision and the principle of transitional bilingual education. Programs that attempt to maintain the student's native language receive almost no support as part of the public educational system. Instead, the model that has been widely adopted provides students with the skills to function effectively in both their native language and in English.

If any generalization can be made about ethnic groups and language, it is that they tend to abandon their native languages and quickly adopt the English language and U.S. cultural values. Grandchildren of immigrants are rarely fluent in the language of their grandparents, and after two or three generations most people speak only English. Many examples demonstrate this point. In Chicago and Buffalo where large numbers of Polish immigrants settled at the beginning of this century relatively few people remain fluent in Polish. Walking through the Polish neighborhoods, one finds that most of those people who are still fluent in Polish are the older people in the community. The same point can be made with any number of other ethnic groups, whether Italian Americans in New York or German Americans in St. Louis.

Clearly the forces of assimilation are powerful. Television, radio, and newspapers present a constant variety of materials in English. The schools are geared toward English instruction; the business community conducts business in English. Bilingualism becomes an asset for individuals in ethnic communities. In most instances it is the key to economic, social, and political advancement.

Most immigrants, despite nostalgia for the old country and its language and traditions, have come to the United States to transcend the limitations imposed by their countries of origin. The Germans who came to the United States in the 1840s, for example, fled the war and revolution overtaking their country, as did their modern counterparts, the Vietnamese, during the 1970s. The Russian Jews who came to New York at the beginning of this century fled poverty and religious persecution, while today the constant stream of Mexicans coming into this country reflects a quest for greater economic opportunity and stability. That these immigrant and ethnic groups should turn to English as a means of quickly joining the economic and social mainstream is easy to understand.

■ THE NEW IMMIGRATION

INTASC Standards
Principle #3

In most instances, the immigrants who came to the United States throughout the nineteenth and early twentieth centuries left their homelands for economic reasons. With its open immigration policy the United States was a land of seemingly unlimited opportunity. In contrast, immigration in our own era has been mostly politically motivated. During the great Cuban exodus of the early 1960s approximately six hundred thousand Cubans fled the Castro government. The influx of immigrants during the 1970s and 1980s from countries such as Cuba, Vietnam, Russia, Nicaragua, and Thailand have nearly always been motivated by political rather than economic conditions.

Significantly, opposition to and fear of massive waves of immigration continues. Although most people in the United States embrace the rhetoric of the United States having an open-door policy, they are nonetheless often confused by and unable to respond to the pressure and demands placed on them by new immigrants. In Miami, for example, the more established groups within the community oppose the recent influx of immigrants from Cuba and Haiti. Opposition to these new immigrants often focuses on their lack of education and job-related skills as well as on their inability to speak English. Whereas it might be

TABLE 8.2 ■ Total and Foreign-Born U.S. Population:
1900–1990 (numbers in thousands)

Year	Total U.S. Population	Foreign Born	
		Total	*Percent*
1990	248,710	19,767	7.9
1980	226,546	14,080	6.2
1970	203,210	9,619	4.7
1960	179,326	9,738	5.4
1950	150,845	10,431	6.9
1940	132,165	11,657	8.8
1930	123,203	14,283	11.6
1920	106,022	14,020	13.2
1910	92,229	13,630	14.8
1900	76,212	10,445	13.7

Source: Department of Commerce, Bureau of Census, Ethnic and Hispanic
Branch. (Available online at the Immigration and Naturalization website:
http://www.ins.usdoj.gov/graphics/aboutins/statistics/304.htm.)

said (perhaps romantically) that Miami has become a more interesting
and exciting city because of the new immigrants, it must be admitted that
it has also become a more complex and difficult city in which to live.

Newly arrived immigrants compete for jobs, living space, and educational opportunities. Although they have brought with them the richness and diversity of their own cultures and traditions, they have also
created problems that demand solutions. In Miami—the greatest immigrant city of the late twentieth-century United States—over 500,000
Cuban exiles currently live in the city. Approximately 124,000 of them
set off from the port of Mariel across the Straits of Florida and landed
in Key West in 1980. Older members of the Miami Cuban community
dislike and distrust the Marielitos whom they (like Castro) claim are *es-
coria* or "scum," nothing more than criminals Castro could no longer
tolerate it.

Such generalizations may be unfair, but they do reflect real divisions
within seemingly homogeneous immigrant groups. Members of the An-
glo community in Miami often discuss the Latins. But who are the
Latins? Are they the Cubans? What about the tens of thousands of
Nicaraguans who fled their country with the downfall of the political
dictatorship of Anastasio Somoza? What about other exiles from coun-

tries such as El Salvador or Colombia? What about the fifty thousand Puerto Ricans who live in the city? Although they share the common language of Spanish and often a tradition of Catholicism, each group represents distinctly different cultural traditions.

Miami's incredible cultural mix is further complicated by other newly arrived immigrants—legal and illegal. Recent immigrants from Russia, Korea, Vietnam, and the Middle East add to the city's heterogeneous population. Miami is exceptional, but other cities in the United States maintain significant enclaves of immigrants too. Currently, 450,000 Asian Americans live in the San Francisco area; many maintain contacts with the countries from which they or their forebears emigrated. In fact, they were in large part responsible for approximately $46 billion worth of trade between California and the Pacific Rim in 1980.

In Houston, Los Angeles, and New York other immigrant populations represent virtually every part of the world. In addition to their energy, intellect, and physical resources, these newcomers bring with them a unique set of experiences that contribute to the definition of what it means to be an American. In doing so they continue a tradition that extends throughout our history.

■ SUMMARY

Most people in the United States assume that immigration is a historic issue—a part of our past rather than an integral part of our present. In fact, immigration is an ongoing part of our experience as a nation. Today, approximately one-tenth of the U.S. population is foreign born—as large a number as any since the colonial period. In places such as Miami-Dade County, Florida, more than half the population is foreign born.

Along with immigration, issues of cultural diversity are an ever-present reality in our classrooms. This is a type of cultural diversity that is becoming increasingly complex compared to that found in classrooms at the beginning of the twentieth century. In 1900, for example, a multicultural class might have included Chinese, German, Spanish, Polish, Russian, Greek, Irish, and Italian students. A culturally diverse class today could easily include Vietnamese, Cambodian, Cuban, Bosnian, and Nicaraguan students.

Although most of these students are concentrated in immigrant centers, such as Miami, New York, Chicago, and Los Angeles, immigrants and culturally diverse populations are making their way into the interior and rural areas of the United States. They move in search of work and the possibilities of a better life. In doing so, they continue the tradition of the people of the United States: they add to the complex mix of cultures and traditions whose needs and perspectives must be clearly understood by educators who are border crossers.

■ DISCUSSION QUESTIONS ■

1. What are the advantages of the diversity in the United States? What are some of the serious problems that arise from this country being a multicultural society?
2. How important is it for the schools to Americanize immigrant children? What are some of the problems that can occur when the schools take on this task?
3. Should quotas be set on the number of people allowed to immigrate to the United States? If yes, how should the quotas be determined?
4. What ultimately defines the United States and its people?
5. What do you understand to be meant by the term *cultural pluralism*?
6. Do you think immigration will continue be an important social process in years to come?
7. Is bilingual education something that should be supported by the schools and the culture in general?
8. In heavily second-language areas such as Miami, Florida, and Los Angeles, California, should a language such as Spanish be considered an official language along with English?

■ SOURCES CITED ■

Banks, James A. 1981. *Multiethnic education: Theory and practice.* Boston: Allyn & Bacon.

Cordasco, Francesco, ed. 1976. *Bilingual schooling in the United States: A sourcebook for educational personnel.* New York: McGraw-Hill.

Cremin, Lawrence. 1964. *The transformation of the school: Progressivism in American education 1876–1957.* New York: Vintage Books.

Elementary and Secondary Education Act of 1965, Public Law 89-10.

Freidlaender, Israel. 1919. *Past and present.* Cincinnati, Ohio: Ark Publishing.

Glazer, Nathan, and Daniel P. Moynihan. 1970. *Beyond the melting pot.* Cambridge, Mass.: MIT Press.

Gollnick, Donna M., and Phillip C. Chinn. 1983. *Multicultural education in a pluralistic society.* St. Louis: C. V. Mosby.

Gordon, M. M. 1964. *Assimilation in American life: The role of race, religion and national origins.* New York: Oxford University Press.

Gunderson, Doris V. 1982. Bilingual education. *Encyclopedia of educational research*. Vol. 1, 202–210. New York: Macmillan and the Free Press.

Hall, Edward T. 1973. *The silent language*. New York: Anchor Books.

———. 1977. *Beyond culture*. New York: Anchor Press.

Itzkoff, Seymour W. 1970. *Cultural pluralism and American education*. Scranton, Penn.: International Textbook.

———. 1976. *A new public education*. New York: David McKay.

Kallen, Horace M. 1924a. *Culture and democracy in the United States*. New York: Boni & Liveright.

———. 1924b. *Cultural pluralism and the American idea*. University of Pennsylvania.

Kloss, Heinz. 1976. *The American bilingual tradition in education and administration*. Rowley, Mass.: Newbury House.

Lai, H. L. 1980. Chinese. In *Harvard encyclopedia of American ethnic groups*. Edited by Stephan Thernstrom. Cambridge: Harvard University Press.

Lau v. Nichols. Supreme Court of the United States, 1974. 414 U.S. 563, 94 S. Ct. 786.

Marzio, Peter. 1976. *A nation of nations*. New York: Harper and Row.

McLaren, Peter. 1998. *Life in schools: An introduction to critical pedagogy in the foundations of education*. 3d ed. New York: Longman.

Nelli, Humber S. 1980. Italians. In *Harvard encyclopedia of American ethnic groups*. Edited by Stephan Thernstrom, 545–560. Cambridge: Harvard University Press.

Peterson, William. 1980. Concepts of Ethnicity. In *Harvard encyclopedia of american ethnic groups*. Edited by Stephan Thernstrom, 234–242.Cambridge: Harvard University Press.

Pratte, Richard 1982. Culture and education policy. *The encyclopedia of educational research*. Vol. 1, 394–400. New York: Macmillian and the Free Press.

Schermerhorn, R. A. 1970. *Comparative ethnic relations: A framework for theory and research*. New York: Random House.

Sleeter, Christine E., and Carl A. Grant. 1999. *Making choices for multicultural education: Five approaches to race, class, and gender*. New York: John Wiley.

Sowell, Thomas. 1981. *Ethnic America: A history*. New York: Basic Books.

Teselle, Sallie. 1974. *The rediscovery of ethnicity: Its implications for culture and politics in America*. New York: Harper and Row.

Weiss, Bernard J. ed. 1982. *American education and the European immigrant*. Urbana, Ill.: University of Illinois.

Zangwill, Israel. 1909. *The melting pot*. New York: Macmillan.

CHAPTER 9

Childhood, Adolescents, and the Family

The forces of a rapidly changing society are reflected in many different aspects of contemporary culture and schooling. Perhaps nowhere is this as evident as in the profound changes that have occurred in the last fifty years that have had an impact on children, **adolescents,** and the family.

In this chapter, we look at how the experiences of U.S. children, adolescents, and families have changed since the late 1950s. We believe that being a child or adolescent today is very different than it was forty or fifty years ago. Likewise, families are different. The influence of media such as television and film, the growth of consumerism, the movement of women out of the home and into the workplace, the increase in the divorce rate, and the growth of single-parent families are just some of the factors that need to be considered.

Understanding how the experience of children, adolescents, and families is changing is critical for teachers. As discussed earlier in this book, most learning comes outside of the formal organization of schools. Children and adolescents carry into the school setting constructions of the world obtained through their experience in families, by interacting with peer groups, and with media such as television, video games, and films. Imagine how much more children know entering school today than they did seventy-five years ago. Because of television and other forms of electronic media (radio, videotapes, film, the Internet), children not only carry with them enormous amounts of knowledge, but even new ways of learning.

How do changes in work patterns for both men and women affect the social and developmental experience of children? Does the increased

INTASC Standards
Principle #9

adolescents
Teenagers who have not yet become adults.

INTASC Standards
Principle #9

199

FIGURE 9.1 ■ A late nineteenth-century U.S. family.

Source: Courtesy of the National Archives.

FIGURE 9.2 ■ A contemporary U.S. family (multicultural).

divorce rate affect children? Does the steady increase in the number of single-parent households significantly change the demands placed on teachers in the classroom? What is the significance of **alternative family models?**

These are crucial questions. New and alternative family models are changing the experience of childhood. The traditional nuclear family (mom, dad, and two or three children) is giving way to a much more complex and fluid model of family—what the child psychologist David Elkind refers to as the **"permeable" family.** The permeable family is dynamic and has many different forms. It is a distinctly postmodern phenomenon. As Elkind explains:

> Over the past half century, profound shifts in our ways of perceiving, valuing and feeling about ourselves and our world have radically altered American society and reconfigured the American family. We find these changes—which have been described as the movement from modernity to postmodernity—both liberating and stressful. The modern nuclear family, often idyllically portrayed as a refuge and a retreat from a demanding world, is fast disappearing. In its stead we now have a new structure—the postmodern permeable family—that mirrors the openness, complexity, and diversity of our contemporary lifestyles. (Elkind 1994, 1)

Most people, including teachers, assume that the concepts of childhood, adolescence, and the family have been constant throughout history. This is not the case. The meaning of childhood, adolescence, and family is widely different across cultures and historical time periods. Contemporary attitudes toward childhood, for example, differ markedly from those of our parents and grandparents. Attitudes in the eighteenth and nineteenth centuries seem even more distant from ours.

In this chapter we examine the role of the family in the socialization and education of the child and adolescent. We begin by assuming that "the family is always a setting in which important educational encounters occur" (Leichter 1977, 2). We also assume that the U.S. family, and in turn U.S. childhood and adolescence, have been going through a process of radical redefinition over the past forty or fifty years.

INTASC Standards
Principle #2

alternative family models
Models of the family other than the traditional nuclear family model consisting of a mother, a father, and children. A single parent or a gay couple with children would represent an alternative family model.

permeable family
A complex model of a family, reflecting patterns of divorce and so on.

? **WHAT DO YOU THINK?**

The Family and Compulsory Education

The case of *Wisconsin v. Yoder* (1972) raised some interesting questions concerning the rights of Amish children and of their parents who refused to comply with the state's compulsory education law. The parents maintained that Wisconsin's compulsory attendance law threatened their survival as a social and religious group; they argued that secondary education was not only superfluous but also detrimental to their way of life. Because the Amish maintain that the knowledge received from books represents a distraction from the message of God provided in the Bible and tends to divide the religious community, their children do not ordinarily attend school beyond the eighth grade.

Of the three children involved, only one said she shared her parent's religious beliefs. Although the Court ruled in favor of the parents, Justice William O. Douglas dissented, arguing that not only the parents' but also the children's point of view needed to be heard.

What should be done when parents' feelings and beliefs oppose their children's? What are the rights of children? What are the rights of parents? Which, if either, should take precedence? What do you think?

■ THE GREAT CHANGE IN CHILDHOOD

How has our understanding of childhood changed over the course of time? Imagine for a moment that you are an alien anthropologist landing on the planet Earth for the first time. You have been sent by the leaders of your civilization across the galaxy to conduct a survey of the habits, attitudes, and cultural values of earthlings.

Unlike the inhabitants of Earth, you come from a planet where people are born fully grown; on your planet children do not exist. Finding them on Earth is your most exciting discovery. At first, you think they are a separate race of miniature humans. Although similar in many ways to the larger earthlings, these smaller earthlings wear different clothes and participate in many different functions and activities. After further investigation you discover that these are "children"—immature earthlings. Through extensive observation and research you finally come to the conclusion that children have a life set apart from adults that includes toys, games, special books, and different clothes.

If your spaceship had landed on Earth three or four hundred years ago, instead of today, you would have discovered a very different situation. The activities of children would not have been as clearly differentiated from those of adults. Until recently, children dressed as adults—simply in miniature. The games children played were the same as those adults played. Rarely if ever were children excluded from adult activities. Children and adults lived their lives together. No separate world of childhood existed.

FIGURE 9.3 ■ Children dressed like adults with teachers.

Source: A Rational Way of Teaching (1688).

Many sources, including paintings, letters, and personal diaries reveal how different childhood was, as compared with our own era, in the sixteenth and seventeenth centuries. The French historian Philippe Aries explored precisely how different these two worlds were in *Centuries of Childhood,* first published in France in 1960 with the title *L'Enfant et la vie familiale sous l'ancien regime.* Aries studied the diary of a doctor named Heorard, the childhood physician of the French king Louis XIII (born in 1601). In his diary Heorard described the daily activities of the future king.

From a very young age the young dauphin was regularly involved in court life. At seventeen months he was given a fiddle. By the time he was two, he sat at dinner with the Queen. At the age of four he was taking part in adult ballets—even dancing as a naked cupid in one performance. According to Aires:

> At five, he was watching farces, and at seven comedies. He sang and played the violin and the lute. He was in the front row of the spectators at a wrestling-match, a ring-tilting contest, a bullfight or a bearfight, or a display by a tightrope walker. (Aries 1962, 67)

Young and old participated in the same activities. Children were treated as miniature adults.

Aries speculates that childhood was different in the fifteenth and sixteenth centuries because of the high infant and child mortality rate. Most children did not survive to adulthood. French essayist Michel de Montaigne (1533–1592) commented, "I have lost two or three children in their infancy, not without regret, but without great sorrow" (Aries 1962, 38–39). Aries cites many similar comments.

During the sixteenth and seventeenth centuries formal schooling was the exception rather than the rule. When children went to school, they usually went for short periods and generally only to learn to read and write. Of course the Latin grammar schools and church-affiliated schools educated a small number of the elite in advanced subjects, particularly Latin. But most education took place in the community, the church, and the family. Significantly, this education transmitted cultural values across generations, not just the book learning of formal schooling. It included both boys and girls.

The reality of the sixteenth and early seventeenth centuries seems to have been that the death of children was commonplace and expected. Adults felt a responsibility to feed and shelter children, but made little effort to protect them from the realities of life. In the middle of the seventeenth century the average child, if he or she survived birth, had a 50/50 chance of reaching the age of ten.

Children began to be treated differently by adults in the late seventeenth and eighteenth centuries as the mortality rate began to decline. This occurred because of improvements in medicine and nutrition. But even as late as the beginning of the eighteenth century, conditions were still harsh. A study focusing on the year 1730 was conducted by the modern French historian Jean Fourastie and his students. It revealed

1. A very high infant mortality rate—one in four newborn children
2. A life expectancy of less than twenty-five years
3. That the average marriage lasted only seventeen years before one of the spouses died
4. That there were an average 4.1 births per marriage; and the average child lost a parent by the age of fourteen
5. That a man who reached fifty years of age had seen, on the average, nine members of his family die (based on Muller 1969, 8)

Until recently, life for most children was short and harsh. Of necessity, children took on adult responsibilities early. Little in the way of special experiences or training was provided to them because the likelihood they would not live to adulthood was great. Children were expected to grow up as quickly as possible.

In our own age we have extended the period of dependency in most children and adolescents. The lovers Romeo and Juliet were respectively fifteen and thirteen years of age—adults for their time. Even less than a century ago, it was common in the United States to find children as young as nine or ten working in factories and mines. As late as the 1890s, high schools enrolled only 7 percent of the population between fourteen and seventeen years of age. The other 93 percent worked in the adult labor force (Postman 1988, 148). Today, most people are not considered adults until they reach the age of twenty or twenty-one—just a few years less than the average age of death for a person in the early seventeenth century. Our concept of childhood is a relatively recent innovation of Western culture and society.

An extremely important concept is at work here: childhood and adolescence are social rather than biological constructs. The educational and media theorist Neal Postman explains:

> Childhood is a social artifact, not a biological category. Our genes contain no clear instructions about who is and who is not a child, and the laws of survival do not require that a distinction be made between the world of the adult and the world of the child. (Postman 1988, 148)

Our modern conception of childhood is only about four hundred years old. The concept of adolescence was created about a hundred years ago, as young adults began to spend more time making the transition from

FIGURE 9.4 ■ Breaker boys working in a mine in Pennsylvania in 1911.

Source: Photograph by Lewis Hine. Courtesy of the National Archive.

childhood to adult life. In fact, the term *teenager* has only been used since the beginning of the Second World War.

As the new century and millennium begin, postmodern forces are causing childhood and adolescence to be redefined in profoundly important ways. So too, is the work of teachers in the schools being redefined.

■ CHILDHOOD AND CONTEMPORARY CULTURE

INTASC Standards

Principle #9

As previously argued, the term *childhood* is defined by how a culture defines both children and adults. It is a social reality or construct, as much as a matter of age. Childhood, like education, reflects the social, political, and economic conditions of the culture. In our own era we are seeing the radical redefinition of childhood and in turn the redefinition of the family. Ironically, the model that is emerging at the beginning of the twenty-first century is similar to the model of children as miniature adults that existed until the late seventeenth and early eighteenth centuries. The reasons for this, however, have nothing to do with high infant mortality rates, but instead with the exposure of children to media and other postmodern trends in the culture.

Neil Postman, Marie Winn, David Elkind, and other contemporary authors have pointed out that the distance separating children from adults has narrowed and in many instances has become negligible. Children today are again wearing clothes identical to those worn by adults. Look in a typical college classroom. Students typically wear the same types of clothes that their younger counterparts do (jeans, T-shirts, and running shoes).

Adult sexuality is less concealed from children. A young mother going around without a bra beneath her blouse may be making a statement about personal freedom and liberation, but she may also be revealing a different attitude to her children about sex than she herself was exposed to as a child. A gay couple raising a child in a nontraditional or alternative family is likewise redefining social and cultural norms.

Information of all types is more available to children than it was even a generation ago. Young children watch adult films and television. Children and adolescents are targeted by commercials for fast food companies such as McDonald's and Burger King, as well as clothing companies such as the Gap, Old Navy, and Calvin Klein. As Postman has pointed out, before television became so dominant in our culture, it was easier to limit the amount of adult knowledge children were exposed to. Books and magazines with adult ideas and information could be kept from children. Exposure to television cannot be regulated to the same degree.

> . . . Television erodes the dividing line between childhood and adulthood in three ways, all having to do with its undifferentiated accessibility: first, because it requires no instruction to grasp its form; second because it does not make complex demands on either the mind or behavior; and third because it does not segregate its audience. (Postman 1982, 80)

According to Postman, television recreates the conditions of communication that existed in the fourteenth and fifteenth centuries. It provides children and adults with the same messages and information. Children and adults are exposed to the same material. Therefore, the notion of the child being an innocent, to be protected from the harsh realities of adult life, is becoming less plausible.

In the past, you had to learn to read to have access to the "secret" knowledge often found in books. Today, television provides ample information about sex, violence, and any number of adult subjects. Movies with primarily adult content are easily available to children and adolescents through broadcast and cable sources. How many children watch

chat room
An electronic meeting place on the Internet where people can engage in the exchange of information.

electronic bulletin board
A site on the Internet devoted to leaving or posting messages.

erotic movies and softcore pornography available in their parents' videotape collection or piped in late at night on a special movie channel? Increasingly, knowledge about the world is being controlled—and made available to children—not by parents and teachers, but by television writers and producers.

How has the Internet and World Wide Web changed children's access to previously prohibited types of information and knowledge? Despite electronic filtering devices, children have virtually unlimited access to information on the Internet. They often come across information by accident. By typing in the website address www.whitehouse.com, for example, you could easily assume that you were going to visit a website that dealt with the residence and offices for the president of the United States. Instead, the address is a pornography site.

Chat rooms and **electronic bulletin boards** on the Internet do not necessarily screen out children. This is the point of a famous *New Yorker* magazine cartoon in which two dogs are sitting next to each other in front of a computer screen. One of them comments to the other that "On the Internet nobody knows you're a dog."

■ CHILDREN AND THE ADULT WORLD

The lives of children and adolescents mirror the changes in adult society. U.S. society has gone through a profound series of changes since the early 1960s. The sexual revolution, the drug epidemic, the assaults on the conventional two-parent family, the women's movement, and the growth of television as a medium of education and socialization have all contributed to the loss of childhood (Winn 1983b, 18). The image of the average U.S. middle-class family so popular during the 1950s and early 1960s is increasingly rare. Most women no longer stay at home to raise children. In fact, two out of three mothers now go to work by the time their children have reached the age of six. Half of all marriages end in separation or divorce. Actually, these conditions have almost always existed for the poor and working classes in the United States. What is new is the extent to which these conditions spread through the entire population by the end of the twentieth century.

It is clear that during the last decade or so, children have been forced into adult responsibilities at earlier and earlier ages. Annie Hermann, director of the New York Child's Development Center, has argued that forcing children to take on adult responsibilities sooner does not necessarily mean that they are mature.

. . . Innocence, once considered the right of children, may be seen as simply the absence of weight and burden. Maturity, meanwhile, may be defined as the capacity to carry a burden successfully. But it you are given the heavy burden of knowledge before you have the capacity to deal with it—and knowledge is burdensome, because it requires mental and psychological work to deal with it—the results may be those distressing signs parents and teachers are observing among children today; confusion, fear, feelings of incompetence. (Winn 1983b, 28)

Children who must cope with divorce, with raising themselves, and who must "act like adults" are being asked to cope with responsibilities and decisions that may well be beyond their capability. The specific forces at work in the experience of postmodern children and adolescents can be identified most clearly by analyzing the changes that have been taking place in families.

? WHAT DO YOU THINK?
The Rights of Children

A major controversy in recent years concerns the rights of children. Two opposing viewpoints have emerged: one argues that children are the same as adults and should be accorded equal rights with them; the second maintains that children are different and should be treated differently.

As children become increasingly integrated into the adult world, should their responsibilities change as well? Adolescents under the age of sixteen, for example, are treated as juveniles by our legal system, and the juvenile justice system is much more lenient than the adult criminal justice system. If a juvenile commits an adult crime, first-degree murder, for example, should he or she be subject to the punishment normally given to adults? Should juveniles have the right to move out of their parent's home over their parent's objections? Should a child be able to divorce her parents? When is a child ready to assume the burden of adult responsibilities? Does this point occur at different ages for different children? Should children's rights be defined differently as a result? What do you think?

■ THE CHANGING U.S. FAMILY

As part of the emergence of a more diverse and postmodern culture, many changes have taken place in the construction of families since the

INTASC Standards

Principle #3

demographic
Refers to the idea of population and social characteristics.

social capital
Human resources—specifically people—available in a culture.

1960s. A look at the **demographic** characteristics of families clarifies the point. More specifically, smaller families, the increase in the work force of women of child-bearing age, the postponement of marriage and child rearing, the increasing number of single parents, and the growing numbers of children who are part of blended families, are all demographic variables that have come to characterize U.S. families in recent years (Kagen 1987, 170).

Divorce has grown at an extremely rapid rate over the past one hundred years. In 1900, 0.3 percent of the population was divorced; in 1960, 1.8 percent; in 1970, 2.2 percent; in 1980, 4.8 percent; in 1990, 6.8 percent; and in 1998, 8.2 percent (*Statistical Abstracts of the United States 1999*, 873). Increased divorce rates have profoundly affected the living arrangements of children. In 1996, approximately a quarter (25.4%) of all children lived with a single parent—usually their mothers (*America's Children 2000*). Compare this figure to the 23 percent who lived with one parent in 1980, 12 percent in 1970, and 9 percent in 1960 (U.S. Department of Commerce 1985, 8). Among selected populations, these statistics are even more marked. In 1996 58.1 percent of all black non-Hispanic children lived with a single parent; 26.4 percent of all Hispanic children, and 14.1 percent of white non-Hispanic children, lived with one parent (U.S. Department of Commerce 1985, 8).

Along with the growth in single-parent families has been the movement of women out of traditional household settings and into the workplace. Among married women with children between the ages of six and seventeen, 39 percent worked outside of the home in 1960; 49.2 percent in 1970; 61.7 percent in 1980; 73.6 percent in 1990 and 76.8 percent in 1998. Between 1980 and 1998, the number of single women with children between the ages of six and seventeen increased from 67.6 percent to 81.2 percent (*Statistical Abstracts of the United States 1999*, 417).

INTASC Standards

Principle #9

The growth of single-parent families as a result of divorce and the increased movement of women into the labor force results in what theorists, such as James S. Coleman, regard as a decrease in parental presence in the household and a significant erosion of the **social capital** available to children. Social capital represents the human resources available to family or community. It can be in the form of a grandparent or aunt or uncle involved in raising a child. It can be a neighbor down the street or a volunteer willing to work with a child such as a Sunday school teacher, or a Boy Scout or Girl Scout leader.

In the context of the loss of social capital in the community, Coleman explains that

The earlier migration of father from household and neighborhood during the day, and the very recent migration of mothers from the household

TABLE 9.1 ■ Percentage of Children under Age Eighteen Living in Various Family Arrangements by Race and Hispanic Origin, 1996

Characteristic	Total	White, Non-Hispanic	Black, Non-Hispanic	Other, Non-Hispanic	Hispanic
Total children ages 0 to 17					
Number (in thousands)	71,694	46,657	11,003	3,277	10,428
Living with two parents	70.9	79.0	26.9	73.1	61.2
Two bio./adopt. married	62.4	70.1	29.9	72.7	51.7
Two bio./adopt. cohab	1.8	1.4	1.8	1.5	4.2
Bio./adopt. parent and step. married	6.4	7.3	4.9	4.6	4.8
Bio./adopt. parent and step. cohab.	0.3	0.2	0.3	0.1	0.4
Living with a single parent	25.4	18.5	54.9	18.0	27.5
Single mother	20.0	13.4	50.2	14.0	22.2
Single mother with partner	2.1	2.1	2.3	1.4	2.4
Single father	2.1	2.4	1.7	1.3	1.3
Single father with partner	0.4	0.4	0.3	0.2	0.4
Stepparent	0.2	0.2	0.3	0.5	0.1
Stepparent with partner	0.0	0.0	0.0	—	—
Living with no parents	2.7	2.5	3.2	3.3	4.3
Grandparents	1.8	1.1	5.0	1.7	1.4
Other relatives only–no grandparent	0.8	0.4	1.6	2.8	1.3
Nonrelatives only–not foster parents	0.4	0.4	0.4	2.1	0.3
Other relatives and nonrelatives	0.3	0.2	0.3	0.4	0.3
Foster parent(s)	0.4	0.3	0.7	2.1	0.7
Own household or partner of householder	0.1	0.1	0.1	—	0.2

Source: America's Children 2000 (http://childstats.gov/ac2000/toc.asp).

into the labor force has meant reduced participation in community organizations, like the PTA, Scouting, and others. In addition, the society has been invaded by an advanced individualism, in which cultivation of one's own well-being has replaced interest in others. Indicators are the extensive growth in concern with one's health (jogging, health clubs, etc.) personal appearance, and career advancement. (Coleman 1987, 32–38)

Coleman argues that the loss of social capital has had profound implications for U.S. child rearing, and in turn for the schools. Child rearing, which used to take place informally as a by-product of community activities involving the household, extended families, and neighborhood-based organizations, has "crumbled" as traditional institutions have declined. Traditional neighborhoods and community organizations have been replaced by shopping malls, cocktail parties, and rock concerts, which serve as alternatives to the traditional extended family, but do not encourage an equally rich and valuable exchange of social capital between children and adults.

INTERNET @ CONNECTIONS

Online Information about Families

The federal government's Forum on Child and Family Statistics is one of the best places on the Internet to find national and state statistics and reports on children and their families, including population and family characteristics, economic security, health, behavior and social environments, and education. Among the major reports to be found are the annual federal monitoring report on the status of the nation's children America's Children: Key National Indicators of Well-Being at http://www.childstats.gov/ac2000/ac00.asp and Nurturing Fatherhood, the federal government's main annual report on the condition of fatherhood in U.S. society, at http://fatherhood.hhs.gov/CFSForum/c4.htm.

The social forces previously outlined profoundly affect the work of teachers and schools. In subsequent chapters we discuss the influence of other forces, such as television and how changing attitudes toward family are redefining sexuality. Considering issues involving social capital only, such as divorce, the growth of single-parent families, and the return of women into the workforce, it is clear that the contemporary U.S. family and its children have fewer human resources than was the case even a generation ago.

Because of the types of demographic factors already outlined, traditional and nontraditional families are playing less of a role in educating and socializing their children. As a result, children and adolescents are turning to peers, the media, and schools for help and guidance in their growth and development. In the case of media and peers this influence is not always positive. As a result, schools are being given even more responsibility in the upbringing of our children. Simply stated, the work of teachers and schools is more complex as increasing demands are placed on them.

If schools are taking on more and more responsibility for socializing children, it can be argued that it is even more important that children be required, or compelled, to attend the schools.

■ COMPULSORY EDUCATION

Compulsory education is a tradition in the United States dating from the colonial period. In the Massachusetts Bay Colony local compulsory education laws passed in 1642 and 1648 were justified on the premise that if children were to be good Christians, they would have to be able to read and interpret Scripture. The first statewide compulsory education law was passed in Massachusetts in 1852. By 1918 education through the elementary grades was compulsory throughout the nation; by the end of the Second World War education was compulsory through the secondary grades (or, age sixteen) in most states. Whether we should force children to attend school is a question that must be addressed by all those entering the field of education. In examining the issue of compulsory education we must consider whether the reasons our society compels students to remain in school may have more to do with the needs of our economy than with the needs of our youth.

Until the beginning of this century young people tended to assume responsibility earlier. People married earlier and soon took over adult responsibilities. Most people went to work after only six or eight years of schooling. Many agricultural and industrial workers had their first job when they were only twelve or thirteen years old. Work required less complex training than now, and the demand for labor was greater.

The need for young workers diminished as the country became more industrialized. Historians such as Joel Spring have indicated that whereas the male labor force increased from 50 percent to 62 percent between 1890 and 1900, the employment figures for the same group declined to 51.2 percent by 1920 and to 44 percent by 1944 (Spring 1978, 73). Jobs traditionally given to young workers dwindled as advances in technology were made. As adolescents became less important to the work force, the school-age population increased. In 1900, 78.7 percent of the population between the ages of five and seventeen attended school. By 1926, this figure had increased to 90.4 percent (Spring 1978, 73).

Compulsory education has become an increasingly controversial issue in recent years. It has been argued that youths who are compelled to go to school do not learn what they need to and instead distract other students from learning. In many large city high schools across the country, as few as 50 percent of the students attend class on any given day.

Enforcement of attendance is lax. Why then do we maintain the illusion of universal attendance? Why are we determined to keep children in school?

One explanation lies in the fact that for many students—particularly at the upper secondary level—school attendance serves a custodial function. Schools keep adolescents off the streets and out of the job market. We require students to complete their high school degree before they can get any type of reasonable job; the high school diploma is a "union" or entry card, required to enter the world of adult work. As an idea, compulsory education is closely linked to our concept of childhood and adolescence. Although on the surface we compel attendance for the good of the student, we may in fact also do so for the good of the economic system. It may well be that we cannot expect schools to educate everyone. We may be at a point in the development of our educational system when we need to propose alternatives to our traditional models of schooling.

Educators such as Theodore Sizer have argued that we may be making many schools much more difficult, if not impossible, places in which to teach and learn by compelling unwilling students to attend. Sizer suggests we consider setting up schools where only interested students may attend classes, where attendance is not compulsory, and where drop-outs can re-enter when they have matured and are ready to learn (Sizer 1984).

INTASC Standards

Principle #9

? WHAT DO YOU THINK?
Should We Require School Attendance?

A popular argument claims the problem with kids these days is that they spend too much time going to school. Many students clearly attend school against their will, and as a result bring to the learning process and to the classroom an inevitable degree of hostility. Many educators maintain that a teacher cannot do much teaching in an institution in which "so many of the inmates are waiting to get out." They make forceful arguments that instead of compelling students to remain in school, we should allow them to go out and discover the real world. When they are ready—and only if they want to—they can return to school to complete their education.

Educators as distinguished as Theodore Sizer, the former dean of the Harvard Graduate School of Education, have proposed solutions such as these. Taking such steps would mean eliminating compulsory education laws. What would be the consequences of such an action? What would be the potential benefits for the student and society? What would be some of the potential problems? What do you think?

■ HOME SCHOOLING

Questions about compulsory schooling are closely linked to whether people should be able to educate their own children themselves. The dissatisfaction many people feel with public schools has led some to undertake the instruction of their children themselves. **Home schooling** has become increasingly popular in the United States. Approximately two million children are currently home schooled.

Parents decide to home school their children for many reasons. Some are disappointed with the quality of education provided by their local schools. Others do so on the basis of their religious beliefs, feeling that public education provides learning in a godless context. Home schooling has met with considerable opposition from local school officials. They argue that most parents are not properly trained to educate their children. Even when a parent does have a degree in teacher education, they argue that a single family cannot adequately provide the resources necessary for proper instruction, such as library facilities, athletic training, and laboratories—all important and necessary services provided by the public school system.

Critics of home schooling also argue that by isolating children in the home environment and within a protective family circle, parents deprive their children of the contact with their peers that leads to a normal and healthy social development. If indeed one important function of the school system is to socialize the child, home schooling presents a serious threat to that objective. If the state's values are in opposition to those of the parent's, should the state have the right to introduce to the child, through the vehicle of its schools, a set of beliefs different from those of the child's family? What if the family objects to the information and ideas presented in the school curriculum? What are the rights of the family?

Questions such as these become particularly controversial in areas such as sex education. Many Christian fundamentalist families, for example, object to introducing sex education in the schools. Tim LaHaye, a **religious fundamentalist** leader, has argued that ". . . the purpose of sex education is to eradicate Christian values and Christian behavior relating to sexual activity and to replace them with Humanist values and behavior" (quoted by Provenzo 1989, 69). The Constitution, and more specifically the Supreme Court, has tended to support the idea that parents have the right to determine what their children should or should not learn in the schools. In the 1972 Supreme Court case *Wisconsin v. Yoder,* the issue of compulsory education was challenged by a group of Amish parents who for religious reasons did not want their

INTASC Standards

Principle #3

home schooling
National movement where children are educated at home by their parents.

religious fundamentalism
A Protestant conservative movement in the nineteenth and twentieth centuries in the United States that emphasized the literal interpretation of the Bible.

INTASC Standards

Principle #3

children to attend school beyond the eighth grade. According to the decision,

> . . . a State's interest in universal education, however highly we rank it, is not totally free from a balancing process when it impinges on the fundamental rights and interests, such as those specifically protected by the Free Exercise Clause of the First Amendment, and the traditional interest of parents with respect to the religious upbringing of their children so long as they, in the words of *Pierce*, "prepare (them) for additional obligations." (quoted by Provenzo 1989, 69)

Decisions like *Wisconsin v. Yoder* make it legally possible for parents to withdraw their children from public education and educate them on their own. In doing so, they must provide certain minimal curricular standards—the argument being that the state, although not superseding the rights of parents, has an interest in the education of its children.

INTERNET @ CONNECTIONS
Home Schooling Resources

Extensive resources on home schooling are available online. Particularly valuable are the American Homeschool Association and its *Home Education Magazine*. The website for *Home Education Magazine* presents free online newsletters, discussion boards, a networking list, and selections from the magazine. You can visit American Homeschool Association at http://www.home-ed-press.com/AHA/aha.html and *Home Education Magazine* at http://www.home-ed-magazine.com/.

■ SUMMARY

The changing nature of childhood and the family in the postmodern era has altered our traditional understanding of education. As educators, we increasingly need to take into account how demographic and cultural shifts are changing the work of teachers and schools. We also need to understand the rights of parents and children, as well as the rights of the state. What is clear is that the conditions and purposes of schooling are changing as the nature of the family and our social system is changing. Schools almost certainly need to take on new roles—ones that will change the meaning and purpose of what we do as educators.

■ DISCUSSION QUESTIONS ■

1. What are the good and bad characteristics of the traditional nuclear family? What are the advantages and disadvantages of Elkind's model of a permeable family?
2. Define what sets children apart from adults in our society. Where and how does the experience and activity of childhood cross over into adulthood?
3. Should children be shielded or protected from certain types of adult knowledge? Can this be considered a restriction of their personal freedom?
4. How has the condition of the family changed since the Second World War? How do these changes alter the experience of childhood in the United States?
5. What is a sufficient education for a child? Should a child be compelled to attend school against her wishes or those of her family?
6. Should parents be allowed to provide home education for their children? To what degree should such education be regulated by the state?

■ SOURCES CITED ■

Aries, Philippe. 1962. *Centuries of childhood.* Translated by Robert Baldrick. New York: Vintage Books.

Arons, Stephen. 1983. *Compelling belief: The culture of American schooling.* New York: McGraw-Hill.

Coleman, James S. 1966. *Equality of educational opportunity.* Washington, D.C.: U.S. Government Printing Office.

———. 1987. Families and schools. *Educational Researcher* 16(6): 32–38.

De Mause, Lloyd, ed. 1974. *The history of childhood.* New York: The Psychohistory Press.

Elkind, David. 1981. *The hurried child.* Reading, Mass.: Addison-Wesley.

———. 1994. *Ties that stress: The new family imbalance.* Cambridge: Harvard University Press.

Federal Interagency Forum on Child and Family Statistics. *America's Children 2000.* Available online at http://childstats.gov/ac2000/toc.asp.

Holt, John. 1976. *Escape from childhood.* New York: Ballantine.

Huizinga, Johan. 1950. *Homo ludens.* Boston: Beacon Press.

Kagan, S. L., ed. 1987. Home–school linkages: History's legacies and the family support movement. In *America's family support programs: Perspectives and prospectives.* New Haven: Yale University Press.

Katz, Michael. 1976. *A history of compulsory education laws.* Bloomington, Ind.: Phi Delta Kappa.

Leichter, Hope Jensen. 1977. *The family as educator.* New York: Teachers College Press.

Maeroff, Gene I. 1982. *Don't blame the kids: The trouble with America's public schools.* New York: McGraw-Hill.

Muller, Philippe. 1969. *The tasks of childhood.* Translated by Anita Mason. New York: McGraw-Hill.

Plumb, J. H. 1971. *The great change in childhood.* New York: Delacorte.

Popenoe, David. 1999. *Life without father: Compelling new evidence that fatherhood and marriage are indispensable for the good of children and society.* New York: The Free Press.

Postman, Neil. 1982. *The disappearance of childhood.* New York: Delacorte.

———. 1985. *Amusing ourselves to death: Public discourse in the age of show business.* New York: Viking.

———. 1988. *Conscientious objections: Stirring up trouble about language, technology and education.* New York: Vintage Books.

Provenzo, Eugene F., Jr. 1990. *Religious fundamentalism and American education: The battle for the public schools.* New York: State University of New York Press.

Sizer, R. Theodore. 1984. *Horace's compromise: The dilemma of the American high school.* Boston: Houghton Mifflin.

Spring, Joel. 1978. *American education: An introduction to social and political aspects.* New York: Longman.

State of Wisconsin v. Yoder. Supreme Court of the United States, 1972. 406 U.S. 205, 92 S. Ct. 1526.

U.S. Census Bureau. 1999. *Statistical abstract of the United States.* Washington, D.C.: U.S. Government Printing Office.

U.S. Department of Commerce, Bureau of the Census. 1985. *Marital status and living arrangements.* Washington, D.C.: U.S. Government Printing Office.

Winn, Marie. 1983a. *Children without childhood.* New York: Pantheon Books.

———. 1983b. The loss of childhood. *The New York Times Magazine,* 8 May.

CHAPTER 10

Education and Dominated Cultures

As discussed at length in Chapter 8, the United States is a pluralistic society representing a wide range of backgrounds and traditions. The majority of people in the United States have settled in this country voluntarily, coming here to pursue personal freedom and economic opportunity. This has not been the case, however, for some American people, including Native Americans, Hawaiians, Puerto Ricans, Mexican Americans, and African Americans.

Historically, these groups represent **dominated cultures:** people who were conquered as part of the European settlement of North America, or were brought here as slaves, or were colonized as part of the U.S. global expansion during the decades immediately preceding the First World War. This chapter discusses dominated cultures and studies their place in the educational system and in society at large.

INTASC Standards

Principle #9

dominated cultures
Cultural groups that have been forced to become part of U.S. culture such as African Americans, Native Americans, and colonized groups such as Hawaiians and Puerto Ricans.

dominant culture
The cultural group in a society whose values and beliefs dominate and who consciously or unconsciously enforce that domination.

■ DOMINATED CULTURES

The concept of a dominated culture is based on the work of the educational theorist Joel Spring. According to Spring, ". . . *dominated cultures* refers to those cultures in the United States that representatives of European culture have attempted to control and change" (Spring 1994, xi). Several ideas are key to the concept of a dominated culture. One is that that the dominating or **dominant culture** strips away the culture of the dominated group. Thus, in the case of Native Americans during the nineteenth century, the European-based white culture tried

INTASC Standards

Principle #5

deculturalization
Eliminating or discouraging the cultural traditions and beliefs of a cultural group.

to replace, or strip away, the religion and tradition of the Native American cultures. This process of assimilation, which has already been described in Chapter 8, is referred to as **deculturalization** (Spring 1994, xi).

Groups who have been deculturalized are by definition considered inferior by the dominant culture. Although attempts may be made to assimilate them into the dominant culture, they are not provided equal rights. Historically, dominated groups have been physically segregated. They are often taught in their own schools by members of the dominant group, rather than by people from their own cultural group. They have limited access to economic and social opportunities. Often their language, traditions, and values are trivialized and considered inferior—not part of the "superior," or mainstream culture.

According to Spring, deculturalization programs use a range of methods in educational settings:

1. Segregation and isolation [The dominated group is isolated from their cultural traditions and leaders.]
2. Forced change of language [The use of the dominated culture's language is eliminated or de-emphasized.]
3. Content of curriculum reflects culture of dominant group [Curricular content is used that emphasizes the values and traditions of the dominant culture.]
4. Content of textbooks reflects culture of dominant group [Textbooks are used that emphasize the values and traditions of the dominant group.]
5. Dominated groups are not allowed to express their culture and religion [Important cultural and historical events are not allowed to be celebrated by the dominated group.]
6. Use of teachers from dominant group [Teachers representing the dominant culture provide instruction to the dominated group.] (Spring 2001, 91)

Each of these methods is closely related to the characteristics of colonized educational systems described in Chapter 4. There it was argued that in a colonized educational system the individual becomes increasingly alienated from his or her native culture; colonized people are directed, they do not direct themselves. The creative power of dominated peoples is impaired; they are objects, not subjects. Such a model clearly fits historically dominated groups such as Native Americans, Hawaiians, Puerto Ricans, Mexican Americans, and African Americans.

■ NATIVE AMERICANS: A DOMINATED CULTURE

The Native American population numbers approximately two million people, or slightly less than 1 percent of the United States population (Davis 1994, 463). Large Native American populations are concentrated in California, New Mexico, Arizona, Oklahoma, and North Carolina (U.S. Bureau of the Census 1995). Approximately 383,000 Native American children were enrolled in K–12 education in 1990. This represents approximately 1 percent of the total K–12 school population in the United States. Only 7 percent of Native American children go to schools sponsored by the Bureau of Indian Affairs, whereas 5 percent attend private or parochial schools. The rest are enrolled in public education (Champagne 1994, 864).

INTASC Standards
Principle #3

Attempts to educate Native American groups began when the first European explorers arrived in North America. The European newcomers consistently disregarded the traditions, identity, and cultural roots of the Native American people. Even the word *Indian* obscures the complexity and diversity of the Native American population. To describe Native Americans with a single descriptive term is like describing Italians, Greeks, Norwegians, and Russians as Europeans. Clearly such a limited description fails to take into account important differences between these various peoples. Native Americans speak at least two hundred different languages. They have widely differing linguistic, religious, economic, and cultural backgrounds. "Indians" include people as diverse as the Aleuts in Alaska and the Seminoles in Florida (Iverson 1978, 153).

? WHAT DO YOU THINK?

What's in a Name?

What is the best term to describe the widely diverse group of people who make up the indigenous or native populations of North America? The name given to these people as part of the European conquest/settlement was *Indian*, a term derived from explorer Christopher Columbus's false impression that he had discovered a new people at the edge of the Indian subcontinent. In Canada, the term *First Peoples* has come into widespread use. Other terms are *Aboriginal Peoples* and *Indigenous Peoples*. Consider the political significance of each term. Which is the most useful and/or correct term to use? What do you think?

From the first European settlement more than three hundred fifty years ago until the last twenty years, Native American education has rested largely in the hands of either religious groups or the state. Religious involvement in the education of Native Americans in North America dates to the beginning of the European settlement. In 1611 the Jesuits brought missionary education to Native Americans for the first time in French Canada. Shortly afterward, other religious groups, such as the Franciscans, began to set up mission communities and schools throughout the Southwest (Thompson 1978, 4).

The primary goal of the missionaries educating Native Americans during the colonial period was to convert them to Christianity. Secondarily, they wanted to "civilize" them by persuading them to adopt European values. Of course, for the natives to adopt European values, it was necessary for them to reject their own traditional beliefs and culture.

Native American education remained primarily in the hands of church groups until the mid–nineteenth century. At that time the federal government became more involved. Following the Civil War, religious groups were excluded from being involved in Native American education. Because Native American populations were the responsibility of the federal government, church involvement with these groups of people, particularly if funded by the government, represented a violation of the principle of separation of church and state.

As early as 1842 the federal government sponsored thirty-seven "Indian" schools. Emphasizing a policy of assimilation, these federal schools taught Native Americans to reject their tribal beliefs and tradi-

FIGURE 10.1 ■ Native American students before and after their education at the Carlisle Indian School.

Source: Harper's New Monthly Magazine, April 1881, 660–661.

tions and to adopt a Western point of view. In 1879 the first such federally sponsored school, the Carlisle Indian School, was established in Carlisle, Pennsylvania. Captain Richard H. Pratt, the first superintendent of the school, summarized its purpose when he said, "All the Indian there is in the race should be dead. Kill the Indian in him and save the man" (quoted by Iverson 1978, 161). Reverend Lyman Abbot at the Sixth Lake Mohonk Conference of Friends of the Indian in 1888 argued in a similar vein that it was cheaper to feed the Native American than to fight him, and that, "It costs less to educate an Indian than to shoot him" (quoted by Iverson 1978, 161).

Native American children came to Carlisle from their homes in the West. During its first year, the school enrolled forty-seven Pawnees, Kiowas, and Cheyennes. By 1900, more than twelve hundred students from seventy-nine different tribes attended Carlisle. Taken away from their tribal homes to attend the boarding school at Carlisle, young students were taught subjects such as industrial arts and homemaking. Assimilating them into U.S. culture was the goal even though racial prejudices of the period precluded Native American people being genuinely accepted into mainstream culture.

Throughout the early decades of the twentieth century the Native American boarding school movement continued to expand. Harsh rules, strict discipline, compulsory attendance, and an emphasis on industrial and vocational training characterized the schools of this period. In 1916 a uniform course of study that deliberately ignored the unique cultural heritage of the Native American was established for all federal schools.

Despite all the efforts of the missionaries and the federal government, however, Native Americans were not readily assimilated into the mainstream. Instead, many tribes held on to much of their own culture. By the end of the 1920s it was clear that federally sponsored programs were largely a failure. In 1928 the federally sponsored Meriam Report advised that Native American children be educated in their own communities instead of at boarding schools (Thompson 1978, 5).

It was not until 1934 that the federal government allowed Native American educators to teach in Native American schools. Under the direction of John Collier, Franklin D. Roosevelt's commissioner for Indian Affairs, programs were established for the first time on reservations throughout the country that took into account Native American languages, traditions, and culture. This policy was abandoned, however, shortly after the Second World War when the federal government decided to terminate its connection with Native American populations.

In 1946 Congress passed the Indian Claims Commission Act, which allowed tribes to sue the federal government over disputes between

FIGURE 10.2 ■ Portrait of Native Americans from reservation in southeastern Idaho, 1897.

Source: Courtesy of the National Archives.

Native American groups and the government. Passed by the Congress to encourage Native Americans to move off the reservations (where it was believed they stayed only to collect payments from the federal government), the results have been described as follows:

> . . . a reversal of the government's Indian policy directed at curtailing Bureau activities and eventually terminating all federal protection sent a new wave of anxiety and suspicion of the white man's intent over the Indian country. The economic and political developments and activities of Indian communities were retarded or obstructed . . . Tribal members moved into lower class white neighborhoods and re-formed Indian groups, but they lost the potential of their income from timber and their own lands on which to work out a new community life. (quoted by Fuchs and Havighurst 1972, 14)

Throughout the 1950s Native American populations were compelled to give up the federal protection and aid guaranteed by earlier treaties. Numerous tribal groups and communities were terminated, including two major tribes, the Klamath in Oregon and the Menominee in Wisconsin (Fuchs and Havighurst 1972, 14). When the tribes were terminated, many Native Americans moved into urban areas. They faced a new and alien environment, and often lacked an adequate educational background to find a good job. Many were confronted with the persistent prejudice of the mainstream culture and became part of a new urban poor.

By the middle 1960s various government task forces had been set up to address the Native American problem. Among the most important was a special subcommittee on Native American education headed by Robert Kennedy, and after his death by Edward Kennedy. After holding meetings for eighteen months, the committee urged that these groups of people be given increased control of their own education, that a National Board of Indian Education be established, and that a model federal system of Native American schools be set in place (Fuchs and Havighurst 1972, 17).

On July 8, 1970, President Nixon reversed the federal government's policy of termination. In a speech dealing with Native American policy, he argued that termination was morally and legally unacceptable. Instead, he argued in favor of the federal government working in conjunction with Native American groups to help them develop educational, cultural, and economic resources of their own. Self-determination and cultural identity were crucial elements in the proposed policy change.

Statistics assembled for congressional hearings in the late 1960s indicate the severity of the crisis in Native American affairs, and particularly in education. Senator Paul J. Fannin reported to a Senate subcommittee that of the 142,000 Indian children in school, 50 percent dropped out before they reached the twelfth grade. General conditions of Native American life were atrocious. Fifty percent of all Native Americans were unemployed; 90 percent of all Native American housing was substandard. The average life expectancy of a Native American was 42 years compared to 62.3 years for the general population in the United States at that time. Infant mortality of the Native American population was five times greater than that of the rest of the population. The incidence of tuberculosis was seven times greater than the national average (quoted by Kaplan 1972, 157).

These statistics reflected a poverty-stricken, demoralized, and dependent people, as well as the federal government's failure for nearly one hundred fifty years to deal with its Native American population. By the mid-1970s legislation that dealt with the specific cultural, economic, and educational needs of Native American groups was set in motion for the first time. The Education Act of 1975, the Indian Controlled Community College Assistance Act of 1978, and the Educational Amendments of 1978 are examples of legislation that gave Native Americans greater control over and involvement in the education of their people (Tippeconnic and Gipp 1982, 127).

Self-determination was more strongly emphasized in the education of Native Americans in the late 1970s and early 1980s. This was despite the fact that funding decreased under the Reagan administration. By the late 1980s, one-third of schools run by the Bureau of Indian Affairs were contract schools run by Native American groups or tribes (Davis 1994, 184).

INTERNET @ CONNECTIONS

Native American Resources on the World Wide Web

The Internet and World Wide Web have a wide range of resources available that deal with different aspects of Native American culture. The main federal agency responsible for Native American issues is the Bureau of Indian Affairs at http://www.doi.gov/bureau-indian-affairs.html. For more information a list of websites follows.

Index of Native American Resources on the Internet
(http://www.hanksville.org/NAresources/)
Visit this site for a highly comprehensive list of Native American resources on the Internet.

National Museum of the American Indian
(http://www.si.edu/nmai/nav.htm)
The Smithsonian Institute's museum dealing with the history and culture of Native Americans can be found at this site.

Native Web
(http://www.nativeweb.org/)
This site contains an electronic database on Native American culture and traditions that deals with current political and social issues.

Federally Recognized American Indian Tribes
(http://www.indiancircle.com/links.shtml)
Visit this site for a comprehensive list of Native American tribes, with links to related websites.

Indian Mascots
(http://www.pitt.edu/~lmitten/mascots.html)
You can find information on stereotyping through the use of "Indian" mascots at this site.

■ PUERTO RICAN AMERICANS: A DOMINATED CULTURE

A Spanish colony until the end of the nineteenth century, Puerto Rico was taken over by the United States during the Spanish American War. This move was part of U.S. colonial expansion into places such as Cuba and the Philippines.

INTASC Standards
Principle #3

Although the establishment of Puerto Rico as a U.S. commonwealth has typically been portrayed in U.S. history textbooks as a liberation of the island from Spain's domination, the facts suggest that Puerto Rico was actually well on its way to independence. In 1897, for example, Spain had declared Puerto Rico an autonomous state. Although a governor appointed by Spain maintained limited control, it was clear that the Puerto Rican people were moving toward independence and a democratic form of government.

Puerto Rican independence was brought to a standstill with the invasion of the country in 1898. Following the landing of U.S. military forces, the island was placed under military rule. The Puerto Rican population, despite its Spanish, African, and Native American roots, was forced to assume U.S. citizenship. All this took place as an attempt on the part of the U.S. military government to assimilate—or as Joel Spring argues, "deculturalize"—the Puerto Rican population (Spring 2001, 84).

Following a classic colonization model, the United States did not afford Puerto Ricans the same rights afforded other citizens. When military rule ended in 1900, a colonial government under the control of the U.S. Congress was put into place. Schools were viewed as vehicles by which to Americanize the Puerto Rican population. Teachers were retrained and expected to teach in English rather than in Spanish. U.S.–trained teachers and administrators were introduced onto the island. U.S. textbooks and curriculum were introduced, along with patriotic exercises such as the Pledge of Allegiance. Organizations with quasi-military and patriotic overtones such as the Boy Scouts were introduced as well (Spring 2001, 84–85).

Puerto Rico is not the only dominated culture to have emerged out of the U.S. colonial expansionist movement of the late nineteenth century. Hawaii and the Philippines represent other examples. Mexican Americans, in areas such as southern California and Texas, can also reasonably claim that their treatment and history reflects that of a dominated culture. Of all the groups that fit this category, however, Blacks, or African Americans, represent the largest single group of any dominated culture in U.S. society.

■ AFRICAN AMERICANS: A DOMINATED CULTURE

INTASC Standards

Principle #3

In 1619 a ship brought twenty Africans to Jamestown, Virginia, to be sold. They were the first slaves introduced to the mainland of British North America. Their arrival in this country set in motion a series of events, the consequences of which are still being felt to this day.

Slavery flourished in the United States because of the desire for cheap labor. European settlers could commercially develop the North American continent only if they had an adequate work force. As the colonies expanded, so too did the importation of slaves. By the middle of the seventeenth century, ten thousand slaves were being transported from Africa to North America each year; by the eighteenth century, at the peak of the slave trade, sixty thousand slaves were entering the United States each year. When the importation of slaves was finally outlawed in the 1820s, over ten million Africans had been brought to North America (Sowell 1981, 185).

The great Black historian and sociologist W. E. B. DuBois once commented that U.S. history could best be understood by studying the status and treatment of black people (Council on Interracial Books for Children 1977, 15). Certainly many of the most important and dramatic

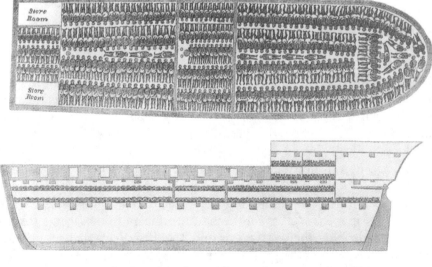

FIGURE 10.3 ■ The interior of an eighteenth-century slave ship.

Source: Courtesy of the Library of Congress.

moments of U.S. history are rooted in the African American experience. The Civil War and the civil rights movement of the 1950s and 1960s are obvious examples.

❓ WHAT DO YOU THINK?
Naming a People

Just as using the term *Indian* to describe people of Native American descent, the use of different terms to describe African Americans is a highly charged issue and reflects changes in values across different historical periods. Throughout much of the nineteenth and early twentieth century, the words *colored* and *Negro* were used to describe African Americans. By the 1960s the term *Black* came into widespread use. More recently the term African American has become widely accepted. Does the use of these different terms mean that much? Do the terms mean different things to different people? What do you think?

Except for the free Blacks who came to America as sailors, explorers, and soldiers during the Spanish and Portuguese conquest of the New World, most Blacks came to this hemisphere unwillingly. Forced to adopt an alien culture, they often lived under inhumane conditions. Racial prejudice, **miseducation,** and the lack of equal opportunity have dominated the experience of Black Americans. Perhaps more than any other ethnic or social group in the United States, African Americans have been shaped by their history.

> Black Americans are among the oldest Americans, and their cultural heritage is one formed almost exclusively on Black soil. In another sense, blacks are among the newer Americans—entering the larger society as a free people with an independent existence of their own only in 1863, with the abolition of slavery. (Sowell 1981, 183)

Even with emancipation, equality has been realized by many African Americans only within the last few decades and only as a result of the enforcement of federal legislation. Residual prejudices rooted in values and traditions going back to our earliest history still need to be overcome.

If the political and social experience of African Americans has been characterized by prejudice and the lack of equal opportunity, their educational experience has reflected the same prejudice and lack of opportunity.

miseducation
Educating people in ways that are contrary to their own best interests.

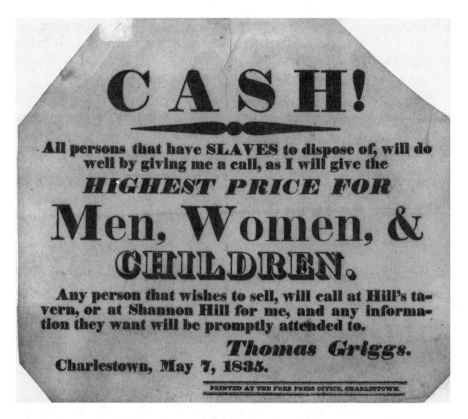

FIGURE 10.4 ■ A broadside offering cash for slaves.

Source: Courtesy of the Library of Congress.

Until recently, the mainstream culture has consistently denied them adequate schooling. North and South, African Americans have had to fight for equal education in nonsegregated settings. Their struggle has been difficult, and despite significant advances—particularly in the past fifty years—an ongoing one.

■ AFRICAN AMERICANS AND U.S. EDUCATION

Colonial Americans had little interest in educating Blacks. In a slave society, these Africans were merely tools for the benefit of their owners. Formal education for them was rare; slaves were taught only what would help them in their work (usually agricultural skills).

Because they lacked formal education, informal education was probably even more important to the slaves than is normally the case. An important oral tradition closely linked to African customs and folkways developed. So powerful was this oral tradition that two hundred fifty years after his great-great-grandfather Kunte Kinte was brought as a slave from Gabon to the New World, novelist Alex Haley could trace his family history through stories passed down as an oral history from generations born and raised in slavery to later free generations. Haley's *Roots* continues a tradition of storytelling that represents a basic way of transmitting cultural knowledge.

Essentially, compulsory ignorance was the policy established for African children under slavery. As early as 1740 South Carolina adopted the first laws prohibiting the teaching of reading and writing to slaves. By the first half of the nineteenth century restrictions placed on the education of African Americans became even more widespread. In 1830, Louisiana passed a law that made the teaching of reading to a slave punishable by a year in jail (Miller 1982, 212). Slave uprisings, such as the 1831 Nat Turner Rebellion in West Virginia, precipitated even harsher legislation to prohibit the education of African Americans. By the time of the Civil War, not one southern state allowed African Americans to be instructed in either reading or writing. Enforced ignorance provided an important means of controlling slave populations. Slaves were kept "ignorant, dependent, and in fear" (Sowell 1981, 187).

Slave Narrative: Frederick Douglass (1817?–1895)

Frederick Douglass was the most famous escaped slave prior to the Civil War. His autobiography, *Narrative of the Life of Frederick Douglass,* was first published in 1845. Subsequent autobiographies written by him were published in 1855 and 1881. The following excerpts are taken from the first chapter of an 1845 edition published in Boston, Massachusetts. Even in this brief selection, he has clearly communicated the extraordinary violence of slavery—not only for slaves, but also for masters.

> I WAS born in Tuckahoe, near Hillsborough, and about twelve miles from Easton, in Talbot county, Maryland. I have no accurate knowledge of my age, never having seen any authentic record containing it. By far the larger part of the slaves know as little of their ages as horses know of theirs, and it is the wish of most masters within my knowledge to keep their slaves thus ignorant. I do not remember to have ever met a slave who could tell of his birthday. They seldom come nearer to it than planting-time, harvest-time, cherry-time, spring-time, or fall-time. A want of information concerning my own was a source of unhappiness to me even during

childhood. The white children could tell their ages. I could not tell why I ought to be deprived of the same privilege. I was not allowed to make any inquiries of my master concerning it. He deemed all such inquiries on the part of a slave improper and impertinent, and evidence of a restless spirit. The nearest estimate I can give makes me now between twenty-seven and twenty-eight years of age. I come to this, from hearing my master say, some time during 1835, I was about seventeen years old.

My mother was named Harriet Bailey. She was the daughter of Isaac and Betsey Bailey, both colored, and quite dark. My mother was of a darker complexion than either my grandmother or grandfather.

My father was a white man. He was admitted to be such by all I ever heard speak of my parentage. The opinion was also whispered that my master was my father; but of the correctness of this opinion, I know nothing; the means of knowing was withheld from me. My mother and I were separated when I was but an infant—before I knew her as my mother. It is a common custom, in the part of Maryland from which I ran away, to part children from their mothers at a very early age. Frequently, before the child has reached its twelfth month, its mother is taken from it, and hired out on some farm a considerable distance off, and the child is placed under the care of an old woman, too old for field labor. For what this separation is done, I do not know, unless it be to hinder the development of the child's affection toward its mother, and to blunt and destroy the natural affection of the mother for the child. This is the inevitable result.

I never saw my mother, to know her as such, more than four or five times in my life; and each of these times was very short in duration, and at night. She was hired by a Mr. Stewart, who lived about twelve miles from my home. She made her journeys to see me in the night, traveling the whole distance on foot, after the performance of her day's work. She was a field hand, and a whipping is the penalty of not being in the field at sunrise, unless a slave has special permission from his or her master to the contrary—a permission which they seldom get, and one that gives to him that gives it the proud name of being a kind master. I do not recollect of ever seeing my mother by the light of day. She was with me in the night. She would lie down with me, and get me to sleep, but long before I waked she was gone. Very little communication ever took place between us. Death soon ended what little we could have while she lived, and with it her hardships and suffering. She died when I was about seven years old, on one of my master's farms, near Lee's Mill. I was not allowed to be present during her illness, at her death, or burial. She was gone long before I knew any thing about it. Never having enjoyed, to any considerable extent, her soothing presence, her tender and watchful care, I received the tidings of her death with much the same emotions I should have probably felt at the death of a stranger.

Called thus suddenly away, she left me without the slightest intimation of who my father was. The whisper that my master was my father, may or may not be true; and, true or false, it is of but little consequence to my purpose whilst the fact remains, in all its glaring odiousness, that slaveholders have ordained, and by law established, that the children of slave women shall in all cases follow the condition of their mothers; and this is done too obviously to administer to their own lusts, and make a gratification of their wicked desires profitable as well as pleasurable; for by this cunning arrangement, the slaveholder, in cases not a few, sustains to his slaves the double relation of master and father.

I know of such cases; and it is worthy of remark that such slaves invariably suffer greater hardships, and have more to contend with, than others. They are, in the first place, a constant offence to their mistress. She is ever disposed to find fault with them; they can seldom do any thing to please her; she is never better pleased than when she sees them under the lash, especially when she suspects her husband of showing to his mulatto children favors which he withholds from his black slaves. The master is frequently compelled to sell this class of his slaves, out of deference to the feelings of his white wife; and, cruel as the deed may strike any one to be, for a man to sell his own children to human flesh-mongers, it is often the dictate of humanity for him to do so; for, unless he does this, he must not only whip them himself, but must stand by and see one white son tie up his brother, of but few shades darker complexion than himself, and ply the gory lash to his naked back; and if he lisp one word of disapproval, it is set down to his parental partiality, and only makes a bad matter worse, both for himself and the slave whom he would protect and defend.

Every year brings with it multitudes of this class of slaves. It was doubtless in consequence of a knowledge of this fact, that one great statesman of the south predicted the downfall of slavery by the inevitable laws of population. Whether this prophecy is ever fulfilled, or not, it is nevertheless plain that a very different-looking class of people are springing up at the south, and are now held in slavery, from those originally brought to this country from Africa; and if their increase will do no other good, it will do away the force of the argument, that God cursed Ham, and therefore American slavery is right. If the lineal descendants of Ham are alone to be scripturally enslaved, it is certain that slavery at the south must soon become unscriptural; for thousands are ushered into the world, annually, who, like myself, owe their existence to white fathers, and those fathers most frequently their own masters.

I have had two masters. My first master's name was Anthony. I do not remember his first name. He was generally called Captain Anthony—a title which, I presume, he acquired by sailing a craft on the Chesapeake Bay. He was not considered a rich slaveholder. He owned two or three farms, and about thirty slaves. His farms and slaves were under the care of an overseer. The overseer's name was Plummer. Mr. Plummer was a miserable drunkard, a profane swearer, and a savage monster. He always went armed with a cowskin and a heavy cudgel. I have known him to cut and slash the women's heads so horribly, that even master would be enraged at his cruelty, and would threaten to whip him if he did not mind himself. Master, however, was not a humane slaveholder. It required extraordinary barbarity on the part of an overseer to affect him. He was a cruel man, hardened by a long life of slaveholding. He would at times seem to take great pleasure in whipping a slave. I have often been awakened at the dawn of day by the most heart-rending shrieks of an own aunt of mine, whom he used to tie up to a joist, and whip upon her naked back till she was literally covered with blood. No words, no tears, no prayers, from his gory victim, seemed to move his iron heart from its bloody purpose. The louder she screamed, the harder he whipped; and where the blood ran fastest, there he whipped longest. He would whip her to make her scream, and whip her to make her hush; and not until overcome by fatigue, would he cease to swing the blood-clotted cowskin. I remember the first time I ever witnessed this horrible exhibition. I was quite a child, but I well remember it. I never shall forget it whilst I remember any thing. It was the first of a long series of such outrages, of which I was doomed to be a witness and a participant. It struck me with awful force. It was the blood-stained gate, the entrance to the hell of slavery, through which I was about to pass. It was a most terrible spectacle. I wish I could commit to paper the feelings with which I beheld it.

This occurrence took place very soon after I went to live with my old master, and under the following circumstances. Aunt Hester went out one night,—where or for what I do not know,—and happened to be absent when my master desired her presence. He had ordered her not to go out evenings, and warned her that she must never let him catch her in company with a young man, who was paying attention to her, belonging to Colonel Lloyd. The young man's name was Ned Roberts, generally called Lloyd's Ned. Why master was so careful of her, may be safely left to conjecture. She was a woman of noble form, and of graceful proportions, having very few equals, and fewer superiors, in personal appearance, among the colored or white women of our neighborhood. Aunt Hester had not only disobeyed his orders in going out, but had been found in company with Lloyd's Ned; which circumstance, I found, from what he said while whipping her, was the chief offence. Had he been a man of pure morals himself, he might have been thought interested in protecting the innocence of my aunt; but those who knew him will not suspect him of any such virtue. Before he commenced whipping Aunt Hester, he took her into the kitchen, and stripped her from neck to waist, leaving her neck, shoulders, and back, entirely naked. He then told her to cross her hands, calling her at the same time a d—d b—h. After crossing her hands, he tied them with a strong rope, and led her to a stool under a large hook in the joist, put in for the purpose. He made her get upon the stool, and tied her hands to the hook. She now stood fair for his infernal purpose. Her arms were stretched up at their full length, so that she stood upon the ends of her toes. He then said to her, "Now, you d—d b—h, I'll learn you how to disobey my orders!" and after rolling up his sleeves, be commenced to lay on the heavy cowskin, and soon the warm, red blood (amid heart-rending shrieks from her, and horrid oaths from him) came dripping to the floor. I was so terrified and horror-stricken at the sight, that I hid myself in a closet, and dared not venture out till long after the bloody transaction was over. I expected it would be my turn next. It was all new to me. I had never seen any thing like it before. I had always lived with my grandmother on the outskirts of the plantation, where she was put to raise the children of the younger women. I had therefore been, until now, out of the way of the bloody scenes that often occurred on the plantation.

When public education was provided to African Americans, it was almost always segregated—a practice that continued in both the North and the South, even after the Civil War. Although guaranteed equal rights as citizens under the Fourteenth Amendment (1867), African

Americans were nonetheless consistently thwarted by the educational system. Court cases challenging the legality of compulsory segregation were pursued unsuccessfully during the decades following the Civil War. *Plessy v. Ferguson* (1896), among the most important cases, ruled that separate but equal facilities were constitutional; African Americans could be sent to segregated schools as long as those schools were provided essentially the same level of public support as white schools. Three years later, in the case of *Cummings v. Richmond County Board of Education* (1899), the Court went even further in restricting the educational rights of African Americans by declaring that a Georgia school board could close down an African American high school while it continued to run a white segregated school (Miller 1982, 213).

Unable to obtain equal access to education, African Americans frequently established their own schools at all levels. In the North, where about two hundred fifty thousand free African Americans lived just prior to the Civil War, their children had limited access to public education. African Americans frequently established their own elementary schools. During the Civil War, schools were established for freedmen throughout

FIGURE 10.5 ■ Primary school for freedmen in the charge of Mrs. Green at Vicksburg, Mississippi.

Source: Harper's Weekly, June 23, 1866. Courtesy of the Library of Congress.

the South. As the Union armies advanced, teachers from the North arrived to educate African American children and adults. The federal Freedman's Bureau was set up in 1865 to provide relocation, health, and educational services to recently freed slaves. By 1869 six hundred thousand African Americans had attended schools under the direction of the Freedman's Bureau.

Black colleges and universities were also established in the decades following the Civil War. Fisk University was founded in 1865 in Nashville, Tennessee; Talladega College in Alabama was founded the same year. Essentially, early African American colleges and universities provided an expanded secondary-level curriculum because many of their students had had only limited previous instruction.

Despite a great deal of promise in the period immediately following the Civil War, African Americans were increasingly denied access to equal educational opportunities. Discriminatory laws and Black Codes (which defined African Americans as legally subordinate to whites) were enacted throughout the South as early as 1865 (Mendes 1999, 249). The fact that in 1900 half of all African Americans remained illiterate confirms the limited access they had to education. Educational discrimination was widespread. In 1912, for example, expenditures per African American students in the South were one-third the amount spent on white students. African American classes were consistently larger than white classes, and African American teachers were consistently less well trained than their white counterparts (Sowell 1981, 214).

■ OPPOSING MODELS OF AFRICAN AMERICAN EDUCATION: BOOKER T. WASHINGTON AND W. E. B. DuBOIS

accommodation
A policy involving one cultural group accommodating itself to the dominant groups.

The most important debate to emerge from the late nineteenth century about African American education and culture took place between Booker T. Washington and W. E. B. DuBois. Washington (a former slave) was the founder of the Tuskegee Institute in Tuskegee, Alabama. Established in 1881 with the help of northern philanthropists, Tuskegee was an industrial school in the heart of rural Alabama. Under Washington's leadership the school rose rapidly from obscurity to national recognition. A gifted fundraiser and politician, Washington supported a policy of **accommodation**. In his famous address before the Cotton Exposition of 1895, he rejected the idea of social equality between African Americans and whites and instead called for accommodation.

Washington proposed a social system in which African Americans would be "as separate as the fingers" from the white population but, like the fingers on a hand, inevitably linked. Washington's system relegated African Americans to a second-rate citizenship that deferred to white society. Washington's position, although widely accepted by the dominant white population, was increasingly rejected by the African American community. The most prominent figure to oppose Washington was the gifted historian and sociologist W. E. B. DuBois.

W. E. B. DuBois was born in 1868 in Great Barrington, Massachusetts. After completing an undergraduate degree at Fisk University in Nashville, Tennessee, he took a second undergraduate degree at Harvard. Going on to graduate studies at the University of Berlin and Harvard, he became the first African American Ph.D. to graduate from Harvard in 1895. DuBois, who eventually became an important leader in the National Association for Colored People (NAACP), and the leading African American intellectual of the first half of the twentieth century, publicly broke with Washington in his 1903 book *The Souls of Black Folks.*

DuBois had initially been guardedly positive about Washington's Atlanta Exposition Speech. But he attacked its assumptions in the *Souls of Black Folks* in a chapter entitled "Of Mr. Booker T. Washington and Others." According to DuBois, Washington's "compromise" threatened the political power of African Americans, their civil rights, and the possibility of higher education and its benefits. Referring to Washington, DuBois argued:

1. He [Washington] is striving nobly to make Negroes artisans, businessmen and property owners, but it is utterly impossible under modern competitive methods, for workingmen and property owners to defend their rights and exist without the right of suffrage.
2. He insists on thrift and self-respect, but at the same time counsels a silent submission to civic inferiority such as is bound to sap the manhood of any race in the long run.
3. He advocates common-school and industrial training and depreciates higher institutions of learning, but neither could common schools, nor Tuskegee itself remain open a day if not for teachers trained in Negro colleges, or trained by their graduates. (DuBois 1986, 399)

In subsequent writings, DuBois argued that what was needed was the training of a "talented tenth" of the African American population to

Victorian
Referring to the moral standards, attitudes, or conduct of the reign of the English Queen Victoria (1837–1901)—especially the notion of being conservative or stuffy.

serve in positions of leadership in education, the ministry, politics, and business. According to DuBois:

> The Negro Race, like all races, is going to be saved by its exceptional men. The problem of education, then among Negroes must first of all deal with the Talented Tenth; it is the problem of developing the Best of this race that they may guide the Mass away from the contamination and death of the Worst in their own and other races. (DuBois 1986, 843)

Although DuBois's position was essentially elitist, it recognized the need to develop an educated leadership class among the African American population in the United States.

Critics such as Cornel West have argued that DuBois's model of the Talented Tenth represents the **Victorian** belief that a cultural elite "are worthy of leadership because they are educated and trained, refined and civilized, disciplined and determined. Most important, they have 'honesty of heart' and 'Purity of motive' (West 1999, 1970). Although admirable, Cornell argues that such an interpretation can also be seen as somewhat naïve. Education does not necessarily guarantee that people will either be good or virtuous. Highly educated people can also be self-serving and discriminatory.

What DuBois's approach fails to take into account is the concept of social and economic class. In other countries, models of discrimination based on social and economic standing are more common than in the United States. The United States likes to view itself as a classless society—an idea many people would argue does not fit reality. DuBois eventually adopted a socialist philosophy when he became a communist toward the end of his life, and exiled himself to Ghana. It can be argued that an essentially elitist model was the foundation of his educational approach.

Timeline of African American History

1493	Columbus brings the first African slaves to the New World.
1619	Dutch ship brings twenty Africans to Jamestown, Virginia.
1641	Massachusetts passes the first law in the English colonies recognizing slavery.
1665	New York legally recognizes slavery.
1723	Due to the increase in slave revolts, Virginia passes laws forbidding free Africans to bear arms.
1770	Crispus Attucks, a free African man, is killed in the Boston Massacre.

1772   Slavery is abolished in England.

1773   Phillis Wheatley publishes *Poems on Various Subjects, Religious and Moral,* the first book published by an African American woman in North America.

1774   Connecticut bans the importation and sale of slaves but allows them to be owned.

1777   Vermont becomes the first state to abolish slavery.

1790   757,208 African Americans live in the United States, which represents 19.3 percent of the U.S. population. Of these, 59,527 are free and 697,681 are slaves.

1793   Eli Whitney invents the cotton gin, which makes cotton cultivation easier and encourages the use of slave labor in the South.

1817   New York passes a law to abolish slavery within the next decade.

1822   Denmark Vesey's plan for revolt, involving nine thousand slaves in Charleston, South Carolina, fails.

1831   Nat Turner leads a major rebellion in Virginia.

1839   Joseph Cinque leads a revolt of slaves aboard a Spanish ship, the *Amistad.* In an 1841 Supreme Court decision, Cinque and his companions are freed.

1857   In the Dred Scott case, the U.S. Supreme Court rules that residence in a free state does not confer freedom on a slave.

1859   John Brown leads a raid against the federal arsenal in Harpers Ferry, West Virginia.

1863   The Emancipation Proclamation is issued on January 1, freeing all slaves in the Confederacy.

1878   Two hundred six African American emigrants set sail aboard the *Azor* from Charleston, South Carolina, for Liberia.

1881   Booker T. Washington founds the Tuskegee Institute in Alabama.

1895   Booker T. Washington delivers his "Atlanta Compromise" speech at the Cotton Exposition in Atlanta, Georgia.

1896   In *Plessy v. Ferguson* the U.S. Supreme Court rules that segregated, or "separate but equal," facilities are constitutional.

1900   According to the census, 8,833,994 African Americans live in the United States, representing 11.6 percent of the total U.S. population.

1903   W. E. B. DuBois publishes *The Souls of Black Folk.*

1905   W. E. B. DuBois helps launch the Niagara Movement, which demands equal rights for African Americans and challenges the more conservative approaches of thinkers such as Booker T. Washington.

1909   A group of African American and white activists, including W. E. B. DuBois and Mary White Ovington, found the National Association for the Advancement of Colored People (NAACP).

1936   Jesse Owens wins four gold medals in track and field at the Berlin Olympics.

1940   The first sit-in at a segregated restaurant is conducted by the Congress of Racial Equality (CORE) in Chicago.

1947	Jackie Robinson becomes the first African American major league baseball player.
1954	In *Brown v. Board of Education of Topeka, Kansas,* the U.S. Supreme Court rules unanimously against school segregation, deciding that "in the field of public education the doctrine of 'separate but equal' has no place."
1955	Rosa Parks triggers the Montgomery, Alabama, bus boycott by refusing to give up her seat to a white person.
1957	In Little Rock, Arkansas, U.S. soldiers escort nine African American students to school after the Arkansas National Guard has been called to keep them out.
1960	The Civil Rights Act of 1960 is passed. The bill provides for the protection of voting rights by authorizing judges to appoint referees who can help African Americans register to vote.
1963	The March on Washington draws 250,000 people to the Lincoln Memorial to lobby Congress for the passage of a civil rights bill. Martin Luther King Jr. delivers his "I Have a Dream" speech.
1964	The Civil Rights Act of 1964 prohibits discrimination in public accommodations and employment.
1965	Martin Luther King Jr. leads his freedom march from Selma to Montgomery, Alabama.
1968	Martin Luther King Jr. is assassinated.
1970	According to the census, 22,580,289 African Americans live in the United States, or 11.1 percent of the total U.S. population.
1984	The Reverend Jesse Jackson runs for president.
1993	Toni Morrison wins the Nobel Prize for Literature. (Facts on File 1999; Earle 2000, 132–135)

■ THE MOVEMENT FOR CIVIL RIGHTS

black codes
Laws restricting the rights of African Americans following the Civil War (1861–1865) in the United States.

slave codes
Laws that restricted the rights of slaves during the antebellum period (pre-1861) in the United States.

Following the Civil War and the emancipation, southern African Americans were given voting rights and, supposedly, equality under the law. In 1866, for example, Congress passed the Fourteenth Amendment granting citizenship to African Americans. In 1869, the Fifteenth Amendment was passed, giving African American men the right to vote. Yet the acquisition of greater freedoms was quickly challenged, particularly in the South, through a reign of segregation, violence, and legal manipulation.

Black codes (laws) restricting the rights of newly freed African American populations were put into place throughout the South. These laws, which were basically a continuation of earlier **slave codes,** made it illegal to marry across racial lines, made voting dependent on property ownership, eliminated African Americans from serving on juries, and so on (Mendes 1999, 248–249). According to W. E. B. DuBois, "the slave went free; stood a brief moment in the sun; then moved back again towards slavery" (quoted by Earle 2000, 94).

By the time of the First World War, a wide range of groups were founded by both African Americans and whites to improve the condition of the African American people. Organizations such as the National Association of Colored People (NAACP), the National Urban League (NUL), and the United Negro Improvement Association (UNIA) began to fight for greater political equality on the legal front. Although the struggle for African American civil rights was fought on many levels by many people throughout the 1960s and 1970s, and continues today, the key court case that brought an end to legal segregation in the United States was the 1954 *Brown v. Topeka* decision.

FIGURE 10.6 ■ At the bus station, Durham, North Carolina, May 1940.

Source: Photograph by Jack Delano. Courtesy of the Library of Congress.

■ *BROWN V. BOARD OF EDUCATION OF TOPEKA*

Despite discrimination and segregation, African Americans made advances in education throughout the first half of the twentieth century. Nonetheless, significant disparities in education between the African American and white populations existed. In 1930, the average African American had six years of schooling; the average white, ten years (Sowell 1981, 214). By the beginning of the Second World War about one-eighth of the African American population in the United States remained illiterate.

The watershed for the modern era came with the 1954 Supreme Court decision on *Brown v. Board of Education of Topeka*. In *Brown v. Board of Education* the Supreme Court concluded that segregated schools effectively generated in African American children "a feeling of inferiority as to their status in the community that may affect their hearts and minds in a way unlikely ever to be undone." According to the Court, separate educational facilities, which had been justified under the 1896 case *Plessy v. Ferguson*, were argued to be inherently unequal; such facilities were essentially seen as depriving black children equal protection under the law.

Desegregation was immediately called for throughout the South. But despite efforts to achieve racial equality in the schools, segregation continued. Eventually the courts drew distinctions between *de jure* and *de facto* segregation. *De jure* segregation promoted the segregation of the races through consciously undertaken laws, policies, and practices. *De facto* segregation was unofficial and more impersonal; no overt action, but rather community settlement patterns segregated the schools. The concentration of African Americans or whites in specific neighborhoods led in turn to segregated neighborhood schools.

? WHAT DO YOU THINK?
Should We Be Ashamed of George Washington?

History, and in turn the curriculum we teach in the schools, is constantly revised by historians and educators. Values and customs change; we learn more about a certain historical figure or incident from our past; and new groups are empowered. Thus, our history has to be rewritten. An example of this can be seen in a recent incident involving the naming of public schools in New Orleans.

In 1992 the New Orleans School Board made the decision that it would rename any school that was named for "former slave owners or others who did not respect equal opportunity for all." In keeping with this policy, in October of 1997 the school board renamed George Washington Elementary to Dr. Charles Drew Elementary.

Dr. Charles Drew was a pioneering African American surgeon who made a number of important discoveries about blood plasma during the Second World War. He is a noteworthy figure and certainly deserves recognition for his accomplishments. But should he take the place of a major U.S. historical figure such as George Washington? Washington was a Virginia aristocrat. He reflected the values of his era. Slavery was legal and widespread in the society in which he lived. Although he owned slaves throughout his life, he freed them when he died.

Washington was also one of the greatest U.S. leaders. He led the Continental Army throughout the Revolutionary War and was our first president. Is it fair to judge Washington and others like him by today's standards? Should the New Orleans School Board change its policy? What do you think?

■ DESEGREGATING LITTLE ROCK'S CENTRAL HIGH SCHOOL

The 1954 *Brown v. Board of Education* decision provided legal justification for dismantling segregated schools. Eliminating segregated programs and transforming racial attitudes throughout the nation became a necessity. It was a difficult process, however, because it meant overcoming deeply rooted traditions of prejudice (Ravitch 1983, 114). For the first time in the nation's history, the law called for genuine equality in U.S. schools.

Implementing the principles defined by the *Brown* decision was not easy. In a May 31, 1955, decision known as *Brown II*, the Court left desegregation to local school authorities under the direction of federal district judges. However, students were to be admitted to the public schools on a nondiscriminatory basis "with all deliberate speed." Resistance to desegregation developed throughout the South; it soon became clear that the federal government would have to intervene locally if desegregation was to be effected. The federal government's authority to do so was tested in Little Rock, Arkansas, in 1957.

INTASC Standards
Principle #9

The local school board in Little Rock had proposed a plan to desegregate the schools beginning in September 1957, with the admission of nine African American students to the city's main high school. African American students would gradually be added to the school's enrollment in succeeding years. Local African American leaders objected that the plan was inadequate, and the district federal court upheld their position. Local whites challenged the court's opinion and threatened violence.

KEY SUPREME COURT CASES

Civil Rights Cases Affecting Segregation

1896 *Plessy v. Ferguson*

This decision upheld an 1890 Louisiana law requiring "separate but equal" facilities on railroads. The case provided the basis for racial segregation in public schools and housing.

1908 *Berea College v. Kentucky*

This case upholds a state law prohibiting integrated classes at Berea College, which historically had a tradition of mixed-race education.

1948 *Sipuel v. Board of Regents of the University of Oklahoma*

The state of Oklahoma is required by the Court to provide a legal education to an African American student denied entry to its all-white law school.

1954 *Brown v. Board of Education of Topeka*

The Court concludes that segregating elementary and secondary students by race is unconstitutional, overturning the Court's 1896 decision of *Plessy v. Ferguson.*

1955 *Brown v. Board of Education of Topeka*

This Court ruling further builds on the 1954 *Brown* decision emphasizing that desegregation of the schools be undertaken with "all deliberate speed."

1971 *Swann v. Charlotte-Mecklenberg Board of Education*

This ruling authorizes mandatory busing to enforce desgregation of the schools.

At this point the governor of Arkansas, Orval Faubus, sent Arkansas National Guard troops to Central High School in Little Rock to prevent the African American students from entering. Supposedly, his goal was to maintain and restore order, although there had been no violence until that time, only threats. Federal District Judge Ronald Davies ordered the school board to proceed with the desegregation plan. On September 4, 1957, African American students attempted to enter the school but were turned back by the National Guard (Ravitch 1983, 136). The governor acted in opposition to the Court, the school board, and the mayor of Little Rock as well. After meeting with President Eisenhower, however, he pledged to accept the Court's decision.

Little Rock became a center for southern opposition to forced deseg-regation. On September 23, 1957, a riot involving nearly one thousand protestors broke out at the high school. African American students were sent home in police cars and President Eisenhower demanded that those blocking the implementation of the court order cease their actions im-mediately. On the following day, as commander in chief of the military, Eisenhower federalized the Arkansas National Guard and sent troops of the 101st Airborne Division into Little Rock to enforce the court's order.

The National Guard successfully helped desegregate the school and restore order. In November 1957 regular troops withdrew from Little Rock; the federalized Arkansas National Guard remained until the end of the school year. In the middle of the school year the Little Rock school board sought to have the implementation of the desegregation plan de-layed because of the disruptions, but the Court refused the board's re-quest (Ravitch 1983, 138). Little Rock represented the first real test of the desegregation laws. Other challenges were made in succeeding years throughout the South, but the process of social change had begun.

In a certain sense, the numerous court cases, protests, and laws of the 1960s were a logical extension of the social and legal revolution set in motion by the 1954 *Brown v. Board of Education* decision. Title IV of the 1964 Civil Rights Act, for example, empowered the attorney general of the United States to initiate suits leading to the desegregation of schools across the country. For the first time, schools in the North as well as the South were affected. As might be expected, cases brought against northern school districts maintained that a system of *de facto* segrega-tion was in effect in many schools.

? WHAT DO YOU THINK?

Reverse Discrimination

Title VI of the Civil Rights Act prohibits discrimination and setting quotas in any pro-gram receiving federal financial assistance. The equal protection clause in the Four-teenth Amendment declares that no state may "deprive any person of life, liberty, or property, without due process of law; nor deny to any person within its jurisdic-tion the equal protection of the laws."

The Fourteenth Amendment and laws like Title VI have often been used most to defend the rights of minorities. In the early 1970s, however, a number of cases before the Supreme Court applied these laws to whites who felt they were being denied their rights as part of a process of reverse discrimination. In the cases of *De-Funis v. Odegard* (1974) and the *University of California Regents v. Bakke* (1978), white students claimed they faced discrimination because they were not admitted into graduate law and medical school programs while less qualified African American candidates were.

The Supreme Court found the DeFunis case moot because DeFunis was admitted to law school as his case went to trial. In the Bakke case a 5–4 decision by the Court struck down the system of racial quotas established by the medical school at the University of California at Davis. In its decision the Court was explicit in maintaining it was not always opposed to racial quotas, but in this case the civil rights of the plaintiff Alan Bakke had been violated. The split decision of the Court and its argument that quotas can still be employed in some cases suggests that presently no clear policy addresses reverse discrimination. What are the arguments for both sides? Are quotas fair? What do you think?

■ BUSING

Many plans were proposed to bring about racial equality throughout the country. Among the most controversial was busing. Busing children to school to achieve greater racial equality has been used since the early 1970s. In *Swann v. Charlotte-Mecklenburg Board of Education* (1971) the Court concluded that although the schools in the Charlotte-Mecklenburg school district in North Carolina had been technically integrated after the *Brown* decision, concentrations of African Americans and whites in particular neighborhoods of the school district had led to *de facto* segregation in the schools.

In the *Swann* decision the Court pointed out that schools had the obligation to prepare children to become members of a pluralistic culture. The schools were expected to reflect the populations of the districts in which they were located, not just the neighborhoods. Although the Court agreed that neighborhood schools were probably desirable under normal circumstances, the inequality that had characterized the history of U.S. schooling was not normal. The argument concluded that busing children throughout a school district to bring about true desegregation was indeed a worthwhile inconvenience. Because bus transportation had been an integral part of the public educational system for years, there was no reason why it could not be used as a tool of public policy (Ozmon and Craver 1972, 11–12).

Another Supreme Court case, *Keyes v. Denver School District No. 1* (1973), applied the same arguments for desegregation to Denver as had been applied to Charlotte-Mecklenburg. Busing was no longer simply a regional concern in the South—it had become a national issue. Busing faced strong opposition from the public. A Harris survey in 1972 showed that 73 percent of the public opposed busing to achieve racial balance. At the time of the survey, 3 percent of the students in the country were being bused to school as a result of court orders whereas 42 percent were being bused for other reasons (Mills 1979, 1).

In 1975 Congress passed a bill forbidding the Department of Health, Education, and Welfare to order school districts to bus children beyond their neighborhoods. Sentiment among both African Americans and whites had become even stronger against busing as a means to achieve desegregation. A 1977 survey made by the National Opinion Research Center reported that 85.3 percent of African Americans opposed busing. Yet the same survey indicated that 91.4 percent of African Americans and 84.8 percent of whites thought African Americans and whites should go to the same schools (Chambers 1982; 1957).

The social and political issues underlying busing are by no means simple. Whereas busing has helped to integrate schools and to encourage greater equality, it has also forced children to travel from the security of neighborhood settings into new and often alien environments. At best, busing has proved to be an imperfect way to overcome past inequalities and discrimination.

WHAT DO YOU THINK?
Busing in South Boston

By the middle of the 1970s many communities were using busing to desegregate schools. During the summer of 1974 in a case brought by the NAACP, Federal Judge W. Arthur Garrity ruled the nation's oldest school system had to desegregate. In September, 1974, the first buses of African American students began to arrive at traditionally white South Boston High School.

The "Southies," located in a blue-collar Irish neighborhood, opposed the integration of their school with a vehemence that recalled earlier civil rights struggles in Selma, Alabama, and Little Rock, Arkansas. The Massachusetts National Guard, ordered to protect bused students, was attacked by mobs. Racial hatred manifested itself with gangs of African American and white youths beating up innocent people. A white auto mechanic was beaten beyond recognition by a group of African American youths after stopping his car at a stoplight in the African American Roxbury neighborhood.

The anti–busing forces in Boston portrayed themselves as victims. In suburban areas such as Brookline and Newton, busing was not being enforced. The Southies maintained that they were being singled out to deal with busing and integration whereas the schools of their more affluent neighbors were left alone. For the Southies, integration meant students had to be bused across town. Traditions and values had to be changed and ways of looking at the world had to be redefined. To what extent should they have been compelled to face these changes by themselves? To what extent was the obligation to face desegregation an obligation for the entire Boston community? What did the busing in South Boston suggest about the relationship between different economic and power groups? What do you think?

■ COMPENSATORY EDUCATION

Included among the important efforts to achieve greater educational opportunity for African Americans and other groups historically discriminated against, was the implementation of compensatory education programs. In 1965 the Elementary and Secondary Education Act (ESEA) was passed. Under the act $1 billion in Title I funds were assigned to school districts to help disadvantaged children (defined as children whose families lived below the government's poverty level).

Beginning in 1965 a wide range of compensatory education programs (e.g., infant education, early childhood education, basic skills, counseling, and dropout prevention programs) were set up throughout the nation's schools. Probably the best known of these was Head Start, which attempted to provide disadvantaged children with a preschool readiness program to prepare them for the first grade.

Underlying the establishment of compensatory educational programs was the recognition of significantly different patterns of social class and educational achievement in the United States. In general, people from lower socioeconomic backgrounds—backgrounds that were frequently the result of sustained discrimination—did not do well in school settings. Assuming that education provided the key to social and economic advancement, compensatory education programs would provide the means by which the disadvantaged might catch up and advance in the system. A considerable debate has emerged in recent years as to how effective compensatory education has been in closing the gap between the disadvantaged and the privileged in the United States. It has been argued that the public schools are middle-class and upper-class institutions that automatically place the poor at great disadvantage. Early research on compensatory education has suggested that disadvantaged children achieved little sustained gain in these programs.

Historically, U.S. schools have contributed to the perpetuation of racial inequality and discrimination against African Americans. In doing so they have often acted as a means of withholding economic and social advancement. At the same time, the educational system has provided important opportunities. The number of African Americans who finished high school in 1960 was half that of whites. By 1980 the figure had risen to 80 percent. Since 1960 the number of African Americans who have completed college has increased fourfold (Thomas 1983, 4).

? WHAT DO YOU THINK?

"Nappy Hair"

Ruth Sherman was a twenty-seven-year-old, third-grade teacher in Brooklyn, New York, whose students loved for her to read them stories. Their favorite story, "Nappy Hair," was about an African American girl named Brenda who had the "kinkiest, the nappiest, the fuzziest, the most screwed up, squeezed up, knotted up, tangled up, twisted up" hair one could imagine. The African American and Hispanic American children in Miss Sherman's class loved the sound of the story with its musical rhythm. They also liked the fact that the story's main character looked like them. Some of the children liked the story so well that they begged Miss Sherman to photocopy the story so they could take it home.

Then the trouble began. Miss Sherman, who is white, was accused by some parents of putting down her students by reading the story to them. *Nappy*, a term used to describe curly African American hair, is sometimes used as a put-down in African American communities. The book's author, Carolivia Herron, is African American. According to her, "children understand right away that this book is about acceptance and celebration" (Clemetson 1998, 39).

Parents organized a protest and, with media coverage, attacked Sherman with epithets such as "cracker" and threats of "You'd better watch out." Miss Sherman felt sufficiently threatened as a result of the incident that she asked to be reassigned to another school, despite the fact that school administrators asked her to remain.

Had Miss Sherman done anything wrong? Would she have had the same problem if she had been a minority herself? Should she have fought to stay in the school? What do you think?

■ DOMINATED CULTURES AND THE CONCEPT OF PRIVILEGE

As a social group, teachers and those who plan to become teachers, are usually white and middle class. Their orientation is typically more suburban than urban and their cultural references are Eurocentric. As

INTASC Standards
Principle #9

representatives of the culture, or cultural agents, whose job it is to pass on values and beliefs from one generation to another, they tend to be moderately conservative and circumspect in what they do.

If we think about Emile Durkheim's idea that schooling has as its primary purpose the "conservation" of the culture, it should not be surprising that in general teachers accept many of the norms, or status quo, of the culture. These norms, however, carry with them assumptions about the world that may or may not be justified. Historically dominated groups, such as Native and African Americans, have good reason to resent many of the assumptions and values that are taken for granted by the mainstream or dominant culture.

It is essential for any teacher—even if they belong to a historically dominated group—to understand the extent to which dominated groups may resent the assumed privileges of the mainstream culture. For those who are part of the mainstream culture, these privileges are often taken for granted. In the final third of this chapter, I would like to introduce privilege as a social concept.

At the beginning of this book, reference was made to Albert Einstein's notion that fish are the last to notice the water that surrounds them. In a similar fashion, I would argue that how we construct the world is often so taken for granted that we do not even think about it. In the case of Western European culture, for example, we are used to Europe and Western society being the center of things. Maps of the world almost always put Europe in the center. One could argue that this is because the zero degree of longitude is Greenwich, England. But why is this the case? Where zero longitude was set was an arbitrary decision—one that was made as a result of the politics of England and Europe during the Age of Exploration more than four hundred years ago.

Likewise, how maps are drawn, what is included on them, and how they are designed, is often a political and social issue, and not necessarily objective. This is particularly clear in the case of the type of map known as a **Mercator projection**. We all know Mercator projections from the maps that were on the walls in our elementary and secondary schools and from world globes.

Mercator projection
A type of map created during the Renaissance in which the parallels of latitude are drawn with increasing separation as they progress away from the equator.

The first Mercator projection map was created by Gerardus Mercator (1512–1594), the Latin name of the Flemish cartographer, geographer, and mathematician Gerhard Kremer. Mercator projections construct the surface of the earth mathematically. In a Mercator projection the parallels of latitude, which are equal distances apart on a globe, are drawn with increasing separation as the areas are being mapped. This creates its own problems, however, because areas are exaggerated as they get more and more distant from the equator. Thus, the size of

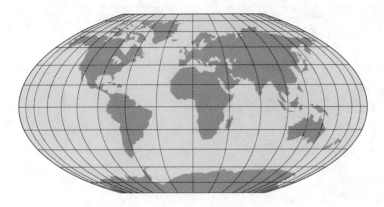

FIGURE 10.7 ■ The world mapped using a Mercator projection.

Greenland and Antarctic are enormously exaggerated in a Mercator projection, although their shape is preserved.

As a result of a Mercator projection, the relative sizes of the world's countries are incorrectly represented. In Figure 10.8, for example, Greenland looks larger than any other country or region. But, in fact, it is the smallest area, measuring only 0.8 million square miles, versus 3.7 million square miles for China, 3.8 million square miles for Europe, and

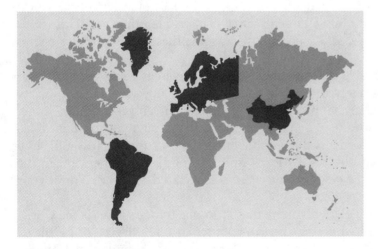

FIGURE 10.8 ■ Apparent sizes of different parts of the world based on a Mercator projection.

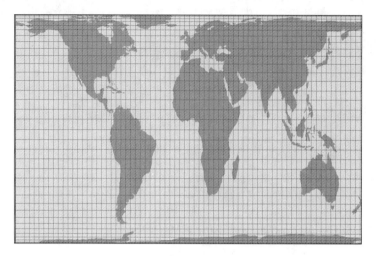

FIGURE 10.9 ■ The Peters equal-area map of the world.

6.9 million square miles for South America. In 1974, the cartographer Arno Peters created an "equal-area" map, which shows the actual relative size of different countries, continents, and oceans of the world. As a result, more accurate comparisons become possible than when using a Mercator projection.

It can be argued that a clear cultural bias is operating when the world is portrayed using a Mercator projection. Obviously we cannot entirely avoid these problems. Maps are useful tools. Instead, we need to know the extent to which they unconsciously influence our view of the world by establishing a **normative practice.** This is also the case with issues such as privilege, and especially what some theorists have described as **white privilege.**

Being white in the United States is perceived as being the norm—or what is often referred to as the mainstream. Being white in U.S. society carries with it special privileges. If you are eighteen years of age, white, male, and wearing baggy pants as you walk through a suburban shopping mall, you are less likely to be hassled by security guards and shop owners than if you are African American or Latino American. In the United States, the degree of privilege is associated with the color of your skin.

Privilege is not an attribute that is unique to one's race. Being Christian in the United States also contributes to one's degree of privilege. Holidays and religious observances are organized around being Catholic or Protestant. Christmas is observed as a holiday, but not **Passover** or **Ramadan.** Christian religious privilege is so taken for granted that even

normative practice
Cultural practices that are considered the norm.

white privilege
The idea that whites and their culture are considered the norm or the mainstream and that being white carries special privileges.

Passover
Jewish holiday commemorating the Hebrews' liberation from slavery in Egypt.

Ramadan
The ninth month of the Islamic year observed as sacred with fasting practiced daily from dawn to sunset.

challenging it is considered absurd by many people: "After all, it's American," or, "that's the way things have always been."

Indeed, this is precisely the point. Privilege associated with dominant groups is simply taken for granted. It is so much a part of the culture that it is not even noticed. When I was in high school in the late 1960s, slightly more than half my classmates were Jewish. Yet no Jewish holidays were celebrated. We had a Christmas assembly every year and sang Christmas carols, but had no Hanukah assembly nor songs. No special recognition was ever given to the Jewish holidays or to the religious beliefs of the majority of my classmates.

What was at work was a type of privilege—what can be defined as **invisible privilege.** Invisible privilege is related to the idea of hegemony. Earlier in this book, I referred to Peter McLaren's definition of hegemony: "the maintenance of domination not by the sheer exercise of force *but primarily through consensual social practices, social forms, and social structures produced in specific sites such as the church, the state, the school, the mass media, the political system and the family*" (McLaren 1998, 177–178). Invisible privilege—whether racial, religious, or gender based—is a mechanism of hegemony and domination in U.S. society. It is part of the power structure in U.S. society and is so powerful and entrenched that it is difficult for people even to recognize it exists. To understand this mechanism, think about an image referred to previously: the water that surrounds a fish is so much a part of its environment that it is difficult even to recognize its presence.

White privilege, and the idea that it is largely invisible, is an essential concept for teachers to understand if they are to work effectively as border crossers. Understanding the concept makes it possible to contextualize what goes on in a particular classroom, school, or community in light of existing power structures and traditions. Also, working with groups who have been historically dominated and deculturized makes understanding their point of view much easier. Of course, doing so may make many people uncomfortable. What happens, for example, when we recognize that white privilege is a reality in our culture? Again, we return to a concept outlined previously in this book: John Fiske's idea of the power bloc.

According to Kincheloe and Steinberg:

The highlighting of the white power bloc enables individuals to see the previously invisible role of whiteness as the norm, the standard by which everyone is measured. Thus, another important moment in this education involves denormalizing whiteness. White ways can no longer be universalized, white communication practices can no longer be viewed

INTASC Standards
Principle #9

invisible privilege
Special privileges afforded a cultural group that are so taken for granted that the privileged group has little or no awareness that they exist.

unproblematically as the standard and issues of race can no longer be relegated to the domain of those who are not White. (Kincheloe and Steinberg 1998, 18)

Kincheloe and Steinberg call for a cultural reassessment of whiteness in U.S. society. They ask educators to become what they term *critical multiculturalists* and to question fundamental assumptions about U.S. culture. They ask them to make "a cultural commitment to rethinking the basis of [a] multicultural society" (Kincheloe and Steinberg 1998, 18).

WHAT DO YOU THINK?

Is There Such a Thing as Whiteness?

What does it mean to be white? Is this a valid question to ask people who plan to teach? According to Ruth Frankenberg:

> Whiteness *does* have content in as much as it generates norms or ways of understanding history, ways of thinking about self and others, and even ways of thinking about culture itself. Thus, whiteness needs to be examined and historicized. We need to look more closely at *the content of the normative* and attempt to analyze both its history and consequences. Whiteness needs to be delimited and "localized." (Frankenburg 1993, 231)

Is whiteness something that can be studied? Do whiteness and the corollary of invisible privilege simply represent the superiority of Western cultural and intellectual traditions, or is it part of the construction of a system of power and influence in Western culture? Can you find examples in your own experience of invisible white privilege? Is the analysis of whiteness threatening? If yes, why? What do you think?

■ SUMMARY

The United States is in many regards a remarkable and admirable country. Perhaps more than any single nation we have championed the ideas of freedom, democracy, and equality. Yet we have done so imperfectly. We are a nation that was founded on the conquest of native or indigenous people. Slavery—almost certainly the most brutal and inhuman treatment possible of another human being—has played a critical role in our historical experience.

The reality is that, although we have accomplished much that is great in this country, we have also consistently assigned privilege and power to groups based on their racial origins, economic power, and geography. Whiteness and white privilege have dominated our culture. As teachers, and as border crossers, it is essential that we understand the experience of dominated cultures. Not to do so is a basic error that diminishes us not only in our work, but also as a culture and a society.

The idea of privilege, and the oppression that often accompanies it in the United States, is not limited to historically dominated cultures such as the ones described in this chapter. In Chapter 12 ("Gender and Education") and Chapter 13 ("The Education of Students with Special Needs"), we continue to explore the idea of privilege and how its assumptions shape our society and our schools.

■ DISCUSSION QUESTIONS ■

1. How are the ideas of a theorist such as Paulo Freire relevant to the experience of dominated culture groups such as Native Americans, African Americans, and others?
2. How has U.S. history been shaped and influenced by slavery and the tradition of racial discrimination?
3. How has education been used to promote racial discrimination?
4. What are the arguments both for and against busing as a means of achieving greater racial equality in our schools?
5. How have U.S. public schools been affected in recent years by the attempts to eliminate racial discrimination in the schools?
6. Does the idea of reverse discrimination have any validity?
7. What are the arguments for and against elite culture, or elite cultural groups?
8. Should racial quotas be used to compensate for discriminatory practices in the past? Can they compensate?
9. Is invisible privilege something you can identify in your own life?

■ SOURCES CITED ■

Berry, Mary Frances. 1997. Ashamed of George Washington? *New York Times,* 29 November, A25.

Brown v. Board of Education of Topeka (I). Supreme Court of the United States, 1954. 347 U.S. 483, 74 S. Ct. 686.

Brown v. Board of Education of Topeka (II). Supreme Court of the United States, 1954. 349 U.S. 294, 75 S.C. 753.

Bullock, Henry Allen. 1970. *A history of the Negro education in the South: From 1619 to the present.* New York: Praeger.

Civil Rights Act of 1968. Public Law 90-284.

Clemetson, Lynette. 1998. Caught in the cross-fire, *Newsweek,* 14 December, 38–39.

Council on Interracial Books for Children. Racism and Sexism Resource Center for Educators. 1977. *Stereotypes, distortions, and omissions in U.S. history textbooks.* New York: Author.

Champagne, Duane, ed. 1994. *The Native American almanac: A reference work on native North Americans in the United States and Canada.* Detroit, Mich.: Gale Research.

Cumming v. Richmond County Board of Education. Supreme Court of the United States, 1899. 175 U.S. 528, 20 S. Ct. 197.

The Elementary and Secondary Education Act of 1965, Public Law 89-100.

Davis, Mary, ed. 1994. *Native America in the twentieth century.* New York: Garland Publishing.

Fellman, David, ed. 1962. *The Supreme Court and education.* New York: Teachers College Press.

Fiske, John. 1994. *Media matters: Everyday culture and political change.* Minneapolis: University of Minnesota Press.

Frankenburg, Ruth. 1993. *The social construction of whiteness: White women, race matters.* Minneapolis: University of Minnesota Press.

Haley, Alex. 1976. *Roots.* New York: Doubleday.

Iverson, Katherine. 1978. Civilization and assimilation in the colonized schooling of Native Americans. In *Education and colonialism,* edited by Philip G. Altbach and Gail P. Kelly, 149–180. New York: Longman.

Jencks, Christopher, ed. 1972. *Inequality: A reassessment of the effect of family and schooling in America.* New York: Basic Books.

Keyes v. Denver School District No. 1. Supreme Court of the United States, 1973. 413 U.S. 189, 93 S. Ct. 2686.

Kincheloe, Joe L., and Shirley R. Steinberg. 2000. Addressing the crisis of whiteness: Reconfiguring white identity in a pedagogy of whiteness. In *White reign: Deploying whiteness in America,* edited by Joe L. Kincheloe, Shirley R. Steinberg, Nelson M. Rodriguez, and Ronald E. Chenault. New York: St. Martin's Griffin.

Lapides, Frederick R., and David Burrows, eds. 1971. *Racism: A casebook.* New York: Thomas Y. Crowell.

———. 1965. The all-white world of children's books. *Saturday Review* 48: 63–85.

McLaren, Peter. 1998. *Life in schools: An introduction to critical pedagogy in the foundations of education.* New York: Longman.

Miller, Lamar P. 1982. Black education. In *Encyclopedia of educational research.* Vol. 3, 211–219. New York: McMillian and the Free Press.

Mills, Nicolaus, ed. 1979. *Busing U.S.A.* New York: Teachers College Press.

Milner, David. 1975. *Children and race.* Baltimore, Md.: Penguin Books.

Mosher, E. K., A. H. Hastings, and J. L. Wagoner. 1979. *Pursuing equal educational opportunity: School policy and the new activists.* Urban Diversity Series, no. 64. New York: ERIC Clearing House for Urban Education.

Myradel, G. 1944. *An American dilemma: The Negro problem and modern democracy.* New York: Harper & Brothers.

Ozmon, Howard, and Sam M. Craver. 1972. *Busing: A moral issue.* Bloomington, Ind.: Phi Delta Kappa Educational Foundation.

Plessy v. Ferguson. Supreme Court of the United States, 1896. 163 U.S. 537, 16 S. Ct. 1138.

Price-Curtis, W. 1981. Black progress toward educational equity. *Educational Leadership* 38: 277–280.

Ravitch, Diane. 1983. *The troubled crusade: American education, 1945–1980.* New York: Basic Books.

Regents of the University of California v. Bakke. Supreme Court of the United States, 1978. 438 U.S. 265, 98 S. Ct. 2733.

Sleeter, Christine E., and Carl A. Grant. 1999. *Making choices for multicultural education: Five approaches to race, class, and gender.* New York: John Wiley & Sons.

Sowell, Thomas. 1981. *Ethnic America.* New York: Basic Books.

Spring, Joel. 2001. *Deculturalization and the struggle for equality.* New York: McGraw-Hill.

Stickney, Benjamin D., and Virginia R. T. Plunkett. 1983. Closing the gap: A historical perspective on the effectiveness of compensatory education. *Phi Delta Kappan* (December) 65.

Swann v. Charlotte-Mecklenburg Board of Education. Supreme Court of the United States, 1971. 402 U.S. 1, 91 S. Ct. 1267.

CHAPTER 11

Gender and Education

The concept of privilege outlined in Chapter 10 does not simply apply to dominated historical groups such as Native Americans and African Americans. This concept can also be applied to gender. In the United States, for example, men have always been afforded special and, what some people would argue, invisible privileges. Likewise, heterosexuality has been the privileged sexual orientation because it is considered the norm.

INTASC Standards

Principle #1

Principle #6

This chapter argues that because gender is such a critical factor, teachers need to understand it better. Returning once again to Henry Giroux's concept of teachers as border crossers, we need to factor in the extent to which gender issues influence and shape what goes on in the classroom. We need to understand that gender, like childhood, is not simply a biological construction, but also a social one. What do we mean when we use the term *gender*? How is gender constructed? What role does gender play in the education of children?

According to Joan Wallach Scott, the word *gender*

> becomes a way of denoting 'cultural constructions'—the entirely social creation of ideas about appropriate roles for women and men. It is a way of referring to exclusively social origins of the subjective identities of men and women. Gender is, in this definition, a social category imposed on a sexed body. (Quoted by deMarrais 2000, 161)

This definition pertains to all people—women, men, heterosexuals, and homosexuals. Our discussion begins with issues involving women and U.S. society and moves on to questions involving women and education, and alternative sexual orientations and schooling.

■ WOMEN AND U.S. SOCIETY

INTASC Standards

Principle #9

Western culture, and specifically U.S. society, has always assigned special privileges to men. Men have been perceived as political and corporate leaders, as the "stronger of the two sexes," and as deserving preferential treatment. Traditionally, women have had a secondary role in U.S. society; they have been expected to define themselves not in terms of personal aspirations and achievements but in relation to their families or their spouses. Until recently most women have been restricted to the home and domestic duties; they have been discouraged from pursuing anything beyond a basic education or from seeking positions of leadership in the work force or political system.

But women have played a much more important role in the labor force than has been recognized. In 1890, for example, they represented 17 percent of all people employed in the United States. By 1970, 38.1 percent of the working population were women (Schmuck 1980, 80). If we look at male versus female employment figures from 1970 to the present, for those sixteen years of age and over, it is clear that women are becoming not only increasingly represented in the U.S. work force, but that their numbers are close to those of men. In 1970, for example, 79.7 percent of all men were employed compared to 43.3 percent of women. In 1980 these figures were 77.4 percent for men and 51.5 percent for women; in 1990, 76.4 percent for men and 57.5 percent for women; in 1998, 74.9 percent for men and 59.8 percent for women. Projections for 2008 estimate 73.1 percent of all men employed versus 61.4 percent of all women. If the trend continues, within a few decades male and female employment in the United States will be equal (*Statistical Abstracts of the United States 1999*, 411).

These figures are all the more remarkable when we take into account that women shoulder significantly greater domestic and childrearing obligations than men. Although attitudes about men and women sharing housekeeping and child-rearing tasks has changed significantly since the late 1960s, women still carry a disproportionate share of these duties. They frequently begin their "second job" at home after they return from their 9-to-5 jobs outside the home.

Historically, the career paths open to women have been limited. Until recently, their careers were usually limited to "feminized occupations" such as teaching and nursing. A majority of working women are part of the pink-collar labor force that provides basic secretarial services to business and government. Only in the past few decades have the traditional careers of women and men begun to be seriously examined and questioned. Deeply rooted in our educational and cultural traditions, stereotypes about male and female roles and jobs pervade our cultural consciousness. Visualize for a moment a nurse, a first-grade teacher, a college president, a doctor, a secretary, an architect, and a scientist. Did you associate these positions with a particular sex? Most people assume that the nurse, the first-grade teacher, and the secretary are women; whereas the college president, the doctor, the architect, and the scientist are men. In reading this chapter, several helpful questions should be kept in mind:

INTASC Standards
Principle #9

1. Have the schools and the educational system played a part in reinforcing gender stereotyping?
2. Have men and women been denied opportunities by the educational system because of their sex? If so, how?
3. What can be done to increase equal opportunity for both men and women?
4. How can schools overcome prejudices within the culture that encourage sexual discrimination?

WHAT DO YOU THINK?

Sexism and Language

Traditional language usage emphasizes male pronouns and nouns to describe both men and women. History books discuss *forefathers* rather than *foremothers,* *mankind* rather than *womankind,* and *brotherhood* rather than *sisterhood.* In the world of work we have *firemen, foremen,* and *repairmen.* Determine how the following sentences could be rewritten to be neutral and gender free.

1. A good teacher is concerned not only with her students' intellectual development, but also with their personal needs.
2. Our forefathers brought to this country many values and traditions based on the cultures in which they were born and raised.
3. Neanderthal man was a sophisticated hunter and tool maker.
4. Businessmen in the community were in favor of the tax increase.
5. The freshmen were reluctant to study for the mathematics exam.

Examine the following sentences and determine how they may be sexually biased.

1. Will Durant and his wife are well-known authors.
2. Sit up, stop crying, and act like a man.
3. The woman lawyer did her job surprisingly well.
4. Boys make the best mechanics and athletes.
5. God watches over us with his wisdom and love.

Is the use of language important? Does it really affect children and our culture that much? What do you think?

▪ WOMEN AND U.S. EDUCATION

During the colonial period women were trained for domestic work or served as apprentices under master craftsmen. In states such as Virginia and Massachusetts, laws were passed as early as the 1640s requiring that women be taught to read. The laws, however, were frequently difficult to enforce, and women often went without any formal education (Sexton 1976, 42).

With the coming of the American Revolution the emphasis on education for women increased. In 1769, for example, women were admitted to Boston public schools for the first time. By 1826 the first public high school for women opened in Boston. Men and women were usually segregated in the schools. Elementary classes were often separated into male and female groups although coeducational groups became common by the beginning of the nineteenth century. Secondary schools were typically either male or female, not coed. This was particularly true with the early academies and seminaries so popular for men and women at the beginning of the nineteenth century.

Women's seminaries became common in the early 1820s. Carefully modeled after English finishing schools, they achieved great popularity throughout New England. Chartered by the state but privately funded, the most famous was Emma Willard's female seminary founded in Troy, New York, in 1821. Willard's school was basically a secondary school intended for daughters of the wealthy. It trained them to be successful wives and mothers. Willard outlined her plans for the school in an 1819 address to the New York State legislature. Its curriculum would consist of four major areas: religious and moral instruction, literary instruction, domestic training (household management), and ornamental instruction (music and the arts) (Cohen 1974, 1575–1576).

Seminaries received widespread support from the educational leaders of the period, including common school leaders Horace Mann and Calvin Stowe. With Mann's help, Catherine Beecher (one of the founders of the Hartford Female Seminary) lobbied for women to be given greater opportunities to become teachers. Through her work with the National Board of Popular Education, Beecher eventually placed more than four hundred east-coast women in teaching positions throughout the West.

Teaching provided women not only with a meaningful profession, but also, as time went on, with greater access to higher education. Yet beginning in the nineteenth century and continuing until recently, female teachers have been paid less than their male counterparts. Married women were not often allowed to teach. Men still usually administered schools, even though women had dominated the profession for many years. But despite these disadvantages, teaching provided an important means of advancement and professional development for many women. By the beginning of the twentieth century, women teachers outnumbered men teachers approximately two to one (Sexton 1976, 46).

Protests against the unequal treatment of women have taken many forms and occurred as early as the end of the eighteenth century. In the early 1790s, Mary Wollstonecraft's *A Vindication of the Rights of Women* maintained that sexual tyranny was no different from political tyranny. According to Wollstonecraft it was imperative that women be sufficiently educated so they could be not only the intellectual equals of their husbands and sons, but also capable individuals able to support themselves if necessary (Button and Provenzo 1983, 137).

By the mid–nineteenth century different groups of women in the United States began to organize and lobby for their rights. In 1848 a women's rights convention, the most important meeting of feminist leaders up to that time, was held in Seneca Falls, New York. It adopted a series of resolutions, patterned on the Declaration of Independence, that proposed the principle that men and women are equal and endowed with certain inalienable rights. Important women's rights leaders, such as Susan B. Anthony (1820–1906), argued that women should have not only equal educational opportunities, but also equal opportunities in the workplace.

FIGURE 11.1 ■ Women suffragists marching in Washington, D.C., in 1913.

Source: Courtesy of the Library of Congress.

Rosie the Riveter
A slang term describing a female industrial worker during World War II (1939–1945).

The women's rights movement achieved its most important victory in 1920 with the ratification of the Nineteenth Amendment. For the first time women had the right to vote. Although few opportunities developed for women during the depression, opportunities to work expanded during the Second World War. Because of labor shortages, women began to work in many businesses and industries from which they had previously been excluded. **Rosie the Riveter** demonstrated to people in the United States that women could work effectively in occupations traditionally held only by men.

Unfortunately, despite their important contribution to the war effort, most women were not allowed to keep their jobs when the men came back after the war. Yet they had taken an important step forward in the cause of women's rights. By demonstrating their ability and willingness to work in nontraditional fields, women exposed the inherent unfairness and inequality of our society.

FIGURE 11.2 ■ Women industrial workers became common during the Second World War to make up for men fighting overseas.

Source: Courtesy of the National Archives.

■ WOMEN AND CONTEMPORARY EDUCATION

The modern women's rights movement began in the 1960s as an outgrowth of the larger civil rights movement. Protests against racial discrimination were responsible not only for raising the consciousness of men and women across the country, but also for leading to the passage of a series of civil rights acts protecting the rights of individuals. The most important federal civil rights legislation affecting women was the 1964 Civil Rights Act prohibiting discrimination on the basis of race or sex. In June 1972, Title IX, an amendment to the 1964 Civil Rights Act, was passed by Congress, but it did not go into effect until July 21, 1975. Title IX states explicitly: "No person in the United States shall, on the basis of sex, be excluded from participation in, be denied the benefits of, or be subject to discrimination under any education program or activity receiving Federal financial assistance." This law applies to all public school districts in the United States and almost all institutions at the collegiate level (Sexton 1976, 137).

A number of major issues emerged as a result of the enactment of Title IX. Physical education classes were to be offered for men and women on an equal basis. For the first time women were to have equal access to sports programs and facilities. Elementary, secondary, and collegiate administrators were advised to make sure their athletic programs provided equal facilities, equipment, coaching staffs, publicity, practice time, and opportunities for women to participate.

Enforcing Title IX in athletics has forced schools, from the elementary through the collegiate levels, to reconsider the support they provide for women's athletic programs. Administrators complain that expenditures for women's athletic programs required by Title IX have taken money away from men's athletic programs. In fact, expenditures for both men's and women's athletic programs have increased, and despite complaints to the contrary, gains made by women have not been at the expense of men.

Various court cases relating to athletics have arisen as a result of the passage of Title IX. The case of *Yellow Springs . . . Board of Education v. Ohio High School Athletic Association* (1978) challenged the segregation of the sexes in contact sports. Two female basketball players at Yellow Springs High School had been awarded positions on the school's team, but, because of their sex, the school board excluded them. The federal district court in Ohio ruled that the school board's decision was discriminatory because it did not allow the female players the opportunity to play at the level of their ability and as a result violated not only the Constitution but also Title IX.

Athletics is just one area affected by Title IX. It also prohibits hiring policies based on sex. Thus, a female applicant applying for a teaching job cannot be denied the position on the basis that she *might* get pregnant and be absent from her job as part of a maternity leave. Title IX prohibits policies establishing a quota for admissions on the basis of sex. A private coeducational college receiving federal funds cannot decide to accept more men or more women in any given year because all qualified applicants must be considered equally. Title IX also prohibits screening methods, like admissions tests, that favor one sex over the other, or lists that rank applicants separately by sex. Counseling, employment programs, and curricula are also included under the jurisdiction of Title IX.

Although arguments over whether federal legislation like Title IX should interfere with the wishes and desires of local communities are numerous, an even more important consideration is whether people are being provided the opportunity to become all they are capable of becoming. This idea is by no means new; it was articulated by Thomas Jefferson more than two centuries ago. We have the obligation as educators and as members of a just society to remove sex barriers in both training and employment. It is the purpose of Title IX and similar legislation to do precisely this—whatever the difficulty.

■ SEXUAL DISCRIMINATION IN THE CLASSROOM

INTASC Standards

Principle #6

Legislation like Title IX represents only the beginning of the battle against sexual discrimination in the classroom. Inequity can involve male and female students being given unequal access to learning materials. For example, boys tend to dominate and control the building-block area in nursery schools. If playing with blocks is an important part of the developmental process for both boys and girls, the instructor must make sure both boys and girls have access to the materials. Similarly, many researchers have observed boys monopolizing computers in classrooms. If computer skills are important for both men and women, no one group should be allowed to dominate the use of these resources.

Gender discrimination can be subtle. Behavior often reflects norms that are simply taken for granted in society. As an example, several years ago I was **field testing** a new online curriculum for middle school students. Students were paired together (often boys with girls) to work with one another. With no prompting from anyone, the boys working on the project assumed the role of "running" the computer whereas the girls

field testing
Testing or trying out materials in an actual or real setting.

took notes and kept things "organized." When asked why they weren't running the computers, the girls explained that having the boys run them was "just easier." In this case, they had assumed, for themselves, stereotypical gender roles.

Sex stereotypes represent, according to Jean Stockard, "reified notions of what men and women are like. Sometimes stereotypes correspond to reality, but more often they are rigid and untrue perceptions" (Stockard et al. 1980, 24). Such preconceptions are almost always prejudicial and diminish the individual they supposedly depict. Referring to female students as "skirts," or "cookies," or women as "ladies" may not seem important. But such comments can, in fact, be indicative of stereotypes that allow only women to be perceived in limited roles—ones that do not allow them to exercise fully their potential as individuals.

Student–teacher interactions too are often associated with gender. Studies have shown that teachers tend to give boys both negative and positive feedback about what they are doing more often than they give similar feedback to girls. Teachers react more forcefully to aggressive behavior in boys than in girls, and they are more likely to use a harsh, angry voice when reprimanding a boy than a girl (Stockard et al. 1980, 13).

The educators Myra and David Sadker are the most well-known researchers in this field and have spent their professional careers looking at the role gender plays in U.S. classrooms. In extensive videotape observations of classrooms, the Sadkers have concluded that boys are given much more attention than are girls:

INTASC Standards
Principle #6

> Our research shows that boys call out eight times more often than girls. Sometimes what they say has little or nothing to do with the teacher's questions. Whether male comments are insightful or irrelevant, teachers respond to them. However, when girls call out, there is a fascinating occurrence. Suddenly the teacher remembers the rule about raising your hand before you talk. And then the girl, who is usually not as assertive as the male students, is deftly and swiftly put in her place. (Sadker and Sadker 1994, 43)

Boys gain more attention for many reasons. Attention-getting behavior is more readily acceptable in our culture for boys than girls. Who among us cannot remember in our own education situations when girls were told to "act more like a young lady," whereas boys exhibiting the same behavior are seen as funny and amusing, or perhaps just a little bit rambunctious. After all, "boys will be boys." A teacher who encourages a boy to be curious and a girl to be "more polite and ladylike" impresses a hidden curriculum on the child based on sexual stereotypes.

male hegemony
Male domination.

male-based gender privilege
Privilege based on being a male.

Actually, boys are not necessarily "just boys" in terms of their behavior. Instead, they are under enormous pressure to conform to certain types of normative behavior. Notions such as "boys don't cry" and "boys are interested in toys such as cars and trucks and video games," are examples of cultural constructions, just as is belief that girls should play with dolls and keep house. Societal expectations about gender are pervasive and unrelenting. Why are pink tags used on the identification tags of female babies in hospitals, and blue ones for boys? Why are boys expected to lead, and girls expected to participate and be part of a group?

The Sadkers often found that most teachers had little notion that they were perpetuating sexual stereotyping in their classrooms. Yet, such a fact should not be surprising. Teachers, whether male or female, are part of the culture. If gender inequality dominates much of our culture through a system of **male hegemony** and **male-based gender privilege**, there is little reason to expect teachers, who have been educated as part of our culture, not to accept these cultural norms and assumptions.

■ SEXISM IN CHILDREN'S BOOKS AND TEXTBOOKS

INTASC Standards

Principle #6

Where do children pick up their attitudes about gender? Many come from families; some from peers. A great many notions about gender come from the media. No one source is responsible for how we view the world. Many of the values we hold about gender are found in the materials we teach.

Numerous studies since the late 1960s have analyzed curricular materials for sexual stereotyping. One important work, *Dick and Jane as Victims* (1972), analyzed 2,760 stories in 134 elementary school readers published by fourteen companies. The study found the following ratios:

Boy-centered to girl-centered stories: 5:2
Adult male to adult female main characters: 3:1
Male to female biographies: 6:1
Male to female animal stories: 2:1
Male to female folk or fantasy stories: 4:1

In these stories, boys consistently demonstrate traits such as ingenuity, creativity, bravery, curiosity, and autonomy. In contrast, girls are depicted as passive, incompetent, fearful, and domestically oriented (*Women on Words and Images* 1975).

Texts such as the ones analyzed in *Dick and Jane as Victims* play an important role in the sex-role socialization of the average child. Boys readily identify with the masculine roles presented to them and girls with feminine roles. Girls and boys learn from these texts that boys are more highly valued than girls in our society and that they are expected to initiate actions and lead more than girls (Weitzman et al. 1976, 6). Boys seem to have greater possibilities for careers than do girls.

Sex-role stereotypes are harmful not only to women but also to men. Men and boys have consistently been discouraged from openly showing their emotions, from admitting that they might be afraid, or from being gentle and compassionate. Limited to specific roles and experiences, boys and men are denied the opportunity to develop the full range of their intellectual and emotional beings (Weitzman et al. 1976, 18).

Obviously, the Weitzman study is dated. We would like to argue that problems of this sort are being corrected. Yet read the following account of Myra and David Sadker's experience in this regard:

> During the summer of 1992 we analyzed the content of fifteen math, language arts, and history textbooks used in Maryland, Virginia, and the District of Columbia. When we counted pictures of males and females, we were surprised to find that the 1989 language arts textbooks from Macmillan and D. C. Heath had twice as many boys and men as girls and women. In some readers the ratio was three to one. A 1989 upper-elementary history textbook had four times as many males pictured as females. In the 1992 D. C. Heath *Exploring Our World, Past and Present,* a text for sixth graders, only eleven female names were mentioned, and not a single American adult woman was included. In the entire 631 pages of a textbook covering the history of the world, only seven pages related to women, either as famous individuals or as a general group. (Sadker and Sadker 1994, 72)

The tradition of sexually stereotyping women and ignoring their contributions extends beyond the elementary and secondary levels. In a study of sexism in teacher education texts from the early 1980s, the Sadkers found a wide range of omissions and stereotypes. In introductory foundations texts similar to this one, leading female educators were almost completely overlooked whereas important male figures were discussed in detail; John Dewey, Jean Piaget, and Benjamin Bloom were frequently mentioned, but Catherine Beecher, Sylvia Ashton Warner, and Maria Montessori were excluded. Similar patterns of discrimination appeared in other textbooks for teachers, including standard works in educational psychology and social studies methods (Sadker and Sadker 1982, 39–42).

WHAT DO YOU THINK?

Single-Sex Classrooms

Would boys and girls learn more if they were separated by gender? A traditional argument for the single-sex education of women is that they are given more opportunity to excel and are given more attention in single-sex classrooms. Current research does not indicate whether coeducation is better than single-sex education (American Association of University Women 1998, 2). For those educated in a coeducational setting, how do you think your experience might have been different if you were educated in a single-sex setting? Would certain conditions make single-sex education better for some students than for others? What do you think?

■ ALTERNATIVE SEXUAL ORIENTATIONS

INTASC Standards

Principle #6

Alternative sexual orientations, including homosexuality and bisexuality, are rarely discussed in schools, for many reasons. Among the most important is the fact that these orientations are offensive to many people in the mainstream population—whose attitudes are often rooted in their religious faith. Ignoring homosexuality in our communities and schools does not mean it does not exist. Approximately 10 percent of the youth population in the United States is homosexual or bisexual. As argued in a recent report by the American Association of University Women:

> By never raising the issue of sexual orientation as a legitimate developmental issue, by not placing informative and nonpejorative books in the school library, and by not seriously confronting homophobia in the classrooms schools abdicate their responsibility not only to adolescents who are questioning their sexual orientation but to all students. (AAUW 1995, 141)

It is my belief (a "white," heterosexual male) that sexual identity is a personal choice. Although heterosexuality is the norm—and clearly the most privileged sexual orientation in our culture—it should not be the only acceptable orientation. Toleration of difference on the part of both heterosexual and homosexual populations is absolutely necessary. This position recognizes not only the sexual diversity inherent in U.S. culture, but also takes into account the civil rights of nontraditional populations. It can be argued that the last frontier of the civil rights movement involves achieving gender equity for male or female heterosexuals, male or female homosexuals, and male or female bisexuals.

Homosexuality is actually against the law in some states. Gays who openly profess their orientation are banned from the military, and **gay bashing** is tolerated in many public settings such as schools. Think for a moment about your own experience in school. You have likely heard a fellow student referred to as a *fag* in an extremely negative context. What you may have heard is almost certainly tolerated. Imagine an African American student being referred to as a *nigger*. That almost certainly would not be tolerated today, although it was acceptable not so long ago.

gay bashing
Discriminating against gays.

■ DOES HOMOSEXUALITY ENCOURAGE HOMOSEXUALITY?

One of the assumptions about tolerating homosexuality is that doing so encourages people to be gay. This model suggests that being a homosexual is like having a disease that is contagious. Scientists do not have a totally clear understanding of why people are gay. Psychological tests (going back to the 1950s) show that no differences exist between homosexuals and other populations, and no clear physiological, or even psychological, causes explain why people are gay. Why is there even a need to know a cause? As the psychologist Evelyn Hooker argues: "It's a mistake to hope that we will be able to modify or change homosexuality. . . . If we understand its nature and accept it as a given then we come closer to the kinds of attitudes which will make it possible for all homosexuals to lead a decent life in society" (quoted by Hersch 1993, 56).

In the mid-1970s, former Miss America Anita Bryant waged a campaign in southern Florida that tried legally to exclude gay teachers from working in the public schools. The implication was that their values were unwholesome and would corrupt the children they taught. The campaign also implied that homosexual teachers might prey on or seduce their students. Statistical evidence, however, indicates that sexual assaults against minors are most often committed by heterosexual men (Khayatt 1992, 8). Bryant's activities received national attention and support.

The fact is that, except to provide general counseling and support, neither heterosexual nor homosexual teachers should under any circumstances be sexually involved with their students. Teachers, by definition, are authority figures and have potentially unfair influence over the students whom they teach. The privilege provided by a position of authority must not be abused. Any teacher, straight or gay, ought to be able to counsel a student appropriately—perhaps concerning depression about a boyfriend or girlfriend—whether the student's relationship is heterosexual, homosexual, or bisexual.

■ THE RIGHTS OF GAY TEACHERS

It can be argued that teachers are hired with the expectation that they conform to certain standards. As discussed previously, teaching is a conservative profession that is expected to reproduce, to a large extent, the values, beliefs, and traditions of the culture. Homosexuality is a difficult issue, in that the culture is still in a significant state of conflict concerning it.

> **INTASC Standards**
>
> Principle #9

We need to ask some serious questions. Should a homosexual teacher be forced to "stay in the closet"? This was the dilemma faced by Wendy

FIGURE 11.3 ■ A man holds a sign while marching in a gay rights parade.

Weaver, a high school psychology teacher and volleyball coach in a conservative town in central Utah. Shortly after completing an MA in the mid-1990s at the University of Utah and returning to the high school, Weaver divorced her husband who was a school district psychologist. Weaver had decided to "come out of the closet" and moved in with another woman. Weaver did not try to conceal her relationship and was seen in public holding hands with her companion. While organizing a new volleyball team in July 1997, a senior asked her whether she was gay. Weaver responded yes, and the student then told her that she would not play on the team with her as coach.

A response to the situation came from the district a couple of days later. The school administration already had some knowledge of Weaver's personal situation. She was contacted by the school district's human resource director, Larry Kimball, and told that she would not be coaching (an after-school activity) the following year. A day later she was summoned back to Kimball's office and given a letter with two directives: (1) she was not to discuss her homosexual orientation with students, staff, fellow teachers, or parents of students; and (2) if she was asked anything about it by members of the school or the parents of students, she should tell them that the subject is private and personal, and inappropriate to discuss with them. The letter concluded with a warning that she could be fired if she did not conform to these restrictions.

A second letter was eventually sent to Weaver that explained that the restrictions placed on her only applied in the context of her work in the school district. Part of the justification for this restriction was that she represented for her students an "authority figure, and role model." Challenging her treatment, Weaver filed a suit in federal district court the following November. Concluding that her First Amendment right to free speech had been violated, the court found in Weaver's favor, awarding her legal fees and a small damage claim. The letters that were sent to her by the school district were purged from her personnel file.

On the surface, Weaver's case is straightforward. Homosexual or heterosexual involvement with students provides clear grounds for termination. Although some communities still have laws making homosexuality illegal, these laws are not necessarily enforced and are potentially subject to court challenge if they are. The real question is whether the homosexual orientation of a teacher interferes with him or her doing a reasonable job in the classroom. In the Weaver case, it is clear that it did not (Zirkel 1999).

James Dale joined the Boy Scouts of America when he was eight years old, and eventually reached the rank of Eagle Scout before he became an assistant scoutmaster. In 1990 he was expelled from the Scouts when a local newspaper identified him as the leader of Rutgers University Lesbian/Gay Alliance. Dale eventually sued the Scouts, arguing that they had violated his civil rights.

In August 1999, the New Jersey State Supreme Court ruled in a 7–0 decision in favor of Dale. Chief Justice Deborah T. Portiz wrote the following about her court's decision:

> The sad truth is that excluded groups and individuals have been prevented from full participation in the social, economic and political life of our country. The human price of this bigotry has been enormous. At a most fundamental level, adherence to the principle of equality demands that our legal system protect the victim of invidious discrimination.

One of the other justices, Alan B. Handler, argued that historically homosexuals had been discriminated against by being identified as inherently immoral. According to Handler:

> That myth is repudiated by decades of social science data that convincingly establish being homosexual does not, in itself, derogate from one's ability to participate in and contribute responsibly and positively in society. In short, a lesbian and gay person, merely because he or she is a homosexual, is no more or less likely to be moral than a person who is heterosexual.

The Boy Scouts of America plan to appeal the case to the Supreme Court of the United States. The case has obvious implications for the teaching profession. Should gay men be allowed to work with young boys in organizations like the Scouts? Should gay and lesbian teachers be allowed in the classroom? What do you think?

The unfortunate reality of U.S. society is that it remains extremely **homophobic.** Teachers who are homosexuals need to be cautious. Although tolerance and understanding is increasing, it is by no means universal or dependable. Homosexual teachers are not allowed the privilege of displaying their sexual affections in the way afforded to most heterosexuals. As Madiha Kayatt explains about lesbian teachers:

homophobia
Fear leading to discrimination against homosexuals.

Frequently, women teachers suspected of being lesbians will be tolerated as long as they are not recognizable as lesbians or as long as it is not a matter of public knowledge. This means that they cannot afford to display their relationship to a woman—a privilege accorded most heterosexual liaisons—nor can they be seen to participate in a gay-related activity. What this means in the everyday life of a lesbian teacher is that she may not wear a ring or a labrys or give any indication of her sexuality. She cannot talk openly about her weekend activities—in short, her life must remain invisible. (Kayatt 1992, 72)

In contrast, a heterosexual teacher can wear a wedding ring, talk openly about dating or living with a member of the other sex, and so on. Privilege is afforded to those who are in the heterosexual mainstream.

■ COUNSELING AND NURTURING HOMOSEXUAL STUDENTS

Homosexual students need to be afforded the same rights and treatment from the schools as any other population. As a historically persecuted group, they need to be protected. Some gay students may negotiate their way through hostile school settings with relatively little difficulty. Many have to deal with issues of identity conflict, and feelings of isolation and stigmatization (Marinoble 1998).

INTASC Standards
Principle #5

To be equitable, school policies need to take into account the special needs of homosexual students. A few selected strategies follow:

■ Lobby for the inclusion of nondiscrimination clauses in teacher contracts and related documents
■ Establish school policies that forbid slurs and jokes concerning homosexuality
■ Run staff training that deals with sexual diversity issues
■ Allow books and reading materials in libraries that portray homosexuality in positive ways
■ Permit the discussion of gay/lesbian issues in school publications such as newspapers
■ Include positive images of homosexuals in curricular materials
■ Accurately portray gay/lesbian history and culture
■ Provide support services to homosexual students
■ Provide information to parents that portrays homosexuality in a realistic and sensitive manner (Marinoble 1998)

If such policies are pursued, students with a homosexual orientation may be treated equitably and have the opportunity to realize their full potential.

WHAT DO YOU THINK?

Reading Rainbow

The inclusion of children's books depicting lesbian and gay couples has caused considerable controversy in different school systems in recent years. In the 1990s books such as *Heather Has Two Mommies* and *Daddy's Roommate,* depicting the family life of lesbian and gay couples, were included as part of the Rainbow Curriculum in the New York City public schools. So much controversy arose over the inclusion of the books that it led to the removal of Joseph A. Fernandez as the superintendent.

In 1997, Planet-Out, a lesbian and gay online service, donated six thousand dollars for the purchase of books for local schools in Seattle, Washington, that portrayed homosexual families in a positive light. Individual school committees with parent representation considered whether to accept the gift. Eventually some Seattle parents protested to the school district about the gifts, arguing that their content violated their religious beliefs and represented an attempt to indoctrinate their children to accept a pro-homosexual point of view.

Should the school district have accepted the gift of the books? What do you think?

■ SEX EDUCATION AND THE SCHOOLS

INTASC Standards

Principle #9

Related to the issue of gender is the question of whether sex education should be taught in the schools. Many conservative and fundamentalist Christian groups feel that sex education represents an imposition of moral values on students by the school system and the general culture. They perceive this as usurping the authority of the family. The question of parents' rights in determining what and how their children learn about a sensitive subject such as sex education is a difficult one. Parents' rights need to be balanced against those of the state and its need to educate children.

In the Supreme Court case *Wisconsin v. Yoder* (1972), the Court upheld the religious rights of parents. The Court explained its ruling:

> The State's interest in universal education is not totally free from a balancing process when it impinges on other fundamental rights, such as those specifically protected by the Free Exercise Clause of the First Amendment and the traditional interest of parents with respect to the religious upbringing of their children.

This becomes a difficult issue in contexts such as the dissemination of information about contraception and **sexually transmitted diseases** (e.g., AIDS.) The state, through the voice of local schools, can legitimately argue that they must provide help to prevent the spread of disease. Not to do so is irresponsible and harmful to society at large.

In contrast, conservative groups argue that by providing sex education, schools are imposing on the rights and duties of the family. Jerry Falwell, one of the most important conservative Christian leaders of the past two decades, argues that the schools cannot, and should not, take the place of the family. According to him:

> The most important function performed by the family is the rearing and character formation of children, a function it was uniquely created to perform and for which no remotely adequate substitution has been found. The family is the best and most efficient "department of health, education and welfare." (Quoted by Provenzo 1990, 72)

Personal family beliefs about issues such as sex education and homosexuality reflect deeply held differences in U.S. cultural values—ones that are highly explosive for schools and their local communities.

sexually transmitted diseases
Diseases transmitted through sexual contact.

AIDS
Acquired Immune Deficiency Syndrome. A viral infection that emerged on a worldwide basis in the early 1980s.

■ SUMMARY

In *Writing a Woman's Life,* the feminist scholar Carolyn Heilbrun notes that

> It is a hard thing to make up stories to live by. We can only retell and live by the stories we have read or heard. We live our lives through texts. They may be read or chanted, or experienced electronically or come to us like the murmurings of our mothers, telling us what conventions demand. Whatever the form or medium, these stories have formed us all; they are what we must use to make new fictions, new narratives. (Heilbrun 1988, 37)

Heilbrun's passage suggests several things. Concerning the issue of gender, we need to create new narratives in U.S. culture. By doing so, we can combat the destructive effects of gender discrimination in our society.

Gender discrimination and stereotyping diminish all people. As educators on the front line in the classrooms and the culture, we need to take a direct role in combating gender discrimination and stereotyping.

We need to examine carefully our own personal attitudes and beliefs and consider how they may or may not reflect gender stereotyping and bias. We need to discuss these issues. We need to make sure that no discriminatory action goes unchallenged. We need to inform people about their rights. In doing so, we will help to achieve a more just and equitable society.

Although gender stereotyping and discrimination have been constants in U.S. history, we need to keep in mind that they are learned behaviors and can be overcome through education and careful critical thought. In the end, if discrimination exists in the schools and is part of the educational system as a whole, it is only because the teaching profession and the public allow it to exist.

■ DISCUSSION QUESTIONS ■

1. How are women stereotyped in advertising on television and in popular magazines? What does this stereotyping say about the roles U.S. society expects women to fill?
2. How does the sexual stereotyping of women affect men? How might such stereotyping ultimately be destructive for men as well as for women?
3. Do any activities or experiences within the public school justify teaching the sexes separately? Defend your position.
4. Does gender bring with it privilege?
5. What are some ways that sexual discrimination manifests itself in the classroom? Can you recall personal experiences with such discrimination? How can this type of discrimination best be overcome and eliminated?
6. How is sexism evident in our day-to-day use of language? Are there ways of overcoming these problems with language?
7. What do you think should be the rights of homosexual teachers and students?
8. Should we have sex education in the schools? What rights do parents have in regard to sex education?

■ SOURCES CITED ■

American Association of School Administrators Advisory Commission on Sex Equality. 1975. *Sex equality in schools*. Vol. 5, AASA Executive Handbook Series. Arlington, Va.: American Association of School Administrators.

The New York Times. 1999. Bigotry in the Boy Scouts. Editorial, 5 August, A22.

Button, H. Warren, and Eugene F. Provenzo, Jr. 1983. *History of education and culture in America.* Englewood Cliffs, N.J.: Prentice-Hall.

Civil Rights Act of 1964. U.S. Code 1976, Title 28, Section 1447.

Cohen, Sol. 1974. *Education in the United States: A documentary history.* Vol. 3. New York: Random House.

Council on Interracial Books for Children. 1977. *Stereotypes, distortions and omissions in U.S. history books.* New York: Council on Interracial Books.

Darrin v. Gould. 85 Wash. 2d 859, 1975.

DeMarrais, Kathleen Bennett. 2000. Gender. In *Knowledge and power in the global economy: Politics and the rhetoric of school reform,* edited by David A. Gabbard, 161–169. Mahwah, N.J.: Lawrence Erlbaum.

Frazier, N., and M. Sadker. 1973. *Sexism in school and society.* New York: Harper and Row.

Gollnick, Donna M., and Phillip C. Chinn. 1983. *Multicultural education in a pluralistic society.* St. Louis, MO: C. V. Mosby.

Gough, Pauline. 1976. *Sexism: New issue in American education.* Bloomington, Ind.: Phi Delta Kappa.

Grossman, Herbert, and Suzanne Grossman. 1994. *Gender issues in education.* Boston: Allyn and Bacon.

Heilbrun, Carolyn. 1988. *Writing a woman's life.* New York: W. W. Norton.

Hanley, Robert. 1999. New Jersey court overturns ouster of gay Boy Scout. *The New York Times,* 5 August, A1 and A21.

Hornblower, Margot. 1999. He? She? Whatever! *Time,* 11 October, 76.

Khayatt, Madiha. 1992. *Lesbian teachers: An invisible presence.* Albany: State University of New York Press.

National Project on Women in Education. 1978. *Taking sexism out of education.* Washington, D.C.: U.S. Department of Health, Education, and Welfare.

Pipher, Mary. 1994. *Reviving Ophelia: Saving the lives of adolescent girls.* New York: Ballentine Books.

Sadker, David, and Myra Sadker. 1980. Sexism in teacher education texts. *Harvard Educational Review* 50: 36–46.

Sadker, Myra, and David Sadker. 1994. *Failing at fairness: How America's schools cheat girls.* New York: Charles Scribner's Sons.

Safilios-Rothschild, Constantina. 1979. *Sex role socialization and sex discrimination: A synthesis and critique of the literature.* Washington, D.C.: U.S. Department of Health, Education, and Welfare.

The New York Times. 1997. Schools' books on gay families stir Seattle. Editorial, 2 November, 20.

Schmuck, Patricia A. 1980. Differentiation by sex in educational professions. In *Sex equity in education,* edited by Jean Stockard, Particia A. Schmuck, Ken Kempner, Peg Williams, Sakre K. Edson, and Mary Ann Smith. New York: Academic Press.

Sexton, Patricia. 1976. *Women in education.* Bloomington, Ind.: Phi Delta Kappa.

Shapiro, June. 1981. *Equal their chances: Children's activities for non-sexist learning.* New York: Prentice Hall.

Stockard, Jean, Patricia Schmuck, Ken Kempner, Peg Williams, Sakre Edson, and Mary Ann Smith. 1980. *Sex equity in education.* New York: Academic Press.

Streitmatter, Janice. 1994. *Toward gender equity in the classroom: Everyday teacher's beliefs and practice.* Albany: State University of New York Press.

Talburt, Susan, and Shirley Steinberg. 2000. *Thinking queer: Sexuality, culture, and education.* New York: Peter Lang.

Trecker, J. 1971. Women in U.S. history textbooks. *Social Education* 35: 249–261.

U.S. Census Bureau. 1999. *Statistical abstracts of the United States.* Washington, D.C.: U.S. Government Printing Office.

Weitzman, Lenore J., Deborah Eifler, Elizabeth Hokada, and Catherine Ross. 1976. Sex-role socialization in picture books for preschool children. In *Sexism in children's books: Facts, figures and guidelines,* 5–30. London: Writers and Readers Publishing Cooperative.

Wisconsin v. Yoder. Supreme Court of the United States, 1972. 406 U.S. 205.

Wirtenberg, J., S. Klein, B. Richardson, and V. Thomas. 1981. Sex equity in American education. *Educational Leadership* 38: 311–319.

Women on Words and Images. 1975. *Dick and Jane as victims: Sex stereotypes in children's readers.* Princeton, N.J.: Author. (ERIC Document Reproduction Service No. ED 065 832)

Woody, T. A. 1966. *History of women's education in the United States.* New York: Octagon Books.

Writers and Readers Publishing Cooperative. 1976. *Sexism in children's books: Facts, figures and guidelines.* London: Author.

Yellow Springs Exempted Village School District Board of Education v. Ohio High School Athletic Association. 433 F. Supp. 753 (S.D. Ohio 1978).

CHAPTER 12

The Education of Students with Special Needs

INTASC Standards

Principle #3

Approximately 12 to 15 percent of the population falls within a special education category (i.e., having special educational needs). One out of nine public school students is officially classified as "handicapped" (Hehir and Latus 1992, v). These diverse categories include children with emotional disturbances, learning disabilities, visual disabilities, hearing disabilities, speech disabilities, and physical disabilities; mentally retarded and gifted children also require special education.

According to the 1994 National Health Interview, 650,000 of all U.S. children (1.3%) are limited in mobility, 470,000 (0.9%) have a self-care limitation, 2,743,000 (5.5%) have a communication limitation, and 5,237,000 (10.6%) have a limitation in terms of their ability to learn. Overall, 6,075,000 U.S. school-age children (12.3%) have some type of functional limitation (Hogan et. al. 1997).

INTASC Standards

Principle #9

What is society's obligation to provide its citizens with special needs and equal educational opportunities? Clearly all people are not equal in ability to learn or take advantage of opportunities provided by the educational system. Others have exceptional potential and ability outside the normal range. How much should the educational system try to meet their special needs?

We are faced with an ethical dilemma. If we are indeed a democracy in action and not just in name, it is the obligation of the educational system to help—within reason—each and every student to become all he or she is capable of becoming. This includes people who are intellectually gifted and physically disabled, artistically talented and mentally retarded.

■ THE GROWTH IN SPECIAL EDUCATION

Although every state mandates free instruction for children in public schools, historically children with special educational needs have in large part been denied equal educational opportunities. Since the early 1970s, however, more and more parents of children with physical and mental impairments have begun to insist that their children have as much a right to be educated as the rest of the population. Drawing on legal precedents established during the civil rights movement, advocates of special education have successfully promoted a number of laws that increase the educational opportunities of special students.

Special education has its origins in the nineteenth century. Although children with special educational needs certainly existed earlier, they rarely received the attention they needed. This occurred for many reasons. Limited resources and limited knowledge about students with special needs restricted what could be done. In addition, prior to the nineteenth century, children who were born with physical problems or who had contracted crippling diseases did not usually survive. With improvements in medical care beginning in the late seventeenth century, children with physical problems had a greatly increased chance of surviving to adulthood.

Limited interest in special education dates back to ancient Greece and Rome. In *The Republic* Plato (427–347 BC) proposed a system in which children would be taken from their parents for special training. Children of "better" parents (those who belonged to the aristocracy of wealth or intellect) would receive training suitable for their stations in life; those born of "inferior" parents would receive instruction suited to their needs. Children with birth defects would "be hidden away, in some appropriate manner, that must be kept secret" (Cornford 1945, 107).

Plato was particularly interested in the education of the gifted and talented. In his idealized **republic** children with superior intelligence (whether from wealthy or poor families) would be provided with special training in science, philosophy, and metaphysics. It was these children who would eventually assume responsibility for the governance and administration of the state, and on whom Greek democracy depended for its survival.

During the Middle Ages and the Renaissance, people who were mentally retarded or psychologically disturbed were often considered either divinely possessed or controlled by demons. Little attempt was made to understand their needs or their problems. During the early modern period (sixteenth and seventeenth centuries), this attitude gradually changed. By the early 1600s, for example, programs were developed for

republic
A type of government in which power resides in its citizens and is exercised by elected officers and representatives.

the first time to teach the deaf to communicate on a systematic basis using sign language.

Among the most important pioneers in special education in the eighteenth century was the Abbe de l'Epee (1712–1789), who in 1760 founded the National Institute for Deaf Mutes in Paris. Recognized by many as the first publicly sponsored school for the disabled, the school's most famous instructor was the physician Jean-Marc Gaspard Itard (1775–1880).

Itard is most noted for the work he did with a young deaf and dumb child brought to him in 1799. A young boy (a feral, or "wild" child) had been discovered in the forest of Aveyron in southern France. When he was "captured," he was about eleven or twelve years of age, naked, dirty, mute, and for all appearances totally wild. When brought to Itard in Paris, the child generated tremendous interest. Here was a child apparently brought up outside civilized society. People wondered what the nature of such an individual would be. Would he be pure and uncorrupted (a notion suggested some years before by the French philosopher Jean

FIGURE 12.1 ■ Portrait of Victor, the "Wild Child of Aveyron."

Source: J. M. Itard, *An Historical Account of the Discovery and Education of a Savage Man* (London: Richard Phillips, 1802).

Jacques Rousseau), or would he be primitive and ignorant, not having had the benefit of living with and learning from other people?

Itard began to work with his young patient. Over a period of five years Itard undertook an intensive program of re-education for the boy whom he called Victor. In his description of his work with Victor (published under the title *Rapports et Memoires sur le Sauvage de L'Aveyron*), Itard outlined five goals he had attempted to achieve with Victor.

1. To interest him in social life by rendering it more pleasant to him than the one he was then leading and above all more like the life which he had just left.
2. To awaken his nervous sensibility by the most energetic stimulation, and sometimes by intense emotion.
3. To extend the range of his ideas by giving him new needs and by increasing his social contacts.
4. To lead him to the use of speech by inducing the exercise of imitation through the imperious law of necessity.
5. To induce him to employ the simplest mental operations over a period of time upon the objects of his physical needs, afterwards inducing the application of these mental processes to the objects of instruction. (Itard 1962, 11–37)

Itard began his work with Victor in 1801. Over a period of nine months he not only helped Victor develop acceptable patterns of personal hygiene, eating, and sleeping, but also taught him to communicate on a very limited basis. During the second phase of his work, a period of four years, Itard managed greatly to extend Victor's understanding of and ability to deal with the world.

Ultimately, Itard achieved only limited success. Victor never learned how to speak and, despite Itard's monumental efforts, was never able to undertake a normal life; he lived well into adulthood, dying in 1828. Itard himself considered his efforts with Victor a failure. Yet his work was probably the first systematic attempt by an educator to meet the particular needs of a special person and to help him develop as fully and completely as possible.

Itard was followed by other educators during the nineteenth century. French educator Edouard Sequin (1812–1880), for example, developed a system for treating the mentally retarded that emphasized clinical observation and the development of sensory and motor skills. Sequin's work influenced other researchers, including Italian physician and educator Maria Montessori (1870–1952). Other nineteenth-century leaders in special education were Samuel G. Howe (1801–1876), who started the first school for the blind in the United States, and Thomas H. Gallaudet (1787–1851), who organized the first school for the deaf in the United States. In France Louis Braille (1809–1852) developed the system of writing named after him that enables the blind to read by touch.

Scientific research gradually contributed to the more accurate diagnosis and treatment of special students throughout the late nineteenth and early twentieth centuries. Yet the needs of special students were for the most part overlooked until the early 1970s. Although some treatment and useful educational programs existed, the extent to which special education was a priority and the needs of individuals were being specifically met was limited.

Significant changes in attitudes toward special education began in the early 1960s. In 1961 President John F. Kennedy (who himself had a sister who was mentally retarded) appointed a special committee on mental retardation. As a result of that committee's recommendations, laws were passed that allocated funds for training experts in special education and expanding special education facilities. In 1967 the Bureau of the Handicapped was established by the United States Office of Education to administer research, education, and training programs in special education. The groundwork had been laid for the major reforms of the early 1970s.

■ THE VOCATIONAL REHABILITATION ACT OF 1973

During the early 1970s various state and federal court decisions supported the rights of disabled students to receive equal treatment in the public school system. In response to the judicial initiative, Congress initiated legislation supporting the rights of special students.

Of the eight million children identified as disabled in the early 1970s, only half had access to educational programs appropriate to their needs. At least one million children were being excluded from the public schools. Many disabled children were not receiving adequate diagnoses of their problems. In 1973 as part of the Vocational Rehabilitation Act, Congress made major provisions to guarantee and protect the rights of disabled people. Section 504 of the Act stipulated that

> no otherwise qualified handicapped individual in the United States . . . shall, solely by reason of his handicap, be excluded from the participation in, be denied the benefits of, or be subjected to discrimination under any program or activity receiving federal financial assistance.

The language of the Act closely paralleled the Civil Rights Act of 1964 that dealt with racial discrimination and Title IX of the Education Amendment Act that dealt with discrimination in education based on sex.

The significance of the Vocational Rehabilitation Act lies in its being the first legislation that guaranteed full rights for the disabled and recognized they had been systematically discriminated against over the years. The practical outcome of the passage of Section 504 of the Vocational Rehabilitation Act has been that employers must provide equal recruitment and employment opportunities to disabled individuals; all new public facilities must be accessible to the disabled; disabled children must be provided a free and appropriate public education; discrimination in admission to higher education for the disabled is prohibited; and discrimination is prohibited in providing social services such as health and welfare. Section 504 provides an important extension of the rights of disabled individuals. Its passage was followed just a few years later by an equally important piece of legislation, Public Law 94-142, commonly known as the Education for All Handicapped Children Act.

INTERNET @ CONNECTIONS

Special Education Resources

Extensive resources on special education subjects including legal rights, specific disabilities, early intervention, special education and related services, individualized education programs, family issues, disability organizations, professional associations, education rights, and transition to adult life are available online at several government sponsored sites.

The National Information Center for Children and Youth with Disabilities (NICHY)
http://www.nichcy.org/index.html

Federal Resource Center for Special Education
http://www.dssc.org/frc/

Americans with Disabilities Home Page (Department of Justice)
http://www.usdoj.gov/crt/ada/adahom1.htm

National Council on Disability
http://www.ned.gov/index.html

■ PUBLIC LAW 94-142

PL 94-142 was passed and signed into law by President Gerald Ford on November 29, 1975. The law was enacted in 1978, amended in the 1980s and reauthorized in 1990 as the Individuals with Disabilities Education Act of 1990 (IDEA) (PL 101-476). PL 94-142 was passed as a result of congressional studies and the pressure of various special education lobbying groups. The key point of the law was the requirement that every child be provided with a "free appropriate public education," defined as:

> a program of special education and related services which (a) have been provided at public expense, under public supervision and direction, and without charge, (b) meet the standards of the state educational agency, (c) include an appropriate preschool, elementary, or secondary school education in the state involved, and (d) are provided in conformity with the individualized education program. . . .

IDEA (PL 101-476), the 1990 revision of Law 94-142, defines "children with disabilities" as having any of the following types of disabilities: autism, deaf, deaf-blindness, hearing impairments (including deafness), mental retardation, multiple disabilities, orthopedic impairments, other health impairments, serious emotional disturbance, specific learning disabilities, speech or language impairments, traumatic brain injury, and visual impairments (including blindness) (NICHY 1997).

Among the most controversial conditions of PL 94-142 is the provision that children with disabilities be educated with nondisabled children whenever possible—a process that came to be known as *mainstreaming*. This provision was a logical outgrowth of the Supreme Court's 1954 *Brown* decision that argued separate but equal education is inherently discriminatory. The logic of the court in the *Brown* decision could be applied equally to children with disabilities.

The crucial issue in mainstreaming is whether a child with special needs can in fact receive the special support he or she needs in a regular classroom. This certainly can be done in many instances, but does require that "regular" teachers receive special training and that supplementary resources are available. Teachers who have special children mainstreamed into their classes frequently say these services are in fact not being adequately provided.

Key to interpreting Public Law 94-142 and IDEA (PL 101-476) has been the policy of placing students with special needs into "the least restrictive environment" possible. Defining precisely what such an

INTASC Standards
Principle #2

INTASC Standards
Principle #3

FIGURE 12.2 ■ Mentally disabled children in a mainstreamed classroom.

environment is, is open to considerable interpretation. Questions arise concerning the rights of teachers and students. Should non–special education teachers be required to work with students with special needs? If so, what type of training and support should they have? Do the demands created by students with special needs interfere with the "normal" conduct of the classroom?

Underlying mainstreaming and the idea of teaching students with special needs in the least restrictive environment possible is the philosophy of **inclusion.** Inclusion assumes that schools reflect the communities of which they are a larger part. According to Strully and Strully:

> Inclusion does not mean a self-contained special education classroom with opportunities to be with nonlabeled children for recess, art, music and lunch. Inclusion does not mean bringing nonlabeled children into special education class and working on a project. Inclusion means the process of making whole, of bringing together all children, and having all children learn together. Inclusion means helping all people (children and adults) recognize and appreciate the unique gifts that each individual brings to a situation or a community. (Strully and Strully 1996, 149)

inclusion
Including students with special needs into the schools and communities of which they are a part.

An interesting example of an early case of the types of demands placed on local districts by Law 94-142 can be seen shortly after the law was enacted. In 1980 Raul Espino Jr. entered school for the first time in San Antonio, Texas. Raul had suffered damage to his nervous system that made it impossible for his body to control its temperature. As a result, he had to be in an air-conditioned environment.

Because Raul's school lacked air conditioning, it was decided that it would be most equitable and cost-effective to place him in a specially air-conditioned glass box in his classroom. If the entire classroom were air conditioned, the other students in the class would unfairly benefit. Raul's parents argued that the glass box unfairly restricted their child and set him apart from the other students in the class. Eventually the case made its way to the Supreme Court; the Court decided that Raul had indeed been placed in an unfairly restrictive environment.

WHAT DO YOU THINK?

Is Mainstreaming Always Justified?

Mainstreaming and inclusion represent specific ideological and philosophical positions concerning education and democracy. According to Anastasios Karaggiannis, William Stainback, and Susan Stainback:

> Exclusion in schools sows the seeds of social discontent and discrimination. . . . By educating all students together, persons with disabilities have the opportunity to prepare for life in the community, teachers improve their professional skills, and society makes the conscious decision to operate according to the social value of equality for all people with the consequent results of enhanced social peace. (Karaggiannis, Stainback, and Stainback 1996, 3)

Some populations with special needs, such as people with hearing disabilities, believe that they should have a separate educational experience from the mainstream. The argument is that through the use of sign language, hearing impaired and deaf individuals have a rich culture and language system and unique sense of community. American Sign Language is the third most widely used language in the United States.

Many sign language advocates maintain that being mainstreamed in a hearing culture presents extremely frustrating conditions for most hearing impaired and deaf students. Even for those individuals who have good speech and auditory skills, living in a non–sign language culture is extremely isolating and limiting.

Is mainstreaming necessarily desirable for populations with hearing disabilities and deafness? What about other populations with special needs? Is mainstreaming always justified? What do you think?

■ EQUAL ACCESS AND THE STUDENT WITH SPECIAL NEEDS

INTASC Standards

Principle #3

The passage of Public Law 94-142 has forced local school systems to reevaluate their physical plans in light of the needs of special students. Until the passage of the law in 1975 most facilities were designed exclusively for the nondisabled. Problems with this assumption become apparent when we consider, for example, the needs of a wheelchair-bound student.

Sinks in bathrooms have most always been set at heights comfortable for the average population. But wheelchair arms must fit under the rim of the sink, and disabled individuals need faucets they can turn on and off easily. This means having large and easily reachable handles. Whether space has been left beneath a countertop in a biology or chemistry laboratory may determine accessibility for a wheelchair-bound student. Assembly halls and stages have rarely been designed to be easily accessible to a wheelchair. In the past if students were to participate in an activity involving the use of an auditorium stage (performing in an orchestra, giving a speech in front of an assembly, or receiving a diploma upon graduation), they had to be lifted from their wheelchairs and carried onto the stage. Such restrictions often meant that students did not participate at all or were singled out because they caused disruption.

Normally, concepts of physical planning before the passage of PL 94-142 did not take into account the **nonambulatory** population. As a result, we now have many schools two or three stories high with no elevators, long flights of stairs, multiple changes of levels, and libraries, cafeterias, auditoriums, and specialized classrooms (for example, science or language laboratories) that are completely inaccessible to nonambulatory students, teachers, and visitors to the school.

Imagine for a moment being blind in the school you attended in your senior year of high school. If there was an elevator in your school, did it have an embossed sign written in braille to help you determine what buttons to push? Were large objects—objects easy to trip over—left in hallways? Were safeguards (like railings around sharp drop-offs) both inside and outside the building? How safe would you have felt going around the school?

If you have access to a wheelchair, a set of crutches, or even a cane, try the following experiment. With all your books and other personal paraphernalia (purse, briefcase, and umbrella, etc.), try getting around to your classes the same way a disabled student must. Start from a distant point in a parking lot. This will give you a sense of what it is like when a nondisabled individual inconsiderately takes the special parking place designated for a disabled person. Make your way around the pot-

nonambulatory
Not being able to walk, that is, nonwalking.

FIGURE 12.3 ▪ Photograph showing wheelchair access.

holes or loose gravel. Next, negotiate over a curb. Maneuver over the grass and finally onto a sidewalk. How much longer will it take to get to class? Were you even able to get around? Note what classrooms may be difficult to enter, what doors are hard to open, and what doors are not wide enough for a wheelchair. Then imagine what it is like to deal with these sorts of problems every single day of your life—in the snow, in the rain, in the heat, on a dark night, and on the day you have three final exams back to back.

Many problems the physically disabled or challenged face can be addressed at relatively little cost or trouble when architects are first designing the building. But once a building is built, it becomes difficult and expensive to install elevators, change the height of sinks, change classrooms from one level of a building to another, and build ramps up the side of auditorium stages.

To provide students with physical disabilities equal educational opportunities, we must provide them with equal access. Although it may not be feasible to anticipate every need of every special individual, we need to follow the general spirit and purpose of laws like PL 94-142. Not to do so is to discriminate against a significant portion of our population and give the nondisabled student the false impression that the learning environment and the world in general is a place intended only for nondisabled people.

■ IDENTIFYING INDIVIDUALS WITH SPECIAL NEEDS

INTASC Standards

Principle #9

The question of identifying individuals with special needs has become very controversial in recent years. In the case of individuals with limited intellectual capabilities, testing has historically been used to identify people. In many instances, **mental testing** has proved highly discriminatory and has been used for purposes that were not always in the best interest of the individual.

At the beginning of the twentieth century, it was widely assumed that measuring an individual's intelligence was possible. Psychologists such as the Frenchmen Alfred Binet (1867–1911) and his assistant Theodore Simon (1873–1961) thought that intelligence could be precisely measured through the use of intelligence tests. In 1904 Binet was asked by the French government to produce a measurement system that would identify children who could not work in classrooms at the same level as "normal" children. Binet and Simon developed a set of tests that would measure children's ability to reason, imagine, and carry out simple commands. Over the course of time, these tests were statistically refined and standardized so that they could be administered on a mass basis (Winzer 1993, 267–268).

Binet produced a version of his test in 1908 that measured the mental age of the child. Essentially, the child began the test at the lowest level and worked through each age level until he or she could no longer answer the question. By doing so, a "mental age" or what was later called an intelligence quota (IQ) could be obtained (Gould 1981, 149). Binet felt that his test should provide a general guide to identifying the special needs of students. He did not feel that intelligence could be captured with a single number or measurement.

Commenting on his scale in 1905, for example, he argued that "the scale, properly speaking, does not permit the measure of the intelligence, because intellectual qualities are not superposable, and therefore cannot be measured as linear surfaces are measured" (quoted by Gould 1981, 151). Binet was afraid that his test would be misused to label children, rather

mental testing
Psychological testing of intelligence and ability.

than act as a guide for identifying children who needed special help. In fact, this is exactly what happened to his work in the United States.

Binet's test was translated into English in 1908 by Elizabeth Kite, who was working with the psychologist Robert Goddard at the New Jersey Institution for Feeble-Minded Boys and Girls at Vineland. Other versions were eventually developed by Lewis Madison Terman at Stanford University.

Under the leadership of Goddard and other "hereditarian" thinkers, Binet's work was adapted and used in ways he would have strongly objected to. Tests were gradually developed and used, including mass-administered instruments during the First World War (Alpha and Beta tests), which screened 1.7 million military recruits in terms of their supposed intelligence. The problem with these and subsequent IQ tests was that they were highly biased in terms of their cultural content and did not in fact measure intelligence.

The military's Alpha and Beta tests provided a foundation for the development of mass-administered intelligence tests during the 1920s and 1930s. Despite criticisms of these tests and their scientific validity, they had widespread use in public schools in the United States. The educational historian Clarence J. Karier has shown how these tests did not measure intelligence, but instead specific U.S. mainstream cultural values, such as the **Puritan work ethic.**

For example, on Form D of the army test, the following question was asked:

> 10. Why should you not give money to beggars on the street? Because
>   ■ it breaks up families
>   ■ it makes it hard for the beggar to get work
>   ■ it takes away the work of organized charities
>   ■ it encourages living off of others (Karier et al. 1973, 13)

The correct answer, according to the test developers is "it encourages living off of others." While that answer might represent the types of values put forward by the public schools and the mainstream culture, the question does not measure intelligence, but instead a specific set of social values. This is particularly clear in the following item included on Form D of the test.

> 1. If the grocer should give you too much money in making change, what is the thing to do?
>   ■ take the money and hurry out
>   ■ tell him of his mistake
>   ■ buy some candy with it
>   ■ give it to the next poor man you meet (Karier et al. 1973, 13)

Puritan work ethic
An ethic of hard work and diligence that traces its roots back to the early Colonial period in America (during the seventeenth and eighteenth centuries).

meritocratic
A system based on merit.

eugenics
The science of controlled breeding for the supposed improvement of a race or breed.

heredity
The transmission of genetic qualities from one generation to another.

Although the correct answer, according to the testers, was "tell him of his mistake," this answer, once again, reflects a specific set of cultural values. If the grocer had been overcharging you and your family for years, would this have been the correct answer? What about the idea of charity? Would giving the money to someone who needed the money more than the grocer did be the more intelligent thing to do?

Intelligence tests served many purposes in the schools during the 1920s and 1930s. Testing provided a means of ranking and classifying people as part of a supposedly **meritocratic** system. The fact that the tests favored certain cultural groups over others meant that they were selective and often highly prejudicial. Among their most disturbing use was as part of the **Eugenics** movement, which led to the misuse of the exams as a means of identifying "feeblemindedness" in the population.

According to Eugenics theory, problems of mental retardation and social deviance were **hereditarily** based. This notion complimented the idea that intelligence was fixed and inherited, rather than changing and dynamic. Using literacy and intelligence tests, immigrants during the period prior to the First World War were supposedly shown to be inferior—and thus did not warrant admission to the United States.

As a result of the Eugenics movement, assumptions became widespread that mental retardation and immorality were directly correlated. By 1930, twenty-eight states had enacted sterilization laws, and 12,057 people were legally sterilized. By 1932, the number had reached approximately sixteen thousand sterilizations. Under the influence of the Human Betterment Foundation, which included the educational psychologist and intelligence test developer Lewis A. Terman and David Starr Jordan, president of Stanford University, California, conducted a total of sixty-two hundred sterilizations. Most of the people sterilized had committed a minor crime, and on receipt of a low score when tested using an intelligence test, underwent sterilization (Karier et al. 1972, 113).

Educational and psychological researchers such as Henry Herbert Goddard, Edward Thorndike, and Lewis Terman assumed that the "feebleminded" were incapable of moral judgments and therefore were, by definition, potential criminals. According to Terman, one of the most distinguished psychologists and educators of his era:

> All feebleminded are at least potential criminals. That every feebleminded woman is at least a potential prostitute would hardly be disputed by anyone. Moral judgments, like business judgment, social judgment or any other kind of higher thought process, is a function of intelligence. (Quoted by Karier et al. 1972, 115)

Cross racial marriages were particularly frowned on, and viewed as reducing the quality of the gene pool by hereditarian-oriented psychologists.

Hereditarian psychological models maintained themselves throughout the twentieth century. In 1966, for example, Edward Garret, past president of the American Psychological Association and former chairman of Columbia University's Department of Psychology, presented the following argument in a pamphlet titled *How Classroom Desegregation Will Work*:

> You can no more mix the two races and maintain the standards of White civilization than you can add 80 (the average I.Q. of Negroes) and 100 (average I.Q. of Whites) divided by two and get 100. What you would get would be a race of 90s, and it is that 10 per cent differential that spells the difference between a spire and a mud hut; 10 per cent—or less is the margin of civilization's "profit"; it is the difference between a cultured society and savagery. (Quoted by Karier et al. 1972, 118)

Garret goes on to argue: "Therefore it follows, if miscegenation would be bad for White people, it would be bad for Negroes as well. For, if leadership is destroyed, all is destroyed" (quoted by Karier et al. 1972, 118).

Garret's racist comments echo those of Lewis Terman in 1923, when before a meeting of the National Education Association he argued that "the racial stocks most prolific of gifted children are those from northern and western Europe, and the Jewish. The least prolific are the Mediterranean races, the Mexicans and the Negroes" (quoted by Karier et al. 1972, 119). More recently, similar types of arguments have been made by psychologists Richard Herrnstein and Charles Murray in their 1994 book *The Bell Curve: Intelligence and Class Structure in American Life,* in which they maintained that segments of the U.S. population, including African Americans and Hispanic Americans, are genetically unable to learn as well as other segments of the population and therefore do not merit financial investment by the educational system.

Although various researchers responded vigorously to the arguments made by Herrnstein and Murray (Kincheloe, Steinberg, and Gresson 1997), the significance of their work may lie in the fact that it represents a continuation of the hereditarian model of intelligence that dominated U.S. psychology and education during the first half of the twentieth century. Newer models of intelligence, such as Howard Gardner's idea of **multiple intelligences,** suggest that intelligence takes many forms and is not something that is a single measure—least of all one with highly prejudiced and racial overtones (Gardner 1983).

hereditarian
Based on principles of heredity.

multiple intelligences
A model of intelligence developed by the psychologist Howard Gardner that is defined along multiple dimensions (seven, and more recently, nine separate types of intelligence).

■ LABELING AS AN ISSUE IN EDUCATION

INTASC Standards

Principle #3

Whereas testing may be a useful tool in education, it is also, as just demonstrated, potentially dangerous if misused or overemphasized. Researchers such as Beth Harry and Mary G. Anderson, for example, argue that disproportionate numbers of African American males are assigned to special education classes. This trend, according to them, has gone on since the inception of special education in public schools. Citing Supreme Court cases such as the 1974 *Johnson v. San Francisco Unified School District* and *Larry P. et al. v. Wilson Riles et al.* (1979), Harry and Anderson point out how the *Larry P.* case demonstrated that whereas 29 percent of the students in the school district were African American, 66 percent of the students in educable mentally retarded (EMR) classes were African American. Similarly, throughout California, whereas 10 percent of the population was African American, 25 percent of the students in EMR classes were African American (Harry and Anderson 1995, 602–603).

Harry and Anderson argue that "racial, gender, cultural and linguistic biases" function as an integral part of special education placements. In light of the earlier history of discriminatory testing practices in the United States, their argument deserves careful attention. Elsewhere Harry and her coauthor Maya Kalyanpur point out the interesting idea of special education representing a "cultural institution" (Kalyanpur and Harry 1999). According to Kalyanpur and Harry, many families whose children are assigned to special education settings, "do not share or value the principles on which special education policies and practices are built and are too often alienated and excluded from collaboration in the treatment of their children's difficulties" (Kalyanpur and Harry 1999, 13). They argue that special educators and regular teachers need to develop a higher degree of cultural awareness toward special education clients, one that represents a "posture of cultural reciprocity."

? WHAT DO YOU THINK?

Who Gets to Cheer?

Being a high school cheerleader is a dream for a lot of high school students. Callie Smart dreamed of being one too. It didn't make any difference to her that she had cerebral palsy and was confined to a wheelchair. She had school spirit like anyone else. Her dream came true when she became a freshman cheerleader.

Evidently fans and the football team loved having her cheer. So it came as a shock at the end of the sports season when she was thrown off the cheerleading squad. She was told by school officials it was for safety purposes. The following fall (1996) she was made an honorary cheerleader for the junior varsity team. However, as an honorary junior varsity cheerleader, she was no longer allowed to cheer at away games, participate in cheerleading fund raisers, nor to roll her wheelchair up and down the sidelines cheering during games. In addition, she was told that the honorary cheerleader position was being eliminated after her sophomore year and that, if she wanted to stay on as a cheerleader, she would have to try out for the squad as anyone else—demonstrating her physical agility by doing splits and tumbles.

Objections to Callie's participation as a cheerleader came from Peter Francis, a businessman whose daughter Jennifer was the head cheerleader on the junior varsity squad. Francis argued that his concern was one of safety, despite the fact that this had not been a problem during Callie's freshman year as a cheerleader. Should Callie be allowed to be a cheerleader? What do you think?

Drawing on a model developed by Lisa Delpit, Kalyanpur and Harry argue that educators working with populations with special needs need to work on three levels of cultural awareness: (1) overt, (2) covert, and (3) subtle (Kalyanpur and Harry 1999, 117). The overt level refers to being sensitive to obvious differences of language, social space, and manner of dress. The covert level goes somewhat deeper and deals with the "invisible culture" of a group—understanding differences concerning time and punctuality (e.g., When does a scheduled appointment really begin?), the need for group consensus, or deference to selected community leaders based on tradition or religious belief. The subtle level of cultural awareness "involves the recognition of imbedded values and beliefs." These are beliefs that may not be in accord with the mainstream culture, but which are nonetheless strongly held by a specific cultural group. Thus in certain Native American traditions, the idea of the group coming before the individual would be an example operating at the subtle level.

In a certain sense, operating at an *overt, covert,* or *subtle* level of cultural awareness is simply a strategy or tool for becoming an effective border crosser of the type described by Henry Giroux (explored previously in this book). To understand a cultural group, whether an immigrant population, a gender or racial group, or a population with special needs who are either gifted or have disabilities, interpreting that culture at multiple levels—overt, covert, and subtle—is essential. This is true with all populations, including those who are gifted and/or talented.

INTASC Standards
Principle #9

■ THE SPECIAL NEEDS OF STUDENTS WHO ARE GIFTED AND TALENTED

INTASC Standards

Principle #3

Special education includes student who are gifted and talented, as well as physically or mentally impaired. At best our treatment of these students has been ambivalent. One moment we talk about these students being the future leaders of our nation, a cultural asset, and our greatest natural resource. The next moment we hesitate to single out individuals already blessed with natural advantages and to give them additional privileges and opportunities.

This anti-elite attitude, although often springing from a misguided democratic spirit, in fact represents a special sort of discrimination against the student who is gifted or talented. If we accept the premise that each individual should be provided with the opportunity to become all he or she is capable of becoming, then we must apply this premise to students with gifts and talents as much as to those with disabilities. If a child has a particular talent in mathematics or history, why shouldn't she be able to pursue that subject to her maximum potential? If a child is talented in art or music, why shouldn't he be able to get the best training the school system can reasonably offer?

But precisely what makes a person gifted or talented? The former American Commissioner of Education attempted to define the terms.

> Gifted and talented children are those identified by professionally qualified persons (and) who by virtue of outstanding abilities are capable of high performance. These are children who require differentiated educational programs and services beyond those normally provided by the regular school program in order to realize their contributions to self and society. (Marland 1972, 2)

Children capable of high performance in general intellectual ability, specific academic aptitude, creative or productive thinking, leadership ability, visual and performing arts, psychomotor ability, or a combination of these areas are to be considered gifted or talented (Marland 1972, 2). Significantly, Marland's definition does not take into account motivational factors, and the six general categories he lists are not necessarily comparable. Visual and performing arts and psychomotor abilities are likely to manifest themselves as subsets of the first four areas (Renzulli and Delisle 1982, 273).

The problem of identifying students who are gifted and talented is not new. Numerous historical examples may be cited of gifted students who were ridiculed or considered stupid in school: Issac Newton,

Thomas Edison, Albert Einstein, and Winston Churchill, to name a few. In light of their subsequent success one must assume that somehow the schools' means of assessing them were inadequate.

In his collection of short stories *Welcome to the Monkey House*, Kurt Vonnegut Jr. includes a piece entitled "Harrison Bergeron," set in the year 2081 when everyone is finally equal. "They weren't only equal before God and the law, they were equal in every which way" (Vonnegut 1950, 7). No one was smarter or better looking than anyone else. Those who were outstanding in any way were given handicaps. Good dancers were forced to carry sandbags; beautiful or handsome people were forced to wear masks; highly intelligent people were required to wear headphones that would emit ear-piercing shrieks every twenty seconds to prevent them from taking unfair advantage of their brains (Vonnegut 1950, 7).

When we fail to support programs in our schools for students who are gifted, we too are providing them with handicaps, almost as if to make sure they do not have an unfair advantage in life. Ironically we contradict this approach when we award scholarships and grants to gifted students entering our best public and private universities. The law school at Harvard is essentially a professional school for the gifted, as is the Stanford University Medical School (Passow 1979, 41).

In the future, programs for students who are gifted and talented must address issues ranging from training teachers to work with these students to developing a research base for understanding their special needs. Among the most interesting challenges for educators in the coming decades will be developing effective educational programs and support systems for these students. Local boards and states have attempted to achieve this end, but it may take federal legislation, as in the case of educating students with disabilities, to make the goal a reality.

■ SUMMARY

Our discussion of the needs and rights of students with special needs echoes many of the questions we raised about educational equity in preceding chapters. Perhaps the ultimate test of a democracy is the degree to which it allows its citizens to fully realize their potential. In our Constitution we proclaim the right to "life, liberty and the pursuit of happiness." Implied in this notion is also the idea of citizens being able to realize their potential (as opposed to simply pursuing it) as fully as possible. It is clear we have only partially realized this ideal. Effective programs in special education at all levels and for all types of students is a necessity for our culture and society.

We need to be particularly concerned that special education is not used as a means to discriminate or manipulate certain populations in our culture. Although such a notion obviously flies in the face of what is the stated purpose of most special education programs, historically, as is clear from the testing movement, the potential for abuse is real.

■ DISCUSSION QUESTIONS ■

1. To what degree should public schools provide special education for students who are especially gifted or especially disabled?
2. What is an appropriate education for a student with special needs?
3. Why has interest in the needs of special students in the United States increased since the early 1960s?
4. What are the arguments for and against mainstreaming students with special needs into regular classrooms?
5. Should all students be mainstreamed?
6. What is meant by the idea that educational inclusion represents a specific philosophy or ideology?
7. Does the idea of inclusion have political overtones?
8. Why is physical access an important issue in education?
9. What have been the limitations of intelligence testing? Do such tests have appropriate uses?
10. How does providing special educational programs for the gifted relate to larger questions of educational equity within our society?

■ SOURCES CITED ■

Education for All Handicapped Children Act (1975). Public Law 94-42.

Gardner, Howard. 1983. *Frames of mind: The theory of multiple intelligence.* New York: Basic Books.

Goldberg, Steven. 1982. *Special education law: A guide for parents, advocates and educators.* New York: Plenum Press.

Gould, Stephen Jay. 1981. *The Mismeasure of Man.* New York: W. W. Norton.

Harry, Beth, and Mary G. Anderson. 1994. The disproportionate placement of African American males in special education programs: A critique of the process. *Journal of Negro Education* 63(4): 602–619.

Hehir, Thomas, and Thomas Latus. 1992. *Special education at the century's end: Evolution of theory and practice since 1970.* Cambridge: Harvard Educational Review.

Herrnstein, Richard, and Charles Murray. 1994. *The bell curve: Intelligence and class structure in American life.* New York: The Free Press.

Hogan, D. P., M. E. Msall, M. L. Rogers, and R. C. Avery. (1997). Improved disability population estimates of functional limitation among American children aged 5–17. *Maternal and Child Health Journal* 1(4): 203–216.

Itard, Jean. 1962. *The wild boy of Aveyron.* New York: Appleton-Century Crofts.

Karier, Clarence J., Paul C. Violas, and Joel Spring. 1972. *Roots of crisis: American education in the twentieth century.* Chicago: Rand McNally.

Kalyanpur, Maya, and Beth Harry. 1999. *Culture in special education: Building reciprocal family–professional relationships.* Baltimore: Paul H. Brookes.

Kincheloe, Joe L., Shirley R. Steinberg, and Aaron D. Gresson, III. 1997. *Measured lies: The bell curve examined.* New York: St. Martin's Press.

Lane, Harlane. 1976. *The wild boy of Aveyron.* Cambridge: Harvard University Press.

Marland, Sidney P., Jr. 1972. *Education for the gifted and talented.* Vol. 1. Report to the Congress of the United States by the U.S. Commissioner of Education. Washington, D.C.: U.S. Government Printing Office.

National Information Center for Children and Youth with Disabilities (NICHY). 1997. General information about disabilities which qualify children and youth for special education services under the individuals with Disabilities Education Act. Available online at http://www.nichcy.org.

Nondiscrimination on the Basis of Handicap. 1977. *Federal Register* 42(86), 4 May.

Passow, Harry, ed. 1979. *The gifted and the talented: Their education and development.* The Seventy-Eight Yearbook of the National Society for the Study of Education. Chicago: University of Chicago Press.

Pressley, Sue Anne. 1996. Disabled cheerleader kicked off school squad. *The Miami Herald,* 15 November, 8A.

Renzulli, Joseph S., and James R. Delisle. 1982. Gifted persons. *Encyclopedia of Educational Research.* Vol. 2, 723–730. New York: Macmillan and the Free Press.

Reynolds, Maynard C. 1982. Handicapped individuals. *Encyclopedia of Educational Research.* Vol. 2, 757–764. New York: Macmillan and the Free Press.

Stainback, Susan, and William Stainback, eds. 1996. *Inclusion: A guide for educators.* Baltimore: Paul H. Brookes.

Strully, Jeffrey L., and Cindy Strully. 1996. Friendships as an educational goal. In *Inclusion: A guide for educators,* edited by Susan Stainback and William Stainback, 141–154. Baltimore: Paul H. Brookes.

Vonnegut, Kurt, Jr. 1950. *Welcome to the monkey house.* New York: Dell.

Weintraub, F. J., and A. Abeson. 1976. New education policies for the handi-capped: The quiet revolution. In *Public policy and the education of exceptional children,* edited by F. J. Weintraub, A. Abeson, J. Ballard, and M. L. LaVor, 7–13. Reston, Va.: Council for Exceptional Children.

Winzer, Margaret A. 1993. *The history of special education: From isolation to integration.* Washington, D.C.: Gallaudet University Press.

CHAPTER 13

Textbooks and the Curriculum

Textbooks are an important part of the **technology of teaching.** They represent an efficient means to present large amounts of information and data to students. In doing so, they make it possible to establish a consistent and uniform curriculum. But textbooks are rarely value free. Besides teaching a child to read, a **basal reader** or **primer** also introduces a student to social values and role models. A U.S. history text provides a high school student with specific political values. A college textbook like this one attempts to introduce students to, and persuade them to adopt, carefully defined professional goals and standards.

This chapter examines not only the historical development of textbooks, but also their role in the current curriculum of the schools. By the end of this chapter, it should be clear that textbooks not only shape the curriculum, but also reflect issues and concerns found within the culture at large.

INTASC Standards

Principle #9

■ TEXTBOOKS AS CURRICULUM AND CULTURAL CAPITAL

Textbooks represent perhaps the most visible evidence of the curriculum in the schools. They represent a conscious effort by educators, local school boards, writers, publishers, and the society at large to systematize what is to be learned in schools. Textbooks are **consensus** documents. They must meet the needs of many people who have different values, goals, and purposes.

technology of teaching
Various technologies (the chalkboard, computers) that support the work of teaching.

basal reader
A basic or beginning reading text.

primer
Historically, the first or most basic book used in teaching children how to read.

consensus
General agreement or unanimity.

INTASC Standards

Principle #9

To discuss the idea of textbooks as curriculum we, of course, have to define the meaning of curriculum. At the most basic level, the curriculum is what is taught. Families have curriculums, television has a curriculum, and schools have curriculums. Christopher Winch and John Gingell define what is meant by curriculum in the following way:

> ... the curriculum is, perhaps, best thought of as that set of planned activities which are designed to implement a particular educational aim— or set of such aims—in terms of the content of what is to be taught and the knowledge, skills and attitudes which are to be deliberately fostered. (Winch and Gingell 1999, 53)

Any curriculum is by definition a cultural document. It is concerned with fostering not only specific skills, but also specific ways of constructing and viewing the world.

Implicit in any curriculum, and in turn any textbook, is the question of what types of things do we want to teach our children? It is not surprising, therefore, that the content of textbooks is often hotly disputed. Textbooks are unavoidably ideological in nature, whether they promote the values of U.S. democracy or of the Cuban or Nicaraguan revolutions. They are among the most tangible available examples of the cultural capital of society.

INTASC Standards

Principle #1

Textbooks typically work at multiple levels. Besides an **overt curriculum,** they nearly always have an underlying hidden curriculum. This is probably inevitable. What is more remarkable is that this fact often goes unnoticed. For example, when I was in elementary school, I learned to read with the Dick and Jane readers. These books, first developed by the Scott Foresman Company in the late 1920s, are seemingly simple stories portraying the life of a Midwestern family with three children and a dog named Spot.

On the surface these stories were neutral, but as we explore in more detail in this chapter, they presented specific values. No single parents nor people of color (black or brown) are to be found in these stories I learned to read by during the mid-1950s. Nor were gay people depicted. No one was poor. Mothers stayed at home and raised the children. Fathers went off to work everyday. Implicit in these seemingly neutral stories were specific models of family and childhood, of cultural capital. As a child reading these textbooks, I accepted them as the norm, never realizing that they represented a specific way of constructing the world.

overt curriculum
The curriculum that is openly and consciously taught.

■ TEXTBOOKS AND THEIR ROLE IN THE HISTORY OF EDUCATION

Textbooks have always played an important part in the curriculum of modern schools. They are, however, a relatively recent invention. In the early 1500s, as part of the Protestant Reformation, Martin Luther introduced illustrated Bibles and **catechisms** intended for the use of both children and adults. These texts eventually led to the development of the modern textbook.

In 1658, the Czech educator John Amos Comenius (also known as Jan Amos Komensky) published what many people consider to be the first modern textbook for children, the *Orbis sensualium pictus* (1887). The *Orbis sensualium pictus* is also considered by many to be the first modern illustrated book for children. It is remarkable in a number of regards.

To begin with, Comenius's text is in both Czech and Latin (an English/Latin translation of the work was published in 1659). In addition, Comenius tried to present a system of instruction that connected pictures of things found in the world with teaching material. In an early English edition of the work, for example, titled "Head and Hands," Comenius describes the different parts of the head and hand using a numbered illustration. One column of text is in English and another in Latin. Even though today we take illustrated children's books for granted, this book represents a revolutionary educational innovation.

In the American colonies the influence of Comenius can be seen in the publication of the *New England Primer*. The *New England Primer* is widely considered the most popular textbook in the period preceding the Revolution. No first edition of the *Primer* survives. It is believed that the book was first published by Benjamin Harris sometime around 1690. The book introduced children not only to the alphabet and the rudiments of reading but also to basic religious values.

Beginning with a prayer, it lists words for children to recite including primarily religious terms such as *benediction, consolation, purification,* and (by modern standards) as surprising a word as *fornication*. Most of the references in the famous rhyming alphabet in the book are religious. The *Primer* begins, for example, with the letter *A* and the admonition: "In Adam's Fall We Sinned All." Other letters have a moral and even threatening tone. The letter *F,* for example, warns that "The Idle Fool Is whipt at School," while the letter *G* explains that "As runs the Glass Mans life doth Pass."

Textbook writers often saw themselves as having an exalted and special function—one that involved shaping the minds of children who

catechisms
A type of religious text intended to instruct individuals in religious principles.

Words of five Syllables.

A-bo-mi-na-ble	ad-mi-ra-ti-on
Be-ne-dic-ti-on	be-ne-fi-ci-al
Ce-le-bra-ti-on	con-so-la-ti-on
De-cla-ra-ti-on	de-di-ca-ti-on
E-du-ca-ti-on	ex-hor-ta-ti-on
For-ni-ca-ti-on	ser-mon-ra-ti-on
Ge-ne-ra-ti-on	ge-ne-ro-li-ty

Words of six Syllables

A-bo-mi-na-ti-on	Gra-ti-fi-ca-ti-on
Be-ne-fi-ci-al-ly	Hu-mi-li-a-ti-on
Con-ti-nu-a-ti-on	I-ma-gi-na-ti-on
De-ter-mi-na-ti-on	Mor-ti-fi-ca-ti-on
E-di-fi-ca-ti-on	Pu-ri-fi-ca-ti-on
Fa-mi-li-a-ri-ty	Qua-li-fi-ca-ti-on

FIGURE 13.1 ■ Lists of words of five and six syllables from a 1777 edition of the *New England Primer.*

read their books. Thus, Noah Webster, the great American **grammarian** and **lexicographer**, wrote in the introduction to his three-volume *Grammatical Institutes of the English Language,* first published in 1783 (the first volume of which is more commonly known as the *Blueback Spelling Book*), that he intended to instill into the minds of the students reading his book ". . . the first rudiments of language, some just ideas of religion, morals, and domestic economy." Interestingly, Webster also believed he was creating a "national" awareness in his readers' minds. Webster was consciously anti-British and argued that textbooks should reflect a specifically American set of values and traditions. Political discussions in the new American textbooks dealt with presidents and the virtues of a democracy rather than with kingship and the nature of a monarchy.

Throughout the nineteenth century the attitudes and beliefs at work within the society were reflected in the content of textbooks. Elementary geography textbooks, for example, clearly divided and ranked the races. In Peter Parley's 1829 *Method of Telling about Geography to Children,* stereotypes of different racial and ethnic groups were included throughout the text. Malays were described as being "wicked,

grammarian
Somebody who studies grammar.

lexicographer
An editor or author of a dictionary.

G — As runs the Glass,
Our Life doth pass.

H — My Book and Heart
Must never part.

I — JOB feels the Rod;—
Yet bleffes GOD.

K — Proud Korah's troop
Was fwallowed up

L — LOT fled to *Zoar*,
Saw fiery Shower
On *Sodom* pour.

M — MOSES was he
Who *Israel's* Hoft
Led thro' the Sea.

FIGURE 13.2 ■ The illustrated letters *G–M* in a 1777 edition of the *New England Primer.*

ferocious and cruel" (Parley 1829, 79). A Chinese person is depicted by an illustration of a Chinese man selling "rats and puppies for pies." (Parley, 1829, 79)

In most geography textbooks published during the nineteenth century Caucasians and northern Europeans were considered the most highly developed and civilized people. In Arnold Henry Guyot's *Physical Geography* (1866), for example, a striking portrait of the Greek god Apollo represented the white race. Other races were depicted in less flattering terms—Africans looked particularly ugly and slow. Such stereotypes obviously did not conform to reality, but they undoubtedly conveyed to many children false ideas about other nations and other peoples.

The depiction of racial stereotypes in textbooks reinforced the superiority of Western culture. In *Orientalism*, the theorist Edward Said argues that such an approach may tell us more about the people writing

KNOWLEDGE and FAME are gain'd not by surprise;
He that would win, must LABOUR for the prize.
'Tis thus the youth, from lisping A, B, C,
Attains, at length, a Master's high degree.

FIGURE 13.3 ■ The Greek goddess Athena directs the American child toward the temples of Knowledge and Fame in the frontispiece of an 1848 edition of Webster's *Blueback Spelling Book.*

the textbooks than about the subjects they portray. Although Said does not specifically talk about textbooks, his ideas are nonetheless relevant. He argues, for example, that the cultures of North Africa, the Middle East, India, and so on have been specifically constructed by Western writers and intellectuals through a process of **orientalism** in a way that not only distorts the realities of life in these cultures but also allows the West to dominate them (Said 1978). Evidence to support this argument can be found in the content of textbooks.

Descriptions of black Africans in nineteenth-century U.S. textbooks, for example, consistently treated them as inferiors. This can be seen in J. A. Cummings's *An Introduction to Ancient and Modern Geography*

orientalism
A term coined by the scholar Edward Said to describe the distortion of Oriental, or Eastern, life as a means of asserting Western dominance.

A Chinese selling Rats and Puppies
for pies.

FIGURE 13.4 ■ An illustration of a
Chinese man in Peter Parley's *Method
of Telling about Geography to
Children.*

(1817) in which he wrote: "Africa has justly been called the country of
monsters. . . . Every man, in this quarter of the world, exists in a state of
lowest barbarism" (quoted by Miller 1964, 87). After the Civil War and
the emancipation of the slaves, textbooks still treated African Americans as inferiors. Typically, they were depicted as childlike, foolish, and
slow. Stereotypes such as these continued well into the twentieth century,
not only in textbooks but also in movies and literature.

But African Americans were certainly not the only group of people
falsely depicted in nineteenth-century textbooks. Catholics, Jews, and
women were often portrayed in a discriminatory light. Women were consistently depicted as mild, meek, and docile by nature. They gave absolute, unquestioning obedience to their fathers and husbands and
confined themselves to suitable activities such as sewing and reading.
Rarely were they ever represented in strenuous activities such as climb-
ing trees or running, let alone pursuing the diverse careers then open to
men.

Textbooks conveyed popular religious prejudices too. Roman
Catholicism was denounced as a false religion; some texts went so far as

to describe Catholicism as a threat to the continuance and well-being of the U.S. democratic system. The Pope was often described as tyrannical, and priests were more interested in lining their pockets with gold and silver than in helping the poor. In fact, the treatment of Catholics in most textbooks was so derogatory that by the 1840s Catholics, in their own defense, began to manufacture and produce textbooks for their children to use in their parochial schools.

WHAT DO YOU THINK?

Ethnocentrism in Nineteenth-Century Textbooks

Examine the illustration in Figure 13.5 from Von Steinwehr and Brinton's *An Intermediate Geography,* published in 1878. It conveys important cultural information and values. What does each illustration seem to communicate to the student? Pay attention to the placement of each race, the gender of each image, whether full-face or profile views are used, and so on. Do contemporary textbooks reflect specific values and beliefs? What do you think?

Conflicts over the content of textbooks, which often parallel current textbook controversies, reflected regional as well as national values during the nineteenth century. Not having the printing and distribution facilities necessary to produce textbooks, Southern schools were forced to buy textbooks from Northern publishers, despite the fact that the content of these textbooks consistently offended Southern readers. Many of the textbooks were written by Northerners opposed to slavery. Their texts reflected their abolitionist sentiments.

Yet many Southerners objected to the books not just because they promoted antislavery sentiments, but also because they represented a Northern perspective that usually included a strongly anti-Southern bias. From a pedagogical point of view, much of the information included in the texts was either inaccurate or inappropriate. An article in *DeBow's Review* reflected Southern frustration:

> What is to be done with geographies that . . . devote *two* pages to Connecticut onion and broom corn, and ten lines to Louisiana and sugar? of histories that are silent about Texas? of first readers that declare that all spelling but Noah Webster's "vulgar," and "not used in good society?" and of "speakers" that abound in selections for Southern decla-

Mongolian.
Ethiopian.   Caucasian.   American.
Malay.

FIGURE 13.5 ■ A depiction of the different races of man (Mongolian, Ethiopian, Caucasian, American, and Malay) from an 1878 geography textbook by Von Steinwehr and Brinton.

mation, made almost exclusively from Northern debates in Congress, and from abolition poets. (*DeBow's Review* 1852, 262)

Clearly the South was being overlooked as a distinct region, and its particular needs and values were being ignored.

■ THE McGUFFEY READERS

The most famous textbook series from the nineteenth century are the *McGuffey Eclectic Readers*. First published in 1836, they dominated the U.S. textbook market for approximately seventy-five years. Although many supplementary texts were published under the name McGuffey, the basic set consisted of a primer and six graded readers. In this case, *graded* referred to progressive levels of difficulty rather than school-grade levels (Lindberg 1976, xv).

The author of the *McGuffey Readers*, William Holmes McGuffey (1800–1873), was a Presbyterian minister who taught at Miami University in Oxford, Ohio. The *Eclectic Readers* were first published by the Cincinnati publishing company Truman and Smith. Interestingly,

LESSON XXVII.

The Dead Mother.

RULE.—This kind of composition is called *Dialogue*, and requires more care in reading, than any other. The tones should not be *too* familiar, yet still *conversational.*

1. *Fath.* Touch not thy mother, boy—Thou canst not wake her.

2. *Child.* Why, Father? She still wakens at this hour.

3. *Fath.* Your mother's dead, my child.

4. *Child.* And what is dead?
   If she be dead, why, then, 'tis only sleeping,
   For I am sure she sleeps. Come, mother, rise—
   Her hand is very cold!

5. *Fath.* Her *heart* is cold.
   Her limbs are bloodless, would that mine were so!

6. *Child.* If she would waken, she would soon be warm.
   Why is she wrapt in this thin sheet? If I,
   This winter morning, were not covered better,
   I should be cold like her.

7. *Fath.* No—not like her:
   The fire might warm *you*, or thick clothes—but *her*—
   Nothing can warm again!

8. *Child.* If I could wake her,
   She would smile on me, as she always does,
   And kiss me. Mother! you have slept too long—
   Her face is pale—and it would frighten me,
   But that I know she loves me.

9. *Fath.* Come, my child.

10. *Child.* Once, when I sat upon her lap, I felt
    A beating at her side, and then she said
    It was her heart that beat, and bade me feel
    For my own heart, and they both beat alike,
    Only mine was the quickest—and I feel
    My own heart yet—but hers—I cannot feel—

11. *Fath.* Child! child!—you drive me mad—come hence, I say.

FIGURE 13.6 ■ The first page of Lesson XVII, "The Dead Mother," in the first edition of the McGuffey *Third Reader.*

FIGURE 13.7 ■ Illustration for the story "George and the Hatchet," based on the legend by Parson Weem in McGuffey's *Second Reader*.

McGuffey was not the publishers' first choice to write the books. Mrs. Catherine Beecher Stowe, the moral educator and abolitionist, was contacted first, but declined to write the books (Lindberg 1976, xix). McGuffey's *Eclectic Readers* are interesting because they provide us with a means by which to reconstruct the social, moral, and political values of their era. In this sense, like many other textbooks, McGuffey's writings are like time machines that can transport us way back into an earlier culture or society.

Themes of death are common in the *McGuffey Readers*. The first edition of the Third Reader, for example, presents a three-page dialogue in which a father and his young son stand in front of a dead body. The first half of the dialogue is included in Figure 13.6. Such a passage reflects not only the frequency of death at an early age in the nineteenth century, but also the sentimental and religious persuasions of the period. Similar passages ask questions such as, "What is Death?" They use the example of a little girl asking her mother about the dead baby lying before them.

Stories about appropriate moral behavior are common—many often taking on political overtones. Parson Weem's **apocryphal** story of George

apocryphal
Of doubtful authenticity.

Washington chopping down a cherry tree, and then declaring, when confronted by his father, that "I cannot tell a lie," has become part of the mythic consciousness of the United States.

Other stories, such as "The Seven Sticks," emphasize the concept of political unity. The story is based on the Aesopic fable "The Old Man and the Bundle of Sticks." It describes how an old man had seven sons who constantly fought with one another. Realizing that he does not have long to live, he calls them together and has them each try to break in half a bundle of sticks that he had tied together—offering a reward of one

FIGURE 13.8 ■ Illustration for the story "The Seven Sticks," based on the Aesopic fable "The Old Man and the Bundle of Sticks." This fable is the likely source of the emblem of the ancient Roman Empire, the *fasces,* derived from the Latin for "a bundle of sticks." The symbol was widely circulated on the backs of Liberty or Mercury dimes from 1916–1946, but became discredited as a result of the Italian Fascists' use of the symbol during the 1930s and 1940s.

hundred dollars if they could do so. Despite their best efforts, none of them could do so. After untying the sticks, the old man proceeded to easily break each stick. In the original Aesopic fable the moral is, "A house divided against itself cannot stand" or "In unity is strength."

It is no accident that the fable was first introduced by McGuffey in 1857, just a few years before the Civil War, nor that Abraham Lincoln drew from the same imagery in his famous "House Divided" speech at the close of the Republican State Convention in Springfield, Illinois, on June 16, 1858. In reference to settling the differences between the North and the South over the slavery question, he explained: "'A house divided against itself cannot stand.' I believe this government cannot endure, permanently half *slave* and half *free*. I do not expect the Union to be *dissolved*—I do not expect the house to *fall*—but I do expect it will cease to be divided. It will become *all* one thing, or *all* the other."

FIGURE 13.9 ■ *Fasces,* which can be seen at the bottom of the illustration, were a faggot of sticks or wooden rods fastened to an axe and held together with a leather strap. They were a symbol of the authority and power of the Roman republic and were carried by Roman judges as a symbol of authority. Their origin can be traced back to the fable "The Old Man and the Bundle of Sticks" included in the *McGuffey Readers.*

■ THE DICK AND JANE READERS

INTASC Standards

Principle #9

One might think that more modern textbooks are less political and **ideological** than older works. In fact, on careful examination, it is clear that current textbooks only appear less biased and value driven because they reflect the culture of which we are a part. Nowhere is this clearer than in the case of the Dick and Jane readers, which are perhaps the most well known textbooks of the twentieth century.

The Dick and Jane readers were developed in the late 1920s by William Gray, a professor of reading at the University of Chicago, and by Zerna Sharp, an educational consultant working for Scott Foresman and Company. The books are important because they became the standard model for teaching reading in the United States.

Allan Luke describes the Dick and Jane readers as being consensus texts, which not only used new methods of instruction to teach reading (phonics), but also represented a vision of democratic life in the 1950s (Luke 1988, 79). Luke quotes Sara Zimet in this context. According to her,

> Contemporary America, as seen through these readers, is an other directed society in which the individual is not motivated to act by traditional institutional pressures but by others whose requests or demands are respected enough to produce compliance. Individuals enter into relationships for specific reasons, and these relationships are generally controlled by the opinions of others. (Zimet quoted by Luke 1988, 85)

If you had no other evidence about U.S. culture in the 1950s than the Dick and Jane readers, you could assume that all the people in the United States were "Caucasian, Northern European in origin and appearance, and quite well to do" (Zimit quoted by Luke 1988, 85). It is interesting that African American characters were not introduced into the series until the mid-1960s. They were depicted as middle class and vaguely "white" looking.

Allan Luke has conducted a revealing analysis of the content of the Dick and Jane readers. Using a story grammar strategy, Luke analyzed key episodes from the First Grade primer, *Fun with Dick and Jane*. Seemingly neutral material is shown to be value laden. Episode 1, "See It Go," is described as follows:

> . . . In the backyard (setting), Dick throws a toy airplane (initiating event); Sally and Jane observe (internal response); the plane goes over the fence beyond the yard; it almost hits father who, in a business suit,

is walking home (consequence); Jane expostulates "This is not fun for Father" (reaction/didactic reiteration). (Luke 1988, 87)

didactic
Designed or intended to teach.

According to Luke, this seemingly neutral text in fact has Dick initiate action while Sally and Jane assume the secondary roles of observers and commentators on male play. Jane provides a **didactic** commentary: "This is not fun for Father." The men (Dick and Father) are in fact the focal points of all that is going on in this seemingly simple story (Luke 1988, 92).

By itself, this story is of little or no consequence. What emerges from Luke's analysis of additional episodes in the book, however, is that a specific set of cultural values is at work in the stories. Male characters initiate the action; female characters provide support and commentary. Men have certain roles in life (going off to work), and women, different roles (taking care of the family). The children in the family assume gender-specific roles that are probably readily assimilated by the readers of the textbook.

In comparison, other contemporary textbooks are much more overt in their promotion of specific values and beliefs. The primer *El amancer del pueblo,* for example, is a beginning reading book, published in 1980, by the communist Sandinista government (following the Nicaraguan revolution). Lesson 1 shows the revolutionary figure Carlos Sandino (after whom the revolution was named) saying: "Sandino: guía de la Revolución" (i.e., Sandino: guide of the Revolution). The term *revolution* is then used to introduce the vowels *A, E, I, O,* and *U* (Ministerio de Educación 1980, 6–7).

Lesson 3 shows a picture of Sandinista military troops with smiling faces, waving their hands and rifles. The sentence introduced is "El FSLN condujo al pueblo a la liberación" (i.e., the FSLN, the Sandinista National Liberation Army, leads the people to freedom) (Ministerio de Educación 1980, 15–16).

The primer *El amancer del pueblo* is overt in its meaning. It takes a specific ideological and political point of view and promotes it. It views the world from a revolutionary and specifically cultural perspective. A seemingly more neutral text such as the Dick and Jane readers actually does the same thing, only much more subtly.

◼ THE TEXTBOOK BUSINESS

Textbooks make up the largest single type of book sold in the United States. They account for approximately a quarter of the roughly $6 billion annual book sales in the United States (Apple 1991, 28). Most textbooks, especially elementary and secondary textbooks, are conservative. Because many different cultural and ethnic groups around the country use their texts, authors and editors often find themselves trying to produce books that are all things to all people. As a result the textbook industry is often accused of producing bland and uninteresting books that avoid taking specific stands on controversial issues.

Textbooks are cultural statements. Imbedded in virtually any textbook are significant social messages. Often what makes a textbook acceptable or unacceptable to an individual or community is its approach to issues rooted in the religious beliefs and moral values of the people using the texts. What is acceptable to one group may not be acceptable to another. A biology textbook emphasizing Darwin's theory of evolution may be perfectly acceptable to a group of parents and students in suburban Boston or St. Louis but unacceptable to a group of West Virginian or Californian parents who believe in creationism and the literal interpretation of the Bible.

Because textbook publishing is an industry whose profit is based on how many books are sold, publishers try to produce textbooks that appeal to as broad a spectrum of the population as possible. This is particularly the case with elementary and secondary books; the profits are potentially the greatest from these books and the pressure from various interest groups is the strongest. And so, to a large extent, textbooks are consensus documents—that is to say, they reflect the norms and values of the mainstream culture.

■ CONTROVERSIES OVER THE CONTENT OF BOOKS

INTASC Standards
Principle #3

Controversies over the content of textbooks and their suitability for the communities where they are used have been a common problem since the 1970s. Particularly notable was the textbook controversy in Kanawha County, West Virginia, in 1974.

The "battle of the books" in Kanawha County had an innocent enough beginning. In March, 1974 a committee of five teachers submitted to the board of education a list of 325 language arts textbooks they wanted to have approved for use in the schools. On April 11, 1974, the members of the school board voted unanimously to adopt the texts, but to delay their purchase until they could be studied in greater detail.

The delay was requested by one of the school board members, Alice Moore. Mrs. Moore, the wife of a self-ordained Protestant minister, argued that ". . . most of the books on the language arts list contained material that was disrespectful of authority and religion, destructive of social and cultural values, obscene, pornographic, unpatriotic, or in violation of individual and familial rights of privacy" (Egerton 1975, 13). Although Mrs. Moore recognized that, according to state law, textbooks needed to reflect multiracial, multiethnic, and multicultural points of view, she argued that this was no excuse to legitimatize the nonstandard English found in the books, or to accept the anti-Christian selections in the books (Jenkinson 1979, 18–19).

On May 16, 1974, at a special meeting of the school board, the members of the textbook selection committee explained their reasons for selecting the proposed textbooks. Mrs. Moore challenged their argument that the texts would enhance the language arts curriculum. Focusing on three books she found particularly objectionable, Moore explained that

> The more I read, the more I was shocked. They were full of negative references to Christianity and God. There was lots of profanity and anti-American and racist antiwhite stories. They presented a warped view of life, as if every black carried a knife, was locked into a slum, and was made to look inferior. (Quoted by Provenzo 1990, 21)

This May meeting was called to a close with the understanding that the textbooks would not be purchased until the board had reached an agreement concerning the various objections.

Mrs. Moore soon launched an antitextbook campaign among fundamentalist church groups within the community. But despite this effort, other parts of the religious community voiced support for the textbooks. On June 24, 1974, ten local ministers approved the textbooks chosen by the school board committee. On June 26, 1974, nearly a thousand people attended the school board meeting. By a vote of three to two, the school board decided to drop the eight most frequently criticized books, but to keep the rest.

The protestors found the textbooks objectionable for many reasons. African American authors such as Gwendolyn Brooks and Eldridge Cleaver were thought unsuitable. Other objections were made to books that included violence, obscene or dirty language, or sad themes. Some protestors even objected to an edition of *Jack and the Beanstalk* because it supposedly taught children to kill and steal (Jenkinson 1979, 19). On September 3, 1974, textbook protestors kept eight thousand children from attending school—20 percent of the school system's forty-five thousand students. On the following day, thirty-five hundred miners walked off their jobs in wildcat strikes protesting the adoption of the textbooks by the school board. Strikes eventually broke out in other local businesses and industries.

School board attempts to conciliate the protestors failed. A board of citizens was appointed to review the content of the textbooks. The school board actually found itself forced to close the schools between September 13 and 16 to protect the students. But violence continued despite the closing of the schools. Two men were shot; another man was severely beaten; a CBS camera crew was assaulted. By September 12 coal companies estimated that they had lost more than $2 million because of the strike. By the end of the month, school officials estimated damage to the schools as part of the protest amounted to $300,000 (Parker 1975, 13).

By November the situation had grown even worse. At that time the citizen's committee reported that the language arts series was educationally sound and should be retained. The board approved the recommendations of the committee. Mrs. Moore dissented. Despite the approval of the list by the citizen's committee, important concessions were made by the board. They prohibited the most controversial titles on the list from being used in the classrooms. These books were shelved in the library instead.

Militant parents met the school board action with considerable hostility. Parents once again removed their children from the schools; buses were hit by gunfire; and a car owned by parents who continued to send their children to school was firebombed (Jenkinson 1979, 4). Shortly after, the school board and the superintendent were served with arrest warrants that charged them with contributing to the delinquency of minors by letting them use un-Christian and anti-American textbooks. The warrants were obtained by the Upper Kanawha Valley Mayors Association—an indication of the extent to which the textbook controversy had become a political issue.

The school board met again five days later and presented a set of guidelines that attempted to appease the protestors. Under these guidelines textbooks had to encourage loyalty to the United States, could not contain profanity, had to recognize the sanctity of the home, could not, by implication, encourage students to criticize their parents, and could not intrude on the privacy of students' home life by requiring them to answer questions about their personal feelings (Jenkinson 1979, 5). Despite occasional outbursts, the conflict over textbooks in Kanawha County quieted down by the beginning of the next year. We are nonetheless left with the question of why the selection of textbooks in Kanawha County provoked such strong feelings. What was at work were powerful forces concerning how the local community defined itself in terms of values and beliefs toward its children.

A similar controversy over reading and textbook content that made its way to the Supreme Court in the early 1980s occurred in Long Island, New York. In 1975, three members of the Island Trees Free School District attended a conservative conference called Parents of New York— United, which distributed a list of "objectionable" books. Returning to their community after the meeting, board members had a number of titles removed from their school library, including works such as Bernard Malamud's *The Fixer,* Kurt Vonnegut's *Slaughterhouse Five,* the anonymous *Go Ask Alice,* Eldridge Cleaver's *Soul on Ice,* and Desmond Morris's *The Naked Ape* (Provenzo 1990, 25–26).

INTASC Standards

Principle #3

Five students at the school sued the board for removing the titles from the library. Protests over the removal of the books became widespread. Some of the books were eventually restored to the library collection, but others remained on the banned list. Eventually, the case made its way to the Supreme Court, which ruled on June 25, 1982, that the books could not be removed simply because of their "anti-American content," but could only be removed if it was shown that they were obscene (*Board of Education, Island Trees Union Free School District No. 26 v. Pico,* 457 U.S. 853).

Yet another important case involving reading materials and textbooks was *Mozert v. Hawkins County Public Schools.* This case involved a group of Christian fundamentalist parents who argued that the way in which women were portrayed and the inclusion of selected folklore and fantasy figures (the witches in a selection from *The Wizard of Oz*) in specific textbooks conflicted with their religious beliefs. The school board denied the parents and their children alternative instructional materials. Although the parents who brought the suit initially won in state court on the basis that they and their children could have been provided an alternative reading program as allowed under Tennessee law, the case was overturned by the federal appeals court in Cincinnati in August 1986.

All these examples reflect how the content of curricular materials (textbooks and library books) can be a source of division in local communities. Implicit in these conflicts is the idea that books represent cultural capital, that they are not neutral, and that a great deal is at stake in terms of their selection and use. Teachers in the schools need to be sensitive to objections that might arise from parents and the local community over the content of specific books. Parents with religious objections to certain materials need to be listened to and respected. You don't necessarily need to agree with their beliefs or opinions, but in most instances you will need to consider providing an alternative reading assignment. If you are at all in doubt about what to do, consult with your principal, your superintendent, and, if necessary, your local school board.

WHAT DO YOU THINK?

Witchcraft and Reading

Margaret Cusack is a fifth-grade teacher in Clarence, New York, whose students love to have her read out loud to them. One of their favorite books is J. K. Rowling's *Harry Potter and the Sorcerer's Stone.* One of her students, Eric Poliner, leaves Ms. Cusack's class to study in the hallway or the library whenever she reads from the *Harry Potter* book.

Eric's parents are born-again Christians. They object to *Harry Potter and the Sorcerer's Stone* because it is about a young boy who attends a school for wizards. The book is full of sorcery, witchcraft, and magical spells. Like many conservative Christians, they feel that evil and witchcraft are at work in the world and that it is not a proper subject—even in fun—for a children's book. Should Eric be excused from class whenever the book is read? Is it fair for him to be sent out into the hallway or off to the library? What do you think?

■ STATE ADOPTIONS OF TEXTBOOKS

Adoption committees in many states review the selection of textbooks for use in the public schools. The most important states using these review procedures are California, Texas, and Florida. Under the system used in most cases, publishers submit their books for approval, the books are put on public display, and a specially appointed legislative committee reviews their content. Whether an elementary reading book is selected or rejected can be enormously important. The adoption of a reading program in Texas, for example, can ensure millions of dollars in sales for the publisher; a book that fails to get on the approved state list can prove a financial disaster.

Because so much is at stake financially, most publishers and authors try to keep their books as uncontroversial as possible. Innovation is often frowned on because it is hard to predict how being different might affect sales. Lyle M. Spencer, the former president of Science Research Associates (SRA), described in a speech in 1965 some of the problems textbook publishers face.

FIGURE 13.10 ■ An eleventh-grade student reviewing a textbook.

. . . We publishers have sometimes been less receptive to fresh, new educational ideas than we might have been, and than we must be in the future. As a young editor . . . I had two publishing maxims painstakingly pounded into me, . . .

The first was that the most damaging publishing mistakes are made by investing heavily in good ideas—not bad ideas, mind you, but good ones—that are too far ahead of their time.

The second mistake is even worse. It is the mortal sin of publishing. This sin is for a publisher to delude himself with the notion that he knows better than professional educators what materials are best for schools to use. You are the service guy behind the cafeteria counter. Your job is to supply the customer with what he wants, not the dietician telling him what he *should* have for dinner.

These maxims are, I think, still generally valid. I doubt seriously whether publishers are likely to become much bolder or more experimental than the educators they serve. (Quoted by Broudy 1975, 26)

The rule in the textbook publishing industry is to appear to be new and innovative, but not too new, and not too innovative.

Some years ago a colleague of mine helped select and edit the materials for a junior high school English textbook. He chose a passage from the beginning of James A. Michener's novel *Centennial*. It described the novel's setting millions of years ago: a primeval jungle dominated the landscape and dinosaurs walked across the landscape. On submitting the materials for use in the textbook, he was informed that, although the Michener selection was interesting, the publisher's science department would have to review it to make sure it would not offend fundamentalist students.

Such fears, as we have seen in the case of the Kanawha County textbook controversy, are certainly justified. Textbook publishers are clearly vulnerable to the demands of the public they serve. From a business point of view—and textbook publishing is first and foremost a business—publishers cannot afford to alienate the public that buys their products. Lyle M. Spencer's comments are as relevant now as they were in 1965. In fact, it may now be more difficult for a publisher to be innovative than ever before.

■ TEXTBOOKS IN A POST-TYPOGRAPHIC CULTURE

INTASC Standards

Principle #4

The textbook represents an educational technology whose history dates to the end of the Renaissance. Along with the teacher in the classroom, it has been the main means of delivering curricular content to students for the past four hundred years. Textbooks are sources of factual information on specific subjects and provide important windows on the world for students. In doing so, their historical importance cannot be overemphasized.

Imagine, for a moment, being a student in a school in rural Ohio or frontier Montana in the late 1880s. Very few books would exist in your community. The most common book available to you would be the Bible. You might see an occasional newspaper or maybe a household manual or almanac. If you were fortunate, some novels might come your way. You would also, of course, have your school textbooks. These textbooks would provide you with much of your information about different subject matter and, at the same time, give you a glimpse of what the world was like outside your community. Your geography textbook would provide you with pictures and maps of faraway people and places; your reading books with stories about different cultures and grand adventures. Whether these textbooks were accurate, they would represent perhaps the most important means available to you for understanding what the world was like beyond your community. They would be the main source of the curriculum and your main way of learning about the world.

icon
A symbol or image representing something.

As we move into an increasingly electronic and post-typographic culture, the culture is losing much of its significance as a cultural **icon** and force. The advent of radio, television, and the computer is profoundly changing the experience of our society and, more specifically, our children. We are increasingly part of what the media theorist Marshall McLuhan called a **global village.** The poorest child in the inner city almost certainly has access to television and, in the years to come, even to computers. Through these and other forms of media, representations of the world, whether accurate or distorted, are brought, for better or worse, to the child, just as textbooks did in the nineteenth and twentieth centuries.

As a result, the importance of the textbook in defining the values and beliefs of children will inevitably diminish. Computer and online curriculums, as well as live and video television are already providing competition. Despite this fact, the textbook will continue to be used because of its convenience and effectiveness as a transmitter of curriculum and cultural capital.

global village
The communication theorist Marshall McLuhan's idea put forward in the early 1960s that the world is becoming increasingly unified through electronic mediums such as television.

■ SUMMARY

Textbooks are the foundation of the curriculum for most schools. As Ian Westbury has argued, they are "the central tools and objects of attention in all modern forms of schooling" (Westbury 1990, 1). Their content is a reflection of the values and beliefs of the culture that creates them. As a technology of teaching, textbooks have been both remarkably durable and highly flexible tools. As a source of cultural capital, they are flashpoints for controversy. For educators, understanding their role and function in the schools and in the culture is critical.

■ DISCUSSION QUESTIONS ■

1. Is it really possible for an author to avoid communicating a political, ideological, or personal point of view when writing a textbook?
2. What is meant by the idea of a textbook being a consensus document?
3. How do textbooks represent a type of cultural capital?
4. How does the fact that textbook publishing is a business affect the content of textbooks?
5. Is bias an issue in textbooks?
6. Should censorship play a role in editing and selecting textbooks?
7. In the United States, who should ultimately be responsible for determining the content of textbooks and other curricular materials used in the schools?

■ **SOURCES CITED** ■

Altbach, Philip G., Gail Kelly, Hugh G. Petrie, and Lois Weis, eds. 1991. *Textbooks in American society: Politics, policy and pedagogy*. Albany: State University of New York Press.

Apple, Michael, and Linda Christian-Smith, eds. 1991. *The politics of the textbook*. New York: Routledge.

Board of Education, Island Trees Union Free School District No. 26 v. Pico, 457 U.S. 853.

Bowler, Mike. 1978. The making of a textbook. *Learning* 8(March): 38–43.

Broudy, Eric. 1976. The trouble with textbooks. *Teachers College Record* 77(1): 13–34.

Comenius, Johann Amos. 1887. *Orbis sensualium pictus*. English and Latin edition translated by C. Hoole for a 1659 edition of the work. Syracuse, New York.

Cruzada Nacional de Alfabetización Heroes y Martires por la Liberacion de Nicaragua. 1980. *El amancer del pueblo*. Nicaragua: Ministerio de Educación.

Cummings, J. A. 1817. *An introduction to ancient and modern geography*. Boston: Cummings and Hilliard.

Egerton, John. 1975. The battle of the books. *The Progressive* 39(6): 13–17.

Elson, Ruth Miller. 1964. *Guardians of tradition: American schoolbooks of the nineteenth century*. Lincoln: University of Nebraska Press.

Faigley, Lester I. 1975. What happened in Kanawha County? *English* 64(5): 7–9.

Fitzgerald, Frances. 1979. *America revised*. Boston: Atlantic Little Brown.

Ford, Paul Lester, ed. 1962. *The New England primer: A history of its origins and development*. New York: Teachers College Press.

Guyot, Arnold Henry. 1866. *Physical geography*. New York: Armstrong.

Hefley, James C. 1979. *Are textbooks harming your children: Norma and Mel Gabler take action and show you how!* Milford, Mich: Mott Media.

Jenkinson, Edward B. 1979. *Censors in the classroom*. Carbondale and Edwardsville: University of Southern Illinois Press.

Kismaric, Carole, and Marvin Heiferman. 1996. *Growing up with Dick and Jane: Living the American dream*. New York: Harper Collins.

Luke, Allan. 1988. *Literacy, textbooks and ideology: Postwar literacy instruction and the mythology of Dick and Jane*. London: The Falmer Press.

McGuffey, W. H. 1836. *McGuffey Eclectic Readers*. Cincinnati, Ohio: Truman and Smith.

New England Primer. 1777.

New York Public Library. 1984. *Censorship: 500 years of conflict*. New York: Oxford University Press.

O'Neil, Robert M. 1981. *Classrooms in the crossfire: The rights of students, parents, teachers, administrators, librarians, and the community*. Bloomington: University of Indiana Press.

Parker, Franklin. 1975. *The battle of the books: Kanawha County.* Phi Delta Kappa Fastback 63. Bloomington, Ind.: Phi Delta Kappa Educational Foundation.

Parley, Peter. 1829. *Method of telling about geography to children.* New York: Collins and Hannay.

Said, Edward W. 1978. *Orientalism.* New York: Vintage Books.

Southern School Books. 1852. *DeBow's Review* 13(September): 260.

Von Steinwehr, and Brinton. 1878. *An intermediate geography.* New York: Van Antwerp, Bragg, and Company.

Webster, Noah. 1810. *Blueback Spelling Book.* Vol. 1 of *Grammatical Institutes of the English Language.* Boston: John West and Company.

———. 1810. Introduction to *Grammatical Institutes of the English Language.* 3 vols. Boston: John West and Company.

Westbury, Ian. 1990. Textbooks, textbook publishers, and the quality of schooling. In *Textbooks and schooling in the United States,* edited by David L. Elliott and Arthur Woodward, 1–22. Chicago: University of Chicago Press.

Wilgoren, Jodi. 1999. Don't give us little wizards, the anti-Potter parents cry. *The New York Times,* 1 November, A1 and A19.

Winch, Christopher, and John Gingell. 1999. *Key concepts in the philosophy of education.* New York: Routledge.

CHAPTER 14

Media, Computers, and Education

In the introduction to this book, I argued that many different sources contribute to the educational process. In the nineteenth century these would have included the family, churches, museums, and newspapers. During the twentieth century, **electronic media** such as radio, television, recorded music, videos, and computers (**video games, hypermedia,** and the **Internet**) have been added to this list.

This chapter examines the issue of electronic media and its impact on children and the schools. I argue that the types of media that children are exposed to, as we move farther and farther into the postmodern era, are not only more varied, but also more complex, than was the case even half a generation ago. **Virtual reality,** interactive mediums, **connected,** and **networked** experiences are all part of the **new media geography** and, significantly, all based on the visual experience of the electronic screen.

■ TELEVISION AND THE ELECTRONIC SCREEN AS CULTURE

Even though television was invented in the mid-1920s, it was not until 1949 that commercial television was first introduced in the United States. This remarkable **medium** has profoundly changed our society. In the case of education, for example, many people (including me) believe that although traditional sources of education, such as family, religion, and schools, remain important, the main source of information

---

INTASC Standards

Principle #4

---

electronic media
Media such as radio, television, recorded music, videos, and computers based on electronic (in contrast to text-based media such as books and newspapers) delivery of information.

video game
An electronic game based on computer technology.

hypermedia
Any combination of text, sound, and motion pictures linked to other sources.

Internet
An experimental network built by the U.S. Department of Defense in the late 1960s, which has evolved into a loosely connected network of millions of computers.

virtual reality
Refers to the idea of creating highly realistic computer simulations of real life.

connected
The idea of being linked electronically.

networked
The idea of computers being connected together by a communication system so that they can exchange programs and information.

new media geography
The conditions being created as a result of the introduction of new media forms such as the Internet and World Wide Web.

medium
The means by which something is communicated.

and education in our culture is now television. The communication theorist George Gerbner maintains that

> For the first time in human history, children are hearing most of the stories, most of the time, not from their parents or school or churches or neighbors, but from a handful of global conglomerates that have something to sell. It is impossible to overestimate the radical effect that this has on the way our children grow up, the way we live, and the way we conduct our affairs. (Gerbner 1994)

Neil Postman argues that *television increasingly is our culture*. It is certainly the one thing in our society that we have in common more than anything else. He explains: "There is no audience so young that it must forgo television. There is no education so exalted that it is not modified by television. And most important of all, there is no subject of public interest—politics, news, education, religion, science, sports—that does not find its way to television" (Postman 1984, 78).

Think for a moment about the things you might have in common with the people who live in your neighborhood. You may, or may not, practice the same religion. You probably have not read the same books, or know the same jokes, but it is likely that you have seen the same television programs and, especially, the same advertisements. Not every person living in the United States knows the folk figures Brer Rabbit, Paul Bunyan, and Pecos Bill, but everyone knows about Ronald McDonald and the Energizer Bunny. Everyone can sing the Coca Cola theme song or the McDonald's theme song, but not necessarily "The Battle Hymn of the Republic" or even "The Star Spangled Banner."

Since its commercial introduction in the late 1940s, television has radically redefined our culture. As a powerful teaching machine it has taught us to consume products, how to dress and present ourselves, how to interpret information, and how to relate to other people. As Neil Postman (1982) and Marie Winn (1983) have pointed out, television has eroded the dividing line between the world of the adult and the world of the child. Television does not segregate its viewers. Children have access to virtually anything that adults have access to.

How has your knowledge of the world been shaped by television? In the 1950s and 1960s, the media sheltered children from sex and extreme violence. It would be rare today to find a child exposed to television that did not know about subjects such as incest and adultery. Words such as *penis* and *vagina* are part of the vocabulary of primetime television, but thirty years ago their use was strictly taboo.

From an ecological point of view, television has created a culture of material desire and consumption. We are taught to want goods and commodities, which will improve our lives if we obtain them. Toothpaste gives you "sex appeal" (Ultrabrite). A hamburger and french fries allow families to bond together (MacDonald's). A bottle of Coca Cola converts a strife-torn world to "perfect harmony." As a result of television, Henry Giroux believes that "culture is increasingly constituted by commerce, and the penetration of commodity culture into every facet of daily life has become the major axis of relations of exchange through which corporations actively produce new, increasingly effective forms of address" (Giroux 1994, 22). Television is the most important conduit or portal through which commercial culture has access to our children. It is the means most used to teach them how to consume and desire commercial products.

It is interesting to note that while television has dominated and defined our culture for the past fifty years, it is losing some of its grip as new screen-based media formats are coming into wider use. Children don't just watch television anymore. According to a recent study by the Annenberg Foundation, the average child in the United States is watching an electronic screen (television, video, or computer) about thirty-eight hours a week, fifty-two weeks a year. Next to sleeping, it is what children do more than anything else. What is interesting, as we enter the new century, is the profound shift underway from learning primarily through television to learning through other screen-based formats, including videos, video games, hypermedia, and the Internet.

This chapter studies the various screen-based technologies that are an important part of the life and learning of children. We first start with an examination of television and then move on to computers and their various functions.

? WHAT DO YOU THINK?

Television as a Type of Learning

The average U.S. household has a television running more than six hours each day. If a child is living in the household, the time increases to eight hours. By its very nature, television is a secondary experience rather than a primary experience. We watch football on television rather than play it. We listen to others interpret the world for us rather than interpret it ourselves. Often, we confuse what we see on TV with reality. People watching television may think they know what it is like to visit India, or to climb the Matterhorn, or to travel under the sea, or even into outer space. But is watching a flickering image in a darkened room the same as actually experiencing it?

What positive learning experiences does television provide? What are the inherent limitations of the medium? By watching television how much do we cut ourselves off from other activities and other people? How much do we limit learning simply to what we can hear and see? To what extent is this an impoverished environment when compared to other types of learning experiences? What do you think?

■ TELEVISION AND U.S. CULTURE

How does television affect U.S. culture? Study the following facts. Consider their meaning and the implications they have for us as a society.

- Ninety-eight percent of U.S. households have a television set (Nielson Media Research 1998).
- The average home has 2.75 televisions (Stanger and Gridina 1999).
- Sixty-five percent of U.S. homes have cable television (*Girls Inc.* 1995).
- The average person in the United States watches television four hours per day or approximately fifty days per year (Nielson Media Research 1998).
- People with low-income levels watch more television than people with higher incomes do, and highly educated people watch less television than do those who are less well educated (American Psychological Association 1992).
- VCRs are owned by 97.8 percent of families (Stanger and Gridina 1999).
- Children spend an average of twenty-eight hours per week watching television (American Medical Association 1996).
- The average child views thirty thousand commercials each year (*Consumer Reports*, February 1998).
- Children between the ages of two and eleven watch approximately 312 hours of children's programming each year (*Los Angeles Times*, 31 December 1997).
- Forty-eight percent of children ages two to seventeen have a television set in their bedrooms (Stanger and Gridina 1999).
- Teenage boys spend nearly twice as much time watching MTV as reading for pleasure (Annenberg 1997).
- By the time the average child reaches the age of eighteen, he or she will have witnessed over two hundred thousand acts of violence including sixteen thousand murders (American Medical Association 1996).
- For children, the likelihood of becoming obese increases by 2 percent with every hour of television watched per day (American Medical Association 1996).

The most widely circulated magazine in the United States is not *Time,* or *Newsweek,* or *Sports Illustrated,* but *TV Guide.* Our folk traditions are being forgotten as television storylines and personalities increasingly dominate our culture.

real time
Something that takes place in actual time.

Yet television has drawn together people in the United States in ways never before possible. When John F. Kennedy was assassinated in 1963, 96 percent of the population in the United States watched the funeral on television. Ninety-four percent watched the Apollo II moon landing (Lichty 1981). Nightly broadcasts from Vietnam brought home a distant war. Television made it impossible for hawks or doves to escape a "personal involvement" in the war. In 1991, we watched the Gulf War unfold in front of us as though it were a video game—even to the point at which we watched, in **real time,** camera-guided missiles zoom in and destroy their targets. Television provides a window on the world and lets people share common experiences in a new way. News is instantaneous

FIGURE 14.1 ■ Family viewing President Kennedy on television during the 1960s.
Source: Courtesy National Archives.

and global. What happens at a local level is less important. We are increasingly connected, up to the minute, yet often distracted with massive amounts of input and information.

In a little more than fifty years, television has come to define U.S. life. Yet in our day-to-day lives we tend to accept its impact uncritically and almost automatically. Coupled with television's potential to communicate ideas and information, however, is the possibility for its misuse and abuse. An ongoing debate focuses on the role television plays in shaping spending habits, voting, attitudes toward sex and violence, and even how children learn at school. Two related questions occupy our discussion of this issue: What do children learn from television? How does television influence what goes on in the classroom? We begin by addressing this second question.

■ TELEVISION AS TEACHING MACHINE

Many contemporary critics of education believe that most of the problems facing the current educational system are due to the way television dominates our culture. They point to students' lack of discipline, concentration, and imagination; their passivity and declining performance on the Scholastic Aptitude Test (SAT); and family instability as problems exacerbated by television's pervasive influence. No doubt these assertions contain some truth and some exaggeration. It can also be argued that television provides many positive experiences for children, such as conveying information and entertainment that are unprecedented.

Think about your own experience as a child watching television. You probably learned how a kangaroo hops or how a lion roars, not from a trip to the zoo or to Australia or Africa, but from watching a television program. And you probably learned about these animals at a very young age, much younger than someone would have one hundred years ago. You probably saw your first murder, real or simulated, at a young age. You learned to want many things you might not have otherwise known about because you saw them in an advertisement or on television. Try to remember how you learned about toys, clothes, or the food you wanted to eat when you were a child. You probably saw it on television!

Television, however, needs to be understood primarily as a teaching machine. This is the basic premise underlying most commercial television—one reflected in the enormous amount of information it directs to children. Think about the earlier cited figure that the average child views thirty thousand television advertisements a year. By defini-

FIGURE 14.2 ■ Contemporary children viewing television.

tion, advertisements are intended to shape the viewer's behavior. Thus, a television viewer is expected to learn something from the advertisements they watch: it may be to buy a car, to purchase certain clothes, or to make their lives better by eating certain types of food. In some industries such as the fast-food business, **cross marketing** (films and videos promoting the sale of foods) is a common practice. A new film from Disney is likely to be promoted through the sale of a special children's meal with a collateral toy to make the advertised product more desirable.

Health experts believe that such constant promotion (particularly realized through television) of fast foods is creating a lifelong preference among many children for fast food. Currently, 25 percent of all children in the United States are overweight, and 50 percent of them will be overweight as adults. Television is seen as contributing to this problem by promoting sedentary behavior and encouraging (some would argue, teaching) poor nutrition (*Children, Health and Advertising* 2000).

Learning about consuming alcohol is also promoted through television advertising. By the time they reach sixteen years of age, average television viewers have seen approximately seventy-five thousand alcohol advertisements. This happens before they reach the legal drinking age. Research suggests that exposure to alcohol advertising may increase

cross marketing
Selling multiple products across different industries in a single promotion.

alcohol consumption by 10 percent to 30 percent (*Children, Health and Advertising* 2000). Television clearly plays a major role in educating children about consumer products. Children between the ages of nine and thirteen, for example, report that their main source of information about new clothing styles is their friends (59%), followed by television (58%), school (38%), and stores (31%) (*Children, Health and Advertising* 2000).

Historically, television has consistently distorted our perceptions of ethnic and minority groups, as well as women. Its content has reflected the privileged status and attention given to northern European and white culture in the United States. For example, in the 1950s African Americans represented 10 percent of the population, yet only 2 percent of all television characters were African American (Calvert 1999). When African Americans were portrayed on television during its early years, they tended to play humorous and not very well respected characters.

During the 1960s, actors such as Bill Cosby broke racial barriers and stereotypes with his role as an international spy in the program *I Spy*. Likewise Cosby's portrayal during the 1980s of an affluent doctor living with his lawyer wife and their family in New York City represented a cultural breakthrough in the portrayal of African Americans on television. African Americans currently represent approximately 12 percent of the population in the United States and roughly 11 percent of the characters seen on television (Calvert 1999). Despite this fact, they often are portrayed in secondary and stereotypical roles.

Historically, Hispanics have also been underrepresented in television programming. In a study of Saturday morning television characters from 1992, Greenberg and Brand, for example, found only one Hispanic character and no Native Americans or Asian Americans (Calvert 1999). Interestingly, Hispanics are often included as characters in advertisements, but not in actual programs (Calvert 1999). This fact suggests that Hispanics are being targeted as commercial consumers but are not considered compelling forces in the culture.

Gender stereotyping has also been widespread in television programming in the United States. Although males and females are almost equally represented in the population, men outnumber women as television characters by a ratio of three to one (Calvert 1999). In 1997, for example, 97 percent of commercials used male **voice-overs.** This suggests that leadership and authority in television advertising is a role assigned to men rather than to women (Calvert 1999).

Ethnic, racial, and gender stereotyping should be evident to almost anyone viewing current programming with a critical eye. Perhaps the prejudices and stereotypes on television are simply reflections of our cul-

gender stereotyping
Making discriminatory judgments based on gender.

voice-over
Recording over an existing voice track in a film or television program.

ture's values, but even so, should television contribute to the perpetuation of these stereotypes? To what extent can television help to diminish or increase discrimination and prejudice? In Canada, for example, women and minority groups are much more consciously included as part of television programming to overcome traditional biases and stereotypes. Perhaps the United States would be well served by following Canada's lead.

? WHAT DO YOU THINK?
How Television Has Changed Family Life

The widespread introduction of commercial television in the early 1950s has had a major impact on family life in the United States. Research has shown that television has changed the nation's sleeping patterns, meal times, and family interactions (the use, for example, of television as an electronic babysitter).

How has television shaped your own life? How many televisions does your family own? Where are they located? When are they turned on? Who watches them? How are they watched? Have your viewing patterns changed significantly with the passage of time? Has television been a positive experience? For your family? For our culture? What do you think?

■ TELEVISION VIOLENCE

Children clearly learn about violence from television. Statistics from the early 1990s indicate that the average child who views two to four hours of television daily witnesses approximately eighty-nine thousand murders and one hundred thousand other assorted acts of violence by the time he or she completes elementary school (Schumer 1992). Experimental studies conducted during the 1960s and 1970s suggest that children exposed to violent television episodes tend to develop more aggressive behavior after the viewing. One famous study involved a group of nursery school-children who were shown a film in which an adult actor performed acts of aggression on a large plastic doll. One group saw only the aggressive acts, a second group watched an additional scene in which the actor was praised and rewarded for his aggressiveness, and a third group saw the actor punished for what he had done. Children in the third group committed fewer aggressive acts than the children in the other experimental groups (Bandura, Ross, and Ross 1963a; 1963b; 1965).

meta studies
A type of research study that takes multiple studies on a topic and combines their results to form a single interpretation.

In another widely cited study from the early 1970s, 136 nine- and ten-year-olds were randomly divided into two groups. One group watched a nonviolent sports film and the other group watched a violent segment of *The Untouchables*, a program about Chicago gangsters during the 1920s. The children were then led into a room that contained a box with two buttons—one labeled *HELP* and the other labeled *HURT*. The children were told that the box was connected to a box in another room where a child was trying to turn a crank connected to a generator as part of a game. When the child turned the crank quickly enough, he or she would be able to turn on the light on top of the box. Finally, the children were told they could either help or hinder the child in the other room by pressing the help or the hurt button. The children who had observed the violent episode of *The Untouchables* pressed the hurt button 33 percent more often than did the children who had seen the nonviolent sports episode (Liebert and Baron 1972).

Many people in the film and television industry maintain that no evidence suggests that a connection exists between media violence and violence in U.S. culture. **Meta studies,** which combine the results of many different research studies, refute this position. In addition, many newer studies suggest that violent television does, in fact, encourage more violent and aggressive behavior in children. Although space does not permit a detailed examination of this issue, reference to several other studies is important.

A study from the mid-1980s investigated the impact of introducing television for the first time to an isolated Canadian community. The community, which was called Notel by the researchers, had never before had television because of signal problems. Using a double-blind research design, forty-five first- and second-graders were observed over a two-year period to see whether aggressive behavior such as hitting, biting, and shoving increased with exposure to television. In the two control groups aggressive behavior did not increase significantly. In Notel, during the same two-year period, however, such behavior increased by 160 percent (Williams, 1986; Williams and Handford, 1986).

In a 1992 article Brandon Centrewall looked at violence in the United States from an epidemiological point of view. He compared homicide rates in the United States and Canada, where television was introduced in the mid-1940s, with the Republic of South Africa, where television was introduced thirty years later. Canada, which had not gone through the political and social unrest of the 1960s, provided a control model for the United States. To rule out the effect of racial conflict in South Africa, only the white homicide rate was considered by Centrewall.

Centrewall found that the homicide rate in both Canada and the United States increased by almost 100 percent between 1945 and 1970. Television ownership increased at almost the same percentage rate as the homicide rate for the same period. In South Africa, the white homicide rate declined between 1945 and 1970. When television was introduced in 1975, the white homicide rate exploded, increasing 130 percent by 1983.

Centrewell concluded from his research that in the United States and Canada ". . . the introduction of television in the 1950s caused a subsequent doubling of the homicide rate, i.e., long-term childhood exposure to television is a causal factor behind approximately one half of the homicides committed in the United States, or approximately 10,000 homicides annually" (Centrewall 1992, 225). Centrewell reasoned that although other factors, such as poverty, crime, alcohol, drug abuse, and stress, might have an impact, the epidemiological evidence suggests that ". . . if hypothetically television technology had never been developed, there would be 10,000 fewer homicides each year in the United States, 70,000 fewer rapes and 700,000 fewer injurious assaults" (Centrewell 1992, 225).

The psychologist Edward Donnerstein suggests that correlational data indicate that media exposure in childhood can account for 5 percent to 10 percent of adult aggressive behavior. The media researcher George Gerbner puts the figure at 5 percent, whereas Karl Erik Rosengren, reporting on a twenty-year study of Swedish children, maintains that direct or indirect effects of television can explain 10 percent to 20 percent of the aggression displayed in schools and neighborhoods (Bok 1998).

These studies and others like them have raised considerable controversy. Actually demonstrating that a specific act of violence like the school shootings at Paducah, Kentucky, or Columbine, Colorado, are directly caused by media such as film, television, or video games is extremely difficult to do. Multiple factors are almost certainly responsible for why an Eric Harris or Dylan Kliebold go on a killing rampage. What we might want to consider, however, is the vision of the world that television and other media construct for the children whom we teach.

George Gerbner argues that television and related media, at the very least, create what is known as "mean world" phenomena, in which television viewers come to believe that the world is a much crueler and meaner place than is in fact justified by actual statistics. According to Gerbner:

> . . . if you are growing up in a home where there is more than say three hours of television per day, for all practical purposes you live in a meaner world—and act accordingly—than your next-door neighbor

who lives in the same world but watches less television. The programming reinforces the worst fears and apprehensions and paranoia of people. (Gerbner 1994)

This mythic quality is perhaps what is most important about television as a medium. Gerbner explains: "People think of television as programs, but television is more than that; television is a mythology—highly organically connected, repeated every day so that the themes that run through all programming and news have the effect of cultivating conceptions of reality" (Gerbner 1994). The task for educators is to understand how media such as television is shaping the children whom they teach. If it is as powerful a mythological system as Gerbner suggests, it is simply too important to take for granted.

■ TELEVISION'S POTENTIAL POSITIVE PROMISE

Many people believe that television has positive potential for children and can lead to significant improvement of schools. In the late 1950s, for example, educators such as Charles Siepmann wrote that television could provide the solution to the problem of too few teachers and of poor instruction: "Education needs television, and that desperately. Television, we hold, while not the *deus ex machina* to solve the crisis, is one indispensable tool that we can and must use to extricate ourselves from the grave trouble we are in, but of which all too few seem to be aware" (quoted by O'Bryan 1980, 6). Instructional television (ITV), whereby master teachers presented lessons to students via television, soon became popular in schools across the country.

With instructional television, regular classroom teachers provided administrative support and supervision for students receiving the main thrust of their instruction from the master teacher. ITV would supposedly provide a solution to the problem of undertrained or inadequate teachers and take pressure off an educational system beginning to experience a shortage of competent instructors because of the increased enrollments as a result of the postwar baby boom (O'Bryan 1980).

Early experiments with ITV proved to be a failure. Classroom teachers resented being superseded by the television master teacher. Teachers who were masters in the classroom were not necessarily master performers on television. Students felt a lack of personal attention. All these problems suggest partial explanations for the failure of instructional television (O'Bryan 1980).

Educational television began to emerge during the 1960s and provided an alternative to instructional television. It was not, however, until 1969 and the first broadcast of *Sesame Street* by The Children's Television Workshop that educational television began to have a major impact on children's viewing habits. The Children's Television Workshop (CTW) was first organized in 1968 and represented a totally new approach to educational programming. For the first time people developing educational materials for television recognized that they were competing with commercial broadcasting. The creators of CTW's first successful program, *Sesame Street*, attempted to combine the successful elements of commercial television with current knowledge in learning and educational psychology. Their success is reflected in the fact that not only have many others imitated *Sesame Street*, but it still remains among the most popular children's programs broadcast today.

Do children learn from educational programming like *Sesame Street*? If so, what do they learn? Early research on *Sesame Street* indicated that children who watched the program scored higher on tests of verbal IQ than children who did not watch it. Frequent viewers had more positive attitudes about school and performed better according to their first-grade teachers (Watkins et al. 1980). Criticisms of some early studies of *Sesame Street* argued that the higher scores of the children who watched the program might have reflected their access to reading materials related to what they were viewing. Some of these materials encouraged parents to become involved in the program with their children. The issue is still open to dispute (Watkins et al. 1980). On a more general level, early criticisms of *Sesame Street* focused on its fast pace and suggested this format may have contributed to increased hyperactivity and behavioral problems among children who watched it. Research has refuted these conclusions, however (Watkins et al. 1980).

Researchers conducted studies on young adults who had participated in early research on viewing *Sesame Street* found that in high school these students had better grades, higher levels of academic achievement, better attitudes about themselves and learning, as well as more positive attitudes toward academic success (Fisch and Truglio, 2001). Evaluations of other educational programming in general suggests that children can learn important intellectual, social, and interpersonal skills from watching educational programming.

INTERNET @ CONNECTIONS
Electronic Media and Education

A wide range of sources are available online for those interested in electronic media and its impact on children and the culture. An excellent site to begin with is the Media Literacy Online Project at the University of Oregon, whose Gateway to

Literacy Media includes a teacher's desk with lesson plans and materials; links to national media literacy groups, bibliographies, and online reading sources in media literacy; information on media violence, advertising and children, race and ethnicity in the media; as well as resources for parents. The Media Literacy Online Project is located at http://interact.uoregon.edu/MediaLit/HomePage.

The Media Education Foundation has a wide range of valuable educational videotapes about the media and its influence. Its website provides some useful compilations of media statistics. Media Education Foundation can be located at http://www.mediaed.org/.

Information on the portrayal of African Americans in media can be found at Center on Blacks and the Media, http://www.afrikan.net/hype/cover1.html.

Mediascope is a public policy organization that addresses a wide range of topics on the media, including ratings, children's TV, violence, the effects of video games, and so on. Mediascope's media policy briefs are particularly valuable, providing information on topics such as how media violence influences viewers, media use in the United States, tobacco advertising in the United States, and video game violence. Mediascope is located at http://www.mediascope.org.

■ COMPUTING AND CONTEMPORARY CULTURE

INTASC Standards

Principle #4

Although the influence of television has been pervasive in U.S. culture since the 1950s, its role is being increasingly eclipsed by computer-based technologies ranging from video games to the Internet and World Wide Web. Since the early 1980s, computers have been increasingly used in classrooms as a means of reforming traditional education and schooling. Consider the following facts:

- Eighty-nine percent of teenagers use a computer at least several times per week (*Newsweek*, 28 April 1997).
- Seventy-six percent of children ages nine to eleven use a computer in school at least once a week (*Inside Kids*, April 1997).
- Fifty-five percent of Asian Americans, 47 percent of whites, 25.5 percent of Hispanic Americans, and about 24 percent of African Americans own computers (*San Jose Mercury News*, 19 March 1999).
- Ninety-four percent of families with annual incomes of $75,000 or more, and 41 percent of families with annual incomes below $30,000, own a computer (Stanger and Gridina 1999).
- The percentage of homes with children aged two to seventeen that own a computer is 68.2 (Stanger and Gridina 1999).
- Thirty-two percent of children in white households use personal computers, compared to 18 percent of children in African American households (Li 1995).

- The average age for first computer usage among children is two years (*KidScreen*, July 1999).
- Teens spend an average of 2.5 weekday hours on a home computer (Goodstein and Connelly 1998).
- U.S. children ages three to seventeen use computers for the following applications: games (70.3%), homework (47.4%), education (31.5%), word processing (30.9%), learning to use the computer (23.7%). Households with Internet access watch television about 13 percent less often than do those not connected (*Daily Variety*, 20 July 1999).
- People in the United States who use the Internet number 100.1 million (*Advertising Age*, 20 December 1999)
- White households are more than twice as likely (29.8%) to own a computer as African American (11.2%) or Hispanic American (12.6%) households (*Internet Access* 1999).
- Eighty-nine percent of public schools in the United States have Internet access; 51 percent of instructional rooms (classrooms, computer labs, and library/media centers) have access (*The American Internet User Survey*, January 1999).
- As of January 1999, 18.6 million children in the United States were online. In five years that number is expected to grow to more than 42 million (Okrent 1999).
- One out of five parents with children ages two to seventeen cite the Internet as the media influence of greatest concern in raising their children (second only to television) (Annenberg Public Policy Center 1999).
- Ninety percent of households with children either rent or own a video game console or computer (Quittner 1999).
- Children who have home video game consoles play with them about ninety minutes a day (Dewitt 1993).

■ THE COMPUTER AS THE CHILDREN'S MACHINE

In his book *The Children's Machine: Rethinking School in the Age of the Computer* (1993), the educational and computer theorist Seymour Papert asks the reader to imagine a group of time travelers visiting from an earlier century:

> . . . among them one group of surgeons and another of schoolteachers, each group eager to see how much things have changed in their profession a hundred or more years into the future. Imagine the bewilderment

of the surgeons finding themselves in the operating room of a modern hospital. Although they would know that an operation of some sort was being performed, and might even be able to guess at the target organ, they would in almost all cases be unable to figure out what the surgeon was trying to accomplish or what the purpose of the many strange devices he and the surgical staff were employing. (Papert 1993, 1)

For the schoolteachers, nearly everything that they would observe in a classroom would be familiar. Perhaps some changes would be found in curriculum and procedures, but the blackboard and textbooks would still be there, along with the other paraphernalia of the classroom. However, other than a television or intercom, the one device they would find as truly startling as the medical equipment was to the doctors would be a computer. More than any single technology, computers have the potential to change the way children learn and the way teachers work.

On the surface computers may appear to be tools simply for writing, doing calculations, and communicating. In an educational context, however, they are much more. Like books, they are deeply cultural and are in the process of revolutionizing the way we teach and learn.

FIGURE 14.3 ■ Students using a computer in a classroom.

WHAT DO YOU THINK?

Censoring the Web

Sean O'Brien did not get along with his band instructor at Westlake High School in Cleveland. He felt that Mr. Walczuk blamed him unfairly for the things that happened in the school. Angry, O'Brien set up a home-based website in which he described his teacher as "an overweight middle-age man." He further described him saying that he was the type of individual who "likes to involve himself in everything you do."

When the school system learned about his website and its content, they suspended Sean for ten days and told him to shut it down. If he refused, they threatened to expel him from school. Sean and his parents then took action against the school system, declaring that his right to free speech was being violated. They sued for restoration of his rights and damages of $550,000.

Eventually an out-of-court settlement was reached with Sean and his family. In addition to an apology, he was paid $30,000. Prior to the settlement, a judge ruled that Sean did have the right as a matter of free speech under the Constitution to run the website. What do you think?

Think for a moment about how the Internet and the World Wide Web have changed our access to traditional sources of information. A student writing a term paper is not simply limited to the books in their school or local library, but can draw on resources from around the world. As a researcher, I have spent a great deal of time and expense visiting the prints and photography collection at the Library of Congress to do research on education and U.S. culture. With the growth of the Internet and the World Wide Web, the resources found at the Library of Congress are increasingly available online through the Library of Congress National Digital Library Program (NDLP). Suddenly, sources that used to be available to scholars only at great expense are now available to students with Internet access.

INTERNET @ CONNECTIONS

Exploring Online Sources

Begun in 1995, after a five-year pilot project, the National Digital Library Program has been digitizing selected collections of documents that deal with different aspects of U.S. cultural heritage. The materials from the National Digital Library Program are available online through the American Memory project at http://leweb2.loc.gov/amhome.html.

Collections going up online as part of the American Memory project include photographs, books, pamphlets, motion pictures, manuscripts, and sound recordings. Documents can be downloaded for free and easily integrated into classroom and research projects.

In terms of African American resources, a good starting point is *African American Perspectives: Pamphlets from the Daniel A. P. Murray Collection, 1818–1907,* at http://memory.loc.gov/ammem/aap/aaphome.html. This is a collection of 351 pamphlets spanning roughly ninety years of African American history and culture. Significant figures found in the collection include Frederick Douglass, Booker T. Washington, Alexander Crummell, and Ida B. Wells-Barnett.

Photographic materials dealing with African American history can be found throughout the American Memory project. As part of the work of the Farm Security Administration, for example, hundreds of thousands of photographs were taken across the country. Many document the discrimination against African and Native Americans. Examples of the photographs of signs enforcing racial discrimination have been conveniently pulled together by staff at the American Memory project. Thirty images can be found at the site Photographs of Signs Enforcing Racial Discrimination, at http://lcweb.loc.gov/rr/print/085_disc.html. These images demonstrate the enforcement of racial segregation throughout the country. Typical is a photograph dating from 1943 of a Colored Waiting Room sign in the Greyhound Bus

FIGURE 14.4 ■ A sign at the Greyhound bus station in Rome, Georgia, September 1943.

Source: Photograph by Esther Bubley. (Location: E-5153. Reproduction No. LC-USZ62-75338).

Station in Rome, Georgia. The documents at this site bring home to students, in a very tangible way, the reality of racial discrimination in the United States in the twentieth century.

Text documents can provide similarly powerful examples. *The African-American Mosaic: A Library of Congress Resource Guide for the Study of Black History and Culture,* for example, provides users with access to a wide range of documents on African American history, including sources on African colonization, abolition, slavery, and African American migration. Links to narratives by ex-slaves, collected as part of the Federal Writers' Project during the 1930s, bring home to students the reality of the experience of slavery in ways that just relating facts and historical timelines cannot do. You may want to visit The African American Odyssey: A Quest for Full Citizenship, at http://lcweb2.loc.gov/ammem/aaohtml/exhibit/aointro.html.

■ COMPUTERS AND THEIR EDUCATIONAL MEANING

How can computers actually be used in the classroom? In his book *The Computer in the School* (1980), Robert Taylor defined three potential roles for the computer: tool, tutor, and tutee. As a *tool*, the computer can do tasks such as word processing, mathematical calculations, or function as a communications device by connecting to the Internet. As a *tutor*, the computer can lead the child through drills in which rote memory and repetition are important. The student's knowledge can be checked easily, and deficiencies overcome by repeating materials or explaining them in different ways. As a *tutee*, the computer can be programmed to carry out specific procedures and operations conceived by the student.

Each of these approaches represents a different pedagogical strategy and a different type of experience for the child. What are the implications of having a student use the computer in each of these three different ways? A computer that used to provide repetitious skill and memory exercises is one type of experience for a child whereas a computer used as a tool to create with is something very different.

INTASC Standards

Principle #4

WHAT DO YOU THINK?

Consequences of the Computer Revolution

U.S. educators have in large part embraced the notion that the use of computers in schools is inevitable and even desirable. Very little effort has been made to ask what problems computers may cause. In many respects, the increasingly wide-spread use of computers in our culture and in our schools parallels the introduction of the automobile at the beginning of the twentieth century. Whereas the automobile made rapid and convenient travel possible, it also engendered high-way construction, air pollution, and frequent accidental deaths. From both a personal and educational point of view, what might be some of the hidden costs of introducing computers into our schools? Can these problems be avoided or are they inevitable? What do you think?

This points to an essential issue about computers and their use as part of the curriculum of schools. Computer use is not neutral, but has specific values and beliefs built into it. As tools for learning computers change the ecology of the classroom (Bowers 1988; 2000). Teachers need to understand the extent to which computers emphasize or de-emphasize certain values and beliefs.

For example, do minority children use computers primarily for drill and memory activities while elite and privileged populations get to program them or use them as tools to create things as part of their education? Is computing provided as an activity more for boys than for girls? Does the use of the Internet and World Wide Web distract children from issues in their local community, by connecting them to a larger global system of information and people? In doing so, are they distracted from the unique local settings where they live and interact with others?

Theorists like C. A. Bowers point to other problems as well. The technology of computers and the Internet often decontextualizes much of the meaning of the information they make available. He explains:

> The technology that allows a search engine to locate thousands of references to a particular word or topic, while creating the impression that the collected knowledge of humankind is instantly accessible anywhere in the world, cannot reproduce what we most need to know in order to make judgment about the context that the data and information are extracted from. (Bowers 2000, 71)

Remarkably, ideas like these are rarely introduced into the discussion of the use of computers in schools. Computers are accepted almost universally as being effective and desirable tools for education. Whether computers do in fact have remarkable potential to improve the quality of education in our schools, this is only possible if they are used appropriately. Like television, the remarkable potential for using computers as part of the educational system often seems less than adequate, and sometimes simply an expensive distraction.

Computers, like television, need to be understood as cultural objects that promote certain values or ways of viewing the world. As Bowers has pointed out, seemingly neutral educational simulations such as the popular educational programs Oregon Trail II and the Sim series (SimLife, SimEarth, SimCity 2000) contain specific ideological and cultural points of view.

In Oregon Trail III, for example, the simulation is undertaken from the perspective of pioneers making their way across the wilderness. In early versions of the game pioneers traveled through land that belonged to Native American tribes—yet the tribes were never identified. They were simply Native Americans, the implication being that all tribes are the same. Likewise, the naming of the land, its rivers and geological formations, (using European names and references), gives credence to the idea that early settlers believed the land was simply empty, simply waiting to be conquered (Bowers 2000, 134).

In the Sim series, according to Bowers, it is assumed

> . . . that complex systems, such as an ant colony, a city, or the earth itself, can be scientifically managed. Ironically, these supposedly environmentally sensitive programs propagate the most extreme expression of Western hubris: that science and technology can solve all the challenges of Nature. (Bowers 2000, 136)

Look, for example, at the following description of the SimLife by its manufacturer, the Maxis Corporation:

> *SimLife* is the first genetic engineering game available for personal computers. It lets players manipulate the very fabric of existence, giving life to creatures that defy the wildest imagination. Players create exotic plants and animals of various shapes, sizes, and temperaments and turn them loose into a custom-designed environment in which only the best-adapted species survive! With *SimLife,* the budding mad scientist can people the landscape with mutagens (agents that cause mutation and indirectly, evolution). Or change the individual genetics of one creature and see what effects its offspring have on the long-term survival of its species and on the ecosystem as a whole. (Quoted by Bowers 2000, 136–137)

Underlying the SimLife program/game is the assumption that humans are better at directing evolution than Nature is, that no particular danger is involved in genetic manipulation, and that it is simply a game or intellectual exercise. We can just imagine some future genetic scientist becoming interested in the field because of playing the game. We should worry, however, about the assumptions he or she might carry away from the game into his or her professional work: that gene manipulation and creation of exotic plants and animals is perfectly all right. Combining human intelligence with a gorilla, for example, might be okay if you need to create a superstrong industrial worker or drone to live and work in the harsh environment of outer space.

WHAT DO YOU THINK?

Are Video Games Teaching Machines?

Computer and video games are typically viewed as harmless child's play. In fact, they are neither harmless nor neutral, but represent powerful types of teaching material. Any computer or video game is ultimately a tool for behavioral reinforcement. You play the game, gradually becoming more skilled with practice, thus learning its lesson. In a sense, players who are particularly skilled are those who have learned the behavioral lesson of the game the best.

Early versions of video games had relatively benign lessons. In the classic game Space Invaders (first introduced in 1978), row upon row of alien spacecraft descended down the screen toward you. The object was to shoot the aliens out of the sky before they devoured you. Space Invaders was, in many regards, like an old-fashioned shooting arcade, where you aimed at a target as it rapidly moved in front of you.

Each successive generation of video games has become more technologically sophisticated, more realistic, and more violent. In 1990, Street Fighter II was the first megahit fighting game. Widely available on the Nintendo video game system, it was followed by the even more popular Mortal Kombat. These games use a side-scroll game format in which players control the action of small figures fighting on the screen. Advanced versions of Mortal Kombat incorporate filmed martial arts fighters to provide even more realism.

By the mid-1990s, increases in computing power led to the introduction of advanced 3-D modeling and graphics into computing and video games. Advanced systems made it possible to have not simply side-scrolled games, but ones that thrust you into the actual action of the game. Among the most interesting early uses of this technology was in first-person shooter games.

First-person shooters are games that provide the player with a real-view perspective of the game. This is very different from the earlier tradition of video games such as Street Fighter II or Mortal Kombat, which had the user view small cartoon figures on the screen and then control their actions by manipulating them through a game controller. In contrast, a first-person shooter actually puts you inside of the action of the game. The barrels of weapons like pistols and shotguns are placed at the bottom, center edge of the computer screen. The player aims the barrel right or left and up or down by manipulating the computer mouse or game controller, or sometimes even a model gun. The effect is that you feel as though you are literally stepping into the action of the game as a participant.

Games that employ a first-person shooter model represent a significant step beyond the tiny cartoon figures that were included in games such as Mortal Kombat in the mid-1990s. More recent games such as Doom and Quake also use the first-person shooter model. Not only are they extremely popular, but also they are highly effective from a conditioning and teaching point of view. It is important to note that games such as Doom have been adapted for military training by the Marine Corps.

Essentially, we have reached a point where we must understand that the current first-person shooter games, running on powerful but widely available computer and video game machines, represent powerful reality simulators that systematically instruct players in the process of hunting and killing other human beings, using weapons such as guns, rockets, and bombs. Are we confusing play with virtual reality simulations that teach us systematically and ruthlessly how to kill other people? Does this matter, or are we simply talking about a harmless sort of play? Has the development of these types of games and other violent media contributed to school shooting incidents such as those at Columbine, Colorado, in April 1998? What do you think?

The point being made is, a simulation is not a neutral technology but represents a value-laden set of assumptions. What is seemingly a harmless game and educational experience may, in fact, represent very important ways of constructing the world. The fact is, technologies shape and define the cultures and societies that create them. Think for a moment about the automobile. How has it shaped and defined our cities, the way we shop, where we work, and where we live? How do our lives differ from those of people who lived a hundred years ago, when the automobile had just been invented? In the Middle Ages, the introduction of stirrups from Asia made it possible for knights to ride armored horses without falling off. This meant that a new type of warfare was possible. It also changed the nature of society by necessitating the development of a feudal culture, in which peasant farmers supported military lords and knights who protected them from invasion and destruction.

Think about how computers and computer-related technologies, such as the Internet, the World Wide Web, cell phones, and personal digital assistants, have changed life in the United States in the past decade. How have they changed the way we do research? How we teach? And how we communicate with our families and in business? As in the case

of earlier technologies such as the automobile or stirrup, the consequences are and will be profound.

■ COMPUTERS AND EQUITY

INTASC Standards

Principle #3

Besides the issue of computers being a value-laden technology, we also
need to address the issue of who gets to use them in educational settings. Clearly, access to computers can be used to perpetuate patterns
of privilege and discrimination that are already at work in our educational system and society. If computers are to play an increasingly important role in the world of work, then the amount of time students
have had to learn about them and to use them as part of their general
education may in fact determine the types of employment open to them
as adults.

Issues of access become terribly important. Will poorer children be
trained to use the machines in school? Will they have access to the Internet and to creative tool programs, or will they simply be encouraged
to use drill-and-practice programs? As I have argued elsewhere:

> The question becomes one of who has access to computer-based educa-
> tional technologies, and what is the nature of that access? Simply hav-
> ing computers in a school or classroom is not enough. There is an
> enormous difference between the data access and knowledge available
> to a student who visits a computer lab for a couple of hours of activi-
> ties per week, as compared to a student who has several computers that
> are in regular use in the back of his or her classroom, or who has com-
> puter access at home. If educational technologies such as computers are
> going to provide the basis for new types of education and schooling—
> and in turn establish new models of discourse—then we need to ask
> questions such as: Who gets access to computers? Boys or girls? Rich or
> poor? Black? White? Brown? People with special needs versus the gen-
> eral population? (Provenzo 2000, 301)

Should children from disadvantaged or historically dominated populations be provided supplemental computer resources? Compensatory education programs such as Head Start are based on just such a premise.
Who shall have access to the machines once they are introduced into the
classroom? Will only students comfortable with them use them? Will we
need to have remedial training for students who have difficulties with the
machines? Who will determine what types of curriculums are used with

them? Because boys tend to be more aggressive and tend to dominate spe-cial activity areas in classrooms, will instructors need to make special ef-forts to ensure that girls receive equal opportunities to use the machines?

■ TECHNOLOGICAL REQUIREMENTS FOR FUTURE TEACHERS

Teacher education programs and their accreditation agencies are in-creasingly emphasizing technological training. Two groups in particular have taken a lead in this area: the National Council for the Accredita-tion of Teacher Education (NCATE), at http://www.ncate.org/, and the International Society for the Study of Technology in Education (ISTE), at http://www.iste.org/. Examine the basic technology skills they are re-quiring for future teachers. Determine whether you have these skills, or are obtaining them as part of your college education.

NCATE's Requirements for the New Professional Teacher

New Understandings

Teachers need to understand the deep impact technology is having on society as a whole: how technology has changed the nature of work and communication and our understanding of the development of knowledge.

New Approaches

Today, teachers must recognize that information is available from sources that go well beyond textbooks and teachers—mass media, communities, etc.—and help students understand and make use of the many ways in which they can gain ac-cess to information. Teachers must employ a wide range of technological tools and software as part of their own instructional repertoire.

New Roles

Teachers should help students pursue their own inquiries, making use of tech-nologies to find, organize, and interpret information and to become reflective and critical about information quality and sources.

New Forms of Professional Development

Teachers must participate in formal courses, some of which may be delivered in nontraditional ways, e.g., via telecommunications; they must also become part of ongoing, informal learning communities with other professionals who share their interests and concerns.

New Attitudes

Finally, teachers need an attitude that is fearless in the use of technology, encourages them to take risks, and inspires them to become lifelong learners.

Source: Technology and the New Professional Teacher: Preparing for the 21st Century Classroom, 1997, NCATE. Available online at http://www.ncate.org/accred/projects/tech/tech-21.htm.

In NCATE's report *Technology and the New Professional Teacher: Preparing for the 21st Century Classroom,* brief case studies demonstrate the innovative use of technology in teacher education programs. You can access these case studies at the NCATE Case Studies of Technology Use in Teacher Education website, located at http://www.ncate.org/accred/projects/tech/caseintro.htm. A list of technology themes included in NCATE's current standards can be found at the Technology Themes in NCATE's Current Standards website, located at http://www.ncate.org/accred/projects/tech/current.htm.

Other groups, such as the International Society for the Study of Technology in Education, have also established national standards in the use of technology both for K–12 students and for teachers. ISTE's standards for K–12 students are available at the National Education Technology Standards for Students website, located at http://cnets.iste.org/index2ss.html. ISTE's standards for teachers are available at the National Education Technology Standards for Teachers website, located at http://cnets.iste.org/index3.html. These standards, though much more detailed and comprehensive than those provided by NCATE, are concerned with many of the same issues.

■ SUMMARY

New forms of media, from television to the computer, have transformed our culture in the past fifty years. New technologies such as television and computers bring with them new ways of viewing the world and of defining culture. They, in turn, change the meaning of literacy and learning.

Rapid changes in media and technology will clearly continue to develop in years to come. Could someone living in the early 1950s, just as television began to emerge as a commercial media, have had any idea how television would change our lives? Who would have predicted in the 1990s that computer-based technologies such as the Internet and World Wide Web would have had such a profound effect on business and education and done so in less than a decade?

The integration of media forms such as television and computers is currently underway. One example is web television, a recent innovation that allows people to access the Internet through their TVs. (The resulting interactive television recalls the "feelies" of Aldous Huxley's **dysutopian** novel *Brave New World*.) Inexpensive handheld electronic books are becoming fairly commonplace and, though expensive for now, will probably become cheaper and more ubiquitous in years to come. Increasingly, words, animations, pictures, and sounds are merged, creating new forms of reading and literacy.

Computer power will certainly continue to increase in years to come, having important consequences for schools. At present, according to Moore's Law, we are seeing computer power double every eighteen months. Video game players available today for two or three hundred dollars are much more powerful than machines that just ten years ago cost thousands of dollars.

New forms of media and educational technology provide opportunities for new ways of presenting traditional information, new methods of problem solving, new ways to organize and structure information, and new ways for students to learn. Although providing interesting opportunities, these technologies also have profound effects on our culture and are a critical force in the emergence of a rapidly changing postmodern culture and society. As teachers, we must try our best to understand what is happening in our classrooms as a result of their increasing influence in shaping how students understand and learn about the world.

■ DISCUSSION QUESTIONS ■

1. To what extent is television a means of education or entertainment? What distinguishes one from the other?
2. How does regular television viewing seem to affect the behavior patterns of a typical family?
3. How does television potentially affect what a teacher can or cannot accomplish in the classroom?
4. How does television change the experience of childhood?
5. Should children be allowed to view violence on television? Should limits be set for the type or amount of violence a child is permitted to see?

6. Should television advertising for children follow specific and carefully regulated guidelines?
7. Do we have reason to believe that computers will succeed when teaching machines have failed in the past? If so, why?
8. How might computer-assisted instruction be misused?
9. How do issues of equity affect the use of computers in instruction?
10. What makes a person computer literate?
11. How might the extensive use of computers in schools in years to come redefine the traditional role and function of our schools?

■ SOURCES CITED ■

The American Internet user survey. 1999. *Cyber Dialogue,* January.
American Medical Association. 1996. *Facts about media violence.*
American Psychological Association. 1992. APA task force explores television's positive and negative influences on society. News Release, 25 February.
———. 1992. *Myths and facts about television viewing in America.*
The Annenberg Public Policy Center. 1999. *Media in the home: The fourth annual survey of parents and children 1999.* Philadelphia: University of Pennsylvania, The Annenberg Public Policy Center.
———. 1997. *Television in the home: The 1997 survey of parents and children* Philadelphia: University of Pennsylvania, The Annenberg Public Policy Center.
Bandura, A., D. Ross, and S. A. Ross. 1963a. Imitation of film-mediated aggressive models. *Journal of Abnormal and Social Psychology* 66: 3–11.
———. 1963b. Vicarious reinforcements and initiative learning. *Journal of Abnormal and Social Psychology* 67: 601–607.
Bok, Sissela. 1998. Mayhem: Violence as public entertainment. Reading, MA: Addison-Wesley.
Calvert, Susan. 1999. *Children's journeys through the information age.* Boston: McGraw Hill.
Centrewall, Brandon S. 1992. Television and violence: The scale and problem and where to go from here. *Journal of the American Medical Association* 267(22): 3059–3063.
Children, health and advertising. 2000. Issue Briefs. Studio City, Calif.: Mediascope.
Consumer Reports, February 1998.
Dewitt, E. P. 1993. The amazing video game boom. *Time,* 27 September.
Diversity in film and television. Issue Brief. 1997. Studio City, Calif.: Mediascope.
Fisch, Shalom M., and Rosemarie T. Truglio, ed. 2001. *"G" is for growing: Thirty years of research on children and Sesame Street.* Mahwah, N.J.: Lawrence Erlbaum Associates.
Gerbner, George. 1994. Reclaiming our cultural mythology: Television's global marketing strategy creates a damaging and alienated window on the world.

In Context: A Quarterly Journal of Sustainable Culture. Available online at http://www.context.org/ICLIB/IC38/Gerbner.htm.

Giroux, Henry A. 1994. *Disturbing pleasures: Learning popular culture.* New York: Routledge.

Goodstein, L., and M. Connelly. 1998. Teen-age poll finds support for tradition. *The New York Times,* 30 April.

Internet access in public schools and classrooms: 1994–1998. 1999. Washington, D.C.: National Center for Educational Statistics and United States Department of Education.

Kakutani, M. 1996. Adolescence rules. *The New York Times,* 11 May.

Kid Think Inc. 1999. *KidScreen,* July.

Kid viewing habits. 1997. *Los Angeles Times,* 31 December.

Li, D. K. 1995. Computer access divides children. *The Oakland Tribune,* 10 May.

Lichty, Lawrence W. 1981. Success story. *The Wilson Quarterly* (Winter): 53–65.

Liebert, R. M., and R. A. Baron. 1972. Short-term effects of televised aggression on children's aggressive behavior. In *Television and social behavior.* Vol. 2 of *Television and social learning,* edited by J. P. Murray, E. A. Rubenstein, and G. A. Comstock. Washington, D.C.: U.S. Government Printing Office.

McManus, Terry. 1998. Home web sites thrust students into censorship disputes. *The New York Times,* 13 August, D9.

Mander, Jerry. 1978. *Four arguments for the elimination of television.* New York: William Morrow and Company.

NAACP to try to narrow racial gap online. 1999. *The Associated Press,* 13 July.

National television violence study. 1996. Studio City, CA: Mediascope.

Nickelodeon. 1997. It's a wired world. *Inside Kids,* April. Television program.

Nielsen Media Research, 1998.

O'Bryan, K. G. 1980. The teaching face: A historical perspective. In *Children and the faces of television: Teaching, violence, selling,* edited by E. L. Palmer and A. Dorr. New York: Academic Press.

Okrent, D. 1999. Raising kids online. *Time,* 10 May.

Otto, M. 1999. Cyperspace's effect on families examined. *Daily News,* 5 May.

Over half of U.S. households now own PCs. 1999. *San Jose Mercury News,* 19 March.

Powell, A. C., III. 1998. Net demographics starting to even out, survey finds. The Freedom Forum Online, 29 April.

Papert, Seymour. 1980. *Mindstorms.* New York: Basic Books.

———. 1993. The children's machine: Rethinking school in the age of the computer. New York: Basic Books.

Piaget, Jean. 1976. *To understand is to invent.* New York: Penguin.

Postman, Neil. 1982. *The disappearance of childhood.* New York: Delacorte.

———. 1984. *Amusing ourselves to death.* New York: Viking.

Provenzo, Eugene F., Jr. 1986. *Beyond the Gutenberg galaxy: Microcomputers and the emergence of post-typographic culture.* New York: Teachers College Press.

———. 1991. *Video kids: Making sense of Nintendo*. Cambridge: Harvard University Press.

———. 2000. Educational technology. In *Knowledge and power in the global economy: Politics and the rhetoric of school reform*, edited by David Gabbard, 297–302. Mahwah, N.J.: Lawrence Erlbaum.

Quittner, J. 1999. Are video games really so bad? *Time*, 10 May.

Re-casting TV: Girls' views. 1995. *Girls Inc.*

Schumer, C. E. 1992. Opening statement of *Violence on television: Hearing before the Subcommittee on Crime and Criminal Justice of the House Committee on the Judiciary*. 102d Cong., 2d sess. Serial 115. 15 December.

Stanger, J. D., and N. Gridina. 1999. *Media in the home: The fourth annual survey of parents and children 1999*. Philadelphia: University of Pennsylvannia, The Annenberg Public Policy Center.

Taylor, Robert. 1980. *The computer in the school: Tutor, tool, tutee*. New York: Teachers College Press.

Teenagers and technology: A *Newsweek* poll shows familiarity and optimism. 1997. *Newsweek*, 28 April.

Watkins, Bruce, Althea Huston-Stein, and John C. Wright. 1980. Effects of planned television programming. In *Children and the faces of television: Teaching, violence, selling*, edited by Edward L. Palmer and Aimée Dorr, 49–69. New York: Academic Press.

Williams, T. M. 1986. Background and overview. In *The impact of television: A natural experiment in three communities*, edited by T. M. Williams, 1–38. Orlando, Fla.: Academic Press.

Williams, T. M., and A. G. Handford. 1986. Television and other leisure activities. In *The impact of television: A natural experiment in three communities*, edited by T. M. Williams, 143–213. Orlando, Fla.: Academic Press.

Winn, Marie. 1983. *Children without childhood*. New York: Pantheon.

The year of the dot-com. 1999. *Advertising Age*, 20 December.

Conclusion

In March 1992, Vaclav Havel, philosopher, playwright, and president of the Czech Republic, wrote an editorial for *The New York Times* entitled "The End of the Modern Era." In it, Havel explained that the end of communism (the fall of the Berlin Wall in 1989, perestroika and so on) "has brought a major era in human history to an end. It has brought an end not just to the nineteenth and twentieth centuries, but to the modern age as a whole."

INTASC Standards

Principle #9

Havel believed that the fall of communism could be understood as a sign. Although he did not use the word *postmodernism* in his editorial, he essentially argued that we have made a transition into a postmodern age. He called for the creation of a more pluralistic culture: "We must see the pluralism of the world, and not bind it by seeking common denominators or reducing everything to a single common equation" (Havel 1992). This is a powerful argument in the context of this book. Havel recognized that we live in a world brimming with different perspectives and cultures and that we are better off when we recognize and cherish our diversity.

Without a doubt, the United States is essentially a pluralistic society. Although some people argue that our diversity is largely historical, the facts contradict this position. As I finish writing this book, the first figures from the 2000 census are being made available to the public. According to Kenneth Prewitt, the director of the Census Bureau: "The twenty-first century will be the century in which we redefine ourselves as the first country in world history which is literally made up of every part of the world." (Alavarez 2001, A7) As of the year 2000, 9.5 percent of the total U.S. population was foreign born. Not since the early colonial period has the foreign-born population been so large. But even then it was not as complex or representative of as many different nations of the world as it is today (Alavarez 2001, A7).

Understanding this diversity—the fundamental, pluralistic nature of the United States—is essential to those who would become teachers in contemporary society. But as I have tried to show, this diversity is not limited simply to immigrants, but is also made up of people who come from widely different experiences. These experiences yield perspectives shaped by race, gender, economic, and cultural domination.

Teachers are the largest and potentially the most important group of border crossers in our culture. No matter how isolated their communities, the process of working across the boundary lines that exist within our society is part of an inevitable process for anyone who teaches. Just as being a pilot requires knowledge of flying, and being a medical doctor requires knowledge of the human body, so too does being a teacher require knowledge of crossing borders. Crossing borders inevitably moves us out of our own frames of reference and into frameworks for viewing the perspectives of others. Although our natural tendency is to think of ourselves—our values and concerns—as remaining constant, we actually continue to evolve and change.

As citizens of the United States in the twenty-first century, we see the world very differently today than in the past. As we have moved from a modern to a postmodern culture, issues and concerns that dominated the United States half a century ago are no longer so significant. In 1950, for example, the Gallup Poll conducted a national survey in which they asked the American public: "What do you think is the most important problem facing the country today?" At that time, 40 percent of the people surveyed reported war, 15 percent reported the economy, 10 percent reported unemployment, and 8 percent reported communism.

In 1970, the responses changed to 27 percent reporting campus unrest, 22 percent reporting the Vietnam War, 14 percent reporting other international problems, and 13 percent reporting racial strife. In 1999, 18 percent of those surveyed reported ethics, morality, and family decline, 17 percent reported crime and violence, 11 percent reported education, and 10 percent reported guns and gun control. This shift in the concerns of the U.S. public is significant for many reasons. It should be of particular concern to anyone interested in becoming a teacher, because it demonstrates that the major social concerns that are likely to affect your classroom and school setting will always be changing (What's the Problem? 1999).

Consider for a moment how different the United States is today compared to a century ago. The population of the United States doubled in the first half of the twentieth century and almost doubled again in the second half: 281 million people call themselves Americans. Compare the statistics of the year 1900 in the following list with your life today.

In 1900, the life expectancy was forty-eight years for whites and thirty-three years for nonwhites. By the year 2000 the gap had narrowed to seven years.

In 1900, children represented 44 percent of the population; at the century's end they represented 29 percent of the population.

In 1900, the Northeast was the center of the country's population. Now it is centered in the South.

In 1900, only 6 percent of married women worked outside the home. In 2000, that figure was 61 percent.

In 1900, women represented 1 percent of lawyers and 6 percent of the doctors. By 2000, those figures had respectively risen to 26 percent and 29 percent.

In 1900, six thousand new books were published. In 2000, approximately sixty thousand were published.

In 1900, each person in the country made an average of 38 telephone calls per year. By 1997, that number had reached 2,325 (America Then and Now 2000).

In 1900, powered flight would not be invented for another three years. Now we think nothing of flying across the country in a matter of hours.

In 1900, no such thing as radio existed, let alone television, or computers. Now these things are part of our daily lives.

Think about the issues that face our culture and teachers working in the schools today. Think about how different they are from the issues faced by the culture and teachers thirty or even fifty years ago. Those of you about to embark on a teaching career will probably work for thirty or forty years—until the middle of the twenty-first century. Think about the changes that will almost certainly take place during your career in terms of media, race relations, gender, and so on.

The challenge of coping with the future, whether you are a teacher or in some other profession or line of work, is to adapt and change, to assume the protean, or shape-shifting, self described in the preface to this book. As teachers and border crossers, you will have the opportunity to work in one of the most challenging and complex settings in our culture. In doing so, you will not only observe the future, but shape it as well. Few professions have such exciting possibilities.

■ SOURCES CITED ■

Alvarez, Lisa. 2001. Census director marvels at the new portrait of America. *The New York Times*, 1 January, A7.

America then and now: It's all in the numbers. 2000. *The New York Times*, 31 December.

Havel, Vaclav. 1999. The end of the modern era. In *Social theory: The multicultural and classic readings*, edited by Charles Lemot (Boulder, CO: Westview Press.) Originally published in *The New York Times*. 1992. 1 March.

What's the problem? 1999. *The New York Times*, 1 August.

Model Standards for Beginning Teacher Licensing and Development

The Council of Chief State School Officers is the main professional organization for state and local school district superintendents in the United States. As part of the effort to improve the training of teachers in the United States, a set of model standards for beginning teacher licensing and development has been developed through the Interstate New Teacher Assessment and Support Consortium (INTASC). In setting these standards, INTASC has envisaged a type of teacher who has the skills necessary to work in the complex cultural settings described throughout this book.

Obviously, defining what skills and insights a teacher should have is a question open to considerable debate. The INTASC standards reflect a specific point of view about what teachers need to know and do. The author of this book believes that the standards provided by INTASC are the best general standards and guidelines available for both beginning and seasoned professionals working in the field of education.

Carefully review the INTASC standards and think about how they relate to the ideas developed in this book. Go back and look at the marginal references found throughout this book that link the INTASC standards to its content in individual chapters. In doing so, you will have the opportunity to link much of the theoretical, historical and sociological content of this work to actual practice in the classroom.

To find out more about the Council of Chief State School Officers and INTASC, please visit the website Council of Chief State School Officers, located at http://www.ccsso.org/index.html. To learn more about the INTASC standards go to the website Interstate New Teacher Assessment and Support Consortium (INTASC), located at http://www.ccsso.org/intasc.html. The following pages provide an excerpt from the INTASC *Model Standards for Beginning Teacher Licensing and Development.*

Preamble

We hold these truths to be self-evident: that all children have the potential to learn rigorous content and achieve high standards and that a well-educated citizenry is essential for maintaining our democracy and ensuring a competitive position in a global economy.

We believe that our educational system must guarantee a learning environment in which all children can learn and achieve their own kind of individually configured excellence—an environment that nurtures their unique talents and creativity; understands, respects, and incorporates the diversity of their experiences into the learning process; and cultivates their personal commitment to enduring habits of life-long learning.

We believe that states must strive to ensure excellence in teaching for all children by establishing professional licensing standards and learning opportunities which enable all teachers to develop and use professional knowledge, skills, and dispositions on behalf of students.

We believe that these standards and opportunities should enable teachers to support the intellectual, social, emotional, moral, and physical development of students; respond with flexibility and professional judgment to their different needs; and actively engage them in their own learning so that they can use and generate knowledge in effective and powerful ways.

We believe that teaching and learning comprise a holistic process that connects ideas and disciplines to each other and to the personal experiences, environments, and communities of students. Consequently, the process of teaching must be dynamic and reciprocal, responding to the many contexts within which students learn. Such teaching demands that teachers integrate their knowledge of subjects, students, the community, and curriculum to create a bridge between learning goals and learners' lives.

We believe that professional teachers assume roles that extend beyond the classroom and include responsibilities for connecting to parents and other professionals, developing the school as a learning organization, and using community resources to foster the education and welfare of students.

We believe that teachers' professional development is a dynamic process extending from initial preparation over the course of an entire career. Professional teachers are responsible for planning and pursuing their ongoing learning, for reflecting with colleagues on their practice, and for contributing to the profession's knowledge base. States and local education agencies must be responsible for investing in the growth of knowledge for individual teachers and the profession as a whole, and for establishing policies, resources, and organizational structures that guarantee continuous opportunity for teacher learning.

Draft Standards

Principle #1: The teacher understands the central concepts, tools of inquiry, and structures of the discipline(s) he or she teaches and can create learning experiences that make these aspects of subject matter meaningful for students.

Knowledge

The teacher understands major concepts, assumptions, debates, processes of inquiry, and ways of knowing that are central to the discipline(s) s/he teaches.

The teacher understands how students' conceptual frameworks and their misconceptions for an area of knowledge can influence their learning.

The teacher can relate his/her disciplinary knowledge to other subject areas.

Dispositions

The teacher realizes that subject matter knowledge is not a fixed body of facts but is complex and ever-evolving. S/he seeks to keep abreast of new ideas and understandings in the field.

The teacher appreciates multiple perspectives and conveys to learners how knowledge is developed from the vantage point of the knower.

The teacher has enthusiasm for the discipline(s) s/he teaches and sees connections to everyday life.

The teacher is committed to continuous learning and engages in professional discourse about subject matter knowledge and children's learning of the discipline.

Performances

The teacher effectively uses multiple representations and explanations of disciplinary concepts that capture key ideas and link them to students' prior understandings.

The teacher can represent and use differing viewpoints, theories, "ways of knowing," and methods of inquiry in his/her teaching of subject matter concepts.

The teacher can evaluate teaching resources and curriculum materials for their comprehensiveness, accuracy, and usefulness for representing particular ideas and concepts.

The teacher engages students in generating knowledge and testing hypotheses according to the methods of inquiry and standards of evidence used in the discipline.

The teacher develops and uses curricula that encourage students to see, question, and interpret ideas from diverse perspectives.

The teacher can create interdisciplinary learning experiences that allow students to integrate knowledge, skills, and methods of inquiry from several subject areas.

Principle #2: The teacher understands how children learn and develop, and can provide learning opportunities that support their intellectual, social, and personal development.

Knowledge

The teacher understands how learning occurs—how students construct knowledge, acquire skills, and develop habits of mind—and knows how to use instructional strategies that promote student learning.

The teacher understands that students' physical, social, emotional, moral, and cognitive development influence learning and knows how to address these factors when making instructional decisions.

The teacher is aware of expected developmental progressions and ranges of individual variation within each domain (physical, social, emotional, moral, and cognitive), can identify levels of readiness in learning, and understands how development in any one domain may affect performance in others.

Dispositions

The teacher appreciates individual variation within each area of development, shows respect for the diverse talents of all learners, and is committed to help them develop self-confidence and competence.

The teacher is disposed to use students' strengths as a basis for growth, and their errors as an opportunity for learning.

Performances

The teacher assesses individual and group performance in order to design instruction that meets learners' current needs in each domain (cognitive, social, emotional, moral, and physical) and that leads to the next level of development.

The teacher stimulates student reflection on prior knowledge and links new ideas to already familiar ideas, making connections to students' experiences, providing opportunities for active engagement, manipulation, and testing of ideas and materials, and encouraging students to assume responsibility for shaping their learning tasks.

The teacher accesses students' thinking and experiences as a basis for instructional activities by, for example, encouraging discussion, listening and responding to group interaction, and eliciting samples of student thinking orally and in writing.

Principle #3: The teacher understands how students differ in their approaches to learning and creates instructional opportunities that are adapted to diverse learners.

Knowledge

The teacher understands and can identify differences in approaches to learning and performance, including different learning styles, multiple intelligences, and performance modes, and can design instruction that helps use students' strengths as the basis for growth.

The teacher knows about areas of exceptionality in learning—including learning disabilities, visual and perceptual difficulties, and special physical or mental challenges.

The teacher knows about the process of second language acquisition and about strategies to support the learning of students whose first language is not English.

The teacher understands how students' learning is influenced by individual experiences, talents, and prior learning, as well as language, culture, family, and community values.

The teacher has a well-grounded framework for understanding cultural and community diversity and knows how to learn about and incorporate students' experiences, cultures, and community resources into instruction.

Dispositions

The teacher believes that all children can learn at high levels and persists in helping all children achieve success.

The teacher appreciates and values human diversity, shows respect for students' varied talents and perspectives, and is committed to the pursuit of "individually configured excellence."

The teacher respects students as individuals with differing personal and family backgrounds and various skills, talents, and interests.

The teacher is sensitive to community and cultural norms.

The teacher makes students feel valued for their potential as people, and helps them learn to value each other.

Performances

The teacher identifies and designs instruction appropriate to students' stages of development, learning styles, strengths, and needs.

The teacher uses teaching approaches that are sensitive to the multiple experiences of learners and that address different learning and performance modes.

The teacher makes appropriate provisions (in terms of time and circumstances for work, tasks assigned, communication and response modes) for individual students who have particular learning differences or needs.

The teacher can identify when and how to access appropriate services or resources to meet exceptional learning needs.

The teacher seeks to understand students' families, cultures, and communities, and uses this information as a basis for connecting instruction to students' experiences (e.g., drawing explicit connections between subject matter and community matters, making assignments that can be related to students' experiences and cultures).

The teacher brings multiple perspectives to the discussion of subject matter, including attention to students' personal, family, and community experiences, and cultural norms.

The teacher creates a learning community in which individual differences are respected.

Principle #4: The teacher understands and uses a variety of instructional strategies to encourage students' development of critical thinking, problem solving, and performance skills.

Knowledge

The teacher understands the cognitive processes associated with various kinds of learning (e.g., critical and creative thinking, problem structuring and problem solving, invention, memorization and recall) and how these processes can be stimulated.

The teacher understands principles and techniques, along with advantages and limitations, associated with various instructional strategies (e.g., cooperative learning, direct instruction, discovery learning, whole group discussion, independent study, interdisciplinary instruction).

The teacher knows how to enhance learning through the use of a wide variety of materials as well as human and technological resources (e.g., computers, audio-visual technologies, videotapes and discs, local experts, primary documents and artifacts, texts, reference books, literature, and other print resources).

Dispositions

The teacher values the development of students' critical thinking, independent problem solving, and performance capabilities.

The teacher values flexibility and reciprocity in the teaching process as necessary for adapting instruction to student responses, ideas, and needs.

Performances

The teacher carefully evaluates how to achieve learning goals, choosing alternative teaching strategies and materials to achieve different instructional purposes and to meet student needs (e.g., developmental stages, prior knowledge, learning styles, and interests).

The teacher uses multiple teaching and learning strategies to engage students in active learning opportunities that promote the development of critical thinking, problem solving, and performance capabilities and that help students assume responsibility for identifying and using learning resources.

The teacher constantly monitors and adjusts strategies in response to learner feedback.

The teacher varies his or her role in the instructional process (e.g., instructor, facilitator, coach, audience) in relation to the content and purposes of instruction and the needs of students.

The teacher develops a variety of clear, accurate presentations and representations of concepts, using alternative explanations to assist students' understanding and presenting diverse perspectives to encourage critical thinking.

Principle #5: The teacher uses an understanding of individual and group motivation and behavior to create a learning environment that encourages positive social interaction, active engagement in learning, and self-motivation.

Knowledge

The teacher can use knowledge about human motivation and behavior drawn from the foundational sciences of psychology, anthropology, and sociology to develop strategies for organizing and supporting individual and group work.

The teacher understands how social groups function and influence people, and how people influence groups.

The teacher knows how to help people work productively and cooperatively with each other in complex social settings.

The teacher understands the principles of effective classroom management and can use a range of strategies to promote positive relationships, cooperation, and purposeful learning in the classroom.

The teacher recognizes factors and situations that are likely to promote or diminish intrinsic motivation, and knows how to help students become self-motivated.

Dispositions

The teacher takes responsibility for establishing a positive climate in the classroom and participates in maintaining such a climate in the school as a whole.

The teacher understands how participation supports commitment, and is committed to the expression and use of democratic values in the classroom.

The teacher values the role of students in promoting each other's learning and recognizes the importance of peer relationships in establishing a climate of learning.

The teacher recognizes the value of intrinsic motivation to students' life-long growth and learning.

The teacher is committed to the continuous development of individual students' abilities and considers how different motivational strategies are likely to encourage this development for each student.

Performances

The teacher creates a smoothly functioning learning community in which students assume responsibility for themselves and one another, participate in decision making, work collaboratively and independently, and engage in purposeful learning activities.

The teacher engages students in individual and cooperative learning activities that help them develop the motivation to achieve, by, for example, relating lessons to students' personal interests, allowing students to have choices in their learning, and leading students to ask questions and pursue problems that are meaningful to them.

The teacher organizes, allocates, and manages the resources of time, space, activities, and attention to provide active and equitable engagement of students in productive tasks.

The teacher maximizes the amount of class time spent in learning by creating expectations and processes for communication and behavior along with a physical setting conducive to classroom goals.

The teacher helps the group to develop shared values and expectations for student interactions, academic discussions, and individual and group responsibility that create a positive classroom climate of openness, mutual respect, support, and inquiry.

The teacher analyzes the classroom environment and makes decisions and adjustments to enhance social relationships, student motivation and engagement, and productive work.

The teacher organizes, prepares students for, and monitors independent and group work that allows for full and varied participation of all individuals.

Principle #6: The teacher uses knowledge of effective verbal, nonverbal, and media communication techniques to foster active inquiry, collaboration, and supportive interaction in the classroom.

Knowledge

The teacher understands communication theory, language development, and the role of language in learning.

The teacher understands how cultural and gender differences can affect communication in the classroom.

The teacher recognizes the importance of nonverbal as well as verbal communication.

The teacher knows about and can use effective verbal, nonverbal, and media communication techniques.

Dispositions

The teacher recognizes the power of language for fostering self-expression, identity development, and learning.

The teacher values many ways in which people seek to communicate and encourages many modes of communication in the classroom.

The teacher is a thoughtful and responsive listener.

The teacher appreciates the cultural dimensions of communication, responds appropriately, and seeks to foster culturally sensitive communication by and among all students in the class.

Performances

The teacher models effective communication strategies in conveying ideas and information and in asking questions (e.g., monitoring the effects of messages, restating ideas and drawing connections, using visual, aural, and kinesthetic cues, being sensitive to nonverbal cues given and received).

The teacher supports and expands learner expression in speaking, writing, and other media.

The teacher knows how to ask questions and stimulate discussion in different ways for particular purposes, for example, probing for learner understanding, helping students articulate their ideas and thinking processes, promoting risk-taking and problem-solving, facilitating factual recall, encouraging convergent and divergent thinking, stimulating curiosity, helping students to question.

The teacher communicates in ways that demonstrate a sensitivity to cultural and gender differences (e.g., appropriate use of eye contact, interpretation of body language and verbal statements, acknowledgment of and responsiveness to different modes of communication and participation).

The teacher knows how to use a variety of media communication tools, including audio-visual aids and computers, to enrich learning opportunities.

Principle #7: The teacher plans instruction based upon knowledge of subject matter, students, the community, and curriculum goals.

Knowledge

The teacher understands learning theory, subject matter, curriculum development, and student development and knows how to use this knowledge in planning instruction to meet curriculum goals.

The teacher knows how to take contextual considerations (instructional materials, individual student interests, needs, and aptitudes, and community resources) into account in planning instruction that creates an effective bridge between curriculum goals and students' experiences.

The teacher knows when and how to adjust plans based on student responses and other contingencies.

Dispositions

The teacher values both long-term and short-term planning.

The teacher believes that plans must always be open to adjustment and revision based on student needs and changing circumstances.

The teacher values planning as a collegial activity.

Performances

As an individual and a member of a team, the teacher selects and creates learning experiences that are appropriate for curriculum goals, relevant to learners, and based upon principles of effective instruction (e.g., that activate students' prior knowledge, anticipate preconceptions, encourage exploration and problem-solving, and build new skills on those previously acquired).

The teacher plans for learning opportunities that recognize and address variation in learning styles and performance modes.

The teacher creates lessons and activities that operate at multiple levels to meet the developmental and individual needs of diverse learners and help each progress.

The teacher creates short-range and long-term plans that are linked to student needs and performance, and adapts the plans to ensure and capitalize on student progress and motivation.

The teacher responds to unanticipated sources of input, evaluates plans in relation to short- and long-range goals, and systematically adjusts plans to meet student needs and enhance learning.

Principle #8: The teacher understands and uses formal and informal assessment strategies to evaluate and ensure the continuous intellectual, social, and physical development of the learner.

Knowledge

The teacher understands the characteristics, uses, advantages, and limitations of different types of assessments (e.g., criterion-referenced and norm-referenced instruments, traditional standardized and performance-based tests, observation systems, and assessments of student work) for evaluating how students learn, what they know and are able to do, and what kinds of experiences will support their further growth and development.

The teacher knows how to select, construct, and use assessment strategies and instruments appropriate to the learning outcomes being evaluated and to other diagnostic purposes.

The teacher understands measurement theory and assessment-related issues, such as validity, reliability, bias, and scoring concerns.

Dispositions

The teacher values ongoing assessment as essential to the instructional process and recognizes that many different assessment strategies, accurately and systematically used, are necessary for monitoring and promoting student learning.

The teacher is committed to using assessment to identify student strengths and promote student growth rather than to deny students access to learning opportunities.

Performances

The teacher appropriately uses a variety of formal and informal assessment techniques (e.g., observation, portfolios of student work, teacher-made tests, performance tasks, projects, student self-assessments, peer assessment, and standardized tests) to enhance her or his knowledge of learners, evaluate students' progress and performances, and modify teaching and learning strategies.

The teacher solicits and uses information about students' experiences, learning behavior, needs, and progress from parents, other colleagues, and the students themselves.

The teacher uses assessment strategies to involve learners in self-assessment activities, to help them become aware of their strengths and needs, and to encourage them to set personal goals for learning.

The teacher evaluates the effect of class activities on both individuals and the class as a whole, collecting information through observation of classroom interactions, questioning, and analysis of student work.

The teacher monitors his or her own teaching strategies and behavior in relation to student success, modifying plans and instructional approaches accordingly.

The teacher maintains useful records of student work and performance and can communicate student progress knowledgeably and responsibly, based on appropriate indicators, to students, parents, and other colleagues.

Principle #9: The teacher is a reflective practitioner who continually evaluates the effects of his/her choices and actions on others (students, parents, and other professionals in the learning community) and who actively seeks out opportunities to grow professionally.

Knowledge

The teacher understands methods of inquiry that provide him/her with a variety of self-assessment and problem-solving strategies for reflecting on his/her practice, its influences on students' growth and learning, and the complex interactions between them.

The teacher is aware of major areas of research on teaching and of resources available for professional learning (e.g., professional literature, colleagues, professional associations, professional development activities).

Dispositions

The teacher values critical thinking and self-directed learning as habits of mind.

The teacher is committed to reflection, assessment, and learning as an ongoing process.

The teacher is willing to give and receive help.

The teacher is committed to seeking out, developing, and continually refining practices that address the individual needs of students.

The teacher recognizes his/her professional responsibility for engaging in and supporting appropriate professional practices for self and colleagues.

Performances

The teacher uses classroom observation, information about students, and research as sources for evaluating the outcomes of teaching and learning and as a basis for experimenting with, reflecting on, and revising practice.

The teacher seeks out professional literature, colleagues, and other resources to support his/her own development as a learner and a teacher.

The teacher draws upon professional colleagues within the school and other professional arenas as supports for reflection, problem-solving, and new ideas, actively sharing experiences and seeking and giving feedback.

Principle #10: The teacher fosters relationships with school colleagues, parents, and agencies in the larger community to support students' learning and well-being.

Knowledge

The teacher understands schools as organizations within the larger community context and understands the operations of the relevant aspects of the system(s) within which s/he works.

The teacher understands how factors in the students' environment outside of school (e.g., family circumstances, community environments, health and economic conditions) may influence students' life and learning.

The teacher understands and implements laws related to students' rights and teacher responsibilities (e.g., for equal education, appropriate education for handicapped students, confidentiality, privacy, appropriate treatment of students, reporting in situations related to possible child abuse).

Dispositions

The teacher values and appreciates the importance of all aspects of a child's experience.

The teacher is concerned about all aspects of a child's well-being (cognitive, emotional, social, and physical), and is alert to signs of difficulties.

The teacher is willing to consult with other adults regarding the education and well-being of his/her students.

The teacher respects the privacy of students and confidentiality of information.

The teacher is willing to work with other professionals to improve the overall learning environment for students.

Performances

The teacher participates in collegial activities designed to make the entire school a productive learning environment.

The teacher makes links with the learners' other environments on behalf of students, by consulting with parents, counselors, teachers of other classes and activities within the schools, and professionals in other community agencies.

The teacher can identify and use community resources to foster student learning.

The teacher establishes respectful and productive relationships with parents and guardians from diverse home and community situations, and seeks to develop cooperative partnerships in support of student learning and well-being.

The teacher talks with and listens to the student, is sensitive and responsive to clues of distress, investigates situations, and seeks outside help as needed and appropriate to remedy problems.

The teacher acts as an advocate for students.

Source: Used with the permission of the Council of Chief State School Officers. This document and its revisions are available online at http://www.ccsso.org/intasc.html.

Glossary

academy An early type of secondary school.

accommodation A policy involving one cultural group accommodating itself to the dominant groups.

adolescents Teenagers who have not yet become adults.

Aesop Ancient storyteller(s) associated with the telling of animal fables.

AIDS Acquired Immune Deficiency Syndrome. A viral infection that emerged on a worldwide basis in the early 1980s.

alternative family models Models of the family other than the traditional nuclear family model consisting of a mother, a father, and children. A single parent or a gay couple with children would represent an alternative family model.

Americanize To acculturate one to hold mainstream American values—that is, those of a largely northern European, and particularly English, origin.

Anansi or **Spiderman** Trickster figure in central African folktales.

Anglo-Saxon English in origin.

Anglo-Teutonic Literally meaning English and German in origin.

apocryphal Of doubtful authenticity.

assimilation The process of becoming like another group or being absorbed in another cultural group.

atomic bomb A bomb whose force is a result of the sudden release of energy resulting from the splitting of nuclei of a heavy chemical element such as plutonium or uranium by neutrons in a very rapid chain reaction.

Auschwitz A concentration camp near Munich, Germany, during World War II (1939–1945).

banking model An idea developed by Paulo Freire in which ideas and information are deposited in people, much like money is deposited in a bank.

basal reader A basic or beginning reading text.

Berlin Wall The guarded wall built by East Germany in 1961 in Berlin to prevent people from passing between East and West Germany during the Cold War.

black codes Laws restricting the rights of African Americans following the Civil War (1861–1865) in the United States.

border crossers Individuals who work across different cultural groups and settings.

botanicas Shops that sell medicinal herbs and spiritual material for the practice of various folk religions such as Santeria.

bureaucracy A highly structured social organization such as a school, the government, or a large business, which includes a hierarchical system of administration and strict rules for its governance.

canon Traditional texts and respected sources.

catechisms A type of religious text intended to instruct individuals in religious principles.

chat room An electronic meeting place on the Internet where people can engage in the exchange of information.

civil rights movement The movement of African Americans for political and social equality, particularly during the 1950s and 1960s.

classical studies Studies emphasizing ancient Greek and Roman sources.

cloning The replication of genetic material.

common school A movement in the 1830s and 1840s calling for common public education for all people.

connected The idea of being linked electronically.

consensus General agreement or unanimity.

Constitution The primary political document of the United States that outlines the rules of our government and the fundamental laws of the nation.

counternarratives Stories or cultural patterns of belief out of the mainstream and opposing traditional values and interpretations.

crack cocaine A crystallized form of the drug cocaine.

critical multiculturalism Model of multiculturalism that draws heavily on critical theory.

It sees humans as being shaped by a wide range of social, economic, and cultural forces.

critical pedagogists Teachers and educators who support a philosophy of critical pedagogy.

critical pedagogy Teaching that involves a critical social and political awareness of issues.

critical theory Philosophical model that sees individuals and their behavior as being shaped by a wide range of social, political, and economic forces.

cross marketing Selling multiple products across different industries in a single promotion.

cultural agents Individuals whose work defines the direction and meaning of a culture or a society.

cultural capital The knowledge and ideas in which a culture or society invests.

cultural diversity The idea of a culture or society being represented by many different cultural groups and their experiences.

cultural literacy Knowledge of cultural events and facts. In recent years this term has taken on significant political overtones.

cultural pluralism Many cultures.

cultural studies An interdisciplinary approach to studying social issues that focuses on culture and identity.

cultural workers People who work in jobs that define and shape a culture or society.

culture The social values and beliefs that define being human and create a society.

culture of silence A concept developed by the Brazilian educator Paulo Freire in which the poor are silenced by not having a voice or a critical role in their own affairs.

curriculum The content of what is taught. It can be both formal and informal.

dame schools Early elementary private schools run by women.

deculturalization Eliminating or discouraging the cultural traditions and beliefs of a cultural group.

demographic Refers to the idea of population and social characteristics.

denominational Referring to a specific religious group or denomination.

desegregation The process of eliminating racially and ethnically segregated social institutions.

dialogue As defined by Paulo Freire, the genuine and meaningful exchange of information and ideas between people—one which leads to greater knowledge and insight for all of those involved.

didactic Designed or intended to teach.

discursive Involving discourse and interaction.

dominant culture The cultural group in a society whose values and beliefs dominate and who consciously or unconsciously enforce that domination.

dominated cultures Cultural groups that have been forced to become part of U.S. culture such as African Americans, Native Americans, and colonized groups such as Hawaiians and Puerto Ricans.

ecological Involving the interaction or the interrelationship of organisms and their environments.

educational colonialism In colonized educational systems a dominant culture imposes its educational ideas and values on a subordinated culture.

electronic bulletin board A site on the Internet devoted to leaving or posting messages.

electronic computer A computer or calculating device whose mechanics are electronic.

electronic media Media such as radio, television, recorded music, videos, and computers based on electronic (in contrast to text-based media such as books and newspapers) delivery of information.

empower To give power to someone.

equity Freedom from bias or favoritism and correspondingly equal treatment.

ethnic Referring to groups of people classed according to common racial, national, tribal, religious, linguistic, or cultural origins or background.

ethnicity Refers to one's cultural affinity or origins based on common racial, national, tribal, or linguistic origins.

eugenics The science of controlled breeding for the supposed improvement of a race or breed.

feminist A person who supports and promotes the idea of gender (usually female) equality.

feminized profession A profession dominated by women such as teaching or nursing.

field testing Testing or trying out materials in an actual or real setting.

formal curriculum The curriculum that is consciously taught.

fundamentalism A conservative movement in U.S. Protestantism that emphasizes the literal interpretation of the Bible.

gay Of, or relating to, homosexuals.

gay bashing Discriminating against gays.

gender stereotyping Making discriminatory judgments based on gender.

generative Referring to words or concepts that generate meaning and which ultimately empower their users.

global village The communication theorist Marshall McLuhan's idea put forward in the early 1960s that the world is becoming increasingly unified through electronic mediums such as television.

gothic A romantic popular culture grouping in which individuals dress in black and focus on themes involving death.

governess A female tutor assigned to the care and instruction of children—almost always within a single family.

grammar schools Early schools that emphasized grammar and the fundamentals of reading and writing.

grammarian Somebody who studies grammar.

Great School Legend The tradition or myth that the public schools have provided students an equal means by which to advance and improve themselves in the culture.

Hanukkah A Jewish holiday commemorating the rededication of the Temple of Jerusalem after its defilement by Antiochus of Syria.

hegemony A concept in which a dominant group maintains its control of a subordinate group or class of people through consensual practices, social forms, and structures. This control can be exercised through educational institutions such as schools, mass media, the political system, and the family.

hereditarian Based on principles of heredity.

heredity The transmission of genetic qualities from one generation to another.

heterosexuality Sexual relationships and activities between males and females.

hidden curriculum Curriculum that is not taught directly or consciously.

hierarchical Involving different levels of authority and responsibility.

high culture Those artifacts of music, art, and literature traditionally associated with the most highly regarded traditions of a culture.

Hiroshima The Japanese city where the first atomic bomb was dropped in 1945.

home schooling National movement where children are educated at home by their parents.

homophobia Fear leading to discrimination against homosexuals.

human capital The idea that we invest in humans as resources much as business people invest in money and goods.

humanistic Referring to a philosophy emphasizing humankind's capacity to live ethically and productively, using human reason.

hypermedia Any combination of text, sound, and motion pictures linked to other sources.

icon A symbol or image representing something.

ideological Relating or concerned with ideas or political values.

inclusion Including students with special needs into the schools and communities of which they are a part.

insurgent multiculturalism A model of multiculturalism similar to critical multiculturalism in which the relationships of power and racialized identities are emphasized.

interactive Refers to the idea of having a user issue a command to a computer and then to have the computer respond.

Internet An experimental network built by the U.S. Department of Defense in the late 1960s, which has evolved into a loosely connected network of millions of computers.

invisible privilege Special privileges afforded a cultural group that are so taken for granted that the privileged group has little or no awareness that they exist.

Kwanza A recently developed holiday introduced by African Americans celebrating African traditions and the family.

Latin grammar schools   Early schools that focused on the teaching of Latin.

left-essentialist multiculturalism   Model of multiculturalism that sees people united by their experience and background in the culture.

lexicographer   An editor or author of a dictionary.

liberal multiculturalism   Generalized model of multiculturalism that assumes universal equity and common humanity.

male hegemony   Male domination.

male-based gender privilege   Privilege based on being a male.

master   Name used for a male teacher during the colonial period in America.

media   Sources of information such as television, movies, books, and newspapers. Media can be print or electronically based.

medium   The means by which something is communicated.

mental testing   Psychological testing of intelligence and ability.

Mercator projection   A type of map created during the Renaissance in which the parallels of latitude are drawn with increasing separation as they progress away from the equator.

meritocracy   A political system based on merit.

meritocratic   A system based on merit.

meta studies   A type of research study that takes multiple studies on a topic and combines their results to form a single interpretation.

microcomputers/personal computers   Small computers introduced in the 1970s for personal and small business use.

miseducation   Educating people in ways that are contrary to their own best interests.

modernism   The historical period having its origins in the French Enlightenment.

modernist tradition   Traditions based on values and traditions from the modern period.

monoculturalism   A model of culture in which a single culture is emphasized to the exclusion of all others.

multiculturalism   The idea of a state or society, such as the United States, being represented by diverse cultural groups and belief systems.

multiple intelligences   A model of intelligence developed by the psychologist Howard Gardner that is defined along multiple dimensions (seven, and more recently, nine separate types of intelligence).

nanotechnology   The creation of materials on an atomic or molecular scale in order to build microscopic machines.

Native American   The populations often equated with the colonial term *Indian*, who occupied North and South America prior to the arrival of the Europeans.

nativism   A social and political movement favoring the interests of established inhabitants over those of immigrants. During the mid-nineteenth century in the United States this movement was also associated with anti-Catholicism.

networked   The idea of computers being connected together by a communication system so that they can exchange programs and information.

new media geography   The conditions being created as a result of the introduction of new media forms such as the Internet and World Wide Web.

nonambulatory   Not being able to walk, that is, nonwalking.

normalization   The process of conforming to the status quo, or assimilating into the dominant culture.

normative practice   Cultural practices that are considered the norm.

null curriculum   The idea that something is taught by not being taught and is excluded from the curriculum.

oppositional groups   Groups that consciously oppose or challenge traditional cultural models.

oral culture   A culture or society based primarily on the oral rather than the written word.

orientalism   A term coined by the scholar Edward Said to describe the distortion of Oriental, or Eastern, life as a means of asserting Western dominance.

overt curriculum   The curriculum that is openly and consciously taught.

paideia   The ancient Greek word for education—literally meaning education is a reflection of the culture of which it is a part.

parochial   Referring to a religious parish—a parochial school being a religious school.

Passover   Jewish holiday commemorating the Hebrews' liberation from slavery in Egypt.

Perestroika   The policy of economic and governmental reform that contributed to the dissolution and end of the Union of Soviet Socialist Republics (USSR).

permeable family   A complex model of a family, reflecting patterns of divorce and so on.

petty schools   Early private schools for younger children.

pluralist multiculturalism   Model of multiculturalism that recognizes the differences between various ethnic and cultural groups.

pluralistic   Referring to the idea of coming from many sources.

postcolonial themes   Themes that have emerged as part of the postcolonial era, typically in opposition to models of colonial power and control.

post-Fordism   The present era following the period of modern industrial production.

postmodern   A model describing the current historical period as being distinct from the modern era. A postmodern society is fragmented, complex, and diverse.

postmodern culture   Culture or society created in the postmodern era.

postmodern perspective   A point of view reflective of the postmodern experience.

post-typographic culture   The contemporary information age in which the printed word has been superseded by electronic media.

power bloc   Political and social groups who subtly hold and maintain power in a culture such as the United States.

primer   Historically, the first or most basic book used in teaching children how to read.

professor   A teacher at the university or college level.

progressive education movement   A movement in education, based originally on the ideas of the philosopher John Dewey (1859–1952), which emphasized the idea of children being part of a community and of "learning by doing."

Proposition 187   A 1994 legal effort in California to restrict the education of undocumented children in the public schools.

protean   Changing and variable.

Puritan work ethic   An ethic of hard work and diligence that traces its roots back to the early Colonial period in America (during the seventeenth and eighteenth centuries).

radical revisionist The most critical of the revisionist theorists.

Ramadan The ninth month of the Islamic year observed as sacred with fasting practiced daily from dawn to sunset.

real time Something that takes place in actual time.

religious fundamentalism A Protestant conservative movement in the nineteenth and twentieth centuries in the United States that emphasized the literal interpretation of the Bible.

Renaissance The historical period in Europe between medieval and modern times, beginning in the fourteenth century and continuing into the seventeenth century.

republic A type of government in which power resides in its citizens and is exercised by elected officers and representatives.

resistance theory The idea that oppressed or dominated groups often develop strategies and effective means to oppose or counter their domination.

revisionist Refers to the group of historians who revised the traditional and highly positive interpretation of the role of education in U.S. culture.

Rosie the Riveter A slang term describing female industrial worker during World War II (1939–1945).

school dame Female teacher during the colonial period in America.

secondary school Schooling at the high school level or junior high school level.

secular Nonreligious.

separation of church and state Policy involving the separation of religion from governmental affairs and actions.

sexually transmitted diseases Diseases transmitted through sexual contact.

singularity An event of such importance that everything that follows it is changed or altered.

slave codes Laws that restricted the rights of slaves during the antebellum period (pre-1861) in the United States.

social capital Human resources—specifically people—available in a culture.

social ecology The interrelationship of individuals and their cultures with their cultural, social, and political environments.

stereotype A discriminatory judgment typically involving race, gender, or ethnicity.

stratified In layers or levels.

superintendent The lead or highest-level administrator in a school district.

teacher Usually used to define an instructor at the elementary or secondary level.

technology of teaching Various technologies (the chalkboard, computers) that support the work of teaching.

tuition tax credits Monetary credits, assigned to parents wanting to send their children to private schools, which are based on the taxes they have to pay.

tuition vouchers Monetary credits that can be used toward paying for private school tuition.

tutor A male instructor assigned to the instruction of children—mostly males and usually within a single family.

typographic culture A culture based on the printed word or on books.

Victorian Referring to the moral standards, attitudes, or conduct of the reign of the English Queen Victoria (1837–1901)—especially the notion of being conservative or stuffy.

video game   An electronic game based on computer technology.

virtual reality   Refers to the idea of creating highly realistic computer simulations of real life.

voice-over   Recording over an existing voice track in a film or television program.

white privilege   The idea that whites and their culture are considered the norm or the mainstream and that being white carries special privileges.

World Wide Web   A graphical user interface for the Internet, often confused with being the Internet.

writing schools   Early schools that emphasized writing.

Index

Puritans, 152
Puritan work ethic, 293

Quake, 351

Racism, 295
Radical revisionist approach, 35
Rainbow Curriculum, 276
Ramadan, 252–253
Reagan, Ronald, 95–96
Recollections of an Immigrant
(Ueland), 181–182
Religion. *See also* Private education
    Christian fundamentalism,
        105–106, 156–157, 215–216,
        276–277, 321, 324
    education of Native Americans,
        222
    and null curriculum, 22–23
    prayer in schools, 22–23,
        154–155
    separation of church and state,
        22–23, 151–153, 154–155, 157
    textbooks and, 309–310
Religious fundamentalists, 105–106,
    156–157, 215–216, 276–277,
    321, 324
Renaissance, 2, 282–283, 324
Republic, 282
Republic, The (Plato), 282
Resistance theory, 23–24, 231
    counternarrative and, 35–37
    need for resistance and, 63–64
    oppositional groups and, 64
Reverse discrimination, 245–246
Revisionist approach, 35
Rice, Joseph Mayer, 124
Rockfish Gap Report (Jefferson), 30
Rodriguez, Richard, 150–151
Roosevelt, Franklin D., 223
Rosengren, Karl Erik, 339
Rosie the Riveter, 264
Rousseau, Jean Jacques, 283–284
Rowling, J. K., 322
Russell, Bertrand, 58
Russian immigrants, 185–187, 193
Ruth, Babe, 185

Sadker, Myra and David, 267–268,
    269
Sagan, Carl, 156
Said, Edward, 307–308
Salaries of teachers, 71–72, 81, 82,
    91, 93–96, 100
San Antonio v. Rodriguez, 127

Sand Country Almanac, A
    (Leopold), 39–41
Saranoff, Jacob, 185–187
Saverin, Brillante, 178
Schaaf, Danielle, 87
Schaeffer, Francis, 156–157
School boards, 117–121
    contemporary, 119–121, 124
    historical foundations, 118–119
    nature of members, 117–118
    superintendents and, 124
    textbook selection and, 318–321
School dames, 80
*School District of Abington
    Township v. Schempp,* 155
School districts, 116–117
Schooling
    critical questions about nature
        and purpose of, 43–46
    nature of (quotes), 67
    as neutral, 19–20
    privilege and, 249–254
Schools
    as bureaucracies, 113–117
    busing and, 244, 246–248
    controls and influences on,
        131–133
    desegregation of, 59, 62, 242–248
    as ecological systems, 29–30,
        37–42
    ethos of, 108
    financial issues, 126–128,
        132–133, 157–159
    new social order and, 42–43
    in postmodern culture, 16
    role in cultural transmission,
        14–15
    role in socialization process, 14
    sexual discrimination in,
        137–138, 266–268
    as social systems, 66–68
*Schools We Need and Why We
    Don't Have Them, The*
    (Hirsch), 17
Schoolteacher (Lortie), 86–89
Schoolteachers and Schooling
    (Provenzo and McCloskey),
    102
Schwartz, Elaine, 88
Scopes Monkey Trial, 105
Scott, Joan Wallach, 259
Scott Foresman and Company, 304,
    316–317
Secondary school, 147
Secular, 157

Seguin, Edouard, 284
Segura, Gloria, 86–87
Self-determination, 225, 226
Seneca Falls convention of 1848,
    263
Separation of church and state,
    22–23, 151–153, 154–155, 157
Service theme, in teaching, 86–87
Sesame Street, 340–341
Sex-change operation, 106
Sex education, 156, 276–277
Sexism, and language, 261
Sexually transmitted diseases
    (STDs), 277
Sexual orientation, alternative sexual
    orientation, 270–276
Sharp, Zerna, 316
Sherman, Ruth, 249
Siepmann, Charles, 340
Simon, Theodore, 292
Sim series, 349–350
Single parents, 9, 104, 210, 211
Single-sex classrooms, 270
Singularity, 2
*Sipuel v. Board of Regents of the
    University of Oklahoma,* 244
Sizer, Theodore, 214
Slave Codes, 240–241
Slavery, 228–230, 231–234,
    242–243
Smart, Callie, 296–297
Smith-Hughes Act of 1917, 134
Social capital, 210–212
Social ecology, 29
Social force, teachers as, 106–107
Social institutions, 1
Socialization
    role of schools in, 14
    sex-role, 268–269
    of teachers, 91–93
Social systems, schools as, 66–68
Soros, George, 170
Souls of Black Folk, The (DuBois),
    237
Spanish language, 191–192
Spark, Muriel, 78
Special education. *See also* Students
    with special needs
    growth in, 282–285
Specialization, 41
Special needs students. *See* Students
    with special needs
Spencer, Lyle M., 322–323, 324
Spiderman, 15
Spring, Joel, 213, 219–220, 227